Engaging. Trackable. Affordable.

CourseMate brings course concepts to life with interactive learning, study, and exam preparation tools that support WRITE 2.

INCLUDES:
Integrated eBook, **interactive teaching and learning tools,** and **Engagement Tracker**, a first-of-its-kind tool that monitors student engagement in the course.

ON THE WEB

WRITE2
Are you in?

ONLINE RESOURCES INCLUDED!

FOR INSTRUCTORS:
- Custom Options through 4LTR+ Program
- Instructor Prep Cards
- Student Review Cards
- Engagement Tracker

FOR STUDENTS:
- Interactive eBook
- Vocabulary Flashcards
- Learning Objectives
- Interactive Quizzes
- Glossary
- Grammar Podcasts
- Graphic Organizers
- Videos
- Writing Models

Students sign in at **login.cengagebrain.com**

WRITE 2: Paragraphs and Essays
Dave Kemper, Verne Meyer, John Van Rys, and Patrick Sebranek

Publisher: Lyn Uhl

Director, Developmental English and College Success: Annie Todd

Development Editors: Leslie Taggart, Karen Mauk

Assistant Editor: Melanie Opacki

Editorial Assistant: Matthew Conte

Media Editor: Amy Gibbons

Marketing Manager: Kirsten Stoller

Marketing Coordinator: Ryan Ahern

Marketing Communications Manager: Stacey Purviance Taylor

Content Project Manager: Rosemary Winfield

Art Director: Jill Ort

Print Buyer: Susan Spencer

Rights Acquisition Specialist, Image: Jennifer Meyer Dare

Rights Acquisition Specialist, Text: Katie Huha

Production Service: Sebranek, Inc.

Text Designer: Sebranek, Inc.

Cover Designer: Hannah Wellman

Cover Image: Gettyimages.com

Compositor: Sebranek, Inc.

Sebranek, Inc.: Steven J. Augustyn, April Lindau, Colleen Belmont, Chris Erickson, Mariellen Hanrahan, Dave Kemper, Tim Kemper, Rob King, Chris Krenzke, Lois Krenzke, Mark Lalumondier, Jason C. Reynolds, Janae Sebranek, Lester Smith, Jean Varley

Library of Congress Control Number: 2010935708

Student Edition:
ISBN-13: 978-0-618-64286-1
ISBN-10: 0-618-64286-2

Annotated Instructor Edition:
ISBN-13: 978-0-618-64287-8
ISBN-10: 0-618-64287-0

Wadsworth
20 Channel Center Street
Boston, MA 02210
USA

Printed in the United States of America
1 2 3 4 5 6 7 14 13 12 11 10

WRITE 2:
Paragraphs and Essays

CONTENTS

Blend Images/ColorBlind Images/Collection Mix: Subjects/Getty Images

David Henley/Dorling Kindersley/ Getty Images

Dougal Waters/Digital Vision/Getty Images

S.Borisov.2010 / Used under license from Shutterstock.com

Part 5: Sentence Workshops 230

online **Online Bonus Chapter**

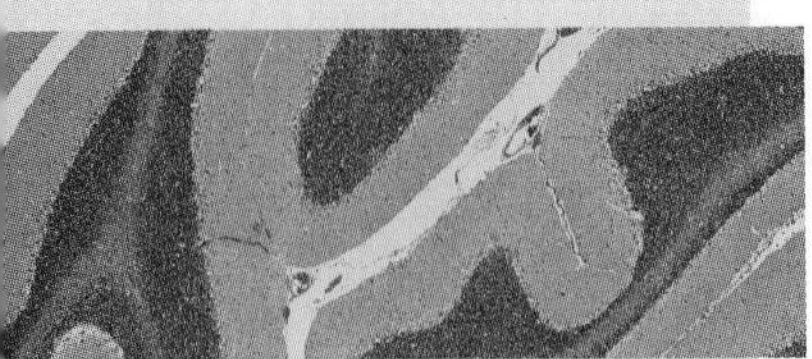

Part 8: Readings 424

Preface

Our objective with *WRITE 2: Paragraphs and Essays* and its companion *WRITE 1: Sentences and Paragraphs* is to help you function, and even flourish, in college and in the workplace. Now more than ever, you need effective communication skills in order to take your place in our information-driven world. There really is no alternative. Writing, speaking, collaborating, thinking critically—these are the survival skills for the twenty-first century. We have kept this crucial directive clearly in mind during the development of *WRITE 1* and *WRITE 2*.

Overview of *WRITE 2*

WRITE 2 covers all of the essential communication skills needed to succeed in the college classroom:

Part 1 features **writing to learn**, **reading to learn**, and making the **writing-reading** connection.

Fuse/Getty Images

Part 2 helps you learn about using the **writing process** and the **traits of effective writing.**

Parts 3 and 4 cover **the forms of paragraph and essay writing** that you will be expected to develop in the college classroom: description, illustration, definition, narration, classification, process, comparison, cause-effect, and argumentation.

Part 5 provides in-depth **sentence workshops** to help you master sentence basics and overcome sentence challenges.

Demetrio Carrasco/Dorling Kindersley/Getty Images

Part 6 offers many **word workshops** to help you understand and master using the parts of speech in your writing.

Part 7 includes **punctuation and mechanics workshops** that cover commas, apostrophes, quotation marks, italics, and capitalization.

Part 8 is **a reader with short, medium, and long professional essays** for the major forms of writing covered in parts 3 and 4.

iofoto,2010 / Used under license from Shutterstock.com

"[Student writers] are frustrated when they are not able to visualize before the first draft what will appear on the page. We must be honest and let them know how much writing is unconscious and accidental."
—Donald Murray

Research-Based Approach

■ **The Writing Process** *WRITE 2* presents writing as a process rather than an end product. Too often, writers try to do everything all at once and end up frustrated, thinking that they can't write.

WRITE 2 shows you that writing must go through a series of steps before it is ready to submit. As you work on the various writing tasks, you will internalize strategies that you can employ in all of your future writing, whether analytical essays in college or quarterly reports in the workplace.

■ **The Traits of Writing** *WRITE 2* not only explains the steps you should take during a writing project but also tells you what to include—the traits. These traits comprise *ideas, organization, voice, word choice, sentence fluency, conventions,* and *design.*

Working with the traits helps you in two important ways: It (1) identifies the key elements of successful paragraphs and essays and (2) provides a vocabulary for discussing writing with others. This information will give you the background knowledge you need to engage thoughtfully with writing.

■ **Connecting the Process and the Traits** *WRITE 2* helps students address the appropriate traits at different points during the writing process. For example, during your prewriting, or planning, you should focus on the ideas, organization, and intended voice in your writing.

The traits are especially useful when revising an initial draft because they help you know what to look for. All of the revising checklists in *WRITE 2* are traits based.

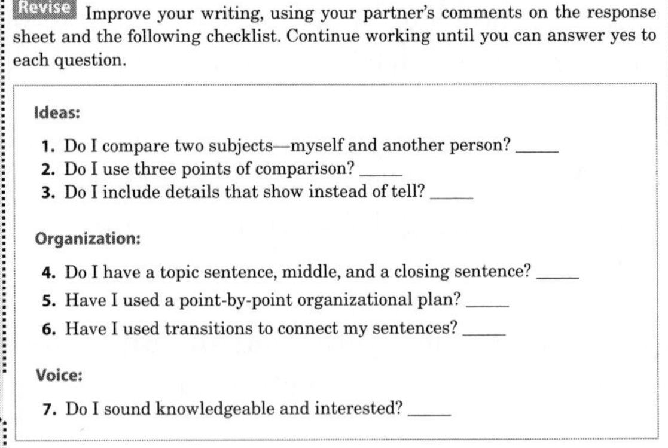

Revise Improve your writing, using your partner's comments on the response sheet and the following checklist. Continue working until you can answer yes to each question.

Ideas:

1. Do I compare two subjects—myself and another person? ____
2. Do I use three points of comparison? ____
3. Do I include details that show instead of tell? ____

Organization:

4. Do I have a topic sentence, middle, and a closing sentence? ____
5. Have I used a point-by-point organizational plan? ____
6. Have I used transitions to connect my sentences? ____

Voice:

7. Do I sound knowledgeable and interested? ____

■ **The Writing-Reading Connection** *WRITE 2* provides you with accessible and exemplary models of sentences, paragraphs, and essays. Before you begin to write, you read and respond both verbally and on the page. And as you write, you will read and respond to other students' works. Numerous activities throughout *WRITE 2* support the reading-writing and speaking-listening connections.

Grammar in Context *WRITE 2* is designed to provide grammar instruction, as much as possible, within the context of your own writing—to merge skills with craft. Study after study has shown this to be the most effective approach to teaching grammar.

In a typical writing chapter, you are introduced to two or three new grammar skills or concepts. After practicing each skill, you apply what you have learned as you edit your own writing. Additional practice activities are provided in the workshop section of the text.

Developmental Design

WRITE 2 employs the following proven strategies:

Helpful Visuals Research shows that visuals help writers learn new concepts and processes. As a result, charts, graphs, and illustrations are used throughout each chapter; and you are encouraged to use graphic organizers as you develop your own writing.

Gathering Details

A Venn diagram will help you gather more details as you plan your comparison-contrast essay. The following diagram compares and contrasts two restaurants, listing unique details about each as well as similarities.

Venn Diagram

Similarities

Beijing Cafe: Chinese food, paper lanterns, Formica tables, booths, bright, lunchtime, carryout, loud, TV playing, cheap

Similarities: good food, friendly people, clean space, strong spices, fortune cookies, chopsticks

Bangkok Garden: Thai food, paintings, tablecloths, chairs/tables, dark, nighttime, dine in, quiet, fountain, expensive

Gather Complete the Venn diagram below. Write the name of one place in one circle and the name of the other place in the other. Next, list the details specific to each place. In the overlapping part, write the things that the two places have in common.

Similarities

Chapter 17 Comparison-Contrast Essay 185

Structured Instruction Each chapter in *WRITE 2* is carefully structured and easy to follow, guiding you through the writing process and helping you produce writing that reflects your best efforts. This approach is essential to help you stay with a piece of writing until it is truly ready to submit.

After completing the work in *WRITE 2,* you will have internalized key strategies for producing effective writing.

Clear Format Objectives, explanations, and directions in *WRITE 2* are clearly marked so you know what you are expected to do and why. In addition, each two-page spread offers definite starting and ending points for your work, eliminating the necessity to page back and forth within a chapter.

Because *WRITE 2* is so easy to follow, it lends itself to small-group work and independent study.

"Students need opportunities to think for themselves, to build intellectual confidence as well as intellectual competence."
—Dave Kemper

■ Reflection and Reinforcement

WRITE 2 asks you to reflect on your writing after completing the various paragraph and essay assignments. This self-assessment or reflection is a critical activity, helping you to internalize the different forms and strategies.

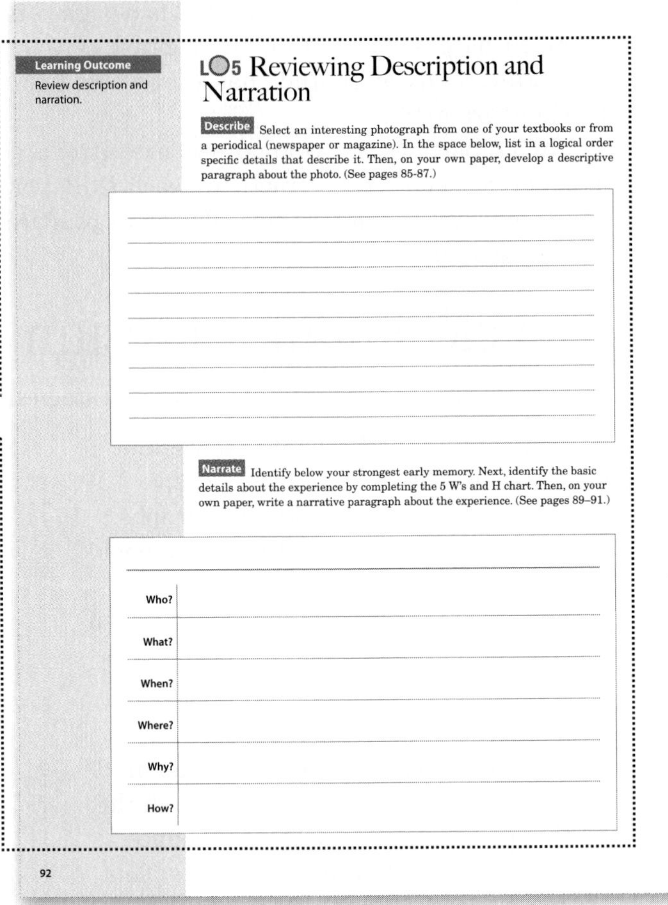

Learning Outcome
Review description and narration.

LO5 Reviewing Description and Narration

Describe Select an interesting photograph from one of your textbooks or from a periodical (newspaper or magazine). In the space below, list in a logical order specific details that describe it. Then, on your own paper, develop a descriptive paragraph about the photo. (See pages 85-87.)

Narrate Identify below your strongest early memory. Next, identify the basic details about the experience by completing the 5 W's and H chart. Then, on your own paper, write a narrative paragraph about the experience. (See pages 89–91.)

Who?
What?
When?
Where?
Why?
How?

92

■ Familiar Connections

WRITE 2 compares new, perhaps difficult concepts with old familiar ones, establishing a comfortable context.

Learning Outcome
Analyze the assignment.

LO1 Understanding the Assignment

Part of making good choices is understanding in advance what you are dealing with. You would, for example, want to know the basics about a job or an internship before you apply for it. The same holds true for each of your college reading and writing assignments. You should identify its main features before you get started on your work.

The STRAP Strategy

You can use the STRAP strategy to analyze your writing and reading assignments. The strategy consists of answering questions about these five features: *subject, type, role, audience,* and *purpose*. Once you answer the questions, you'll be ready to get to work. This chart shows how the strategy works:

For Writing Assignments		For Reading Assignments
What specific topic should I write about?	Subject	What specific topic does the reading address?
What form of writing *(essay, article)* will I use?	Type	What form *(essay, text chapter, article)* does the reading take?
What position *(student, citizen, employee)* should I assume?	Role	What position *(student, responder, concerned individual)* does the writer assume?
Who is the intended reader?	Audience	Who is the intended reader?
What is the goal *(to inform, to persuade)* of the writing?	Purpose	What is the goal of the material?

Test Taking
The STRAP questions help you quickly understand a writing prompt or a reading selection on a test.

The STRAP Strategy in Action

Suppose you were given the following reading assignment in an environmental studies class.

Read the essay "To Drill or Not to Drill" in the online readings. Then write a blog entry, comparing the reading with what you've learned about oil drilling in class discussions.

Here are the answers to the STRAP questions for this assignment:
Subject: Drilling for oil in the Arctic National Wildlife Refuge
Type: Persuasive essay
Role: Advocate of less drilling, more conservation
Audience: General consumers
Purpose: To persuade readers to accept a new line of thinking

Vocabulary
STRAP strategy
a strategy for identifying the main features in a writing or reading assignment

18

■ Vocabulary

Key terms related to instruction are defined.

Additional Special Features

The following features appear as side notes or special call-outs to help you develop your communication skills and to connect your work with other learning situations—both in school and in the workplace.

Traits

The traits are used for writing and reading.

Test Taking

When appropriate, tips for taking exams are provided.

Speaking & Listening

Optional oral activities complement the writing instruction.

WAC

Special notes connect your work to writing in different classes.

Workplace

Special notes connect your work to writing in the workplace.

ESL Support

These features will help those who speak English as a second language to improve their understanding as they complete the activities in *WRITE 2*.

Insight

The insights explain or reinforce concepts for students who are just learning English.

Vocabulary

Challenging words and idioms throughout the book are defined to help ESL students—and any other student.

Insight

As the introduction indicates, native English speakers use this order unconsciously because it sounds right to them. If you put adjectives in a different order, a native English speaker might say, "That's not how anybody says it." One way to avoid this issue is to avoid stacking multiple adjectives before nouns.

Fuse/Getty Images

Part 1 Writing and Reading for Success

"I write to discover what I think."
—Joan Didion

Fuse/Getty Images

1 Writing and Learning

In college, the new concepts flooding your way can seem overwhelming. To succeed you must be able retain new knowledge, connect it to other ideas and subjects, and communicate conclusions with your peers and instructors. Writing can help.

You may not think of writing as a learning tool, but writing can make you a better, more efficient learner. Think about it: writing allows you to sort through your thoughts, form new and thoughtful opinions, and communicate what you've learned with others. And these skills translate directly to the workplace. It is no surprise that today's employers place a premium on effective writers.

This chapter is set up in two parts. The first half introduces you to writing as a learning tool, while the second half introduces writing as a means of sharing knowledge. Becoming an effective writer and learner isn't magic, but the result of focus and practice.

What do you think?

What does the quotation on the previous page say about writing? How does it match up with your opinion of writing?

Answers will vary.

Learning Outcomes

LO1 Write to learn for yourself.

LO2 Write to share learning.

LO3 Consider the range of writing.

LO4 Review writing and learning.

Learning Outcome

Write to learn for yourself.

LO1 Writing to Learn

Gertrude Stein made one of the more famous and unusual statements about writing when she said, "To write is to write is to write is to write. . . ." The lofty place that writing held in her life echoes in the line. As far as she was concerned, nothing else needed to be said on the subject.

What would cause a writer to become so committed to the process of writing? Was it for fame and recognition? Not really. The real fascination that experienced writers have with writing is the frame of mind it puts them in. The act of filling up a page stimulates their thinking and leads to exciting and meaningful learning.

Changing Your Attitude

If you think of writing in just one way—as an assignment to be completed—you will never discover its true value. Writing works best when you think of it as an important learning tool. It doesn't always have to lead to an end product submitted to an instructor.

A series of questions, a list, or a quick note in a notebook can be a meaningful form of writing if it helps you think and understand. If you make writing an important art of your learning routine, two things will happen: (1) You'll change your feelings about the importance of writing, and (2) you'll become a better thinker and learner.

Speaking & Listening

As a class, discuss this writing experience: Did it help you focus your thinking on the topic? Did you surprise yourself in any way? Could you have written more? If so, about what?

Reflect Write nonstop for 5 minutes about one of the three topics below. Don't stop or hesitate, and don't worry about making mistakes. You are writing for yourself. Afterward, checkmark something that surprises you or you learned about yourself.

What are my talents? **Where do I want to go?** **Have I seized opportunities?**

Answers will vary.

Keeping a Class Notebook

Keeping a class notebook or journal is essential if you are going to make writing to learn an important part of your learning routine. Certainly, you can take notes in this notebook, but it is also helpful to reflect on what is going on in the class. Try these activities:

- **Write freely about anything from class discussions to challenging assignments to important exams.**
- **Discuss new ideas and concepts.**
- **Argue for and against any points of view that came up in class.**
- **Question what you are learning.**
- **Record your thoughts and feelings during an extended lab or research assignment.**
- **Evaluate your progress in the class.**

WAC

Note taking is a common form of writing to learn in most classes. Always try to explore your thoughts and feelings alongside the basic notes. This makes note taking more meaningful. (See page 12.)

Special Strategies

Writing or listing freely is the most common way to explore your thoughts and feelings about your course work. There are, however, specific writing-to-learn strategies that you may want to try:

Sent or Unsent Messages	Draft messages to anyone about something you are studying or reading.
First Thoughts	Record your first impressions about something you are studying or reading.
Role-Play	Write as if you are someone directly involved in a topic you are studying.
Nutshelling	Write down in one sentence the importance of something you are studying or reading.
Pointed Question	Keep asking yourself *why?* in your writing to sort out your thoughts about something.
Debate	Split your mind in two. Have one side defend one point of view, and the other side, a differing point of view.

"If you can't explain it simply, you don't understand it well enough."
—Albert Einstein

Practice For one month, make a commitment to writing to learn. In a notebook or on a laptop, take five minutes after or in between classes to write freely about what you just learned. Also, try a few of the strategies on this page as study tools. Afterward, evaluate how writing to learn worked for you. Did you retain more knowledge? Did you come to new conclusions or understandings?

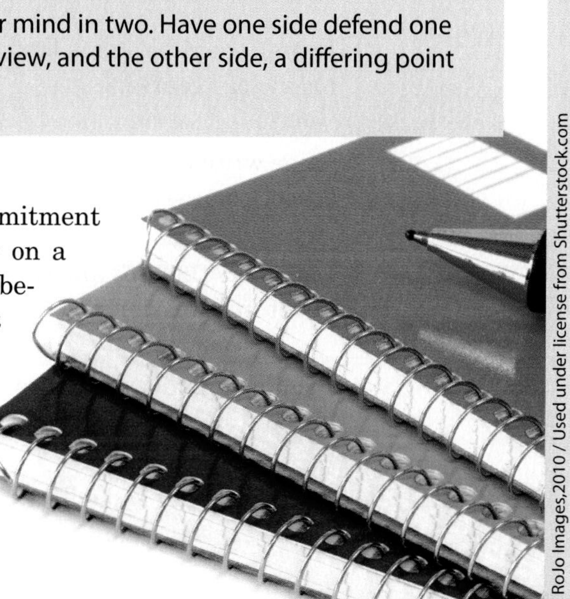

Learning Outcome

Write to share learning.

LO2 Writing to Share Learning

The other important function of writing is to share what you have learned. When you write to learn, you have an audience of one, yourself; but when you write to share learning, you have an audience of many, including your instructors and classmates.

All writing projects (paragraphs, essays, blog entries) actually begin with writing to learn, as you collect your thoughts about a topic. But with a first draft in hand, you turn your attention to making the writing clear, complete, and ready to share with others.

Note: Writing is called a process because it must go through a series of steps before it is ready to share. (See pages 26-81.)

A Learning Connection

As the graphic below shows, improved thinking is the link between the two functions of writing. Writing to learn involves exploring and forming your thoughts; writing to share learning involves clarifying and fine-tuning them.

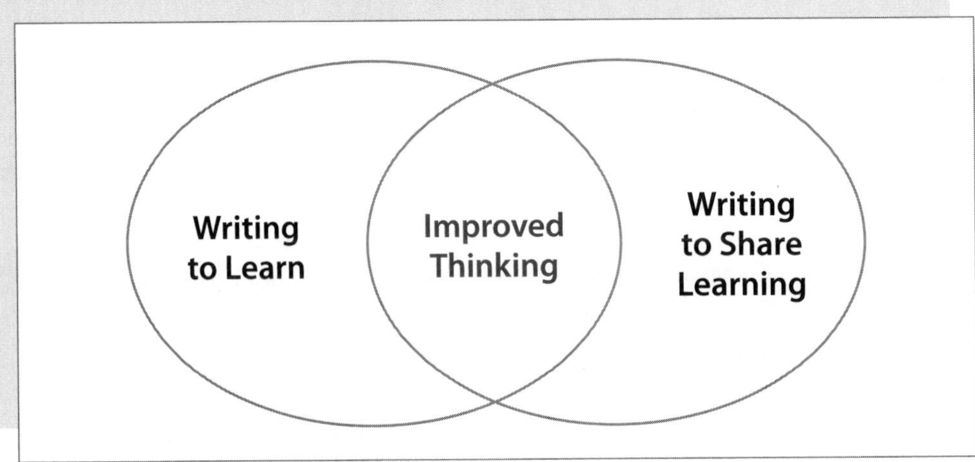

Speaking & Listening

As a class, explore the following question: Why is writing often called "thinking on paper"?

Identify Label each scenario below as an example of writing to learn (WL) or writing to share learning (WSL).

WL 1. Evan freewrites on his laptop about a concept he just learned in his biology course.

WSL 2. Paige writes a blog about last night's basketball game for her school's online newspaper.

WL 3. Liam lists the pros and cons of a political movement he learned about in a Russian and Eastern studies course.

WSL 4. Brianna e-mails new notes from her book review to her study group.

WSL 5. Mia is revising and editing her personal essay for her creative writing assignment.

LO3 Considering the Range of Writing

The forms of writing to share cover a lot of territory as you can see in the chart below. Some of the forms are quick and casual; others are more thoughtful and formal. As a college student, your writing may cover this entire spectrum, but the instruction you receive will likely focus on the more formal types.

Learning Outcome

Consider the range of writing.

The Writing Spectrum

Formal and Thoughtful ↑	Multimedia Reports
	Research Papers
	Stories/Plays/Poems
	Responses to Literature
	Persuasive Paragraphs and Essays
	Expository Paragraphs and Essays
	Business Letters
	Personal Narratives
	Blogs
	E-Mails
	Microblogs
Casual and Quick	Text Messages

Insight

Completeness and correctness are not critical in quick and casual writing, but they are important for all of the other forms on the chart.

React After studying the chart, answer the following questions. Then discuss your responses as a class.

Answers will vary.

1. What form of writing do you most often engage in?

____

____

2. How might your writing approach change at different points on the writing spectrum?

____

____

3. What characteristics do you associate with casual and quick writing? How about formal and thoughtful?

____

____

Learning Outcome

Review writing and learning.

LO4 Reviewing Writing and Learning

Writing to Learn Answer the following questions about writing as a learning tool. (See pages 2-3.) Answers will vary.

1. How is writing to learn different from traditional writing assignments?

2. What are some ways you can write to learn using your classroom notebook or personal laptop?

3. How can pointed questions be used as a writing-to-learn strategy? What about debate?

Writing to Share Learning Answer the following questions about writing to share learning. (See page 4.) Answers will vary.

1. How is writing to share learning different from writing to learn?

2. Why is improved thinking considered the link between writing to learn and writing to share?

The Range of Writing Rank the following forms of writing in order of casual and quick to formal and thoughtful, with 1 being the most casual.

__2__ On your personal blog, you write a review of a new restaurant.

__4__ You complete a research report on sports in Ancient Greece.

__1__ You send your friend a text message about your plans for the evening.

__3__ You argue for a campus-wide smoking ban in a letter to the editor in your college's newspaper.

"Reading furnishes the mind only with materials of knowledge; it is thinking that makes what we read ours."
—John Locke

John Giustina/Stone/Getty Images

2 Reading and Learning

Reading, as you well know, is a gateway to learning. Textbooks, literature, newspaper articles, and Web sites have fueled much of your formal education. It should come as no surprise then to discover that reading is an essential learning tool in college.

But where much of elementary and secondary school reading material is geared toward gaining a basic understanding of new ideas and concepts, college reading assignments demand a more active reader. Your instructors will expect you not only to retain new information, but also to compare it to what you already know and reflect on what makes the information important. This chapter is set up to help you become a successful college reader.

Learning Outcomes

- LO1 Read to learn.
- LO2 Use reading strategies.
- LO3 Read graphics.
- LO4 Review reading and learning.

What do you think?

What message is John Locke trying to get across in his quotation at the top of the page? Do you agree with him?

Answers will vary.

Learning Outcome

Read to learn.

"Some books are to be tasted, others to be swallowed, and some few are to be chewed and digested."
—Francis Bacon

Traits

Effective writing has strong ideas, clear organization, appropriate voice, precise words, smooth sentences, correct conventions, and a strong design. Use these traits to understand what you read.

Vocabulary

context cues
using the words surrounding an unfamiliar term to help unlock its meaning

LO1 Reading to Learn

Thoughtful, active reading encompasses a number of related tasks: previewing the text, reading it through, taking notes as you go along, and summarizing what you have learned. Active reading gives you control of reading assignments and makes new information part of your own thinking.

Effective Academic Reading

Follow the guidelines listed below for all of your academic reading assignments. A few of these points are discussed in more detail later in the chapter.

1. **Know the assignment:** Identify its purpose, its due date, its level of difficulty, and so on.
2. **Set aside the proper time:** Don't try to read long assignments all at once. Instead, try to read in 30-minute allotments.
3. **Find a quiet place:** The setting should provide space to read and to write.
4. **Gather additional resources:** Keep on hand a notebook, related handouts, Web access, and so on.
5. **Study the "layout" of the reading:** Review the study-guide questions. Then skim the pages, noting titles, headings, graphics, and boldfaced terms.
6. **Use proven reading strategies:** See pages 10–15.
7. **Look up challenging words:** Also use **context cues** to determine the meaning of unfamiliar terms.
8. **Review difficult parts:** Reread them, write about them, and discuss them with your classmates.
9. **Summarize what you learned:** Note any concepts or explanations that you will need to study further.

Reflect Which of the tips above do you follow? Which do you not follow? Reflect on one tip that could help you improve.

Answers will vary.

Using a Class Notebook

To thoughtfully interact with a text, you need to write about it, so reserve part of your class notebook for responses to your readings. Certainly, you can take straight notes on the material (see page 12), but you should also personally respond to it. Such writing requires you to think about the reading—to agree with it, to question it, to make connections. The following guidelines will help you get started:

- **Write whenever you feel** a need to explore your thoughts and feelings. Discipline yourself to write multiple times, perhaps once before you read, two or three times during the reading, and one time afterward.
- **Write freely and honestly** to make genuine connections with the text.
- **Respond to points of view** that you like or agree with, information that confuses you, connections that you can make with other material, and ideas that seem significant.
- **Clearly label and date your responses.** These entries will help you prepare for exams and other assignments.
- **Share your discoveries.** Think of your entries as conversation starters in discussions with classmates.

Insight

If you are a visual person, you may understand a text best by mapping or clustering its important points. (See page 39 for a sample cluster.)

Special Strategies

Here are some specific ways to respond to a text:

Discuss Carry on a conversation with the author or a character until you come to know him or her and yourself a little better.

Illustrate Use graphics or pictures to help you think about a text.

Imitate Continue the article or story line by trying to write like the author.

Express Share your feelings about a text in a poem.

Practice For one of your next reading assignment, carry out at least two of the reading-response strategies described on this page. When you have finished, reflect on the value of responding to the reading.

Learning Outcome

Use reading strategies.

Note:
Annotate reading material only if you own the text or if you are reading a photocopy.

Vocabulary

annotating
the process of underlining, highlighting, or making notes in a text

LO2 Using Reading Strategies

To make sure that you gain the most from each reading assignment, employ the additional strategies on the next four pages.

Annotating a Text

Annotating a text allows you to interact with the writer's thoughts and ideas. Here are some suggestions:

- Write questions in the margins.
- Underline or highlight important points.
- Summarize key passages.
- Define new terms.
- Make connections to other parts.

Annotating in Action

You've Got Hate Mail
by Lydie Raschka

First I expected it; now I'm scared.

Hate mail confirms a vague, nagging feeling that you've done something wrong. It's a firm tap on the shoulder that says, "The jig is up." So when the first letter came, it was expected. The second, however, was a shock. By the third I was a wreck. How did he know it would take exactly and only three?

So the hate mail is all coming from one person—a man.

I started writing a few years ago, after I had a baby. I haven't completely figured out what led me to writing, but it was probably tied up with my son's birth and the attendant emotions that needed sorting.

Def: related; associated

I like the solitary work life. I write at a table in the bedroom. I send my ideas out into the void. The bedroom seems a safe enough place. I have been told that I am an introvert. What on earth makes me want to communicate with strangers in this perilous way—standing naked in a field?

I can relate to this. Also, it exhibits her fear of people judging her.

"You have to expect these things when you are a writer," my father says about the hate mail. "When you're in the public eye, anyone can read what you write."

The letters are effective and unsettling, to say the least. I have an unusual name, so he thinks I'm foreign. He calls me "Eurotrash." It's a relief because it means he doesn't really know me—although he makes some pretty accurate guesses. He doesn't know that my parents simply like unusual names.

A shortsighted conclusion

Annotate Carefully read the excerpt below from an essay by John Taylor Gatto. Then annotate the text, according to the following directions:

- Circle the main point of the passage.
- Underline or highlight one idea in the first paragraph that you either agree with, question, or are confused by. Then make a comment about this idea in the margin. AWV
- Do the same for one idea in the second paragraph and one idea in the final paragraph. AWV
- Circle one or two words that you are unsure of. Then define or explain these words in the margin. AWV

Hélène Desplechin/Flickr/Getty Images

Why Schools Don't Educate
by John Taylor Gatto

I accept this award on behalf of all the fine teachers I've known over the years who've struggled to make their transactions with children honorable ones: men and women who are never complacent, always questioning, always wrestling to define and redefine endlessly what the word education should mean. A "Teacher of the Year" is not the best teacher around—those people are too quiet to be easily uncovered—but a standard-bearer, symbolic of these private people who spend their lives gladly in the service of children. This is their award as well as mine.

We live in a time of great social crisis. Our children rank at the bottom of nineteen industrial nations in reading, writing, and arithmetic. The world's narcotic economy is based upon our own consumption of this commodity. If we didn't buy so many powdered dreams, the business would collapse—and schools are an important sales outlet. Our teenage-suicide rate is the highest in the world—and suicidal kids are rich kids for the most part, not poor. In Manhattan, 70 percent of all new marriages last less than five years.

Our school crisis is a reflection of this greater social crisis. We seem to have lost our identity. Children and old people are penned up and locked away from the business of the world to an unprecedented degree; nobody talks to them anymore. Without children and old people mixing in daily life, a community has no future and no past, only a continuous present. In fact, the term "community" hardly applies to the way we interact with each other. We live in networks, not communities, and everyone I know is lonely because of that. In some strange way, school is a major actor in this tragedy, just as it is a major actor in the widening gulfs among social classes. Using school as a sorting mechanism, we appear to be on the way to creating a caste system, complete with untouchables who wander through subway trains begging and sleep on the streets.

Taking Effective Notes

Taking notes helps you focus on the text and understand it more fully. It changes information you have read about to information that you are working with. Personalizing information in this way makes it much easier to remember and use.

Insight

Note taking should be more than writing down what you read. It should also be connecting with and questioning new information.

Note-Taking Tips

- Use your own words as much as possible.
- Record only key points and details rather than complicated sentences.
- Consider boldfaced or italicized words, graphics, and captions as well as the main text.
- Employ as many abbreviations and symbols as you can (vs., #, &, etc.).
- Decide on a system for organizing or arranging your notes so they are easy to review.

An Active Note-Taking System

To make your note taking more active, use a two-column system, in which one column (two-thirds of the page) is for your main notes and another column (one-third of the page) is for comments, reactions, and questions.

Two-Column Notes

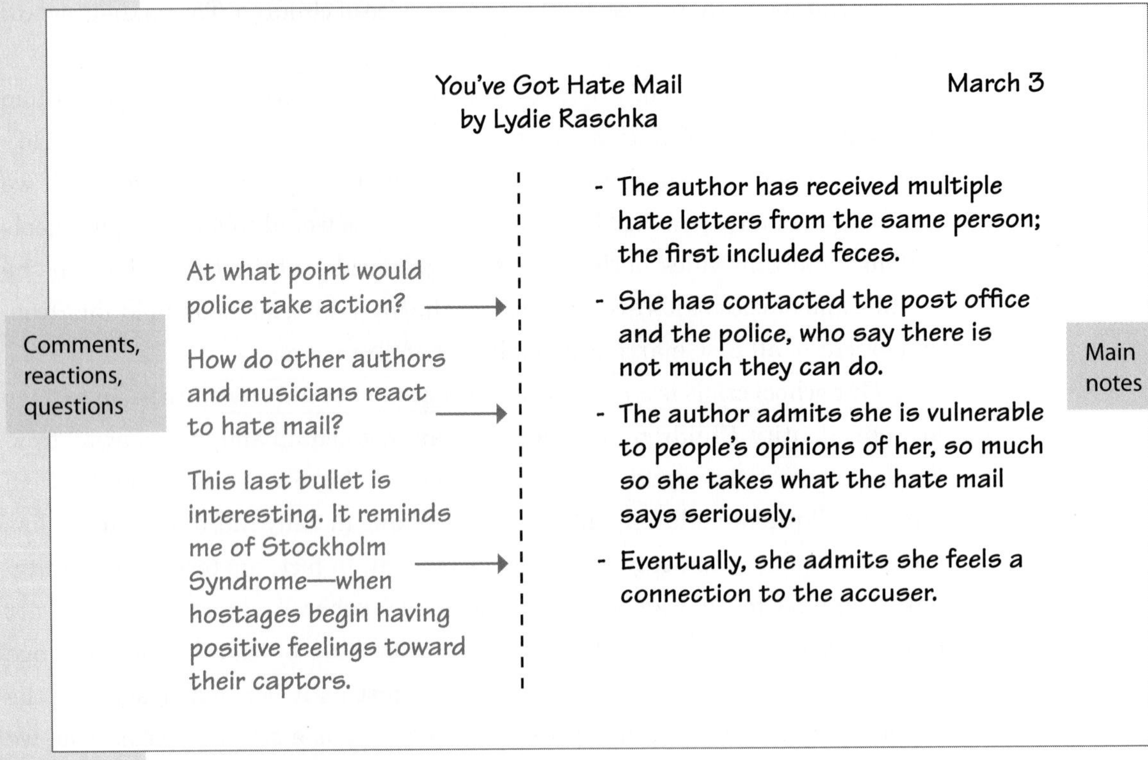

Practice Use the two-column note system for one of your next reading assignments. Use the left-hand column to react with questions, comments, and reflections about the information that you record.

Summarizing a Text

Summarizing a reading assignment is an effective way to test how well you understand the information. **Summarizing** means to present the main points in a clear, concise form using your own words (except for those few words from the original text that can't be changed). Generally speaking, a summary should be no more than one-third as long as the original.

Summarizing Tips

- Start with a clear statement of the main point of the text.
- Share only the essential supporting facts and details (names, dates, times, and places) in the next sentences.
- Present your ideas in a logical order.
- Tie all of your points together in a closing sentence.

WAC

In many classes, you'll find summarizing skills useful to help you understand and retain content.

Example Summary

The example below summarizes a three-page essay by Lydie Raschka concerning hate mail that she received.

Main points (underlined)

Essential supporting facts

Closing sentence (underlined)

Three occurrences of hate mail from the same sender have left author Lydie Raschka consumed with fear and doubt. Even before the hate mail, Raschka, who admits to being an introvert, struggled with the vulnerability of sharing her writing. She expected hate mail, but, when new letters from the same man kept coming, Raschka contacted the post office and police. Neither helped much. As the unsettling feeling increased, Raschka was unable to continue writing. At some point, she became so consumed by the letters that she began relating to her enemy, even feeling some sympathy for him. For example, he talks in his letters about his aunt and disabled sister; Raschka has a sister and a disabled aunt. In the end, Raschka wishes the sender could realize how much he has in common with her.

Practice Summarize the information in one of the essays on pages 424–w499 or in an essay provided by your instructor. Use the tips and sample above as a guide.

Vocabulary

summarizing
presenting the main points of a text in a clear, concise form using, for the most part, your own words

Learning Outcome

Read graphics.

LO3 Reading Graphics

In many of your college texts, a significant portion of the information will be communicated via charts, graphs, diagrams, and drawings. Knowing how to read these types of graphics will help you become a more effective and informed college student. Follow the guidelines listed below when you read a **graphic**.

- **Scan the graphic.** Consider it as a whole to get an overall idea about its message. Note its type (bar graph, pie graph, diagram, table, and so forth), its topic, its level of complexity, and so on.
- **Study the specific parts.** Start with the main heading or title. Next, note any additional labels or guides (such as the horizontal and vertical guides on a bar graph). Then focus on the actual information displayed in the graphic.
- **Question the graphic.** Does it address an important topic? What is its purpose (to make a comparison, to show a change, and so on)? What is the source of the information? Is the graphic dated or biased in any way?
- **Reflect on its effectiveness.** Explain in your own words the main message communicated by the graphic. Then consider its effectiveness, how it relates to the surrounding text, and how it matches up to your previous knowledge of the topic.

Vocabulary

graphic
a visual representation of information that reveals trends, makes comparisons, shows how something changes over time, and so on

horizontal
parallel to ground level, at right angles to the vertical

vertical
straight up and down, at right angles to the horizontal

Analysis of a Graphic

Review the vertical bar graph below. Then read the discussion to learn how all of the parts work together.

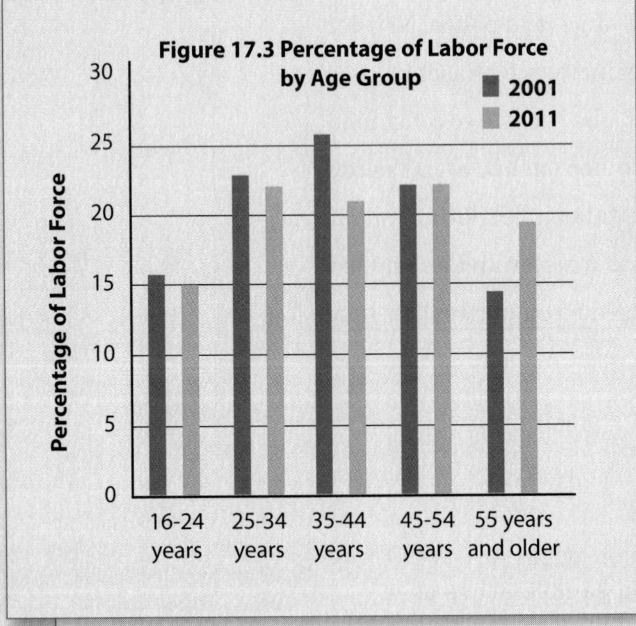

Discussion: This bar graph compares the labor force in 2001 to the labor force in 2011 for five specific age groups. The heading clearly identifies the subject or topic of the graphic. The **horizontal** line identifies the different age groups, and the **vertical** line identifies the percentage of the labor force for each group. The key in the upper right-hand corner of the graphic identifies the purpose of the color coding used in the columns or bars. With all of that information, the graphic reads quite clearly—and many interesting comparisons can be made.

React Read and analyze the following graphics, answering the questions about each one. Use the information on the previous page as a guide.

Graphic 1

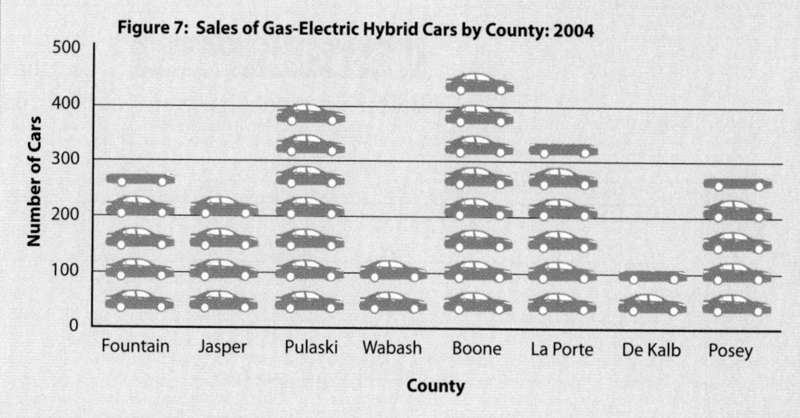

1. This graphic is called a pictograph rather than a bar graph. What makes it a "pictograph"?

   It is built of pictures of cars.

2. What is the topic of this graphic?

   Sales of gas-electric hybrid cars in eight counties

3. What information is provided on the horizontal line? On the vertical line?

   The eight counties appear on the horizontal line. The number of cars sold appears on the vertical line.

4. What comparisons can a reader make from this graphic?

   Numbers of cars sold (in increments of one hundred)

Graphic 2

Figure 36.2 Complex Web Site Map

Home Page
Second level
Second level
Third level
Third level
Third level
Fourth level
Fourth level
Fourth level
Fourth level

1. This graphic is called a line diagram, mapping a structure. What structure does this diagram map?

   A complex Web site

2. What two working parts are used in this diagram: *words, lines,* and *symbols?* Circle the appropriate choices.

3. How are the different navigational choices on a complex Web site shown on this graphic?

   Straight lines show the hierarchy of pages. Curved lines with arrows show links between individual pages.

Learning Outcome

Review reading and learning.

LO4 Reviewing Reading and Learning

Complete these activities as needed to help you better understand the concepts covered in this chapter.

Using a Class Notebook Describe some activities you can do in your notebook to better engage with your reading assignments. (See page 9.)

Answers will vary.

Annotating a Text What is the purpose of annotating a text? (See pages 10–11.)

It allows you to interact with the author's thoughts and ideas.

Taking Effective Notes Identify three helpful note-taking tips. (See page 12.)

1. Use your own words. Record only key points and details.
2. Consider boldfaced or italicized words, graphics, and captions as well as the main text.
3. Use abbreviations and symbols. Use an organizing system.

Reading Graphics Describe the steps you should take to evaluate the graphics you see in your reading assignments. (See page 14-15.)

1. Scan the graphic.
2. Study the specific parts.
3. Question the graphic.
4. Reflect on its effectiveness.

"It's good to rub and polish our brain against that of others."

—Michel de Montaigne

Blend Images/ColorBlind Images/Collection Mix: Subjects/Getty Images

Making the Writing-Reading Connection

Professional writers are well aware of the special connection between writing and reading. Stephen King says, "Reading is the creative center of a writer's life." Joan Aiken says, "Read as much as you possibly can." William Faulkner said, "Read, read, read. Read everything. . . ." These individuals know that reading stimulates writing, while their writing stimulates them to read more.

As a student, you need to make your own special connections between writing and reading. This chapter will get you started because it provides three important strategies that enrich college-level writing and reading.

Learning Outcomes

LO1 Analyze the assignment.

LO2 Use the traits of writing.

LO3 Use graphic organizers.

LO4 Review the writing-reading connection.

What do you think?

How can you connect the de Montaigne quotation to the writing process, the reading process, or both?

Answers will vary.

Learning Outcome

Analyze the assignment.

LO1 Understanding the Assignment

Part of making good choices is understanding in advance what you are dealing with. You would, for example, want to know the basics about a job or an internship before you apply for it. The same holds true for each of your college reading and writing assignments. You should identify its main features before you get started on your work.

The STRAP Strategy

You can use the **STRAP strategy** to analyze your writing and reading assignments. The strategy consists of answering questions about these five features: *subject, type, role, audience,* and *purpose*. Once you answer the questions, you'll be ready to get to work. This chart shows how the strategy works:

For Writing Assignments		For Reading Assignments
What specific topic should I write about?	**Subject**	What specific topic does the reading address?
What form of writing *(essay, article)* will I use?	**Type**	What form *(essay, text chapter, article)* does the reading take?
What position *(student, citizen, employee)* should I assume?	**Role**	What position *(student, responder, concerned individual)* does the writer assume?
Who is the intended reader?	**Audience**	Who is the intended reader?
What is the goal *(to inform, to persuade)* of the writing?	**Purpose**	What is the goal of the material?

Test Taking

The STRAP questions help you quickly understand a writing prompt or a reading selection on a test.

The STRAP Strategy in Action

Suppose you were given the following reading assignment in an environmental studies class.

> Read the essay "To Drill or Not to Drill" in the online readings. Then write a blog entry, comparing the reading with what you've learned about oil drilling in class discussions.

Here are the answers to the STRAP questions for this assignment:

Subject: Drilling for oil in the Arctic National Wildlife Refuge
Type: Persuasive essay
Role: Advocate of less drilling, more conservation
Audience: General consumers
Purpose: To persuade readers to accept a new line of thinking

Vocabulary

STRAP strategy
a strategy for identifying the main features in a writing or reading assignment

Respond Use the STRAP strategy to analyze the assignment that follows for a reading in *WRITE 2*. Then in the box below, analyze another reading assignment as directed.

Assignment 1: Read "Religious Faith Versus Spirituality" starting of page 458 in *WRITE 2*. Then in your class notebook, respond to the reading, noting its key features and your reactions to them.

Subject: What specific topic does the reading address?
Religion and spirituality

Type: What form *(essay, text chapter)* does the reading take?
Essay

Role: What position does the writer assume?
Concerned individual

Audience: Who is the intended audience?
Everyone

Purpose: What is the goal of the material?
To persuade that religion is not required for spirituality

Assignment 2: Answer the STRAP questions that follow for a reading assignment in *WRITE 2* or elsewhere that informs or entertains. Answers will vary.

Subject: What specific topic does the reading address?

Type: What form *(essay, text chapter)* does the reading take?

Role: What position does the writer assume?

Audience: Who is the intended audience?

Purpose: What is the goal of the material?

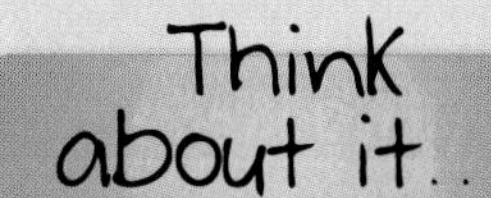

Before you begin any reading assignment, you should also consider these issues:

- The importance of the assignment
- The time you have to complete it
- The way the assignment fits into the course as a whole

Speaking & Listening

Work on the second assignment with a partner or a small group if your instructor allows it.

Learning Outcome

Use the traits of writing.

LO2 Using the Traits

Chapter 4 in *WRITE 2* goes into great detail about using the **traits** to help you with your writing. (See pages 24–34.) You can use these same traits to help you analyze and discuss your reading assignments.

Previewing the Traits

The traits of writing are highlighted below. Each one addresses an important feature in a reading selection, whether an essay, a chapter, an article, or a piece of fiction. (The questions will help you analyze a reading selection for the traits.)

- **Ideas** The information contained in reading material
  What is the topic of the reading?
  What main point is made?
  What supporting details are provided?
- **Organization** The overall structure of the material
  How does the reading selection begin?
  How is the middle part arranged?
  How does the selection end?
- **Voice** The personality of the writing—how the writer speaks to the reader
  To what degree does the writer seem interested in and knowledgeable about the topic?
  To what degree does the writer engage the reader?
- **Word Choice** The writer's use of words and phrases
  What can be said about the nouns, verbs, and modifiers in the reading?
  Are the words too general, or are they specific and effective?
  Does the writer use ***figurative language****?*
- **Sentence Fluency** The flow of the sentences
  What stands out about the sentences?
  Are they varied in length, do they flow smoothly, do they seem stylish, and so on?
- **Conventions** The correctness or accuracy of the language
  To what degree does the writing follow the conventions of the language?
- **Design** The appearance of the writing
  What, if anything, stands out about the design?
  Does it enhance or take away from the reading experience?

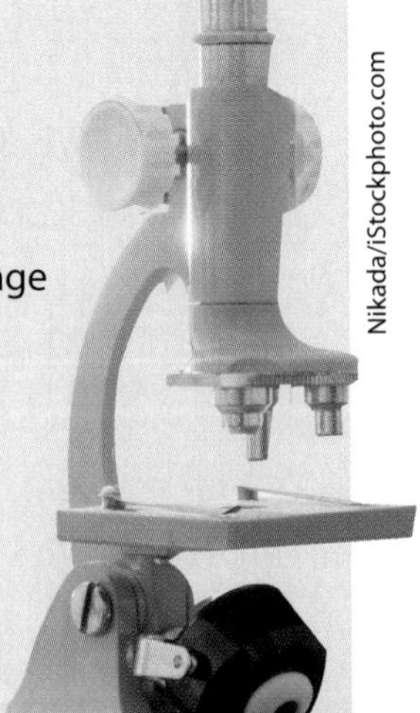
Nikada/iStockphoto.com

Traits

Throughout *WRITE 2*, the traits are used to help you read and write. Watch for this advice in annotations like this one.

Vocabulary

traits
the key elements found in effective writing

figurative language
metaphors, personification, or other creative comparisons used to describe something or to make a point

A Sample Analysis for a Reading Selection

Here is a traits analysis of "A Modest Proposal: Guys Shouldn't Drive Till 25," an argumentative essay on pages 491–493 in *WRITE 2*.

- **Ideas**

  The essay focuses on a bold proposal (rather than a modest one): raising the driving age for males to 25. The writer presents reliable statistics showing the dangers that young male drivers present. She also addresses main objections to her idea as well as many benefits to it.

- **Organization**

  The beginning paragraph uses dramatic statistics to lead up to her proposal.

  The middle paragraphs cover main objections, benefits, and exceptions to her idea.

  The closing paragraph identifies rules and actions that haven't worked in the past as a dramatic contrast to her bold claim, which she restates here.

- **Voice**

  The writer speaks in a friendly, knowing manner. The use of the pronoun "We" in a few paragraphs helps connect the reader with the writer. At times, she speaks in a **tongue in cheek** style. For example, she claims a more fit male population in our "paunchy" society would be a side benefit.

- **Word Choice**

  The word choice reflects an essay intended for a general audience—not too challenging nor too basic. The most challenging terms such as *salient* and *carnage* are defined for the reader.

- **Sentence Fluency**

  The sentences are, for the most part, long, and some of them may require a few readings. The varied sentence beginnings help with the flow of the writer's ideas.

- **Conventions**

  The writer clearly follows the conventions.

- **Design**

  The essay is traditional in design except for one long bulleted list.

Vocabulary

tongue in cheek
an expression or idiom meaning "somewhat humorously" or "not to be taken seriously"

Respond Analyze "Spanglish Spoken Here" (page 473–474) in *WRITE 2* for the traits. To develop your analysis, ask and answer each of the specific questions on page 19, or use the questions as a basic response guide, as is done above. (Use your own paper.)

Speaking & Listening

Work on this activity with a partner or a small group of classmates if your instructor allows it.

Learning Outcome

Use graphic organizers.

WAC

See page 42 for eight common graphic organizers that you can use to organize ideas in any class.

LO3 Using Graphic Organizers

Graphic organizers help you map out your thinking for writing and reading assignments. You can, for example, use a Venn diagram or a T-graph to arrange your thinking for a comparison essay that you are about to write or for one that you have just read. Other common graphics help you organize your thinking for problem-solution, cause-effect, and narrative writing and reading.

Graphing a Reading Assignment

Provided below is a time line charting the main actions in a narrative essay starting on page 432 in *WRITE 2*. (A time line identifies the key actions and events, without the related details and explanations.)

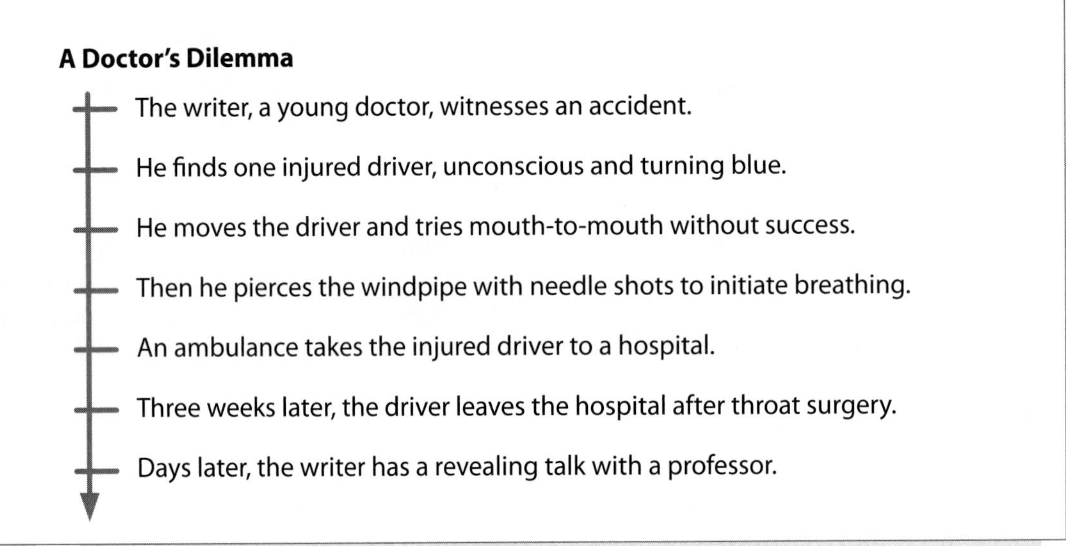

Respond In the space provided, use a time line to chart the main actions from the narrative essay "Shark Bait," starting on page 427. (Remember to focus on key actions, without all of the related details.)

Shark Bait

- Ten males took a motorboat excursion off the Miami coast.
- They ate fried chicken and potato chips.
- The four boys were punching one another.
- The group motored to open sea and dropped anchor.
- They spent some time diving for lobsters.
- Afterward, Larry began fishing and hooked a barracuda.
- Before he could reel it in, a hammerhead shark ate most of it.
- Impressed, the boys were finally quiet.

LO4 Reviewing the Writing-Reading Connection

Learning Outcome

Review the writing-reading connection.

Complete these activities as needed to help you better understand the writing-reading connection.

Analyze the Assignment Use the STRAP strategy to analyze the following reading assignment. (See pages 18–19.)

Read "Why I Changed My Mind on the Death Penalty" starting on page 489 in your text.

Subject: Death penalty

Type: Essay

Role: Concerned individual

Audience: Everyone

Purpose: To convince that the death penalty should be abolished

Use the Traits Analyze the contents of "Why I Changed My Mind on the Death Penalty" for the following traits. (See pages 20–21.)

Ideas: Answers will vary.

Organization:

Word Choice:

Part 2 The Writing Process and the Traits of Writing

"If you start in the right place and follow all the steps, you will get to the right end."
—Elizabeth Moon

Christof Schlotmann/Bridge/Corbis

4 Using the Writing Process and the Traits

Have you ever climbed to the top of a lighthouse? You can't get there in one step. You can't get there in a straight line, either. But if you've ever climbed to the top of a lighthouse and looked out for miles over the ocean, you know it's worth the trip.

Writing is the same way. You can't arrive at a final draft in one step or in a straight line. It's going to take some work and a bit of sweat. You may even feel dizzy sometimes. But if you take the steps in the writing process, you'll reach your destination and see things you've never imagined. This chapter will show you the way.

What do you think?

How can a series of small steps in writing equal a giant leap in thinking?

Answers will vary.

Learning Outcomes

- LO1 Think about writing as a process.
- LO2 Learn about the steps in the writing process.
- LO3 Learn about the traits of effective writing.
- LO4 Connect the process and the traits.

Learning Outcome

Think about writing as a process.

LO1 Understanding the Writing Process

When receiving a writing assignment, most writers ask the same question: How will I *ever* get this done? If you struggle to answer this question, you are not alone. Even professional writers labor for the right answer. But have no fear. As the quotation on the previous page explains, a writing project is much less imposing when you approach it as a process rather than as an end product.

This chapter will introduce you to the manageable steps of the **writing process**. Taking those steps one at a time will help you become a better writer and make your next writing assignment a lot less intimidating.

The Process in Action

The writing process is often considered a process of discovery because while you follow it, you will find out what you want to say.

Read/React Read the following quotations from writers who describe the writing process as a means of discovery. Discuss the quotations with a partner or a small group of classmates. Then explain below what one or two of the statements mean to you.

"Writing became such a process of discovery that I couldn't wait to get to work in the morning: I wanted to know what I was going to say."

—Sharon O'Brien

"For most writers, the act of putting words on paper is not the recording of a discovery but the very act of exploration itself."

—Donald Murray

"If you don't allow yourself the possibility of writing something very, very bad, it would be hard to write something very good."

—Steven Galloway

Reactions: Answers will vary.

Vocabulary

writing process
the process a writer uses to develop a piece of writing, from planning through publishing

Thinking About Your Own Writing

Respond Answer the following questions about your writing experiences. Be sure to explain each of your answers.

1. Rate your experience as a writer by circling the appropriate star:
   negative ★ ★ ★ ★ ★ positive   Answers will vary.

   Explain. ______________________________

2. What is the easiest part of writing for you? ______________________________

3. What is the hardest part of writing for you? ______________________________

4. What types of writing assignments challenge you the most? ______________________________

5. What is the best thing you have ever written? ______________________________

6. What is the most important thing you have learned about writing?

Kristian Dowling/Getty Images

Spotlight on Writing

"Sometimes something discouraging can be encouraging. It's all in how you take it."

The writing career of playwright Suzan-Lori Parks nearly fizzled, thanks in part to resistance from her high school English teacher, who recommended she not pursue an English degree because she was a poor speller. "Still am actually," says Parks.

Following that advice, Parks went to college to pursue a chemistry degree, but rediscovered her passion for writing in a fiction workshop. "What you love comes back to you," she says.

Since that time, Parks has become a renowned playwright. In 2002, her play *Topdog/Underdog* was awarded the Pulitzer Prize for Drama, making her the first African American woman to win the award.

Learning Outcome

Learn about the steps in the writing process.

"The first draft is a skeleton—just bare bones."
—Phyllis Reynolds Naylor

LO2 The Steps in the Process

You cannot change a flat tire in one fell swoop—it takes a number of steps to get the job done right. The same goes for writing. If you expect to finish a paper in one broad attempt, you are going to be disappointed. On the other hand, if you follow the steps of the writing process and pace yourself, you'll get the job done right.

Process	Activities
Prewriting	Start the process by (1) selecting a topic to write about, (2) collecting details about it, and (3) finding your focus, the main idea or thesis.
Writing	Then write your first draft, using your prewriting plan as a general guide. Writing a first draft allows you to connect your thoughts about a topic.
Revising	Carefully review your first draft and have a classmate read it as well. Change any parts that need to be clearer, and add missing information.
Editing	Edit your revised writing by checking for style, grammar, punctuation, and spelling errors.
Publishing	During the final step, prepare your writing to share with your instructor, your peers, or another audience.

Explain On the lines below, tell how the writing process explained above compares with your own way of completing writing assignments. Consider what you usually do first, second, third, and so on.

Answers will vary.

The Process in Action

As the chart indicates, you will likely move back and forth between the steps in the writing process. For example, after writing a first draft, you may decide to collect more details about your topic, which is actually a prewriting activity.

Process Chart

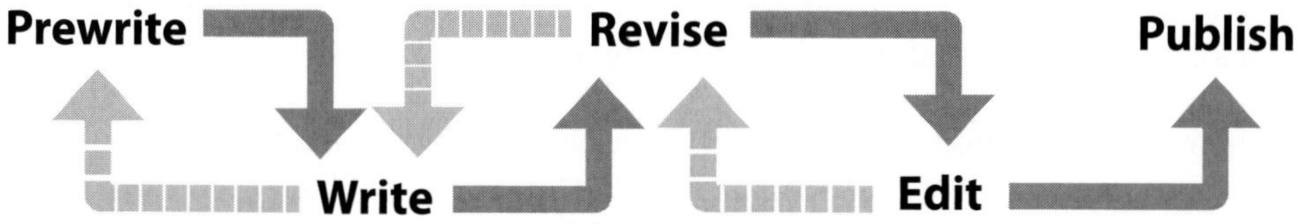

Create In the space provided below, create a chart that shows your own process—the one you described on page 28. Discuss your chart with a partner or small group of classmates.

Speaking & Listening

If you are having trouble explaining your process, talk about it with a partner.

Test Taking

When you respond to a prompt on a test, use an abbreviated form of this process. Spend a few minutes gathering and organizing ideas, then write your response. Afterward, read what you have done and quickly revise and edit it.

Reasons to Write

The four main reasons to write are given below. Always use the writing process when **writing to show learning** and when **writing to share**.

Reason	Forms	Purpose
Writing to show learning	Summaries, informational essays	To show your understanding of subjects you are studying
Writing to share	Personal essays, blog postings, short stories, plays	To share your personal thoughts, feelings, and creativity with others
Writing to explore	Personal journals, diaries, unsent letters, dialogues	To learn about yourself and your world
Writing to learn	Learning logs, reading logs, notes	To help you understand what you are learning

Explain Why is using the writing process unnecessary for **writing to explore** and **writing to learn?**

Answers will vary.

Learning Outcome

Learn about the traits of effective writing.

LO3 Understanding the Traits of Writing

Think about your favorite song. What makes it great? It's a combination of elements, right? The beat is fresh; the lyrics, inventive; the chorus, catchy.

A combination of elements results in good writing, too. The elements, or **traits**, that you find in the best articles and essays are described below.

■ **Strong Ideas** Good writing contains plenty of good information (ideas and details). And all of the information holds the reader's interest.

In the world of cloud enthusiasts, 1951 was a special year. It marked the last time a new cloud category was recognized by the International Cloud Atlas. But that may soon change. A photograph of wavy, violent-looking clouds over Cedar Rapids, Iowa, is at the heart of a 2009 cloud debate. Many say the picture reveals a new cloud category known as *undulatus asperatus*. Others say it is just another example of an *undulatus* cloud. A review is underway to determine the answer. Will 2009 become the new 1951?

— Johanna Ruiz

1. Rate the passage for ideas by circling the appropriate star:

   weak ★ ★ ★ ★ ★ strong

   Explain. Answers will vary.

2. What is the main point? A new cloud category, *undulatus asperatus,* is being debated.

WAC

The traits help you write and read in any subject area. Each discipline has its own ideas and organizational structures that you should learn, and writing always benefits from strong words, smooth sentences, correctness, and effective design.

■ **Logical Organization** Effective writing has a clear overall structure—with a beginning, a middle, and an ending.

I've experienced all sorts of road trips. Some have been great; others have been lousy. But along the way, I've picked up tips for maximizing the experience. The first is preparation. Before you leave, gather snacks, caffeinated drinks, and a minimum of three of your favorite CDs. Next, carry a notebook to record all the stupid things your friends say. And lastly, drive whatever car is least likely to break down. Now go enjoy the open road!

— T. J. Brown

Traits

Transitions (*first, later, for a brief time*) establish logical organization by linking ideas.

1. Rate the passage for organization by circling the appropriate star:

   weak ★ ★ ★ ★ ★ strong

   Explain. Answers will vary.

2. How is this passage arranged—by time, by order of importance, by logic?

   By order of importance

3. What transitional phrases does the writer use?

   "But along the way," "before you leave," "next," "and lastly"

Vocabulary

traits
the key elements, or ingredients, found in effective writing

Fitting Voice In the best writing, you can hear the writer's voice—her or his special way of saying things. It shows that the writer cares about the subject.

> Natural disasters are as ruthless as they are powerful. Too often they leave families, communities, and entire countries broken and helpless. But that's when we must step up and help. You may think one person can't make a world of a difference to people affected by a natural disaster, but you can. Besides donating money, you can give blood, volunteer for relief agencies, and use social media to influence others to help. Will you join the cause?
>
> — Melanie Roberts

1. Rate the passage for voice by circling the appropriate star:
   weak ★ ★ ★ ★ ★ strong
   Explain. Answers will vary.
2. Does the writer seem to care about the topic? Explain.
   Answers will vary.
3. How would you identify the voice in this passage—sincere, silly, bored?
   sincere

Speaking & Listening

Read this model aloud to a partner. Then have the partner read the model. How do your different voices and expression affect the overall impact of the model?

Well-Chosen Words In strong writing, nouns and verbs are specific and clear, and the modifiers add important information.

> The swimmer hunched over the starting line, anticipating the start of the race. "Bang!" The sound thrust her into motion. She dived into the pool, darting through the water like a torpedo. As she approached the other end of the pool, she swiftly spun around, kicked her feet off the concrete side, and swam back to the original end of the pool.
>
> — Joel Gutierrez

1. Rate the passage for word choice by circling the appropriate star:
   weak ★ ★ ★ ★ ★ strong
   Explain. Answers will vary.
2. Which, if any, specific verbs stand out for you?
   hunched thrust darting spun kicked
3. What other words do you find interesting? (Name two.)
   Answers will vary.

Traits

The traits help you in two important ways: (1) They name the key elements that you must consider when writing. (2) They provide a vocabulary to discuss writing with your peers.

■ Smooth Sentences The sentences in good writing flow smoothly from one to the next. They carry the meaning of the essay or article.

> Have you ever sent so many text messages that your thumbs started to ache? If so, you may be suffering from a condition dubbed "Blackberry thumb." It's true. Repetitive stress on your thumbs from texting can cause tendonitis and nerve damage. Doctors say the chance for injury is greater as you age. Naturally, the remedy is to rest your fingers.
>
> — James Jackson

1. Rate the sentences in the passage by circling the appropriate star:
   weak ★ ★ ★ ★ ★ strong
   Explain. Answers will vary.
2. In what ways does the writer vary the sentences he uses?
   Answers will vary.
3. Which sentence do you like best? Why?
   Answers will vary.

■ Correct Copy Strong writing is easy to read because it follows the conventions, or rules, of the language.

> Ella Fitzgerald is one of the most famous jazz vocalists in music history. Known as "the First Lady of Song," Fitzgerald made her singing debut at 17 at the renowned Apollo Theater in Harlem, New York. From there, her career went through three progressions—big band, bebop, and mainstream. In all, her recording career lasted 59 years and produced 13 Grammy Awards.
>
> — Chloe Evans

1. Rate the conventions in the passage by circling the appropriate star:
   weak ★ ★ ★ ★ ★ strong
   Explain. Answers will vary.
2. What punctuation marks, other than periods, are used in this passage?
   commas quotation marks dash
3. What do the quotation marks show? (See page 408 for help.)
   Answers will vary.

■ Appropriate Design In the best academic writing, the design follows the guidelines established by the instructor or school.

LaShawna Wilson

Ms. Davis

Forces in Science

February 11, 2011

Physics of Rainbows

"Why are there so many songs about rainbows?" asks the old tune. Perhaps it's because rainbows are beautiful, multicolored, and huge, arching over cities and mountains. But rainbows have captured human imagination as much because of their mystery as their beauty. In his work with prisms, Sir Isaac Newton demonstrated that something as beautiful and mysterious as a rainbow could be created through the simple property of refraction.

Basics of Refraction

The key to understanding rainbows is refraction. When light passes from one medium to another, it bends. Simply look at a straw in a glass, and the apparent break in the straw when it enters the water demonstrates refraction. Light is bending as it passes through the water, showing the straw in a different place.

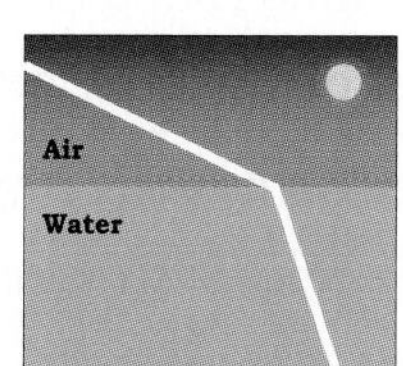

Figure 1: Basic refraction. Light moving from one medium to another slows down. When entering at an angle, the light is more sharply refracted.

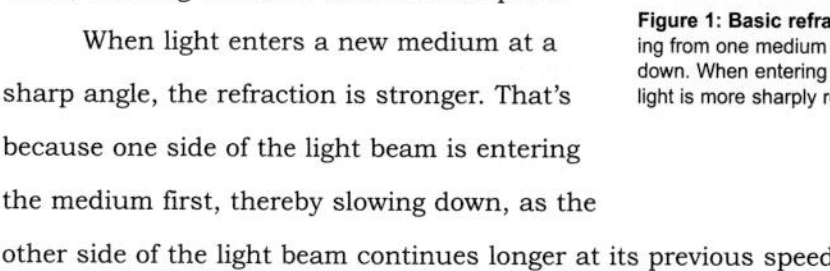

When light enters a new medium at a sharp angle, the refraction is stronger. That's because one side of the light beam is entering the medium first, thereby slowing down, as the other side of the light beam continues longer at its previous speed. The result is a turn in the angle of the light ("Prism" 13). This effect is demonstrated in Figure 1.

Wilson 2

Frequencies and Refraction

Different frequencies of light bend at different angles. The relatively long wavelengths of red light do not bend as much as the relatively short wavelengths of purple light, which is why a prism splits white light into its colors.

A raindrop can do the same thing. Figure 2, derived from the Web site "How Stuff Works," shows how white light is bent when passing through a raindrop.

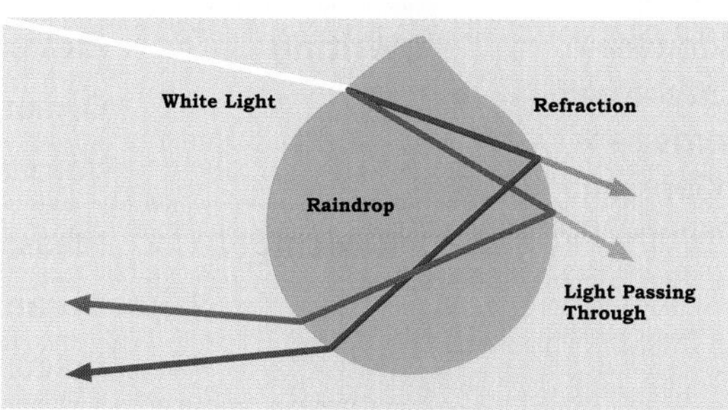

Figure 2: Refraction of light through a raindrop. Note that the purple light exits at a higher angle than the red. Drops lower in the air will reflect violet light to viewers' eyes, while higher drops reflect red light. (Source http://science.howstuffworks.com/rainbow2.htm.)

Bands of Color

The reason that a rainbow looks like bands of color is that the observer sees only one color coming from each droplet. As Figure 2 shows, a droplet that is higher in the sky will refract red into the eyes of the viewer. A droplet that is lower in the sky will refract violet into the viewer's eyes. This same pattern holds for all of the colors in between—orange, yellow, green, blue, and indigo. This effect creates the bands of color that the person sees when looking at the rainbow.

1. Rate the design of these pages by circling the appropriate star:

   weak ★ ★ ★ ★ ★ strong

   Explain. Answers will vary.

2. What one design feature stands out for you? Answers will vary.

3. Why is format and design important for a finished piece of writing?

   Answers will vary.

Workplace

Design becomes especially important when you create a workplace document. Using correct format for letters, memos, and reports helps readers understand the content and projects a professional image.

Learning Outcome

Connect the process and the traits.

Traits

The first three traits—ideas, organization, and voice—deal with big issues, so they dominate the beginning of the writing process. Words, sentences, conventions, and design become important later.

LO4 Connecting the Process and the Traits

The writing process guides you as you form a piece of writing. The writing traits identify the key elements to consider in the writing. This chart connects the two. For example, it shows that during prewriting, you should focus on ideas, organization, and voice.

Process	Traits: Activities
Prewriting	**Ideas:** selecting a topic, collecting details about it, forming a thesis **Organization:** arranging the details **Voice:** establishing your stance (objective, personal)
Writing	**Ideas:** connecting your thoughts and information **Organization:** following your prewriting plan **Voice:** sounding serious, sincere, interested . . .
Revising	**Ideas:** reviewing for clarity and completeness **Organization:** reviewing for structure/arrangement of ideas **Voice:** reviewing for appropriate tone
Editing	**Word choice:** checking for specific nouns, verbs, and modifiers **Sentences:** checking for smoothness and variety **Conventions:** checking for correctness
Publishing	**Design:** evaluating the format

Think Critically Team up with a classmate to discuss the following questions. Record your answers on the lines below.

1. Which writing trait interests you the most? Why?

   Answers will vary.

2. Which step in the writing process should probably take the most time? Explain.

   Answers will vary.

3. How could you use the chart above during a writing project?

   Answers will vary.

"Bring ideas in and entertain them royally, for one of them may be king."
—Mark Van Doren

David Henley/Dorling Kindersley/ Getty Images

5

Prewriting

A process, by definition, is "a series of actions bringing about a result." **Prewriting** is the first action or step in the writing process, and, in many ways, the most important one, because it involves all of the decisions you should make before the actual writing. If you do the necessary prewriting and planning, you will be well prepared to work through the rest of the process. If, on the other hand, you jump right into your first draft, you will find it extremely difficult to develop an effective piece of writing.

In this chapter, you will learn about the following prewriting strategies: selecting a specific topic, gathering details about it, forming a focus or thesis, and organizing your support. Completing each one of these activities puts you in control of your writing. And for extended writing assignments, like research papers, thorough prewriting becomes even more important.

Learning Outcomes

LO1 Analyze the assignment.
LO2 Select a topic.
LO3 Gather details about a topic.
LO4 Use graphic organizers.
LO5 Establish a focus.
LO6 Understand patterns of organization.
LO7 Organize your information.
LO8 Review prewriting.

What do you think?

In the quotation above, what does Van Doren mean by "bring ideas in and entertain them royally"? How does this thought relate to prewriting?

Answers will vary.

Vocabulary

prewriting
the first step in the writing process, preparation for the actual writing

Learning Outcome

Analyze the assignment.

LO1 Analyzing the Assignment

Suppose a student writes an essay explaining the main features of a weight-training program, but the instructor really wanted an evaluation of its effectiveness. The student will have missed the purpose of the assignment (*to evaluate*). To make sure that this doesn't happen to you, always analyze your writing assignments.

Using the STRAP Strategy

In *WRITE 1*, you were introduced to the **STRAP strategy** for analyzing assignments. This strategy asks you to answer key questions about an assignment.

Subject: What specific topic should I write about?

Type: What form of writing *(essay, article, report)* should I use?

Role: What position *(student, citizen, employee, family member)* should I assume?

Audience: Who *(classmates, instructor, government official, parent)* is the intended reader?

Purpose: What is the goal *(to inform, to analyze, to persuade, to share)* of the writing?

Respond Analyze the following assignment using the STRAP strategy.

Assignment: In a class blog posting, reflect on the significance of a social custom from another culture. In your writing, consider the history of the custom, its relationship to similar customs in other cultures, and your reasons for choosing this particular custom.

Subject: What topic should I write about?

A social custom from another culture, its history, its relationship to other customs, and my reasons for choosing it

Type: What form of writing should I use?

Blog post

Role: What position should I assume?

Student

Audience: Who is the intended reader?

Classmates

Purpose: What is the goal of the writing?

To analyze and to share

Test Taking

For some assignments, you may not find a direct answer to every STRAP question. Use your best judgment when this happens.

Vocabulary

STRAP strategy
a strategy helping a writer identify the key features of an assignment—the subject, type of writing, writer's role, audience, and purpose

Understanding Key Words in Assignments

A key word in a writing assignment identifies your purpose; more specifically, it tells you what you should do in your writing. For example, in the assignment on the previous page, the key word is *reflect*. Other common key words include *explain, persuade, describe,* and so on. But what exactly does it mean to reflect or explain? The following chart shares the meanings and implications of key terms in your writing assignments.

Tip

Reflecting may include other writing and thinking moves, such as *explaining, describing,* and *comparing*.

Common Key Words

Here are key words that you will find in many of your assignments.

Analyze	Break down a topic into its parts.
Argue or persuade	Defend a position with logical arguments and support.
Compare	Show the similarities and differences.
Describe	Show in detail what something or someone is like.
Evaluate	Consider the truth, usefulness, or value of something.
Explain or inform	Give reasons, list steps, or discuss something.
Reflect	Share your well-considered thoughts and feelings about a topic.
Summarize	Restate someone else's ideas briefly in your own words.

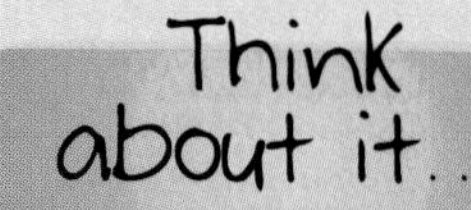

Once you find out the due date for the assignment, set up a schedule to complete your work. Be sure to give yourself enough time for each step in the writing process—prewriting, writing, revising, and editing.

Identify Circle the key word in each of the following assignments. Then explain how this key word will direct your writing. (The first one is done for you.)

1. In a movie review suitable for a school publication, evaluate one of Quentin Tarantino's latest films.

   To evaluate a movie means to identify its main features, its strengths and weaknesses, and its value (whether or not it is worth seeing).

2. In a personal essay, describe a time when the "better angels of your nature" took control.

   Answers will vary.

3. Write a letter to your representative in Congress, arguing for or against a piece of immigration legislation.

   Answers will vary.

4. Explain in an informational essay the causes of a serious health condition affecting a large number of people.

   Answers will vary.

Select a topic.

"There are few experiences quite so satisfactory as getting a good idea. . . . You're pleased with it, and feel good."
—Lancelot Law Whyte

LO2 Selecting a Topic

Personal essayist Andy Rooney of *60 Minutes* fame stated, "I don't pick subjects so much as they pick me." He is lucky in that he can write about anything that interests him, and he comes across so many interesting subjects that they seem to "pick" him. You are not so lucky in most of your writing assignments because your choices are usually limited. Even so, always try to select a topic that you have strong feelings about. Otherwise, you will find it very difficult to do your best work.

Narrowing Your Choices

Some assignments will tell you specifically what you should write about, but in most cases, they will identify a general subject area that serves as a starting point for a topic search. This graphic shows how the selecting process should work, moving from the general subject area to a specific topic.

Assignment: Analyze the cause and effects of an urban health problem.

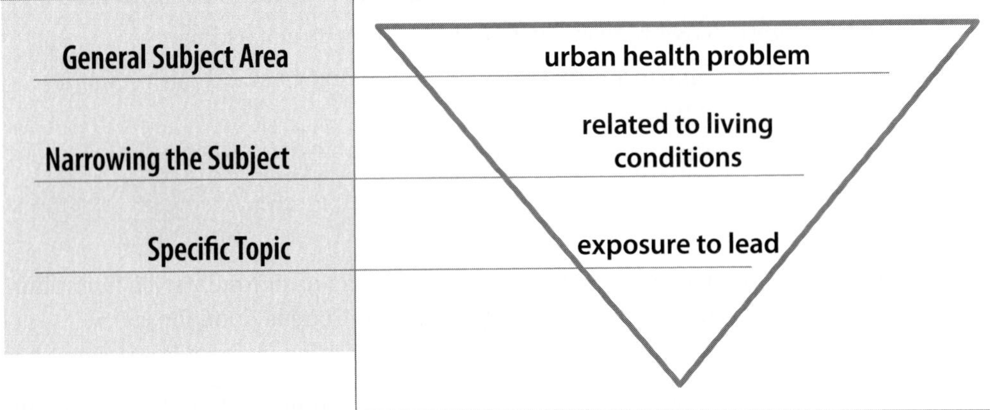

Traits

A topic for an extended assignment such as a research paper must be broad enough to offer plenty of information. For a more limited assignment (a one- or two-page essay), the topic should be more specific.

Choose Identify a specific topic for the following assignment. (Use the example above as a guide.)

Assignment: In a persuasive essay, argue for or against a new or proposed mode of transportation.

A new or proposed mode of transportation

Answers will vary.

Answers will vary.

1. What is the general subject area?
2. How can you narrow this subject?
3. What is one specific topic that you could write about?

Selecting Strategies

If you can't think of a suitable topic for an assignment, be sure to review your class notes, your text, and relevant Web sites for ideas. You may also want to use a selecting strategy to help you identify possible topics.

Clustering Begin a cluster with the general subject area or a narrowed subject. Circle it and then cluster related words around it.

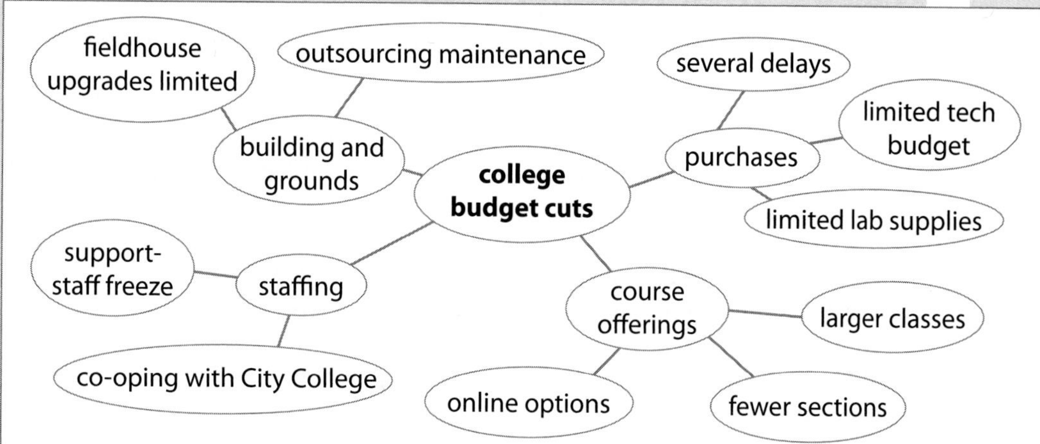

Freewriting Write nonstop for 5–10 minutes about your assignment to discover possible topics. Begin by writing down a particular thought about the assignment. Then record whatever comes to mind without stopping to judge, edit, or correct your writing.

Developing a Dialogue Create a **dialogue** between yourself and another person to identify possible topics for a writing assignment.

Extend

If one of the clustering ideas interests you, write about it for 5 minutes to see what you can discover.

Practice Use the format below to create a dialogue for the following writing assignment. Afterward, circle any possible writing ideas. (Use your own paper to continue the conversation.)

Vocabulary

dialogue
a composition in the form of a written conversation

Assignment: Write a brief personal essay in which you reflect on something that really bugs you about school life or the workplace.

You: So what is one thing that really bugs you about this school?

Other person: Answers will vary.

You: Answers will vary.

Other person: Answers will vary.

Learning Outcome

Gather details about a topic.

LO3 Gathering Details

After selecting a writing topic, you'll need to learn as much as you can about it. Writing your first draft will go smoothly if you have collected plenty of information about your topic, so use strategies like those below and on the next page to gather facts and details.

> "Writing comes more easily if you have something to say."
> —Sholem Asch

Deciding What You Already Know

To review what you already know about a topic, try one of these strategies:

Five W's of Writing Answer the five W's (who? what? when? where? and why?) to identify basic information about your subject. Add *how?* to the list for more thorough coverage.

Listing List your first thoughts about your topic as well as questions about it. Work rapidly, recording ideas nonstop for as long as you can.

Clustering Create a cluster with your specific topic as the starting point. (See page 39.)

Focused Freewriting Write freely about your topic for at least 5 minutes to see what thoughts and feelings you can uncover. Keep writing for as long as you can.

Dialoguing Discuss your topic in a creative dialogue between you and another person of your choice. (See page 39.)

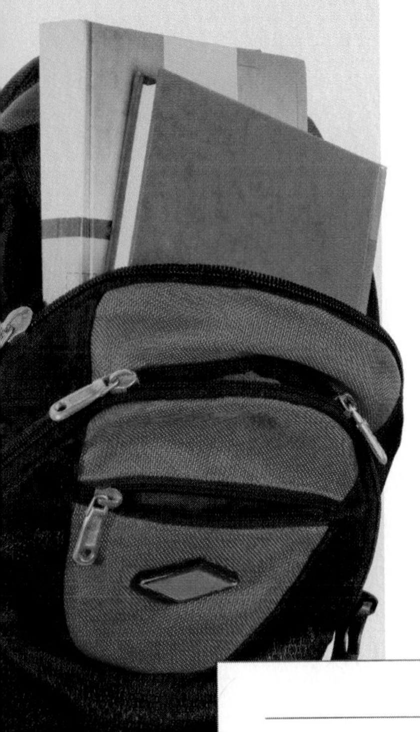

Explore Using one of the strategies above, collect your first thoughts about a topic you identified on the previous page, or one of the topics listed here. (Use your own paper if you need more room.)

- the benefits (or drawbacks) of taking online college courses
- a promising career choice
- a particular trend in fashion or music

Answers will vary.

Collecting Additional Information

For most writing assignments, gathering your own thoughts will just be a starting point, unless, of course, you're writing about a personal experience. Conducting **primary** and **secondary research** is the main way to learn more about a topic. Here is the main difference between the two types of research:

Primary research consists of information you gather by observing the topic in action, participating in it, and so on.

Secondary research consists of learning what others have already written about the topic.

"Knowledge is of two kinds. We know the subject ourselves, or we know where we can find information upon it."
—Samuel Johnson

Questioning

Your questions will naturally guide your search for additional information about a topic. Whether your topic is a **problem** (school budget cuts), a **policy** (graduation requirements), or a **concept** (a weight-training program), the questions in the following chart will lead you to pertinent facts and details.

	Description	Function	History	Value
Problems	What is the problem?	Who or what is affected by it?	What or who caused it?	What is its significance?
Policies	What are the most important features?	What is the policy designed to do?	What brought this policy about?	What are its advantages and disadvantages?
Concepts	What type of concept is it?	Why is it important?	When did it originate?	What value does it hold?

Vocabulary

primary research information gained through firsthand experience such as participating, observing, or interviewing

secondary research information gained through reading what others have learned about a topic

Collect Fill in the first blank below with a specific topic. (See the previous activities in this chapter for ideas.) Then indicate the topic's category—either a problem, policy, or concept. Finally, choose two appropriate questions from the chart above and answer them. (You may have to do some quick research to answer your questions.) Answers will vary.

Topic: ______________________ Category: ______________________

Question 1: ______________________ Question 2: ______________________

______________________ ______________________

Answer: ______________________ Answer: ______________________

______________________ ______________________

Learning Outcome

Use graphic organizers.

Traits

A graphic organizer helps you to put the information you are collecting in good order.

LO4 Using Graphic Organizers

Researching a topic is one thing; keeping track of all of the new information is quite another. To remember key points, take notes, write summaries (see pages 12–13), or use a graphic organizer.

Sample Graphic Organizers

Time Line Use for personal narratives to list actions or events in the order they occurred.

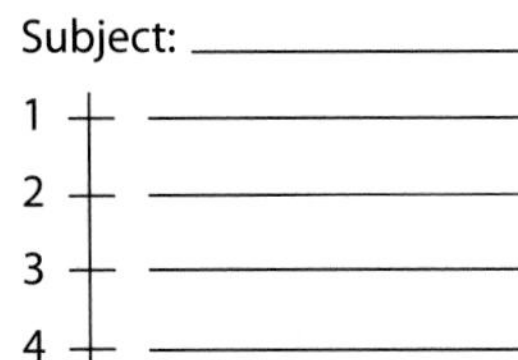

Process Diagram Use to collect details for science-related writing, such as the steps in a process.

Topic:

Step 1 → Step 2 → Step 3

Line Diagram Use to collect and organize details for informational essays.

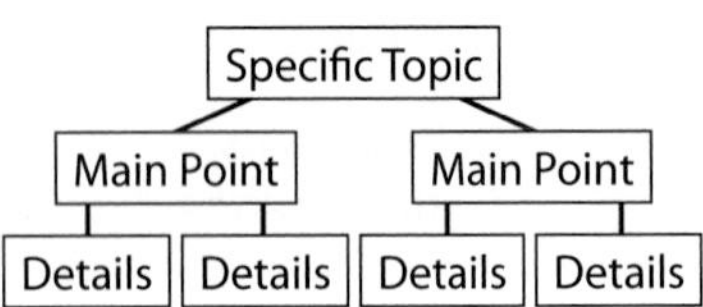

Venn Diagram Use to collect details to compare and contrast two topics.

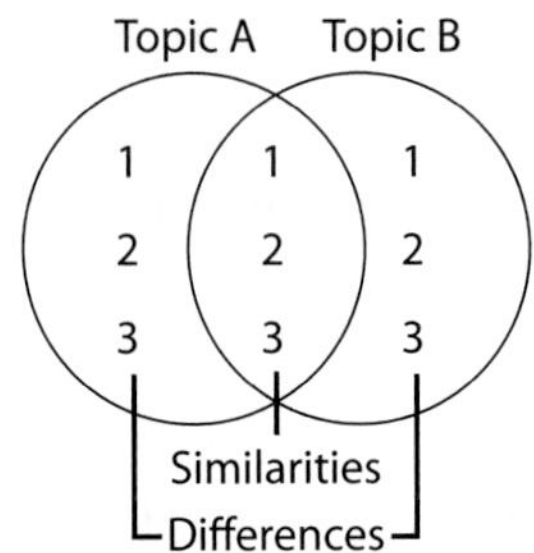

Cause-Effect Organizer Use to collect and organize details for cause-effect essays.

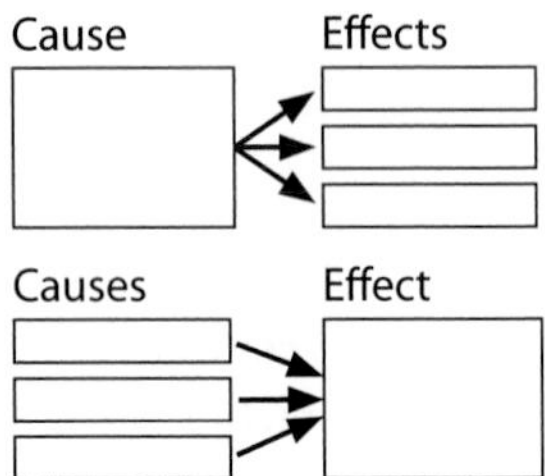

Problem-Solution Web Use to map out problem-solution essays.

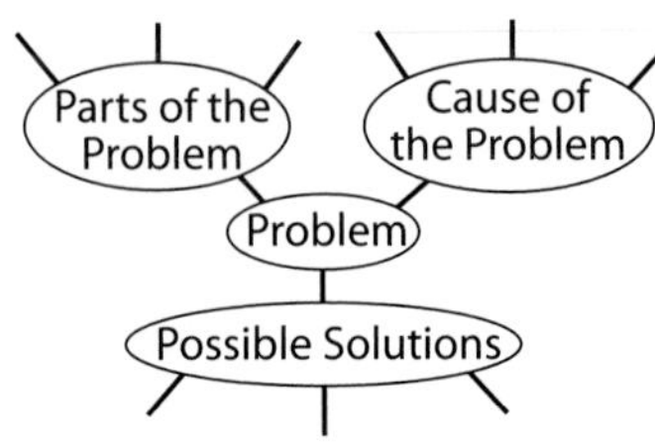

Evaluation Chart Use to collect supporting details for essays of evaluation.

Subject:

Points to Evaluate	Supporting Details
1	
2	
3	
4	

Cluster Use to collect details for informational essays.

Choose Identify the best graphic organizer for collecting information about each of the following topics.

1. A personal experience that changed your thinking

   Graphic organizer: time line

2. The features of a new recycling system

   Graphic organizer: line diagram, process diagram, or cluster

3. Vandalism in the dormitories

   Graphic organizer: cause-effect organizer or problem-solution web

4. Effects of a specific oil spill

   Graphic organizer: cause-effect organizer

5. Examining two similar movies

   Graphic organizer: Venn diagram

Complete Use the appropriate graphic organizer to record information about the topic you worked with on page 41, or for the first topic above. (You may have to do more research to help you fill in the graphic organizer.)

Answers will vary.

Learning Outcome

Establish a focus.

Traits

Your writing will go on and on and be hard to follow if it is unfocused.

Vocabulary

initiate
take the first step, begin

focus
centering on a particular feeling or a specific part of a topic

LO5 Establishing a Focus

There are really two parts to prewriting. Part one involves selecting an appropriate topic and collecting information about it. Part two deals with planning how to use this information in the actual writing. To **initiate** this plan, you must establish a writing focus.

Choosing the Special Part of a Topic

A skilled photographer decides how to **focus** or center the subject before taking a photograph. You should do the same before you begin writing. A thoughtful focus dictates what information to include in your writing, and what information to leave out.

Suppose you were writing an essay on the effects of the 2010 Gulf oil leak on a local shrimping community. To focus your writing and enhance its interest, you could cover how the spill has affected one particular shrimping family or business.

Topic: Effects of 2010 Gulf oil spill on (name of local shrimping community)

Focus: The spill's effect on a particular family or business

Review Rate the effectiveness of each focus below by circling the appropriate star. Consider whether the focus is clear, reasonable, and worth developing.

1. **Topic:** My personal ambitions
   Focus: A direct result of my mother's influence

   weak ★ ★ ★ ★ ★ strong

   strong

2. **Topic:** Barbie dolls
   Focus: Have been around a long time

   weak ★ ★ ★ ★ ★ strong

   weak

3. **Topic:** American art museums
   Focus: Why government funding is questionable

   weak ★ ★ ★ ★ ★ strong

   strong

4. **Topic:** Dog food
   Focus: What does it really taste like?

   weak ★ ★ ★ ★ ★ strong

   weak

Forming a Thesis Statement

You will state your focus in a **thesis statement** for an essay and in a **topic sentence** for a paragraph. An effective thesis statement identifies a special part of a topic or shares a particular feeling about it. The following formula can be used to write a thesis statement or a topic sentence.

A specific topic	+	A particular feeling, feature, or part	=	An effective thesis statement or topic sentence
Wearing *hijab*—Islamic covering		Mixed feelings about it		To wear *hijab*—Islamic covering—invites mixed feelings in me.

Tip

You may have to write two, three, or even four versions of a thesis statement until it says exactly what you want it to say.

Create Identify a focus and then write a topic sentence or thesis statement for each of the following assignments. The first one is done for you.

1. **Writing assignment:** Paragraph describing a specific type of exercise

   Specific topic: Pilates

   Focus: a thoughtful approach to fitness

   Topic sentence: Pilates provides a thoughtful approach to physical fitness.

2. **Writing assignment:** Paragraph explaining a type of ethnic food

   Specific topic: Tex-Mex cuisine

   Focus: Answers will vary.

   Topic sentence: ______

3. **Writing assignment:** Essay reflecting on a modern social problem

   Specific topic: Affordable living spaces

   Focus: Answers will vary.

   Thesis statement: ______

4. **Writing assignment:** Essay analyzing a favorite or important movie

   Specific topic: (Your choice)

   Focus: Answers will vary.

   Thesis statement: ______

Vocabulary

thesis statement
the controlling idea in an essay, highlighting a special part or feature of a topic or expressing a particular feeling about it

topic sentence
the controlling idea in a paragraph

Learning Outcome

Understand patterns of organization.

LO6 Understanding Patterns of Organization

After identifying your thesis, you'll need to decide how to organize the information that supports it. You have many patterns of organization to choose from. Here's how to proceed:

1. **Study your thesis statement.** It will usually indicate how to organize your ideas. For example, consider the following thesis statement:

   > Viewers love *The Simpsons* because it **parodies** daily live in the United States.

   As a point to be proved, this thesis suggests arranging the information by order of importance. As an idea to be shared and explained, it suggests a deductive organization of supporting information.

2. Then **review the information you have gathered**. Decide which ideas support your thesis and arrange them according to the appropriate method of organization. For example, if you are trying to prove a point about *The Simpsons,* you would arrange your reasons either from most important to least important or vice versa.

Patterns of Organization

Listed below are some of the common patterns that you will use in your writing.

- Use **chronological order** (time) when you are sharing a personal experience, telling how something happened, or explaining how to do something.
- Use **spatial order** (location) for descriptions, arranging information from left to right, top to bottom, from the edge to the center, and so on.
- Use **order of importance** when you are taking a stand or arguing for or against something. Arrange your reasons either from most important to least important or the other way around.
- Use **deductive organization** if you want to follow your thesis statement with basic information—supporting reasons, examples, and facts.
- Use **inductive organization** when you want to present specific details first and conclude with your thesis statement.
- Use **compare-contrast organization** when you want to show how one topic is different from and similar to another one.

Traits

For some writing assignments, you will use one main pattern of organization, and **complement** it with one or more additional patterns. For example, in an essay organized by order of importance, you may also need to make a comparison or describe someone or something.

Vocabulary

parody
imitate for comic effect or to prove a point

complement
add something extra to complete or make up a whole

Choose Study each of the following thesis statements. Then choose the method of organization that the thesis suggests. Explain each of your choices. The first one is done for you.

1. **Thesis statement:** The boardwalk makes Coney Island different from any other New York neighborhood.

   Appropriate method of organization: spatial order

   Explain: The thesis suggests that the writer will describe the boardwalk, so spatial organization makes sense.

2. **Thesis statement:** I am a Korean, but I am an American, too.

   Appropriate method of organization: compare-contrast organization

   Explain: Answers will vary.

3. **Thesis statement:** Multicultural education is vital to a society made up of many different peoples.

   Appropriate method of organization: deductive organization

   Explain: Answers will vary.

4. **Thesis statement:** I did something totally out of character for me; I jumped off a bridge with nothing more than a giant rubber band attached to my ankles.

   Appropriate method of organization: chronological order

   Explain: Answers will vary.

5. **Thesis statement:** (Choose one that you wrote on page 45.)

   Appropriate method of organization: Answers will vary.

   Explain: ______

Speaking & Listening

Work on this activity with a partner if your instructor allows it.

"The essay is a literary device for saying almost everything about almost anything."
—Aldous Huxley

Learning Outcome

Organize your information.

LO7 Organizing Your Information

Here are three basic strategies for arranging your supporting information after identifying an appropriate pattern of organization.

Make a quick list of main points.

Create an outline—an organized arrangement of main points and subpoints.

Fill in a graphic organizer, arranging main points and details in a chart or diagram. (See pages 42.)

"Complicated outlines tempt you to think too much about the fine points of organization, at a time when you should be blocking out the overall structure."
—Donald Murray

Using a Quick List

A quick list works well when you are writing a short piece, such as a paragraph, or when your planning time is limited. Here is a quick list for an informational essay about comets. (The main pattern of organization is chronological.)

Sample Quick List

Topic sentence: The appearance of comets in the night skies has puzzled people for thousands of years.

- very early on, thought to be planets
- Aristotle, the result of air escaping from atmosphere
- by 15th & 16th centuries, thought to be heavenly bodies
- all along, considered a sign of impending disaster
- really a gaseous body around a core of ice and dust
- head, hundreds of miles in diameter; tail millions of miles in length

Create Write a thesis statement and a quick list for an essay explaining why a certain book is one of your favorites. Answers will vary.

Thesis statement: ____________________

____

____

Quick list:

____

____

____

____

____

Using an Outline

An effective outline shows how ideas fit together and serves as a blueprint for your writing. Topic and sentence outlines follow specific guidelines: If you have a "I," you must have at least a "II." If you have an "A," you must have at least a "B," and so on. You can also **customize** an outline to meet your own needs.

Sample Customized Outline

What follows is the first part of a customized outline that includes main points stated in compete sentences and supporting details stated as phrases.

Thesis statement: Activist Charlotte Perkins Gilman rejected commonly held notions of male superiority.

1. Gilman's beliefs did little to prepare her for domestic life.
   - in 1884, married Charles W. Stetson
   - gave birth to a daughter
   - visited CA shortly after to mentally and emotionally recuperate
   - while there, wrote a book about a pregnant woman locked in a room
2. During the next stage in her life, Gilman became a leading feminist.
   - delivered speeches on women's rights
   - following a divorce in 1894, edited *Impress* for Women's Press Associate
   - from 1895-1900, continued lecturing on women's rights
   - in 1896, a delegate to the National Socialist and Labor Congress in London

Vocabulary

customize
to change or alter

unregulated
not controlled

Create Develop the first part of a customized outline for an essay about television viewing. A thesis statement and two main points are provided. Put the main points in a logical order and make up two or three details to support each one.

Thesis statement: **Unregulated** television viewing has harmful effects on young viewers.

Main points: Television is reactive, requiring no skill or thinking. Television viewing takes away from study and reading time.

1. Answers will vary. ____________________
   - ____________________
   - ____________________
   - ____________________
2. ____________________
   - ____________________
   - ____________________
   - ____________________

Learning Outcome

Review prewriting.

LO8 Reviewing Prewriting

Complete these activities as needed to help you better understand the key prewriting strategies.

Selecting a Topic Select a specific topic for the following general subject area (or for one of your own choosing): *a helpful Web site.* (See page 38.) Answers will vary.

1. General subject area: ______________________
2. Narrowing the subject: ______________________
3. Specific topic: ______________________

Forming a Thesis Statement Fill in the top spaces with the formula for writing thesis statements. Then write a thesis statement for the topic you identified above. (See page 45.)

A specific topic	+	A particular feeling, feature, or part	=	An effective thesis statement or topic sentence.
Answers will vary.		Answers will vary.		Answers will vary.

Choosing a Pattern of Organization Identify the best pattern of organization for developing each of the following thesis statements. (See pages 46–49.)

1. **Thesis statement:** Believe it or not, the environment can take care of itself.

   Pattern of organization: Deductive organization

2. **Thesis statement:** The animated movie *Fantasia* may be more than 60 years old, but it is still a timeless work of art.

   Pattern of organization: Order of importance

"You have to write a lot; let the words flow. . . ."
—Benjamin Percy

Philippe Colombi/Stockbyte/Getty Images

6 Drafting

When developing a piece of writing, you don't have to get it right the first time, the second time, or even the third time. Knowing this should help you feel less anxious about writing first drafts. You have a **singular** task at this point in the process—connecting your thoughts and feelings about your topic. These thoughts and feelings don't have to be perfectly worded or in the best order; they just have to be put on paper so you have something to work with.

Of course, drafting goes most smoothly when you have done the necessary prewriting, including information gathering, focusing, and organizing. Prewriting provides a road map for the writing that follows.

If you remember to approach a first draft as your *first look* at an emerging writing idea, you'll do fine. This chapter provides many additional tips and guidelines about the drafting process.

Learning Outcomes

LO1 Follow a drafting plan.
LO2 Form a meaningful whole.
LO3 Create an effective opening.
LO4 Develop the middle part.
LO5 Write a strong closing.
LO6 Review drafting.

Vocabulary

singular
one of a kind, unique

What do you think?

How can Benjamin Percy's advice about writing a lot and letting the words flow be applied to writing a first draft?

Answers will vary.

Learning Outcome

Follow a drafting plan.

LO1 Following a Drafting Plan

When writing a first draft, you're writing to see how well you match up with the topic and if your initial planning still makes sense.

Writing a first draft helps you decide how to proceed with your writing idea. If you're lucky, everything will turn out just as you had planned, and you'll continue to develop your writing. On the other hand, you may discover that you need to learn more about the topic, adjust your focus, or start over.

Traits

In order to do your best work, you must have strong feelings about your topic.

A Writing Plan

Use the following points as your drafting guide.

- Focus on developing your thoughts and feelings, not on trying to produce a final copy.
- Follow your prewriting and planning notes, but also feel free to include new ideas that come to mind as you write.
- Continue writing until you cover all of your main points or until you come to a logical stopping point.
- Express yourself honestly and sincerely, using other sources of information to support what you have to say.
- If you get stuck, employ one of these strategies:

  Write as if you are in a conversation with the reader.

  Write in short, fluid bursts of 3-5 minutes.

  Start in the middle by simply identifying your topic and going from there.

Write Answer the following questions related to the drafting process.

1. Why is a first draft commonly called a rough draft?

   Answers will vary.

2. In what way does writing a first draft set in motion the rest of the writing process?

   Answers will vary.

3. Some instructors suggest turning down the **resolution** on your computer if you have trouble writing a first draft. How do you think this action would help?

   Answers will vary.

Vocabulary

resolution
a term used to describe the clarity of the image on a computer screen

LO2 Forming a Meaningful Whole

Learning Outcome

Form a meaningful whole.

Writer Lillian Hellman said, "There are a thousand ways to write, and each is as good as the other if it fits you." That is certainly true when writing a first draft, once you understand that it doesn't have to be perfect. You must also understand that when developing a first draft, your goal is to form a meaningful whole or a complete initial writing.

Forming a meaningful whole for a paragraph means including a topic sentence, body sentences, and a closing sentence. For an essay, it means including an opening paragraph (with a thesis statement), multiple supporting paragraphs, and a closing paragraph.

"Just get it on paper, and then we'll see what to do with it."
—Maxwell Perkins

Graphically Speaking

The graphics below show the structure of both basic forms of writing.

Paragraph Structure

Topic Sentence
A **topic sentence** names the topic.

Detail Sentences
Detail sentences support the topic.

Closing Sentence
A **closing sentence** wraps up the paragraph.

Essay Structure

Opening Paragraph
The **opening paragraph** draws the reader into the essay and provides information that leads to a thesis statement. The thesis statement tells what the essay is about.

Middle Paragraphs
The **middle paragraphs** support the thesis statement. Each middle paragraph needs a topic sentence, a variety of detail sentences, and a closing sentence.

Closing Paragraph
The **closing paragraph** finishes the essay by revisiting the thesis statement, emphasizing an important detail, providing the reader with an interesting final thought, and/or looking toward the future.

Learning Outcome

Create an effective opening.

"The best advice on writing I've ever received is 'Knock 'em dead with the lead sentence.'"
—Whitney Balliett

LO3 Creating an Effective Opening

In many situations, first impressions are important—say, for instance, when you're interviewing for a job or introducing yourself to a roommate or a coworker. First impressions are important in writing, too, because the first few ideas help set the **tone** for the rest of the piece. The information that follows will help you make a positive impression in the opening part of your essays.

The Basic Parts

The opening paragraph (or part) of an essay usually does these three things: (1) identifies the topic, (2) **engages** the reader, (3) and states the thesis. Before stating your thesis, you may also need to include a sentence or two of background information.

Starting Strategies

Listed below are a few strategies to help you introduce the topic and engage the reader.

- Begin with a surprising or little-known fact about the topic.

  Thousands of babies are born each year with alcohol-related defects, making fetal alcohol syndrome one of the leading causes of mental retardation.

jon le-bon/2010. Used under license from Shutterstock.com

- Ask an interesting or challenging question about the topic.

  What exactly do the signs held up by homeless people tell us?

- Start with a telling quotation.

  "We live here and they live there," Bigger Thomas says in *Native Son*. "We black and they white. They got things and we ain't. They do things and we can't."

- Share a brief, dramatic story.

  It was May 1945. World War II had just ended and Yugoslavia had been overtaken. The town of Vrhnika, Yugoslavia, was no longer safe. Russian and communist troops would break into houses, take what they wanted, and even kill.

- Open with a bold statement.

  Barbie's boobs and spacious mansion helped cause the decay of today's youth, or so say some experts.

Vocabulary

tone
the writer's attitude toward his or her topic

engage
attract, instill interest

Sample Opening Paragraph

Analyze Carefully read the following opening paragraph from an essay about a **degenerative** bone disease called Legg-Calve-Perthes (pronounced leg-cal-VAY-PER-theez). Then answer the questions below.

Allie Mason acted like a typical high school freshman. She was bubbly, energetic, and extremely friendly. She was also a **conscientious** student, belonged to the Honors Art Club, and enjoyed golfing. What set Allie apart was a **debilitating** physical condition that caused one of her legs to be noticeably shorter than the other one and forced her to limp. As a result, she had to endure endless medical procedures and missed out on typical school activities such as gym and dances. She also had to endure more than her share of insensitive remarks. She remembered, "My classmates would tease me and call me names." Their comments obviously hurt, especially those made by her friends. The reason for Allie's suffering was Legg-Calve-Perthes, a painful bone disease that truly challenges the sufferer.

1. What strategy does the writer use to introduce the topic and engage the reader? (See the previous page.)

   She gives a brief dramatic story.

2. What, if any, background information is provided about the topic?

   The effects are shaped before the condition is named.

3. What special part of or feeling about the topic is identified in the thesis statement?

   The pain and challenge of Legg-Calve-Perthes disease.

Create Write a sample opening paragraph for an essay about one of the topics that you worked with in "Prewriting" (pages 35–50). Use your own paper if you need more room.

Answers will vary.

Traits

Once the beginning part is set, you'll find it much easier to develop the rest of your writing.

Vocabulary

degenerative
gradual loss of use or function

conscientious
caring, hard-working

debilitating
weakening, draining the strength or health

Learning Outcome

Develop the middle part.

"When your writing is filled with details, it has a lot more impact."
—Ivan Levison

WAC

Most writing assignments use one of these basic writing words to identify the key focus of your work—to *describe,* to *explain,* and so on.

LO4 Developing Your Ideas

In the middle paragraphs, you should develop all of the main points that support your thesis statement. Use your planning (quick list, outline, graphic organizer) as a general guide when you develop this part of an essay. Here are a few tips for getting started:

- **Keep your thesis statement in mind as you write.** All of your main points should support or advance this statement.
- **Develop each main point in a separate paragraph (or two).** State the main point in the form of a topic sentence and follow with detail sentences that support it.
- **Use plenty of details** to fully explain your points.
- **Use your own words,** except on those few occasions when you employ a quotation to add authority to your writing.
- **Be open to new ideas that occur to you,** especially if they will improve your essay.
- **Try any of the following writing moves** that are appropriate to your topic.

Basic Writing Moves

The paragraphs in the middle part of an essay should, among other things, *explain, describe, define, classify,* and so on. What follows is a list and definitions of these basic writing moves.

Narrating — sharing an experience or a story
Describing — telling how someone or something appears, acts, or operates
Explaining — providing important facts, details, and examples
Analyzing — carefully examining a subject or breaking it down
Comparing — showing how two subjects are similar and different
Defining — identifying or clarifying the meaning of a term
Reflecting — connecting with or wondering about
Evaluating — rating the value of something
Arguing — using logic and evidence to prove something is true

Special Challenge Read two different essays on pages 424–499 in *WRITE 2.* On your own paper, list the different moves that the writer uses in the middle paragraphs of her or his writing. For example, the writer may *explain* in one or more paragraphs, *reflect* in another, and so on.

Sample Middle Paragraph

Analyze Carefully read the following middle paragraph from an essay on Legg-Calve-Perthes. Then answer the questions below.

Legg-Calve-Perthes is both rare and mysterious. The disease affects only 5 of every 100,000 children, usually when they are between the ages of five and twelve. While boys suffer from the disease far more frequently than girls do by a ratio of 4 to 1, when girls do develop Legg-Calve-Perthes, they tend to suffer more severely from it. At this point, researchers are not really sure of the cause of the disease. They are, however, fairly certain that it is not genetic. They also know that a reduction of blood flow at the hip joint contributes to the disease and causes the bone tissue to collapse or react in other strange ways. Usually, the rounded part of the femur bone that fits into the hip joint becomes deformed. In Allie's case, the top of her femur bone grew to double its normal size, a condition that produced extreme pain when she tried to walk. It's hard to imagine how Allie or anyone else is able to deal with this condition during the active childhood years.

1. What specific part or special feature of the topic is identified in the topic sentence?

   The rarity and mysteriousness of Legg-Calve-Perthes disease

2. What basic writing move (or moves) does the writer use in this paragraph? (See the previous page.)

   describing, explaining, analyzing, defining

Tip

Keep your reader in mind as you write. Try to anticipate and answer any questions your audience may have about your topic.

Create Write a middle paragraph to go along with the opening paragraph that you wrote on page 55. You may either carry out some quick research or simply make up details to complete your paragraph. Use your own paper if you need more room.

Answers will vary.

Learning Outcome

Write a strong closing.

Traits

You may need to write two or three versions of your closing before it says exactly what you want it to say.

Vocabulary

forfeits
loses or surrenders

agroterrorist
someone who uses diseases to attack a country's agricultural industry

LO5 Writing a Strong Closing

While the opening part of your writing offers important *first* impressions, the closing part should offer important *final* impressions. More specifically, it should help the reader better understand and appreciate the importance of your topic or thesis.

The Working Parts

Consider the strategies below when writing your closing. In most cases, you will want to use more than one of them; but whatever you choose to do, your closing must flow smoothly from your last middle paragraph.

- Remind the reader of the thesis.

  Legg-Calve-Parthes is like a cancer in how it affects an individual and her or his family.

- Summarize the main points or highlight one or two of them.

  Ultimately, both Alan and Bigger (two literary characters) fail to gain real control over the outside forces in their lives. Alan **forfeits** his interest in life, and Bigger forfeits life itself.

- Reflect on the explanation or argument you've presented in the main part.

  It would be a shame to lose these amazing creatures (humpback whales). We don't want their mysterious song to be a thing of the past. And we can't turn to zoos when the numbers shrink to a precious few.

- Offer a final idea to keep the reader thinking about the topic.

  If the country waits until an **agroterrorist** attack happens, people may become ill, the overall economy could be damaged, and the agricultural economy may never recover.

Noam Armonn/2010. Used under license from Shutterstock.com

Sample Closing Paragraph

Analyze Carefully read the following closing paragraph for an essay on Legg-Calve-Perthes. Then answer the questions below.

Legg-Calve-Perthes is like a cancer in how it affects an individual and her family. In Allie's case, the debilitating effects started with her painful efforts to walk and has continued with attempts to address the condition with operations, therapy, and braces. Through all of this, she and her family have missed out on so much. Her mother had to quit her job, and her sister felt ignored. As Allie recalled, "My sister has always felt jealous of all of the attention I get from my parents." But knowing that the condition should, in time, resolve itself certainly must help sufferers like Allie meet each new challenge. It must also help them to know that young people suffering from Legg-Calve-Perthes usually do quite well in the long term. Unfortunately, the chance of permanent hip damage exists as well.

1. In what way does the first sentence remind the reader of the thesis statement?

   It focuses on the way the disease affects the sufferer.

2. What other strategy or strategies does the writer use?

   The author shares more anecdotes about Allie's suffering.

Create Write a closing paragraph to go along with the opening and middle paragraphs that you have written in this chapter. Use the sample above and the information on page 58 as a guide.

Answers will vary.

"Make your writing useful."
—William Zinsser

Traits

Feel free to include new information in your closing, especially if you feel it will help you emphasize the importance of your topic.

Learning Outcome

Review drafting.

LO6 Reviewing Drafting

Complete these activities as needed to help you better understand key strategies in this chapter.

Follow a Drafting Plan What are two things that you can do if you get stuck when drafting? (See page 52.)

1. See the list under the final bullet point on page 52.
2. See the list under the final bullet point on page 52.

Create an Effective Opening What are the three main things that you should accomplish in the opening part of an essay? (See page 54.)

1. Identify the topic.
2. Engage the reader.
3. State the thesis.

Develop the Middle Part Answer these questions about the basic writing moves a writer may use. (See page 56.)

1. What does it mean to narrate in a paragraph?

   Sharing an experience or a story
2. When explaining, what types of information will a writer include?

   Important facts, details, and examples
3. When a writer evaluates, what is she or he actually doing?

   Rating the value of something

Write a Strong Closing What are two strategies that you can use to develop a closing? (See page 58.)

1. See the bulleted list on page 58.
2. See the bulleted list on page 58.

"If [you] write a lot, that's good.
If [you] revise a lot, that's even better."
—Toni Morrison

Micheline Pelletier/Corbis News/Corbis

Revising

You would never expect a musician to perform or record a song after putting lyrics and music together for the first time. In fact, the real work would have just begun. There would be questions to answer: Does the song have potential? If so, what needs to be done to get it performance-ready? Then would come the work of arranging and practicing the song, again and again, until everything—lyrics, rhythm, timing, beat—was just right.

In the same way, you should never expect to share a first draft of your writing as if it were a finished piece. You still have a lot of work ahead of you—reviewing your writing, and then revising any confusing, incomplete, or out-of-order parts. Each revision you make brings you closer to an effective piece of writing.

This chapter provides guidelines and strategies for revising a first draft, with the traits of strong writing, and a fine finished draft, in clear view.

Learning Outcomes

- **LO1** Understand the revising process.
- **LO2** Recognize the traits of strong writing.
- **LO3** Check for completeness.
- **LO4** Check for coherence.
- **LO5** Learn the basics of peer reviewing.
- **LO6** Review revising.

What do you think?

In the quotation, why does Morrison state that revising a lot is even better than writing a lot?

Answers will vary.

Learning Outcome

Understand the revising process.

"If you haven't revised, you're not finished."
—Patricia T. O'Conner

Traits

Don't pay undue attention to surface issues—usage, spelling, punctuation—at this point in the process. Instead, focus on the **content** of your writing.

Vocabulary

content
the ideas covered in a piece of writing

LO1 Understanding Revising

Revising is the process of improving the message in your writing. To make the best revising decisions, follow these guidelines:

- **Take some time away from your writing.** This will help you see your first draft more clearly, and with a fresh outlook.
- **Read your first draft a number of times,** silently and out loud, to get an overall impression of your work.
- **Have a trusted peer or two react to your writing.** Their questions and comments will help you decide what changes to make.
- **Check your overall focus or thesis.** Decide if it still works and if you have provided enough support for it.
- **Then review your work, part by part.** Pay special attention to the opening, since it sets the tone of your writing, and the closing, since it serves as your final word on the topic.
- **Plan a revising strategy** by deciding what you need to do first, second, and third.

Evaluate Rate each sample below in terms of its potential as an effective starting point for a piece of writing. Explain your choices.

I've met a lot of people. Some were interesting and some were enemies. Some I hardly knew. Whenever I see kids building a snow fort, I ask myself, "Whatever happened to Keyton Kaul, the most feared girl in my old neighborhood?" Keyton was a bully, and she had done a lot to earn that label. I also remember Mary Osmond. . . .

weak ★ ★ ★ ★ ★ strong

Weak. Explanations will vary.

Though Howard Hughes died more than 20 years ago, his legend lives on. He represented the American Dream turned on itself because he was a victim of the multibillion-dollar empire he single-handedly created. We all are fascinated by celebrities, heroes, the wealthy, and the sick. Hughes was all of these things and more. . . .

weak ★ ★ ★ ★ ★ strong

Strong. Explanations will vary.

Additional Considerations

What follows are two additional aspects of the revising process to consider.

Revisit Your Purpose and Audience

Before you revise a first draft, be sure to have the purpose of your writing clearly in mind: *Are you writing to explain, to persuade, to describe, or to share?* With a clear understanding of the purpose, you will find it much easier to know what changes to make. Also consider your readers: *Have you anticipated and answered the questions they may have about the topic?*

Understand the Basic Revising Moves

You have four basic ways to make changes in your writing—adding, cutting, rewriting, or reordering information. Each change or improvement that you make will bring you closer to a strong finished piece.

Add information to . . .

- make a main supporting point more convincing.
- complete a specific explanation.
- improve the flow of your writing.

Cut information if it . . .

- doesn't support the thesis.
- seems repetitious.

Rewrite information if it . . .

- seems confusing or unclear.
- appears too complicated.
- lacks the proper **voice.**

Reorder information if it . . .

- seems out of order.
- would be more significant in another spot.

Vocabulary

voice
a writer's manner of expression, the "sound" of his or her words (A strong voice signals an interested, knowledgeable writer.)

React Carefully read this first draft. As you will see, it has a number of problems. Then follow the directions below the writing.

Winning the lottery must be everyone's number one dream! If I won the lottery, my life would be wonderful. First, I'd travel to other countries. I've always wanted to go to Italy and eat spaghetti in a gondola. ~~Yeah I'm definitely going to keep buying those lottery tickets.~~ Then I'd buy a retooled Mustang with a stardust paint job. My dad says that old Fords have mechanical problems. But he's just an old dude who doesn't know cars. Everyone knows Mustangs are totally hot-looking cars. I'd buy my mom a car, too. She'd probably want a dull, dependable car like a Volvo or something dull like that, but a Jeep is something I'd talk her out of undoubtedly for sure. Some 4x4 action would spice up her life.

1. **Underline** one sentence or idea that could be improved if information were added.
2. **Put** a line through one idea that should be cut because it is unnecessary or unneeded.
3. **Draw** a wavy line under one idea that should be rewritten because it is unclear.
4. **Circle** one idea that should be moved; draw an arrow to show where you would move it.
Answers will vary.

Special Challenge Rewrite this paragraph, making the changes that you marked on the original. Feel free to make other changes as well. Afterward, share your revised writing with your classmates.

Learning Outcome

Recognize the traits of strong writing.

"There is no such thing as good writing, only good rewriting."
—Louis Brandeis

Traits

Word choice and sentence fluency are not as important as the other traits at this point. But they become very important during the editing step.

LO2 Recognizing Strong Writing

Understanding the traits of writing will help you revise your first drafts. Think of the traits (*ideas, organization,* and so on) as the key ingredients in writing, each one contributing to the development of a piece of writing. The traits-based checklist below can serve as an effective guide when you revise. If your writing doesn't "pass" certain descriptors, then you should make the necessary changes.

Revising Checklist

Ideas

☐ **1.** Does an interesting and relevant topic serve as a starting point for the writing?

☐ **2.** Is the writing focused, addressing a specific feeling about or a specific part of the topic? (The focus is usually expressed in the thesis statement.)

☐ **3.** Are there enough specific ideas, details, and examples to support the thesis?

☐ **4.** Overall, is the writing engaging and informative?

Organization

☐ **5.** Does the writing form a meaningful whole—with opening, middle, and closing parts?

☐ **6.** Does the writing follow a logical pattern of organization?

☐ **7.** Do transitions connect ideas and help the writing flow?

Voice

☐ **8.** Does the writer sound informed about and interested in the topic?

☐ **9.** In addition, does the writer sound sincere and genuine?

Word Choice

☐ **10.** Does the word choice clearly fit the purpose and the audience?

☐ **11.** Does the writing include specific words as much as possible?

Sentence Fluency

☐ **12.** Are the sentences clear and do they flow smoothly?

☐ **13.** Are the sentences varied in terms of their beginnings and length?

React Carefully read the following paragraphs from a persuasive essay. Then answer the questions below that address the first three traits: *ideas, organization,* and *voice.* (Use your own paper for your answers.)

Learn to Earn

Lack of student motivation is a main topic of discussion when it comes to today's underachieving schools. The experts ask, how can we motivate our students to learn? And how can we keep them in school long enough to prepare for the twenty-first century workplace? These questions are especially important in urban areas, where the drop-out rate is alarming, especially among nonnative English students. One answer appears quite logical: Give them money. In other words, if we want our students to succeed in school, we should pay them.

Students, in one way, are already bribed to attend school. The whole point of academic scholarships is based on receiving a monetary reward for being a good student. Calling a cash award a "scholarship" doesn't alter the fact that what's being offered is money. Presently, only the best students or the best athletes pick up all the cash. That does not seem fair. What about the student that doesn't want to go to college? Why not pay everyone for going to school the same way they would get paid for doing any other job?

Many students drop out of school because they are forced to work to help support their families. When it comes to choosing between going to school or going to work, the latter usually wins out for practical reasons. If these same students were paid a minimum wage for attending school, they wouldn't have to worry about choosing between education and keeping their jobs. In the long run, it would probably be less expensive to keep these students in school by paying them than to have them drop out of school with no skills.

Ideas Answers will vary.

1. Is the topic relevant and interesting? Explain.
2. Is the focus or thesis of the essay clear? Explain.
3. Does the essay contain a variety of specific details? Explain.

Organization

1. Does the first paragraph include the key elements of an effective opening? (See pages 54–55.) Explain. Answers will vary.
2. Do these paragraphs follow a logical pattern of organization? If so, which one? (See pages 46–49.) Deductive organization or order of importance.

Voice Answers will vary.

1. Does the writer sound informed and interested in the topic? Explain.
2. Does the writer sound sincere and honest? Explain.

Learning Outcome

Check for completeness.

"The first great gift we can bestow on others is a good example."
—Thomas Morell

LO3 Checking for Completeness

Your college instructors expect you to support the main points in your essays with plenty of details. Details help you develop complete explanations and arguments.

Types of Details

The following list identifies the common types of details.

Facts and statistics give specific information that can be checked.

> Legg-Calve-Perthes affects only 5 of every 100,000, usually when they are between the ages of five and twelve.

Examples demonstrate or show something.

> Donald, two years younger than me, has always been more daring. (main point)
>
> When we were younger, he was the first to jump off the cliffs at the quarry. (example)

Definitions explain new terms.

> The *American Heritage College Dictionary* defines sexual harassment as "unwanted and offensive sexual advances or sexually **derogatory** remarks."

Reasons answer "why" after a main point.

> Watching television is a **reactive** activity. (main point)
>
> It takes absolutely no skill or thinking. (reason)

Quotations provide the thoughts of people knowledgeable about the topic.

> Tuyen stated, "In the Chinese tradition, the superior person assumes loving responsibility for the inferior, and the inferior person shows respect and obedience to the superior."

Reflections offer the writer's thoughts.

> For most young people, growing up means being told to act like an adult while being treated like a child. It means receiving an abundance of advice but having little patience. It means wanting to be independent but realizing just how dependent you are.

Vocabulary

derogatory
scornful, hurtful, making someone feel less important or smaller

reactive
reacting to rather than initiating or creating

Identify In the essay on page 65, record one example for each type of detail listed below. (Use your own paper if you need more room.) Answers will vary.

Facts: ______________________________

Examples: ______________________________

Reasons: ______________________________

Quotations: ______________________________

Levels of Detail

Effective essays are thorough, meaning that they contain different levels of information to fully explain or develop each main point. Here are three basic levels of detail in writing.

Level 1: A **controlling sentence** names a topic (usually a topic sentence) or makes a main point.

Level 2: A **clarifying sentence** explains a level 1 sentence.

Level 3: A **completing sentence** adds details to complete the point.

Traits

To "complete" some main points, a writer may add another level of detail (level 4).

Details in Action

The passage that follows uses three different levels of detail. Notice that the level 1 sentence (a topic sentence) is supported by three level 2 sentences. Two level 3 sentences complete the last level 2 sentence.

> **(Level 1)** Legg-Calve-Perthes is both rare and mysterious. **(Level 2)** The disease affects only 5 of every 100,000 children, usually when they are between the ages of five and twelve. **(Level 2)** Boys suffer from the disease far more frequently than girls do, by a ratio of 4 to 1, which makes Allie's experience all the more unusual. **(Level 2)** At this point, researchers are not really sure of the cause of the disease. **(Level 3)** They are, however, fairly certain that it is not genetic. (**Level 3**) They also know that a reduction of blood flow . . .

Identify Carefully read the following passage; then label its levels of detail. (Work on this activity with a partner if your instructor allows it.)

> (controlling) Plato, an ancient Greek philosopher and educator, was the first to write about the lost continent of Atlantis in his book *Critias*. (clarifying) Most scholars agree that Plato's book includes only legendary events, not real history. (completing) When Plato described Atlantis, he painted a picture of a people of fabulous wealth who ruled over a great and wonderful empire. (completing) He also claimed that the continent of Atlantis sank beneath the sea in one day's time.

Special Challenge Write a paragraph of at least five or six sentences about one of the following topics: *types of sports fans, your favorite type of music, the best piece of technology ever invented, the one time you really "roughed it."* Afterward, label your sentences with the numbers 1, 2, or 3, depending on the level of detail they include.

Learning Outcome

Check for coherence.

"I tell [students] to use transitions, to start each paragraph with an interlocking nut, a thread, so that the story is seamless."
—Steve Lovelady

LO4 Checking for Coherence

When a paragraph or essay is **coherent**, all of its ideas work together and flow smoothly from one point to the next. Transitions, or linking words and phrases like *such as, on the other hand,* and *in addition,* help create coherence because they connect ideas. Transitions can show location or time, compare and contrast things, and so on.

Words used to show location:

above	behind	down	on top of
across	below	in back of	onto
against	beneath	in front of	outside
along	beside	inside	over
among	between	into	throughout
around	beyond	near	to the right
away from	by	off	under

Words used to show time:

about	during	next	today
after	finally	next week	tomorrow
afterward	first	second	until
as soon as	immediately	soon	when
at	later	then	yesterday
before	meanwhile	third	

Words used to compare things (show similarities):

also	in the same way	likewise
as	like	similarly

Words used to contrast things (show differences):

although	even though	on the other hand	still
but	however	otherwise	yet

Words used to emphasize a point:

again	for this reason	particularly	to repeat
even	in fact	to emphasize	truly

Words used to conclude or summarize:

all in all	finally	in summary	therefore
as a result	in conclusion	last	to sum up

Words used to add information:

additionally	and	equally important	in addition
again	another	finally	likewise
along with	as well	for example	next
also	besides	for instance	second

Words used to clarify:

for instance	in other words	put another way	that is

Vocabulary

coherent
orderly, logical, holding together

Linking Words and Phrases in Action

Note the use of transitions in the following passages. Each one adds to the coherence and readability of the ideas.

- Jazz ballet provides me with all of the exercise that I need. *To begin with,* it combines gymnastics with dance. All of the gymnastic-like splits, leaps, kicks, and high jumps provide the ultimate cardiovascular workout. *(The transition is used to add information.)*
- Alan experiences the pressure of working as a clerk at Bryson's Appliance Store. The customers are demanding, and the many products and brand names are confusing. *Later,* under hypnosis, he admits that his "foes" are the myriad brand names he is challenged to locate. *(The transition is used to show time.)*
- In response to Motz's idea that Barbies make girls dependent on males, I say, "Phooey." I played with the dolls for years, and I have often been free from any type of romantic attachment. *In fact,* I am now a happy single girl. *(The transition emphasizes a point.)*

Traits

Use transitions as needed in your writing, but be careful not to overuse them. Too many transitions can actually get in the way and draw undue attention to themselves.

Identify Circle the transition or transitions used in each of the following passages. In the space below each passage, identify the purpose of the transition—*to show location, to show time,* and so on.

- Humpbacks, like other whales, must migrate. Some humpbacks begin their journey in October. Mature females accompanied by their yearling calves set off first. Next, the immature males and females begin the journey. . . .

  to show time

- American art museums represent a confusing mix of public and private interests. Without question, however, the primary function of the museum is to serve the public.

  to contrast things (show differences)

- What set Allie apart was a debilitating physical condition that caused one of her legs to be noticeably shorter than the other one. As a result, she had to endure endless medical procedures, . . .

  to conclude or summarize

- This crude tent-like structure was to be my home. Around the base, four strong poles stick straight up. On the top, a crisscrossing of long branches and thatch serves as a roof. . . .

  to show location

Special Challenge Review the paragraph you may have written on page 67, looking for transitions. Did you use any? If not, could the paragraph benefit from a transition or two? Which ones?

Learning Outcome

Learn the basics of peer reviewing.

"Keep away from people who try to **belittle** your ambitions." —Mark Twain

Speaking & Listening

Responding to each other's writing builds a community spirit among classmates. It will help you appreciate writing as a process of learning rather than just another assignment.

Andresr, 2010/used under license from www.shutterstock.com

Vocabulary

belittle
lessen, make smaller, criticize

constructively
in a helpful manner

LO5 Reviewing with Peers

Having your peers react to your writing helps you decide what changes need to be made. They can tell you if your writing keeps their interest, answers their main questions about the topic, and makes sense from start to finish.

The Role of the Writer

1. **Have a complete piece of writing to share.** Make a copy for each group member.
2. **Set the scene** by making a few introductory comments about your work. But don't say too much.
3. **Read your work out loud.** Don't stop for explanations; just read the text as clearly as you can.
4. **Afterward, listen carefully to the reactions,** and answer any questions. Don't try to defend yourself or your writing. Just listen and take notes on important points.
5. **Ask for help** if you have concerns about certain parts.

The Role of the Listeners/Responders

1. **Pay careful attention during the reading.** Take brief notes if you think it would help. Then read the text silently.
2. **React positively and constructively.** Instead of saying "Nice start," for example, say something more exact, such as "Sharing that dramatic story in the beginning really made me take notice."
3. **Comment on specific things you noticed.** Saying "It would be good to add more style to your writing" isn't very helpful. But saying "Many of the sentences start in the same way" gives the writer a specific idea for improving the writing.
4. **Question the writer** if you are unsure of something. "What is the purpose of . . . ?" or "Why did you start the . . .?"
5. **Show that you are really interested in helping.** Have at least one positive comment and one suggestion to offer. Also listen to others' comments and add to them.

Write Develop a first draft in which you reflect and/or comment upon a current event in any area of life—political affairs, the environment, sports, entertainment, and so on. (Use your own paper if you need more room.)

Answers will vary.

Share Review your first draft in a peer-responding session, following the guidelines on the previous page. (Work with one partner or a small group of your peers.) Then list two helpful suggestions that were made. Answers will vary.

1. ______

2. ______

Learning Outcome

Review revising.

LO6 Reviewing Revising

Complete these activities as needed to help you better understand the revising process.

Understand the Revising Process List below the four basic revising moves. (See page 63.)

1. Add information.
2. Cut information.
3. Rewrite information.
4. Reorder information.

Recognize Strong Writing What questions should you ask about your writing to check it for effective organization? Identify two of them. (See page 64.)

1. See checklist points 5, 6, and 7 on page 64.
2. See checklist points 5, 6, and 7 on page 64.

Check for Completeness Identify the type of detail used in each of the following examples. (See page 66.)

1. Facts and statistics According to *Modern Style Magazine,* a face-lift costs $5,000-$15,000; nose jobs are $4,000-$8,000; and hair transplants are $6,000–$10,000.
2. Examples Charlotte Perkins Gilman contributed to the women's movement. *(main point)* She developed the idea of collective child care and attacked misconceived notions of womanhood and motherhood.

Check for Coherence Circle the transitions used in each passage and tell the purpose of each one: to show time, to emphasize a point, and so on. (See pages 68–69.)

1. The assortment of food whisking by me is astonishing. Below me, a father and his two sons are just completing their third trip to the food court. to show location
2. I made French toast this morning for my family. It was an American treat, and they praised its taste. Afterward, we all watched an old movie. to show time
3. A tactful person not only expresses herself sensitively, but truthfully as well. Doctors, for example, must be truthful when dealing with their patients and the patients' families. to add information

"I love the taste of words. They have a taste and a weight and a colour as well as a sound and a shape." —Philip Pullman

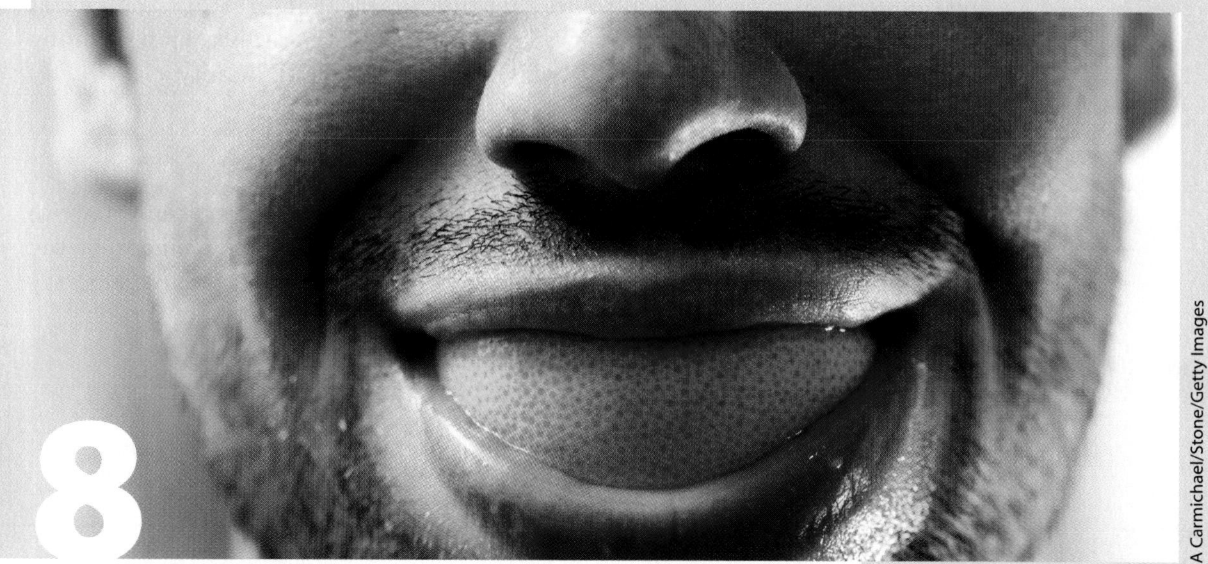

A Carmichael/Stone/Getty Images

Editing

There's a time during the writing process when **editing** for style and correctness makes the most sense. And that time comes after you have done everything possible to make your main message logical and complete. Always think content before anything else.

Editing writing is like buffing out the smudges and scratches on a car after it's been painted. The buffing is certainly important, but only after the main work—the actual painting—is complete.

The first part of this chapter provides tips for checking the word choice and sentence fluency in your writing. The second part provides, among other things, strategies for editing for correctness and an explanation of Standard English.

Learning Outcomes

- LO1 Edit for style.
- LO2 Learn how to check for correctness.
- LO3 Understand Standard English.
- LO4 Use a common errors list.
- LO5 Review editing.

What do you think?

How can Pullman's quotation serve as a guide for selecting words for your writing?

Answers will vary.

Vocabulary

editing
the step in the writing process when you check the style (word choice and sentence fluency) and accuracy of your revised writing

Learning Outcome

Edit for style.

LO1 Editing for Style

When editing your writing for style, you are checking the quality of its words and sentences. You want to make sure that they are clear, interesting, and honest (sounding like they come from you). Trying to force style into your writing by using **flowery language**, for example, will diminish its overall quality.

Checking for Word Choice

Suppose some five-alarm buffalo wings actually bring you to tears. Then you write about the experience: "I ate some hot food." Did you capture the moment, or the pain? Or course not. General words like "hot" and "food" do not compare favorably to specific words like "five-alarm" and "buffalo wings."

Traits

Watch for the overuse of the "be" verbs (*is, are, was, were*) in your writing. Often, a more vivid verb can be made from another word in the sentence.

Using Specific Nouns and Verbs

It's especially important to use specific nouns and verbs because they carry most of the meaning in your writing. Note that the subjects and verbs in the following sentences are specific.

The five-alarm buffalo wings (noun) scorched (verb) my mouth.

Charlotte Perkins Gilman (noun) rejected (verb) the belief in male superiority.

Analyze Study the photograph to the right. Then list examples of specific nouns and verbs that could be associated with it. Afterward, compare lists with your classmates.

Answers will vary.

Specific Nouns	Specific Verbs

Vocabulary

flowery language
writing that uses more sophisticated words than needed

Create On your own paper, write a brief descriptive paragraph about the photograph using some or all of the words that you listed above.

Checking for Sentence Fluency

To check the fluency of your sentences, read your writing out loud, or have someone read it out loud to you.

Sentence Trouble Spots

Pay special attention to the following two problems.

Slow-Moving Sentences

If too many of your sentences contain passive verbs, your writing will plod along. To fix this problem, edit the sentences so that they contain active, forward-moving verbs. (See page 352 for more information.)

Sentence with Passive Verb:

The 16-ounce porterhouse was dragged along the kitchen counter by the Chihuahua. *(The subject "porterhouse" is being acted upon.)*

Sentence with Active Verb:

The Chihuahua dragged a 16-ounce porterhouse along the kitchen counter. *(The subject "Chihuahua" is performing the action.)*

Sentences with Qualifiers

If you use too many qualifiers in your sentences (*maybe, it seems to me, I think*), you will sound unsure of yourself. To sound confident, simply omit these words.

Sentence with Qualifiers:

Although McDonald's is a leading fast-food chain, *it seems to me* that they have *maybe* introduced some healthy alternatives to fried food.
(The qualifiers create uncertainty.)

Sentence without Qualifiers:

Although McDonald's is a leading fast-food chain, they have introduced some healthy alternatives to fried food.
(Removing the qualifiers creates assurance.)

Traits

Also check your writing for series of short, choppy sentences. These sentences can often be combined.

Vocabulary

monarch
a ruler, such as a king or queen, who usually has limited authority

Edit Rewrite these sentences to fix the trouble spots discussed above.

Answers will vary.

1. Ryan Braun was being held at first base by Albert Pulois. The pitcher was signaled by the catcher Yavier Molina to throw a pitch out.

____

____

2. I think that Queen Elizabeth II is the **monarch** of the United Kingdom, but, if I'm not mistaken, the prime minister actually governs the country.

____

____

Learning Outcome

Learn how to check for correctness.

"While I grumble about the imperfections of spellcheckers, mine does find those embarrassing word repetitions (*the the*) I can't see myself."
—Patricia T. O'Conner

LO2 Checking for Correctness

Correctness should be the last element that you address in a piece of writing. When editing for correctness, you check your writing for punctuation, capitalization, spelling, and grammar errors.

Strategies for Editing

When checking for errors, examine your writing word for word and sentence by sentence. The following strategies will help you edit thoroughly and effectively.

- Work with a clean copy of your writing, one that incorporates your revisions and stylistic changes.
- Check one element at a time—spelling, punctuation, and so on.
- For spelling, start at the bottom of the page to force yourself to look at each word. (Remember that your spell-checker will not catch all errors.)
- For punctuation, circle all the marks to force yourself to look at each one.
- Read your work aloud at least once, noting any errors as you go along.
- Refer to a list of common errors. (See page 80.)
- Have an editing guide (see pages 230–422 in this text) and a dictionary handy.
- Ask a trusted classmate to check your work as well.

Preview When you have questions about punctuation, grammar, or any other convention, turn to pages 230-422 in *WRITE 2*. This part of the book is divided into three major workshops. Answer the following questions about this section.

1. What are the names of the three workshops in this section?
   Sentence Workshops, Word Workshops, and Punctuation and Mechanics Workshops
2. How will these workshops prove helpful when you are editing your writing?
   Answers will vary.
3. Which one or two of these workshops will you probably turn to more than the others? Why?
   Answers will vary.

Using Editing Strategies

You can use editing symbols to mark errors in your writing. Listed below are some of the most common symbols.

Symbol	Meaning	Symbol	Meaning
chicago (C)	Capitalize a letter.	my speech (first)	Insert here.
Fall	Make lowercase.	∧ ∧ ∧	Insert a comma, a colon, or a semicolon.
Mr Ford	Insert (add) a period.	∨ ∨ ∨	Insert an apostrophe or quotation marks.
Sp. or (recieve)	Correct spelling.	? ! ∧ ∧	Insert a question mark or an exclamation point.
Mr. Lott he	Delete (take out) or replace.	possible worst	Switch words or letters.

"My attitude toward punctuation is that it ought to be as **conventional** as possible."
—Ernest Hemingway

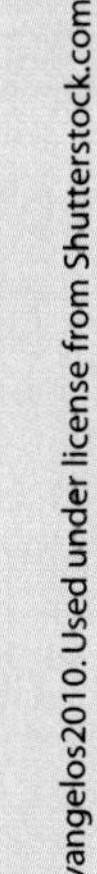

Edit Use the editing symbols above to mark errors in this writing sample and show how they should be corrected. The first error has been marked for you.

During the last few decades this Nation has become obsessed with dieting and **caloric intake**. While many of us are counting calories, not everyone understands what it is were are counting. by definition, a calorie is a measure of the heat similar to that required to raise the temperature of one gram of water by one degree Celsius. Our bodies can be thought of as biocemical machines that burn the food we eat for fuel The amount of burning that takes place is measured in calories. how much energy is produced by burning calories is determined by how active we are. By just sitting and resting we **expend** about a calorie minute. That means that just to stay alive our body it must burn 1440 calories per day. The more active we are, the more calories we will up burn. How many calories do we burn up when we engage hard exercise.

Vocabulary

conventional
usual or accepted

caloric intake
the total number of calories taken in

expend
use up, burn

Learning Outcome

Understand Standard English.

Vocabulary

dialect
a regional or social variety of a language

habitual
formed or acquired by continual use

Insight

A grammatical form that is not used in SE may be acceptable in another dialect. So this chart is identifying variations, not errors.

"Standard English is not a language—but a variety of English among many."
—Peter Trudgill

LO3 Understanding Standard English

Standard English (SE) is the **dialect** of English that is considered appropriate in business, government, and education. You have been learning to use SE throughout your years in school, and just about every career choice you make requires that you know and effectively use SE.

Surprisingly, there are not many grammatical differences between SE and other common dialects, and you may already be aware of most of them. As one linguist put it, "The difference boils down to the details." The chart below shows some of the common differences between non-Standard variations of American English (NS) and SE.

Differences in . . .	NS	SE
1. Expressing plurals after numbers	10 mile	10 miles
2. Expressing **habitual** action	He always be early.	He always is early.
3. Expressing ownership	My friend car . . .	My friend's car . . .
4. Expressing the third-person singular verb	The customer ask . . .	The customer asks . . .
5. Expressing negatives	She doesn't never . . .	She doesn't ever . . .
6. Using reflexive pronouns	He sees hisself . . .	He sees himself . . .
7. Using demonstrative pronouns	Them reports are . . .	Those reports are . . .
8. Using forms of *do*	He done it.	He did it.
9. Avoiding double subjects	My manager he . . .	My manager . . .
10. Using *a* or *an*	I need new laptop. She had angry caller.	I need a new laptop. She had an angry caller.
11. Using the past tense of verbs	Carl finish his . . .	Carl finished his . . .
12. Using *isn't* or *aren't* versus using *ain't*	The company ain't . . .	The company isn't . . .

Analyze Underline any Standard English error that you find in the following descriptive essay. Then write the number that describes each error, based on the chart on the previous page. (The first one has been done for you.)

My grandparents they used [9] to baby-sit for me when my mom had to work weekends. They were never too busy to have me. Whenever I be bored [2] with playing outside, I would head into the two-car garage and "help" Grandpa. His garage was really just a collection place for all of his old machines. He be always putzing [2] around with something in there. I think Grandpa saw hisself [6] as a master repairman.

Upon entering this ancient structure, the burnt smell of oil was the first thing that I would notice. Once my eyes adjusted to the gloom, I could begin to make out different parts of the collection. On the right wall, he had picture of everyone in the Smith family. On certain days I had to stand four inch [1] from the picture to see the grinning faces. Glaring sunbeams would shoot through them dusty, yellowish curtains [7] covering the one window.

In one corner, there was a dirty old refrigerator fill [11] with cans of soda and new canisters of snuff, just in case he ran out while working on a project. You see, Grandpa he [9] always had a pinch of snuff in his mouth. Because of this nasty habit, he would occasionally spit into an old coffee can, object [10] I avoided at all costs. Other than that, he was a great person to be around because he be so patient and interested [2] in working with me.

Occupying the entire left side of the garage was Grandpa pride and joy, [3] his tractor. He could spend hours working on it. And then, of course, there was my grandfather dog, [3] Max, who sometimes chased me and once tried to pull my pants down. When I was eight or nine, I didn't never [5] want to be anyplace else.

Discuss Afterward, discuss your work as a class. How easy or difficult was it to find the errors?

Speaking & Listening

Work on this activity with a partner or in small groups if your instructor allows it.

Vocabulary

putzing
keeping busy; cleaning, fixing, and so on

LO4 Using a Common Errors List

You can find top-ten lists covering just about any topic: top business schools, top crime novels, even top angry comedians. Here is a list of 10 common writing errors to watch for. (The corrections are shown in blue.) Turn to this list whenever you edit your writing.

1. Missing Comma After Long Introductory Phrase(s)

   Because of the fitness craze in this country many people are suffering from sore muscles and pulled tendons.

2. Confusing Pronoun Reference

   While Serena met with Ms. Randall, her cell phone rang two different times. Ms. Randall's

3. Missing Comma in a Compound Sentence

   For job-searching advice, consulting a school's placement service is a good first step but there are many other options to consider as well.

4. Missing Comma(s) with a **Nonrestrictive** Phrase or Clause

   Traveling which is usually tiring is absolutely brutal when you experience flight delays or cancellations.

5. Comma Splices

   People are affected differently by the sun, each person's system produces different amounts of skin pigment or melanin.

6. Subject-Verb Agreement Errors

   Every one of the senators want the president to call a special meeting. wants

7. Missing Comma in a Series

   Stephen Hawkings became a renowned physics professor author and theorist despite suffering from **ALS**.

8. Pronoun-**Antecedent** Agreement Errors

   Neither Carlos nor Manny has completed their first-aid requirements for the job. his

9. Missing Apostrophe to Show Ownership

   The left front tire on Marthas car needs to be replaced.

10. Misusing *Its* and *It's*

    It's Its a fact that a hummingbird beats its it's wings more than 75 times a second.

Learning Outcome

Use a common errors list.

Insight

Throughout the semester, list in a notebook other errors that you commonly make. Then be sure to refer to this list whenever you are editing your writing.

Vocabulary

nonrestrictive
extra, not necessary (A nonrestrictive phrase or clause is set off by commas because it offers extra information, or information that is not necessary to understand the basic sentence. See page 400.)

ALS
amyotrophic lateral sclerosis, a disease of the nervous system that controls muscle movement

antecedent
the noun that the pronoun refers to

LO5 Reviewing Editing

Complete these activities as needed to help you better understand the editing process.

Checking for Sentence Fluency In the space provided below, explain what is meant by the two sentence problems.

Slow-moving sentences: Sentences that plod because of passive verbs (See page 75.)

Sentences with qualifiers: Sentences that seem uncertain due to phrases like "maybe" and "I think" (See page 75.)

Editing for Correctness Edit the following sentences using the symbols on page 77 to mark the errors.

London is a fascinating city, it's filled with historical buildings such as the british museum and st pauls cathedral

Understanding Standard English Answer the following questions about Standard English (SE). (See pages 78–79.)

1. How should you express habitual action when you are using SE versus a typical non-Standard (NS) usage? Conjugate the "be" verb (I am, you are, she is, and so on).

2. How should you express the past tense in SE versus how it is often expressed in a NS dialect? Use the past tense form of the verb (e.g., "ran," "finished," "ate") instead of the infinitive ("run," "finish," "eat").

Using a Common Errors List Answer the following questions about the common errors list on page 80.

1. What punctuation mark is often missing in compound sentences? comma between the clauses

2. What is an antecedent, and what word in the sentence must it agree with? An antecedent is the noun a pronoun refers to. The two must agree.

Learning Outcome

Review editing.

"To write about people you have to know people, to write about bloodhounds you have to know bloodhounds, to write about the Loc[illegible] Ness monster you have to find out

9 Description and Narration

What sets human beings apart from other animals is, among other things, our curiosity. We have a deep-seated need to know what is happening around us, what things look like, and what our world means. It is not an exaggeration to say that the world as we know it would not exist if people weren't obsessed with a need to know.

Whenever you describe a particular topic or explore some aspect of your life, you are satisfying, in one small way, your **innate** curiosity. In the first part of this chapter, you will analyze a descriptive paragraph and then write a paragraph of your own. In the second part, you will analyze a narrative paragraph before recalling and writing about one of your own memorable experiences.

As you develop each of your paragraphs in this section, you will learn valuable strategies that you can apply to all of your writing, including establishing a focus, using specific details, and following a clear pattern of organization.

Jeremy Woodhouse/Photodisc/Getty Images

What do you think?

What does Thurber's quotation say about the importance of research in the writing process, especially as it applies to descriptive writing?

Answers will vary.

Learning Outcomes

- LO1 Analyze a descriptive paragraph.
- LO2 Write a descriptive paragraph.
- LO3 Analyze a narrative paragraph.
- LO4 Write a narrative paragraph.
- LO5 Review description and narration.

Vocabulary

innate
inborn or automatic

Learning Outcome

Analyze a descriptive paragraph.

LO1 Analyzing a Descriptive Paragraph

When writing a description, you are using words to represent a topic. An effective description creates a clear, interesting image in the reader's mind.

Read/React Read the following descriptive paragraph; then answer the questions at the bottom of the page.

Vocabulary

portrait
a photograph or painting showing the face and perhaps the upper part of the body

Matchmaker, Matchmaker

The **topic sentence** identifies the topic and focus of the paragraph.

Body sentences share descriptive details plus interesting background information about the topic.

The **closing sentence** reestablishes the importance of the topic.

One particular Capewell photo is proudly displayed in our house. It is a **portrait**-style black-and-white photograph of two people neatly attired in their best military uniforms, and it was taken during World War II in a small studio in Leicester, England. One of the individuals is wearing the uniform of the British Royal Air Force; the other, the uniform of the United States Army Air Force. Both people are clearly very happy. The person positioned to the left has huge dimples, an infectious smile, and bright, dark eyes. The one to the right has a more understated smile and lighter, happy eyes. The first has thick, wavy black hair worn in a fashionable turned-under military style; the second has neatly trimmed fairer hair. What makes this photograph so special to our family is the occasion that prompted it. It is my great-grandparents' wedding picture. My great-grandmother was born in England and my great-grandfather was born in the States, and they were both on leave to get married. Their honeymoon had to wait until after the war. This photograph is one of the few keepsakes that we have left from their military experience and wedding day, and we take very special care of it.

1. What does the paragraph describe?

   A wedding photograph from the World War II era with a bride and groom from different nations.

2. What physical features of the two people are highlighted?

Specific Features	Woman	Man
uniform	British Royal Air Force	U.S. Air Force
face	dimples, big smile, dark eyes	subtler smile, lighter eyes
hair	black, wavy	fair, neatly trimmed

LO2 Writing a Descriptive Paragraph

The next three pages provide guidelines for writing a descriptive paragraph, starting with prewriting below.

Learning Outcome

Write a descriptive paragraph.

Vocabulary

keepsakes
small items reminding people of specific events or times

indispensable
essential, absolutely necessary

Prewriting

List/Select Under each category below, list potential topics. Then circle the one topic that you will describe in your paragraph. On the lines provided at the bottom of the chart, explain the reason for your choice. Answers will vary.

Favorite Keepsakes	Special Photographs	Indispensable Tools or Gadgets

Collect Study your topic; then list specific details that describe it. Try to list them in a logical order: from top to bottom, bottom to top, side to side, and so on.

Answers will vary.

Create Write a topic sentence for your paragraph following this formula:

A specific topic	+	a particular feeling, feature, or part	=	an effective topic sentence.
a Capewell photograph		proudly displayed in our house		One particular Capewell photo is proudly displayed in our house.

Answers will vary.

Writing

Write Create a first draft of your descriptive paragraph, using the following paragraph outline as a guide.

Traits

The basic paragraph structure can be expanded into an essay structure with an opening, a middle, and a closing.

Paragraph Outline

Topic Sentence: Begin with your topic sentence from the previous page.

Body Sentences: Follow with sentences that describe and explain your topic. Organize your details according to the order that you determined during prewriting.

Closing Sentence: Write a sentence that sums up the topic's essential meaning.

Answers will vary.

Revising

Revise Read your paragraph and, if possible, have someone else read it as well. Then use the following checklist to guide your revision. Keep revising until you can check off each item in the list.

Ideas

- ☐ **1.** Does my paragraph describe a special keepsake, photo, or tool?
- ☐ **2.** Do I include plenty of specific details?
- ☐ **3.** Do I include background information to tie the details together?

Organization

- ☐ **4.** Does my topic sentence name the topic and focus of the paragraph?
- ☐ **5.** Do the body sentences present details in a logical order (top to bottom, left to right, most important to least important)?
- ☐ **6.** Does my closing sentence tell what the object means to me?

Voice

- ☐ **7.** Does my writing voice reflect my feelings about the topic?
- ☐ **8.** Does my voice sound knowledgeable?

Editing

Edit Create a clean copy of your revised paragraph and use the following checklist to check it for style and conventions.

Words

- ☐ **1.** Have I used specific nouns and verbs? (See page 74.)
- ☐ **2.** Have I used specific modifiers? (See page 143.)

Sentences

- ☐ **3.** Have I varied the beginnings and lengths of sentences? (See pages 264, 266.)
- ☐ **4.** Have I combined short, choppy sentences? (See page 262.)
- ☐ **5.** Have I avoided fragments and run-ons? (See pages 297–302, 306–307.)

Conventions

- ☐ **6.** Do I use correct verb forms (*he saw,* not *he seen*)? (See page 356.)
- ☐ **7.** Do my subjects and verbs agree (*she speaks,* not *she speak*)? (See pages 282–291.)
- ☐ **8.** Have I used the right words (*their, there, they're*)?
- ☐ **9.** Have I capitalized first words and proper nouns and adjectives? (See page 414.)
- ☐ **10.** Have I used commas after long introductory word groups? (See page 396.)
- ☐ **11.** Have I carefully checked my spelling?

Learning Outcome

Analyze a narrative paragraph.

LO3 Analyzing a Narrative Paragraph

The starting point for all writers is their own story. Everything they create stems, in some way, from their own experiences. Keeping this point in mind gives you a new perspective whenever you read another's writing.

Read/React Read the following narrative paragraph; then answer the questions at the bottom of the page.

Attention!

The **topic sentence** identifies the topic and focus of the paragraph.

Body sentences shares details about the memory.

The **closing sentence** brings the experience to a satisfying ending.

Mr. Brown, my middle school gym teacher, did not allow any goofing around in his class. Unfortunately two of my friends learned this the hard way. At the end of the first day of flag football, Mr. Brown blew his whistle to signal that time was up. Most of us knew enough to stop and **fall in line**. He had made it very clear on the first day of class that when he blew his whistle, we had to stop whatever we were doing. Immediately! Randy Steger and Joe Johnson, being brave or stupid, decided to test Mr. Brown, so they continued throwing a football to each other. With fire in his eyes, "the drill sergeant" quickly sent us in and went after the two **transgressors**. We all watched from the locker-room doorway while Mr. Brown gave them an earful and then made them **duckwalk** across the field. After 10 yards or so, we could tell that duckwalking was not easy because they were already struggling. He sent them in after another 10 yards when their duckwalk had turned into more of a crawl. We couldn't help giving a few duck calls when Randy and Joe got into the locker room, but we didn't "quack" too loudly. We didn't want Mr. Brown to make us walk like a duck, or any other animal.

1. This paragraph (1) shares a specific experience and (2) introduces you to a memorable individual. What details stand out about either one? Name two.

   Answers will vary.

2. What questions, if any, do you have about the experience?

   Answers will vary.

3. What is the **tone** of this paragraph (serious, sarcastic, interesting/entertaining)? Explain.

   Answers will vary.

Vocabulary

fall in line
an idiom meaning, in this case, to line up as a group

transgressors
people who act in violation of (against) the rules or laws

duckwalk
to walk in a crouching or squatting position

tone
the writer's attitude toward the topic

LO4 Writing a Narrative Paragraph

Learning Outcome

Write a narrative paragraph.

The next three pages provide guidelines for writing a narrative paragraph, starting with prewriting below.

Prewriting

Select List below four or more experiences that you have had with memorable individuals. Consider school-related, work-related, sports-related, and family-related experiences. Circle the one experience that you would like to share in a narrative paragraph. On the lines that follow, explain the reason for your choice.

Answers will vary.

Collect Gather details for your paragraph by answering the 5 W's and H about the experience. Answers will vary.

Who?

What?

When?

Where?

Why?

How?

Writing

Write Create the first draft of your narrative paragraph, using the following paragraph outline as a guide.

Paragraph Outline

Topic Sentence: Begin with a topic sentence that identifies the topic and focus of your paragraph. (See page 85 for a formula to follow.)

Body Sentences: Write sentences that cover the 5 W's and H of the experience. Be sure to include plenty of specific details.

Closing Sentence: Write a sentence that brings the experience to a satisfying or natural stopping point.

Answers will vary.

Revising

Revise Read your paragraph, and, if possible, have someone else read it as well. Then use the following checklist to guide your revision. Continue making improvements until you can check off each item in the list.

Ideas

- ☐ **1.** Does my paragraph share a specific experience related to a memorable person?
- ☐ **2.** Have I answered the 5 W's and H about the experience?
- ☐ **3.** Do I include plenty of specific details?

Organization

- ☐ **4.** Does my topic sentence name the topic and focus of the paragraph?
- ☐ **5.** Do the body sentences present details in chronological (time) order?
- ☐ **6.** Does my closing sentence bring the experience to a satisfying end?

Voice

- ☐ **7.** Does my voice reflect my feelings about the topic?
- ☐ **8.** Does my voice create interest in the reader?

Editing

Edit Create a clean copy of your revised paragraph and use the following checklist to check it for style and conventions.

Words

- ☐ **1.** Have I used specific nouns and verbs? (See page 74.)
- ☐ **2.** Have I used specific modifiers? (See page 143.)

Sentences

- ☐ **3.** Have I varied the beginnings and lengths of sentences? (See pages 264, 266.)
- ☐ **4.** Have I combined short, choppy sentences? (See page 262.)
- ☐ **5.** Have I avoided fragments and run-ons? (See pages 297–302, 306–307.)

Conventions

- ☐ **6.** Do I use correct verb forms *(he saw,* not *he seen)*? (See page 356.)
- ☐ **7.** Do my subjects and verbs agree (*she speaks,* not *she speak*)? (See pages 282–291.)
- ☐ **8.** Have I used the right words (*their, there, they're*)?
- ☐ **9.** Have I capitalized first words and proper nouns and adjectives? (See page 414.)
- ☐ **10.** Have I used commas after long introductory word groups? (See page 396.)
- ☐ **11.** Have I carefully checked my spelling?

Learning Outcome

Review description and narration.

LO5 Reviewing Description and Narration

Describe Select an interesting photograph from one of your textbooks or from a periodical (newspaper or magazine). In the space below, list in a logical order specific details that describe it. Then, on your own paper, develop a descriptive paragraph about the photo. (See pages 85–87.)

Answers will vary.

Narrate Identify below your strongest early memory. Next, identify the basic details about the experience by completing the 5 W's and H chart. Then, on your own paper, write a narrative paragraph about the experience. (See pages 89–91.)

Answers will vary.

Who?	
What?	
When?	
Where?	
Why?	
How?	

"Knowledge is of two kinds: We know the subject ourselves or we know where we can find information upon it."

—Samuel Johnson

Todd Davidson/Getty Images

10 Illustration and Process

The best informational writing succeeds because it (1) focuses on an interesting topic and (2) provides plenty of supporting facts and examples. This fact holds true for newspaper stories, magazine articles, text chapters, blogs, and academic essays. Readers of informational texts want to be **engaged** and informed.

In this chapter you will read examples of two basic forms of informational writing: illustrating a main point and explaining a process. Each one is intended to be interesting and informative. After each sample, you will write an illustration or process paragraph of your own.

What do you think?

According to the Johnson quotation, what are the two kinds of knowledge? How does the quotation relate to informational writing?

Answers will vary.

Learning Outcomes

- LO1 Analyze an illustration paragraph.
- LO2 Write an illustration paragraph.
- LO3 Analyze a process paragraph.
- LO4 Write a process paragraph.
- LO5 Review illustration and process.

Vocabulary

engaged
fully and actively occupied

Learning Outcome

Analyze an illustration paragraph.

LO1 Analyzing an Illustration Paragraph

Illustrating in writing is the process of clarifying or explaining with examples. Think of the examples in this type of writing as the legs that support the tabletop, or main point.

Read/React Read the following illustration paragraph; then answer the questions below.

Super Sleuths

The **topic sentence** states the topic and focus.

Body sentences give examples that illustrate or support the topic sentence.

The **closing sentence** keeps the reader thinking.

The best mystery writers have created **iconoclastic** super **sleuths**. Edgar Allan Poe created the first detective, before the term detective even existed. The name of this character is C. Auguste Dupin, a French gentleman who is able to enter the criminal mind to help him solve murders. Some people say that Arthur Conan Doyle modeled the most famous detective of all after Dupin. Doyle's detective, of course, is Sherlock Holmes, the **eccentric** private investigator who uses his incredible powers of deduction to solve difficult mysteries. Another British writer—Agatha Christie, the **grand dame** of mystery writers—created the well-known Jane Marple, an elderly woman who happens to show up at murder scenes to offer her crime-solving abilities, and Hercule Poirot, an odd, but skilled detective from Belgium. Writer Raymond Chandler became famous in this country with Philip Marlowe, an intelligent, tough, hard-drinking detective. Not to be outdone, writer Robert Parker created Spenser (no first name), a Boston private investigator who is tough, but also philosophical, funny, and afraid of nothing. Lee Child has also created a Spenser-like sleuth named Jack Reacher, who simply wanders around the States solving complicated crimes. It will be interesting to see if future mystery writers will break out of this super-sleuth model, and, if so, in what direction they will go.

1. What is the main point of the paragraph?

   Popular mystery writers create unique, unusual characters as their fictional detectives.

2. List at least four examples that support the main point.

   Answers will vary.

Vocabulary

iconoclastic individualistic, nonconforming, radical

sleuths detectives

eccentric unusual, odd

grand dame a respected woman with experience in a particular field

LO2 Writing an Illustration Paragraph

Learning Outcome

Write an illustration paragraph.

Prewriting

Select To select a topic for your paragraph, answer the following question:

What is your favorite type of television show, movie, music, literature, magazine, or Internet feature? (*The writer of the sample paragraph identified his favorite type of literature—mysteries.*)

Answers will vary.

Focus Then decide on a feature of this topic that you could illustrate in your paragraph. Explain your choice below. (*The writer of the sample paragraph decided to illustrate the memorable detectives created by the best mystery writers.*)

Answers will vary.

Identify List at least four examples that illustrate this feature.

Answers will vary.

Create On the lines below, write a topic sentence for your paragraph. Be sure that your sentence identifies the topic and the feature you are going to illustrate. (See page 85 for a formula to follow.)

Answers will vary.

Writing

Write Develop a first draft of your illustration paragraph, using the outline below as a guide. Be sure to refer to the sample on page 94 for additional help.

Traits

The topic sentence gives the reader a summary of the material in the paragraph.

Paragraph Outline

Topic Sentence: Begin with the topic sentence that you wrote on page 95.

Body Sentences: Present the supporting examples that you listed on page 95. Include explanations or background information as needed to connect the examples.

Closing Sentence: Write a sentence that keeps the reader thinking about your topic.

Answers will vary.

Revising

Revise Read your paragraph, and, if possible, have someone else read it as well. Then use the following checklist to guide your revision. Continue making improvements until you can check off each item in the list.

Ideas

- ☐ **1.** Does my paragraph address an interesting topic?
- ☐ **2.** Have I included at least four examples that illustrate the topic?
- ☐ **3.** Do I include additional background details as needed?

Organization

- ☐ **4.** Does my topic sentence name the topic and focus of the paragraph?
- ☐ **5.** Are the body sentences presented in a logical order?
- ☐ **6.** Does my closing sentence keep the reader thinking about the topic?

Voice

- ☐ **7.** Does my voice reflect my feelings about the topic?
- ☐ **8.** Does my voice create interest in the topic?

Editing

Edit Create a clean copy of your revised paragraph and use the following checklist to check it for style and conventions.

Words

- ☐ **1.** Have I used specific nouns and verbs? (See page 74.)
- ☐ **2.** Have I used specific modifiers? (See page 143.)

Sentences

- ☐ **3.** Have I varied the beginnings and lengths of sentences? (See pages 264, 266.)
- ☐ **4.** Have I combined short, choppy sentences? (See page 262.)
- ☐ **5.** Have I avoided fragments and run-ons? (See pages 297–302, 306–307.)

Conventions

- ☐ **6.** Do I use correct verb forms *(he saw,* not *he seen)*? (See page 356.)
- ☐ **7.** Do my subjects and verbs agree (*she speaks,* not *she speak*)? (See pages 282–291.)
- ☐ **8.** Have I used the right words (*their, there, they're*)?
- ☐ **9.** Have I capitalized first words and proper nouns and adjectives? (See page 414.)
- ☐ **10.** Have I used commas after long introductory word groups? (See page 396.)
- ☐ **11.** Have I carefully checked my spelling?

Learning Outcome

Analyze a process paragraph.

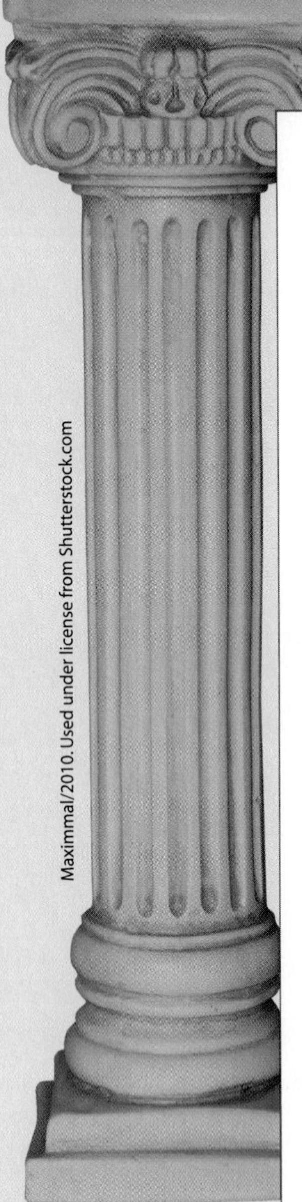
Maximmal/2010. Used under license from Shutterstock.com

LO3 Analyzing a Process Paragraph

Process paragraphs explain how to do something *(apply for a passport)* or how something works *(photosynthesis)*. The paragraph that follows explains how to do something.

Read/React Read the following process paragraph; then answer the questions below.

Two Steps Forward, One Step Back

The **topic sentence** introduces the process.

Body sentences explain the materials needed and the steps to follow.

The **closing sentence** provides the reader with a final thought about the topic.

Walking the streets of Rome for the first time requires patience and a sense of adventure. Before you set out, be sure to wear a comfortable pair of shoes. Roman streets, at least the most interesting ones, are **cobbled**. Also dress in light layers, even if you see most of the **natives** dressed in heavy coats. They must have thinner blood than the rest of us. Then plan a route on a street map by circling the sites you want to visit and the streets you need to follow. As you start, enjoy all that the **cityscape** has to offer. Then within the first 10 or 15 minutes, expect to get lost. Roman streets, other than the main thoroughfares, are never straight, seldom marked, and rarely labeled on the street map you have in hand. When this happens, you can try to retrace your steps or continue on. If you are at all adventurous, just keep going and enjoy what that part of the city has to offer. You won't be disappointed, and sooner or later, you'll come across a plaza or church square that will be marked on your map. Once you get your bearings, proceed, but again, expect to get lost in no time at all. You can continue in this way from plaza to plaza, enjoying the sites that you come across as well as stopping for some refreshments or a meal. When you've had enough, find a taxi or tram for the return trip—you'll never find your way by foot.

1. What specific feeling about the topic is expressed in the topic sentence?

   Amused affection.

2. What steps are offered for the walking tourist in Rome?

   Answers will vary.

Vocabulary

cobbled
uneven, rough

natives
those who are born in a place or country

cityscape
the part of a city viewed, the sights in part of a city

LO4 Writing a Process Paragraph

Learning Outcome

Write a process paragraph.

Prewriting

Select Complete the following sentence starters in at least two ways. (Avoid food-related topics.) Answers will vary.

1. I learned the hard way how to . . .

    ______________________ ______________________

2. I may be one of the few people who knows how to . . .

    ______________________ ______________________

3. In case of an emergency, I would like to be able to . . .

    ______________________ ______________________

4. Choose a topic and explain your choice.

    ____

Collect Identify the materials needed and the steps in your process.

Materials	Steps
Answers will vary.	

Create Write a topic sentence for your paragraph. This sentence should identify the topic and focus of your writing. (See page 85 for a formula to follow.)

Answers will vary.
____

____

Writing

Write Create a first draft of your process paragraph, using the following paragraph outline as a guide.

WAC

Science and history classes often require process writing.

Paragraph Outline

Topic Sentence: Begin with the topic sentence that you wrote on the previous page.

Body Sentences: First, discuss any materials that may be needed. Then clearly explain the steps to complete the process. Add other information as needed to connect all of your ideas.

Closing Sentence: Write a sentence that sums up the process.

Answers will vary.

Revising

Revise Read your process paragraph and, if possible, have someone else read it as well. Then use the following checklist to guide your revision. Continue to make improvements until you can check off each item in the list.

Ideas

- ☐ **1.** Have I selected an interesting process to explain?
- ☐ **2.** Do I identify the necessary materials and provide all of the steps?

Organization

- ☐ **3.** Does my topic sentence identify the topic and focus of my paragraph?
- ☐ **4.** Have I put the body sentences that explain the steps in good order?
- ☐ **5.** Does my closing sentence effectively sum up the process?

Voice

- ☐ **6.** Does my writing voice sound knowledgeable?
- ☐ **7.** Does my voice create interest in this process?

Editing

Edit Create a clean copy of your revised paragraph and use the following checklist to check it for style and conventions.

Words

- ☐ **1.** Have I used specific nouns and verbs? (See page 74.)
- ☐ **2.** Have I used more action verbs than "be" verbs? (See page 348.)

Sentences

- ☐ **3.** Have I varied the beginnings and lengths of sentences? (See pages 264, 266.)
- ☐ **4.** Have I combined short, choppy sentences? (See page 262.)
- ☐ **5.** Have I avoided fragments and run-ons? (See pages 297–302, 306–307.)

Conventions

- ☐ **6.** Do I use correct verb forms *(he saw,* not *he seen)*? (See page 356.)
- ☐ **7.** Do my subjects and verbs agree (*she speaks,* not *she speak*)? (See pages 282–291.)
- ☐ **8.** Have I used the right words (*their, there, they're*)?
- ☐ **9.** Have I capitalized first words and proper nouns and adjectives? (See page 414.)
- ☐ **10.** Have I used commas after long introductory word groups? (See page 396.)
- ☐ **11.** Have I carefully checked my spelling?

Learning Outcome

Review illustration and process.

LO5 Reviewing Illustration and Process

Illustration Fill in the top blank with a career that truly interests you. Then write four statements that illustrate or explain your choice. On your own paper, write an illustration paragraph about this career. (See pages 95–97.)

Career: Answers will vary. ____________________

Example: ____________________

Example: ____________________

Example: ____________________

Example: ____________________

Process On the top blanks, list possible topics for a paragraph explaining how something works. Consider pieces of technology, features on the Internet, a natural phenomenon *(evaporation)*, a governmental process *(how to become a U.S. citizen)*, and so on. Circle the one that you would like to write about.

Next, list any materials needed and the steps taken to complete the process. Then, on your own paper, write a paragraph explaining the process. (See pages 99–101.)

Topics (how something works) Answers will vary.

____________________ ____________________ ____________________

Materials

____

____

Steps

____

____

____

____

____

____

____

"My father told me that words and letters hold the secrets of the universe. That in their shape and sounds I could find everything, could see beyond myself to something special . . . perfect."

—Eliza, in the movie *Bee Season*

Dougal Waters/Digital Vision/Getty Images

11

Definition and Classification

Each new course presents you with a set of words and concepts to learn. (Just think of all of the vocabulary lists you've received over the years.) One of the best ways to understand these new terms and topics is to write about them. Writing **extended** definition and **classification** paragraphs allows you to do just that.

Each type of writing requires you to research a word or concept and then understand and **synthesize** the information you have gathered. As you develop these paragraphs, you may consult several sources—from traditional dictionaries to a variety of online sites. As you hunt down information, your topic will take shape before you

Learning Outcomes

- LO1 Analyze a definition paragraph.
- LO2 Write a definition paragraph.
- LO3 Analyze a classification paragraph.
- LO4 Write a classification paragraph.
- LO5 Review definition and classification.

Vocabulary

extended
fully explained, added to

classification
systematic or organized grouping

synthesize
combine multiple ideas to form new understandings

What do you think?

How can words "hold the secrets of the universe"?

Answers will vary.

Learning Outcome

Analyze a definition paragraph.

LO1 Analyzing a Definition Paragraph

A definition paragraph explains a new or, perhaps, misunderstood term. This type of paragraph may include a dictionary definition, the history of the term, examples of it, related words, and so on. Providing extended definitions like this is an important part of academic writing.

Read/React Read this definition paragraph; then follow the directions at the bottom of the page.

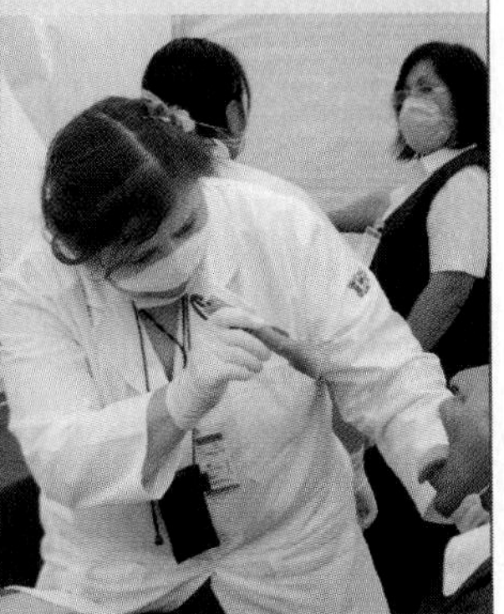

Frontpage/2010. Used under license from Shutterstock.com

Vocabulary

influenza
a contagious viral infection

infectious
capable of being spread from person to person

globetrotting
traveling often and widely

A Word of Warning

The **topic sentence** identifies the term and focus of the paragraph.

Body **sentences** explore the term in a number of ways.

The **closing sentences** keep the reader thinking about the term.

One word in medical reports strikes fear into people everywhere, and that word is *pandemic.* One report might say, "The threat of a pandemic flu hitting the United State exists"; another one might say, "The World Health Organization has raised the level of the **influenza** pandemic alert." Who wouldn't be scared by threats such as these? So what exactly is a pandemic and where did this word come from? A pandemic is an "**infectious** disease covering a wide geographic area and affecting a large proportion of the population." Being "infectious" is a key feature because a disease cannot become a pandemic unless it can be spread by humans over a very wide area. So influenza can be pandemic, but cancer cannot. Some people use *pandemic* interchangeably with *epidemic.* But an epidemic doesn't become pandemic until it covers an extremely widespread area, such as a series of countries. *Pandemic* comes from the Greek *pandēmos:* The Greek root *pan* means "every" or "all" and *demos* means "common people." Thus, *pandēmos* means "all the people," so the connection with pandemic is clear. Two pandemics that are often cited are the Black Death during the Dark Ages and the flu pandemic in 1918 that killed from 40 to 50 million people. Current pandemics include H1N1, an infectious flu virus, and HIV. Here's a scary final thought: **Globetrotting** provides an easy way for pandemics to occur.

This paragraph defines *pandemic* by providing the following types of details. Identify each detail from the paragraph.

Dictionary definition: Infectious disease covering a wide geographic area and affecting a large proportion of the population

History of the word: From the Greek word *pandēmos, pan* meaning "every" and *dēmos* meaning "common people"

Examples: Black Death; flu pandemic of 1918; current H1N1 virus and HIV

Related word: epidemic (though an epidemic isn't widespread)

Explanations: Answers will vary.

LO2 Writing a Definition Paragraph

Learning Outcome

Write a definition paragraph.

The next three pages provide guidelines for writing a definition paragraph, starting with prewriting below.

Prewriting

Identify Read a few articles (online or in print) about medical, scientific, or technological topics. On the blanks below, list four to six terms you encountered that sparked your interest. Then circle one term that you would be interested in writing about. On the lines that follow, explain the reason for your choice.

Answers will vary.

Collect On the lines below, gather information for your paragraph. Look for the following types of details:

Dictionary definitions	History of the word	Related words
Examples	Quotations	Explanations
Interesting facts	Personal definition	What it means to others

Answers will vary.

Writing

Write Create a first draft of your paragraph, using the outline that follows as a guide.

WAC

As the model on page 104 shows, definition writing is key to science.

Paragraph Outline

Topic Sentence: Write a topic sentence that names the term and identifies a personal feeling or special feature about it. (See the formula on page 85.)

Body Sentences: Write sentences that explore the term in a variety of different ways. Organize the details in a logical way, perhaps starting with the dictionary definition.

Closing Sentence: Write a sentence that leaves the reader with a final thought about the term.

Answers will vary.

Revising

Revise Read your paragraph and, if possible, have someone else read it as well. Then use the following checklist to guide your revision. Keep revising until you can check off each item in the list.

Ideas

- ☐ **1.** Does my paragraph focus on an interesting term?
- ☐ **2.** Do I explore the term in a number of different ways?

Organization

- ☐ **3.** Does my topic sentence name the term and focus of the paragraph?
- ☐ **4.** Are the body sentences arranged in a logical way?
- ☐ **5.** Does my closing sentence leave the reader with an interesting final thought?

Voice

- ☐ **6.** Does my writing voice demonstrate a clear understanding of the term?
- ☐ **7.** Does my voice engage the reader?

Editing

Edit Create a clean copy of your revised paragraph and use the following checklist to check it for style and conventions.

Words

- ☐ **1.** Have I used specific nouns and verbs? (See page 74.)
- ☐ **2.** Have I used more action verbs than "be" verbs? (See page 348.)

Sentences

- ☐ **3.** Have I varied the beginnings and lengths of sentences? (See pages 264, 266.)
- ☐ **4.** Have I combined short, choppy sentences? (See page 262.)
- ☐ **5.** Have I avoided fragments and run-ons? (See pages 297–302, 306–307.)

Conventions

- ☐ **6.** Do I use correct verb forms (*he saw,* not *he seen*)? (See page 356.)
- ☐ **7.** Do my subjects and verbs agree (*she speaks,* not *she speak*)? (See pages 282–291.)
- ☐ **8.** Have I used the right words (*their, there, they're*)?
- ☐ **9.** Have I capitalized first words and proper nouns and adjectives? (See page 414.)
- ☐ **10.** Have I used commas after long introductory word groups? (See page 396.)
- ☐ **11.** Have I carefully checked my spelling?

Learning Outcome

Analyze a classification paragraph.

LO3 Analyzing a Classification Paragraph

A classification paragraph identifies the types or varieties of something. Classifying is a common form of thinking and writing used in the sciences.

Read/React Read the following classification paragraph; then answer the questions at the bottom of the page.

Nighttime Blues

The **topic sentence** identifies the topic and focus.

Body sentences provide examples that classify the topic.

The **closing sentence** provides a final thought.

Most people are familiar with eating disorders and learning disorders, but they may not be quite as familiar with sleeping disorders. Experts in the field identify four basic types of sleep disorders. The first one, insomnia, is linked to the other disorders because it covers the inability to fall asleep or stay asleep at night. Sleep apnea is another sleep disorder, and it is characterized by snoring, snorting, and even gasping. These irritating sound effects are produced when the sufferer tries to force air through a blockage of the airway during sleep. Narcolepsy, a third disorder, is characterized by excessive sleepiness during the day. It is caused by a chemical imbalance in the part of the brain that controls sleeping and staying awake. One narcoleptic stated that the sleepiness can come on suddenly in much the same way as an epileptic attack comes on. The fourth type of sleep disorder is restless leg syndrome. People suffering from this disorder feel a twitching, pulling, or aching in their legs, which forces them to move or kick them. The syndrome most often strikes during the night, but it can also occur during the day. Exploring the basics of sleeplessness makes it clear why we have sleep disorder clinics: There are a lot of people who aren't getting a good night's sleep.

1. What are the topic and focus of the paragraph?

   Sleep disorders

2. How many types of the topic are identified? What are they?

   Four types: insomnia, apnea, narcolepsy, restless leg syndrome

3. How does the closing connect with the beginning?

   Answers will vary.

LO4 Writing a Classification Paragraph

Learning Outcome

Write a classification paragraph.

Prewriting

Select On the blanks that follow, list possible topics as they come to mind. Try to fill in the entire chart with ideas. Afterward, review your list and circle one topic that you would like to write about in a classification paragraph. (Two ideas are provided for you.) Answers will vary.

Types of . . .

weight trainers		
instructors		

Collect Complete the following chart to gather details for your paragraph. In the first column, list the types of your topic. In the second column, explain or define each one. (You may have to do some quick research to gather information.)

Types/Varieties	Explanation/Definition
Answers will vary.	

Mikhail Valeev/2010. Used under license from Shutterstock.com

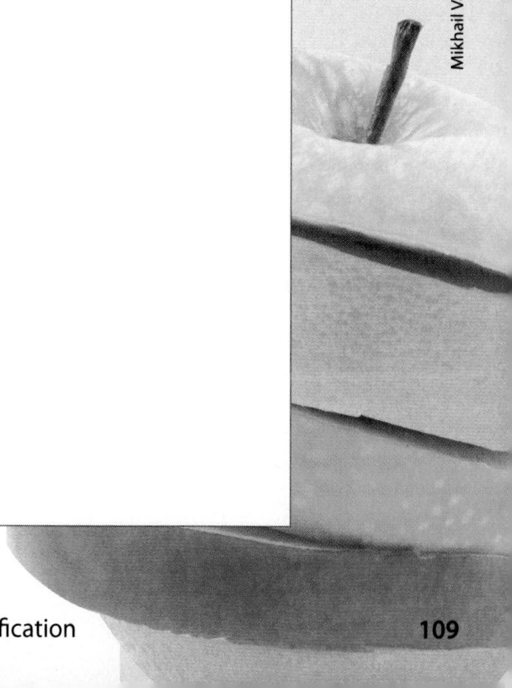

Writing

Write Create a first draft of your classification paragraph, using the following outline as a guide.

Paragraph Outline

Topic Sentence: Write a sentence that identifies the topic and focus of your paragraph. (See page 85 for a formula.)

Body Sentences: Write sentences that name and explain each type. Add information as needed to tie everything together.

Closing Sentence: Write a sentence that connects with the beginning or that keeps the reader thinking about the topic.

Answers will vary.

Revising

Revise Read your paragraph and, if possible, have someone else read it as well. Then use the following checklist to guide your revision. Keep making improvements until you can check off each item in the list.

Ideas

- ☐ **1.** Does my paragraph focus on an interesting or important topic?
- ☐ **2.** Do I fully explain or classify the important types or varieties of the topic?
- ☐ **3.** Do I include plenty of specific details to explain each type?

Organization

- ☐ **4.** Does the topic sentence name the topic and focus of my writing?
- ☐ **5.** Are the body sentences arranged in a logical way.
- ☐ **6.** Does my closing sentence bring the paragraph to a satisfying end?

Voice

- ☐ **7.** Does my writing voice show my interest in the topic?
- ☐ **8.** Do I sound knowledgeable about the topic?

Editing

Edit Create a clean copy of your revised paragraph and use the following checklist to check it for style and conventions.

Words

- ☐ **1.** Have I used specific nouns and verbs? (See page 74.)
- ☐ **2.** Have I used specific modifiers? (See page 143.)

Sentences

- ☐ **3.** Have I varied the beginnings and lengths of sentences? (See pages 264, 266.)
- ☐ **4.** Have I combined short, choppy sentences? (See page 262.)
- ☐ **5.** Have I avoided fragments and run-ons? (See pages 297–302, 306–307.)

Conventions

- ☐ **6.** Do I use correct verb forms *(he saw,* not *he seen)*? (See page 356.)
- ☐ **7.** Do my subjects and verbs agree (*she speaks,* not *she speak*)? (See pages 282–291.)
- ☐ **8.** Have I used the right words (*their, there, they're*)?
- ☐ **9.** Have I capitalized first words and proper nouns and adjectives? (See page 414.)
- ☐ **10.** Have I used commas after long introductory word groups? (See page 396.)
- ☐ **11.** Have I carefully checked my spelling?

Learning Outcome

Review definition and classification.

LO5 Reviewing Definition and Classification

Define In the chart that follows, identify a term that interests you from one of your classes. Next, collect details that will help you define and explain the term. (Complete at least four of the categories.) Then, on your own paper, develop a definition paragraph about the term. (See pages 105–107.)

Term: Answers will vary. __________

Dictionary definition: __________

Personal definition: __________

History of the word: __________

Related words: __________

Quotations: __________

Classify At the top of the chart below, list two or three style-related topics. Consider topics that can be broken down into types or varieties. Circle the one that you would like to write about. Next, complete the chart by identifying the types of your topic and an explanation of each one. Then, on your own paper, write a classification paragraph about the topic. (See pages 109–111.)

Answers will vary. __________ __________ __________

Types/Varieties	Explanation/Definition

"Understanding is a two-way street."
—Eleanor Roosevelt

Digital Composite/Lifesize/Lifesize/Getty Images

Cause-Effect and Comparison-Contrast

We lead cause-effect lives. One person shops for a scooter *(effect)* because he can't afford a car anymore *(cause)*. Another person can still fit into her swimsuit *(effect)* because she's been careful about her diet *(cause)*. Someone else has had it with a neighbor's barking dog *(cause)*, so she's looking for a new apartment *(effect)*.

A lot of academic writing deals with causes and effects as well. Stated in another way, writing often deals with the logical relationship between events and outcomes. Comparing and contrasting related topics is another important form of academic writing. These two-part forms of writing require analytical thinking and planning to complete.

Learning Outcomes

- LO1 Analyze a cause-effect paragraph.
- LO2 Write a cause-effect paragraph.
- LO3 Analyze a comparison-contrast paragraph.
- LO4 Write a comparison-contrast paragraph.
- LO5 Review cause-effect and comparison-contrast.

What do you think?

How would you explain Eleanor Roosevelt's contention that "understanding is a two-way street"?

Answers will vary.

Learning Outcome

Analyze a cause-effect paragraph.

LO1 Analyzing a Cause-Effect Paragraph

These two starter sentences identify the type of thinking involved in cause-effect writing: *Because of . . . , we now . . .* or *Since . . . happened, we have had to . . . .* Keep this thought pattern in mind as you read and analyze cause-effect writing.

Read/React Read the following cause-effect paragraph; then answer the questions at the bottom of the page.

Africa Studio ,2010 / Used under license from Shutterstock.com

Problems in Print

The **topic sentence** identifies the topic and focus of the paragraph.

Body sentences explore the causes and effects.

The **closing sentence** expands on the main point.

Students interested in pursuing a career in traditional journalism may want to think carefully about this decision. The reason is simple: Fewer and fewer people are buying newspapers. Most of them, instead, are getting all or most of their news on the Internet. Fewer buyers of newspapers and magazines mean less income from subscriptions and newsstand sales. Fewer readers also mean fewer ad dollars, a main source of income for publishers. As a result, newspapers are going out of business or cutting back, and magazines are folding. This state of affairs has left publishers unsure about how to re-form for survival. News sources do offer electronic alternatives to their print products, but readers get this news for free or pay a limited fee that in no way offsets the huge losses publishers are experiencing. Because of this situation, there simply are not enough jobs for experienced journalists, let alone recent graduates. So **prospective** journalism students must realize that their chances of working in a traditional newsroom are slim to none. However, all is not lost. The Internet may offer exciting new career options for journalists, especially those who are strong researchers and communicators and well versed in the new opportunities that the **information age** has to offer.

1. What are the topic and focus of this paragraph?

   Traditional journalism as a career is declining dramatically.

2. What are the main causes and effects explained in the paragraph?

   Causes: Fewer buyers of traditional newspapers; less income from electronic news; less income from ads

   Effects: Fewer dollars to pay salaries; more competition for existing jobs

Vocabulary

prospective
likely or expected

information age
a period of widespread electronic access to information

LO2 Writing a Cause-Effect Paragraph

To write a cause-effect paragraph, use the guidelines on the next three pages, starting with prewriting below.

Prewriting

Select In the first column, list careers or jobs that you are interested in or have had some experience with. In the second column, explain the **status** of each one. Afterward, put a check next to the job that you would like to write about in a cause-effect paragraph. On the lines at the bottom of the chart, explain the reason for your choice. (One example is provided.) Answers will vary.

Careers or Jobs	Status
journalist	Career opportunities are shrinking and changing.

Consider To plan your paragraph, consider the causes and effects of the current status of your topic. You may have one main cause and multiple effects, multiple causes and one main effect, or multiple causes and effects. Answers will vary.

Causes	Effects

Learning Outcome

Write a cause-effect paragraph.

Traits

In the sample paragraph, there is one main cause (fewer readers of print media) and one main effect (fewer traditional opportunities).

Vocabulary

status
current situation, standing, or state of affairs

Writing

Write Create a first draft of your cause-effect paragraph, using the following outline as a guide.

Paragraph Outline

Topic Sentence: Begin with a topic sentence identifying your topic and focus. (See page 85 for a helpful formula.)

Body Sentences: Explain the causes and effects of the topic. Arrange these ideas in a logical way, dealing with causes first and then the effects, or vice versa.

Closing Sentence: Write a sentence that revisits or expands upon the main point.

Answers will vary.

Test Taking

By practicing cause-effect writing now, you will be better prepared for cause-effect writing prompts on tests.

Revising

Revise Read your paragraph and, if possible, have someone else read it as well. Then use the following checklist to guide your revision. Keep making improvements until you can check off each item in the list.

Ideas

- ☐ **1.** Does my paragraph address an interesting and **timely** topic?
- ☐ **2.** Do I provide appropriate and clear "cause and effect" information?

Organization

- ☐ **3.** Does my topic sentence identify the topic and focus of my paragraph?
- ☐ **4.** Do the body sentences follow a logical order: causes first, then effects; effects first, then causes?
- ☐ **5.** Does my closing sentence revisit or expand upon the main point?

Voice

- ☐ **6.** Do I sound knowledgeable about the topic?
- ☐ **7.** Does my voice create interest in the topic?

Editing

Edit Create a clean copy of your revised paragraph and use the following checklist to check it for style and conventions.

Words

- ☐ **1.** Have I used specific nouns and verbs? (See page 74.)
- ☐ **2.** Have I used specific modifiers? (See page 143.)

Sentences

- ☐ **3.** Have I varied the beginnings and lengths of sentences? (See pages 264, 266.)
- ☐ **4.** Have I combined short, choppy sentences? (See page 262.)
- ☐ **5.** Have I avoided fragments and run-ons? (See pages 297–302, 306–307.)

Conventions

- ☐ **6.** Do I use correct verb forms *(he saw,* not *he seen)*? (See page 356.)
- ☐ **7.** Do my subjects and verbs agree (*she speaks,* not *she speak*)? (See pages 282–291.)
- ☐ **8.** Have I used the right words (*their, there, they're*)?
- ☐ **9.** Have I capitalized first words and proper nouns and adjectives? (See page 414.)
- ☐ **10.** Have I used commas after long introductory word groups? (See page 396.)
- ☐ **11.** Have I carefully checked my spelling?

Vocabulary

timely
well-timed, important now

Learning Outcome

Analyze a comparison-contrast paragraph.

LO3 Analyzing a Comparison-Contrast Paragraph

Comparison-contrast writing may emphasize both the similarities and differences between two topics, or it may focus more attention on how the topics are either alike or different.

Read/React Read the following comparison-contrast paragraph; then answer the questions at the bottom of the page.

Order in the Court

The **topic sentence** identifies the topics and focus of the paragraph.

Body sentences share details about the two topics.

The **closing sentence** provides a final thought about the topics.

Both solicitors and barristers serve the public in the British legal system, but they do so in different ways. Someone in Great Britain seeking legal help contacts a solicitor, who will usually be part of a law firm. A solicitor then serves as a client's legal representative, providing legal guidance and advice, and even representing a client in some court cases. When a client needs specialized legal help and **advocacy** before the high court, a solicitor will contact his legal **battery mate**, a barrister. Unlike a solicitor, a barrister has no attachment to any firm but instead is a member of chambers, a group of barristers that share legal aides and such. A barrister's main responsibility is to argue a client's case before a judge and jury, so his or her independence from any firm provides an unbiased voice in the law proceedings. When in "uniform" in front of the judge and jury, barristers have traditionally worn elaborate horsehair wigs, stiff white collars, and long gowns. This legal division of power has served the British public well for ages, even though solicitors are now gaining more responsibility before the courts.

1. What are the topics of this paragraph?

   Solicitors and barristers in the British court system

2. Does the paragraph focus on similarities, differences, or both? Explain.

   Both. Answers will vary.

3. What are two important things that you learned about the topics?

   Answers will vary.

Vocabulary

advocacy
active support, arguing in favor of something

battery mate
in terms of baseball, the combination of a pitcher and catcher; in more general terms, partners in an activity or occupation

LO4 Writing a Comparison-Contrast Paragraph

To write a comparison-contrast paragraph, follow the guidelines on the next three pages, starting with prewriting below.

Learning Outcome

Write a comparison-contrast paragraph

Prewriting

Select Think of jobs or positions that are closely related. For example, within the dental profession, there are dental assistants and dental **hygienists**. In the automotive field, there are automotive technicians and car mechanics. After listing a number of related jobs, circle the pair you would like to write about in a comparison-contrast paragraph. Answers will vary.

Related Jobs or Positions

Collect In the space provided below, gather information about your two topics. Consider training, job description, opportunities, and so on. (Use your own paper if you need more room.) Answers will vary.

Job or Position One: ________	Job or Position Two: ________

Plan Decide how you will organize your paragraph: Are you going to share all the information about one topic and then the other? Or are you going to cover the two topics point by point, first showing how they compare or contrast in terms of training, then in terms of job description, and so on?

Vocabulary

hygienists
health specialists

Writing

Write Create a first draft of your comparison-contrast paragraph, using the following outline as a guide.

Paragraph Outline

Topic Sentence: Begin with a topic sentence that identifies the related topics and focus of your paragraph. (See page 85 for a formula.)

Body Sentences: Develop the body sentences, following your planning at the bottom of the previous page.

Closing Sentence: Write a sentence (or two) that provides a final thought about the topics.

Answers will vary.

Revising

Revise Read your paragraph and, if possible, have someone else read it as well. Then use the following checklist to guide your revisions. Keep making improvements until you can check off each item in the list.

Ideas

- ☐ **1.** Does my paragraph address two related jobs in an interesting field?
- ☐ **2.** Do I provide an adequate number of important similarities and/or differences?

Organization

- ☐ **3.** Does my topic sentence identify the topics and focus of the paragraph?
- ☐ **4.** Do the comparisons and/or contrasts follow a logical order?
- ☐ **5.** Does my closing sentence provide an important final thought about the topics?

Voice

- ☐ **6.** Do I sound knowledgeable about the topics?
- ☐ **7.** Does my voice engage the reader?

Editing

Edit Create a clean copy of your revised paragraph and use the following checklist to check it for style and conventions.

Words

- ☐ **1.** Have I used specific nouns and verbs? (See page 74.)
- ☐ **2.** Have I used specific modifiers? (See page 143.)

Sentences

- ☐ **3.** Have I varied the beginnings and lengths of sentences? (See pages 264, 266.)
- ☐ **4.** Have I combined short, choppy sentences? (See page 262.)
- ☐ **5.** Have I avoided fragments and run-ons? (See pages 297–302, 306–307.)

Conventions

- ☐ **6.** Do I use correct verb forms (*he saw,* not *he seen*)? (See page 356.)
- ☐ **7.** Do my subjects and verbs agree (*she speaks,* not *she speak*)? (See pages 282–291.)
- ☐ **8.** Have I used the right words (*their, there, they're*)?
- ☐ **9.** Have I capitalized first words and proper nouns and adjectives? (See page 414.)
- ☐ **10.** Have I used commas after long introductory word groups? (See page 396.)
- ☐ **11.** Have I carefully checked my spelling?

Learning Outcome

Review cause-effect and comparison-contrast.

LO5 Reviewing Cause-Effect and Comparison-Contrast

Cause-Effect Fill in the following chart with causes and effects related to this photograph of a shantytown. Answers will vary.

Causes	Effects

On the lines below, write a topic sentence for a cause-effect paragraph about the shantytown. Write the paragraph on your own paper. (See pages 115–117.)

Topic Sentence: ____________________

____

____

Comparison-Contrast List two pairs of related gestures, actions, or feelings. Giggling and snickering, for example, are two types of laughter. Circle the pair that you would like to write about in a comparison-contrast paragraph.

1. Answers will vary. __________ 2. __________ __________

Next, use this Venn diagram to collect details about your topic. Write the paragraph on your own paper. (See pages 119–121.)

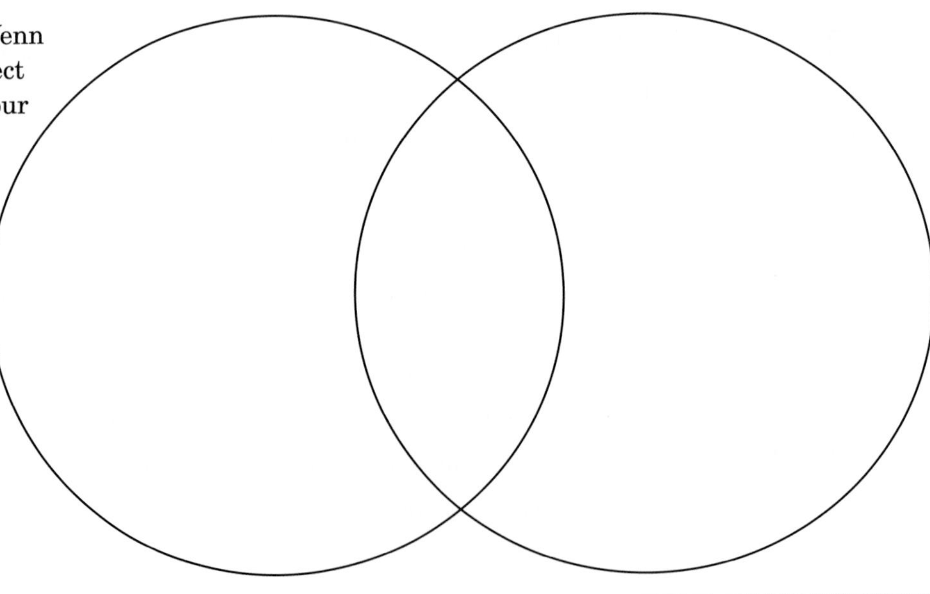

John Wang/Photodisc/Getty Images

"You're entitled to your own opinion. But you're not entitled to your own facts."
—Daniel Patrick Moynihan

David Madison/Photographer's Choice/Getty Images

13 Argument and Problem-Solution

Writing is really thinking on paper. When you explain or describe, you are demonstrating your ability to understand information. When you compare or classify, you are involved in analyzing, a higher level of thinking. When you persuade, you move even higher up the thinking **food chain**.

Writing persuasively is essentially the process of arguing for or against a particular point of view. In order to form a thoughtful opinion, you first must thoroughly understand and analyze the subject. Developing a problem-solution paragraph is a closely related form because it involves analyzing and recommending.

You'll be expected to writing persuasively in almost all of your college course work, so the strategies that you learn in this chapter will prove very helpful.

What do you think?

What does Moynihan have to say about the relationship between opinions and facts?

Answers will vary.

Learning Outcomes

LO1 Analyze a persuasive paragraph.

LO2 Write a persuasive paragraph.

LO3 Analyze a problem-solution paragraph.

LO4 Write a problem-solution paragraph.

Vocabulary

food chain
the connection from the lowest life forms to the highest; here, a metaphor for different levels of thinking

Learning Outcome

Analyze a persuasive paragraph.

LO1 Analyzing an Argument Paragraph

A persuasive paragraph presents a mini-argument by expressing an opinion and supporting it with reliable facts and details. The test of this form of writing is whether or not the reader accepts the **validity** of the argument.

Read/React Read the following persuasive paragraph; then answer the questions at the bottom of the page.

Evening the Odds

The **topic sentence** states the writer's opinion.

Body sentences provide support for the writer's position.

The **closing sentence** reinforces the writer's position.

Barbed hooks should be banned from lure fishing to protect the fish stocks. Fishing was once a way to put food on the table, so using barbed hooks may have made sense in the past, but in today's word, fishing for almost everyone is a form of recreation. A properly set barbed hook often inflicts serious injury to the fish, especially the smaller ones. Many small fish are kept because the angler knows that releasing them would be inhumane, while others are released with portions of their jaws severely damaged or missing. Using a smooth, barbless hook, on the other hand, is much easier to remove from a fish's mouth, leaving only a small puncture in the jaw area, and giving anglers the opportunity to release undamaged fish. In this way, barbless hooks help to preserve our limited fish stocks. Supporters of barbed hooks say that banning them would decrease the number of fish they are able to catch and that their enjoyment would decrease. They are partially correct because playing a fish is difficult without a barb. However, many anglers using barbless hooks report that they actually find fishing more enjoyable because it adds another challenge. To maintain a healthy fish population for recreational fishing, barbed hooks no longer belong in an angler's tackle box.

1. What is the writer arguing for or against?

   Against barbed hooks in lure fishing

2. What part of the paragraph addresses a **counterargument**? (Identify the lines.)

   13-15

3. How would you rate the effectiveness of this argument? Explain your choice.

   weak 1 2 3 4 5 6 7 8 9 10 strong

   Answers will vary.

Vocabulary

validity
effectiveness or strength

counterargument
argument against

LO2 Writing an Argument Paragraph

Learning Outcome

Write a persuasive paragraph.

To write an argument paragraph, follow the guidelines on the next three pages, starting with prewriting below.

Prewriting

Select In the space that follows, list activities (hobbies, sports, other pastimes) that you participate in or have strong feelings about. Then circle one that you could write about in a persuasive paragraph.

Activities:

Answers will vary.

Form After thinking about the topic, write a working opinion statement. (You can always adjust or change it later on.) Use the formula below as a guide.

Topic	+	position	=	opinion statement
Barbed hooks		should be banned from lure fishing to protect the fish stock		Barbed hooks should be banned from lure fishing to protect the fish stock.

Answers will vary.

Collect Fill in the chart below with two or three supporting details (facts, statistics, quotations, and so on), and, if possible, one main counterargument. Answers will vary.

Supporting Details

1.
2.
3.

Counterargument

Writing

Write Create a first draft of your persuasive paragraph, using the following paragraph outline as a guide.

WAC

Problem-solution writing is key to both social sciences and real sciences.

Vocabulary

reaffirm
to restate to emphasize or stress

Paragraph Outline

Topic Sentence: Begin with your opinion statement from page 125.

Body Sentences: Write sentences that develop your supporting details from page 125. Work in a counterargument if you feel it is necessary. (Note how the sentences in the sample paragraph flow from one to another.)

Closing Sentences: Write a sentence that **reaffirms** your opinion.

Answers will vary.

Revising

Revise Read your paragraph and, if possible, have someone else read it as well. Then use the following checklist to guide your revision. Keep making improvements until you can check off each item in the list.

Ideas

- ☐ **1.** Does my paragraph address a timely and/or important topic?
- ☐ **2.** Do I provide a convincing argument (opinion and supporting points)?
- ☐ **3.** Do I address an important counterargument (optional)?

Organization

- ☐ **4.** Does my opinion statement make a **reasonable** claim?
- ☐ **5.** Are the body sentences presented in a logical order?
- ☐ **6.** Does the closing sentence reaffirm my opinion or position?

Voice

- ☐ **7.** Does my writing voice reflect my feelings about the topic?
- ☐ **8.** Do I sound logical and knowledgeable?

Editing

Edit Create a clean copy of your revised paragraph. Then edit your writing for style and conventions using the following checklist as a guide.

Vocabulary

reasonable
practical and intelligent

Words

- ☐ **1.** Have I used specific nouns and verbs? (See page 74.)
- ☐ **2.** Have I used specific modifiers? (See page 143.)

Sentences

- ☐ **3.** Have I varied the beginnings and lengths of sentences? (See pages 264, 266.)
- ☐ **4.** Have I combined short, choppy sentences? (See page 262.)
- ☐ **5.** Have I avoided fragments and run-ons? (See pages 297–302, 306–307.)

Conventions

- ☐ **6.** Do I use correct verb forms (*he saw,* not *he seen*)? (See page 356.)
- ☐ **7.** Do my subjects and verbs agree (*she speaks,* not *she speak*)? (See pages 282–291.)
- ☐ **8.** Have I used the right words (*their, there, they're*)?
- ☐ **9.** Have I capitalized first words and proper nouns and adjectives? (See page 414.)
- ☐ **10.** Have I used commas after long introductory word groups? (See page 396.)
- ☐ **11.** Have I carefully checked my spelling?

Learning Outcome

Analyze a problem-solution paragraph.

LO3 Analyzing a Problem-Solution Paragraph

Problem-solution paragraphs and essays can be expository or persuasive. If the problem and solution happened in the past, the writing is expository. If the essay focuses on a current problem, the writing is persuasive.

Read/React Read the following problem-solution paragraph; then answer the questions at the bottom of the page.

© Glenn Bo/iStockphoto.com

Lead Alert

The **topic sentence** states the topic and focus of the paragraph.

Body sentences explain the problem and offer one or more solutions.

The **closing sentence** reminds readers of the importance of the problem.

Young children unprotected from almost any amount of lead may suffer serious health problems. Lead poisoning can lead to everything from headaches and periods of confusion to learning disabilities and behavioral problems. As the Alliance for Healthy Homes reports, the problem is most **acute** in large urban areas where families live in substandard housing. Inner city dwellings built before 1960 likely contain lead-based paints, the major source of the problem. If the lead paint in these dwellings is peeling, very young children will eat the paint chips, but even the dust from the paint is potentially harmful. It can settle on anything, and eventually get in the mouths of the very young. Unfortunately, once someone suffers from lead poisoning, there are no complete cures. The best solution for families is to take **preventative** measures such as daily house cleaning and regular washing of hands. Long-term measures include painting over old lead paint, but without sanding before hand. The Mayo Clinic Web site on lead poisoning reminds renters that they have rights protecting their health and safety. Landlords by law are required to find and address sources of lead. Growing up poor is hard enough. Problems only become magnified if the living conditions expose dwellers to the dangers of lead.

1. What are the topic and focus of the paragraph?

   Topic: Children exposed to lead paint **Focus:** children of urban poor

2. What are two things that you learned about the problem?

   Answers will vary.

3. What two or three solutions did you learn about?

   Answers will vary.

Vocabulary

acute
intense, serious, or sharp

preventative
intended to prevent

LO4 Writing a Problem-Solution Paragraph

Learning Outcome

Write a problem-solution paragraph.

To write a problem-solution paragraph, use the next three pages as a guide, starting the prewriting below.

Prewriting

Select List two or three problems in your community such as *lack of public transportation* or *loud noises.* Also list two or three problems related to school life such as *crowded classrooms* or *limited access to courses.* Then circle one that you could write about in a problem-solution paragraph. Answers will vary.

Community-related problems:	School-related problems:

Collect Gather information for your paragraph by following the directions below. Answers will vary.

Problem

State the problem: ______

Identify who is affected by it: ______

______

Identify the causes of the problem: ______

______

______

Explain its significance: ______

______

Solutions

State two or three possible solutions: (*Circle the best one.*)

______

______

______

______

Writing

Write Create a first draft of your problem-solution paragraph, using the following paragraph outline as a guide.

Paragraph Outline

Topic Sentence: Start your paragraph with a clear statement of the problem. (See the formula on page 125 for help.)

Body Sentences: Write sentences that explain the problem and offer the best solutions. You may want to lead up to the best solution. Include additional explanations as necessary to connect your ideas.

Closing Sentence: End with a sentence that reminds the reader about the importance of the problem.

WAC

Problem-solution writing is key to both social sciences and natural sciences.

Answers will vary.

Revising

Revise Read your paragraph and, if possible, have someone else read it as well. Then use the following checklist to guide your revision. Keep making improvements until you can check off each item in the list.

Ideas

- ☐ **1.** Does my paragraph address an important current problem?
- ☐ **2.** Do I effectively explore the problem and solutions?
- ☐ **3.** Do I offer additional explanations as needed?

Organization

- ☐ **4.** Does my topic sentence clearly identify the problem?
- ☐ **5.** Are the body sentences arranged in a logical way?
- ☐ **6.** Does my closing sentence stress the important of the problem?

Voice

- ☐ **7.** Do I sound interested in and knowledgeable about the problem?
- ☐ **8.** Do I speak sincerely to the reader?

Editing

Edit Create a clean copy of your paragraph; then use the following checklist to edit your writing for style and conventions.

Words

- ☐ **1.** Have I used specific nouns and verbs? (See page 74.)
- ☐ **2.** Have I used specific modifiers? (See page 143.)

Sentences

- ☐ **3.** Have I varied the beginnings and lengths of sentences? (See pages 264, 266.)
- ☐ **4.** Have I combined short, choppy sentences? (See page 262.)
- ☐ **5.** Have I avoided fragments and run-ons? (See pages 297–302, 306–307.)

Conventions

- ☐ **6.** Do I use correct verb forms *(he saw,* not *he seen)*? (See page 356.)
- ☐ **7.** Do my subjects and verbs agree (*she speaks,* not *she speak*)? (See pages 282–291.)
- ☐ **8.** Have I used the right words (*their, there, they're*)?
- ☐ **9.** Have I capitalized first words and proper nouns and adjectives? (See page 414.)
- ☐ **10.** Have I used commas after long introductory word groups? (See page 396.)
- ☐ **11.** Have I carefully checked my spelling?

Part 4 Developing Essays

"I never travel without my diary. One should always have something sensational to read on the train."

14 Narrative Essay

Memories seemingly alter reality, taking your mind to another time and place. They can flood your brain for hours, make a lengthy car ride go by in a flash, or get you through a particularly mind-numbing classroom lecture. When your mind drifts to that special place and remembers a past experience, you are reflecting on your own unique story.

An essay that shares a memory or story from your own life is called a personal narrative. The goal of such writing is to bring the memory to life with details that will help the reader see, hear, touch, and taste the experience.

This chapter will guide you through the process of writing a narrative essay about an important past experience.

Demetrio Carrasco/Dorling Kindersley/Getty Images

What do you think?

What sensational stories might be included in the diary of your own life?

Answers will vary.

Learning Outcomes

- LO1 Understand narrative essays.
- LO2 Plan a narrative essay.
- LO3 Write the first draft.
- LO4 Revise the first draft.
- LO5 Edit the essay.
- LO6 Reflect on the experience.

Learning Outcome

Understand narrative essays.

LO1 Reviewing a Narrative Essay

A narrative essay tells a story. In the following essay, a writer shares a personal story about a memorable experience.

Read/React Read the following essay. Then complete the analysis on the next page.

Tripped Up Road Trip

The **opening paragraph** starts in the middle of the action.

Jammed in our aging royal blue Chevy Astro van with no air conditioning, no radio, and limited legroom, sat my parents, my two sisters, and our beloved golden retriever, Max. It was mid-June and we were traveling along historic Route 66 near the New Mexico-Arizona border, on our way to Grand Canyon National Park.

The first **middle paragraph** uses dialogue to push the story along.

This was not exactly my idea of a fun family vacation. Sweat beads trickled down my brow, and a feeling of dread washed over me as I noticed the low-battery sign blinking on my mp3 player. Couldn't we go to a resort with a swimming pool? "Just six hours left," Mom commented from the front seat. Six hours? You could watch *Avatar* twice in that same amount of time.

The next **paragraph** describes the key moment in the narrative.

What happened next seemed like a scene from a bad comedy movie. Out of nowhere, grayish smoke billowed from under the hood of the van and up the windshield, completely blocking my dad's view of the road. As Dad pulled off to the side, Max started barking, startling my slumbering sisters, who started screaming as smoke spilled into the car through the open windows. When the car was parked, I flung open the door and ran out into the desert sun. This was the worst vacation ever.

The **closing paragraph** describes the action that followed the key moment and provides closure.

Dad discovered the engine had overheated, and we were stuck. "Is this thing going to blow up?" asked my younger sister Michelle. "I have like a bunch of clothes in there." Luckily Mom had brought a cooler stocked with bottled water and snacks, so we survived the hot sun while we waited for a tow truck. It must have been a funny sight for the truck driver when he pulled up. All six of us sat in a circle, sweating and looking miserable. We did eventually make it to the Grand Canyon, but not before Mom admitted, "A pool would feel really nice right now."

A Closer Look

This essay relied on three basic building blocks of narrative writing: action, dialogue, and description. **Action** uses active verbs to describe what is happening. *Out of nowhere, grayish smoke billowed from under the hood of the van.* **Dialogue** reveals the unique personalities of the people involved in the story. *"I have like a bunch of clothes in there," said Michelle.* And **description** uses vivid details to describe people, places, and things. *Sweat beads trickled down my brow.*

Analyze Reread the essay on the facing page. As you do, record any examples of action, dialogue, and description in the following chart. Answers will vary.

Action	Dialogue	Description

Explain What type of sensory detail are you most interested in hearing about from a writer? Why? Answers will vary.

Learning Outcome

Plan a narrative essay.

LO2 Prewriting: Planning

In your own essay, you will write about an experience from your past. Think of a time, a place, or an event that sticks out as a particularly memorable moment in your life.

Selecting a Topic

Select In the space below, list four experiences from your own life to consider for a narrative essay. Remember, the experiences don't have to be big or life altering. Small events, even ones that may seem inconsequential, can make interesting topics for narrative essays. Answers will vary.

1. ______________________ 2. ______________________

3. ______________________ 4. ______________________

Using Chronological Order

Once you have selected a topic, think carefully about the order of events in your memory. In almost all cases, narrative essays are arranged **chronologically**, or according to time.

Vocabulary

chronological order
time order; relating details in the order that they occurred

Identify Use the time line below to list the main details of your topic in chronological (time) order. Answers will vary.

1. ______ | ______________________________
2. ______ | ______________________________
3. ______ | ______________________________
4. ______ | ______________________________
5. ______ | ______________________________
6. ______ | ______________________________
7. ______ | ______________________________
8. ______ | ______________________________

Gathering Details

The most vivid narrative essays use plenty of sensory details. Such details allow the reader to picture, hear, and touch what you describe. The following chart describes the sensory details in a narrative essay about a special memory.

Sights	Sounds	Smells	Tastes	Textures
ceiling fan egg in the frying pan sparkle of brown eyes arthritic hands	buzz of the phone conversation with Mom Grandpa's deep laugh	eggs frying	burn of the bourbon drink	lump in the throat watery eyes

Traits

The best dialogue captures a person's unique voice, so write the way a speaker actually speaks.

Gather Complete the sensory chart below. Collect any sights, sounds, smells, tastes, or textures about your subject in the appropriate column. Answers will vary.

Sights	Sounds	Smells	Tastes	Textures

Learning Outcome

Write the first draft.

WAC

Though some academic forms of writing restrict use of first-person pronouns, *I, you,* and *we,* are acceptable in narrative essays.

LO3 Writing: Creating a First Draft

In a first draft you follow your plan and organize your details to create a narrative story. Provided below is a sample narrative essay about a memorable moment in the writer's life.

Read/React Read the essay, noting how the writer created an effective opening and closing for his personal narrative.

Remembering Gramps

Opening paragraph

It was sometime after eight o'clock on a Saturday morning when I received the call about my grandfather's death. I was already awake, cracking eggs into a skillet, when my cell phone buzzed on the countertop. A little early for a phone call, I thought. It was my mom. "Are you awake?" she asked, her voice cracking. Sensing her distress, I asked what was wrong. She told me my grandfather had suffered a stroke during the night and didn't make it.

Middle paragraph 1

After talking through the funeral plans, I wobbled over to my cushy, leather couch and stared blankly at the circulating blades on the ceiling fan. Memories of my grandfather spun around in my head, like the time he taught me how to throw a curveball, and the fishing trip we took together on the Gulf Coast, and the day he poured me a Coke, but instead mistakenly handed me his glass of bourbon and ice.

Middle paragraph 2

Of course, those were old memories. By the time I reached college, Grandpa wasn't as active anymore. Tired and overworked from his years of hard labor at the steel yard, his back eventually gave out and his joints swelled up with arthritis. He lived alone in the modest two-bedroom home he built for my grandmother after they married. But even after she was gone, he never lost the sparkle in his brown eyes. Nor did he lose his sense of humor, punctuated by a deep baritone laugh.

Closing paragraph

And so I sat there, staring at the ceiling and reminiscing about Grandpa. Sure, I had a lump in my throat and tears filled my eyes; but I felt thankful for the memories of times we had together, and hopeful that one day I could be as good a grandfather as he had been to me.

Laura Doss/Fancy/Corbis

Creating an Opening Paragraph

The opening paragraph should capture attention and lead the reader into the story. Here are some strategies for beginning your narrative:

- **Set the stage.**
  Show where things happen. Describe the place by using precise details that appeal to the five senses.
  > It was sometime after eight o'clock on a Saturday morning when I received the call about my grandfather's death.
- **Jump into the action.**
  Quickly establish the setting, introduce the characters and topic, and have them do or say something.
  > Jammed in our aging royal blue Chevy Astro van with no air conditioning, no radio, and limited legroom, sat my parents, my two sisters, and our beloved golden retriever, Max.
- **Focus on an interesting detail.**
  Offer a powerful sensory or **thought detail** to introduce an amazing or surprising part of the story.
  > I should have listened to my brother. I never should have walked in that room.

Vocabulary

thought details
a writer's impressions, emotions, or reflections about an experience

Write Create your opening paragraph. Start with a sentence that uses one of the strategies above. Then write sentences that continue to introduce the story.

Answers will vary.

Traits

Transition words that show time: after / at / before / during / finally / first / later / next / next week / now / second / soon / suddenly / third / then / today / until / when / while / yesterday

Creating Middle Paragraphs

Write As you write your middle paragraphs, include action, description, and dialogue. (See page 135.) Use these narrative elements to build suspense until the story reaches its most exciting moment. Finally, use transition words to move the story along in time order. (Refer to "Traits" at the left.) Answers will vary.

Creating a Closing Paragraph

The closing paragraph should explain the outcome of the narrative. Consider the following strategies:

- **Use a final piece of dialogue.**
  Close with an appropriate quotation from someone involved in the narrative.
- **Explain the event's impact.**
  In a sentence, describe how you or the world around you changed after the experience.
- **Reveal a new understanding.**
  Explain what you learned from the experience.

Write Create the closing paragraph for your narrative essay. Answers will vary.

Learning Outcome

Revise the first draft.

Speaking & Listening

Have your partner read your essay aloud. Then complete the response sheet.

LO4 Revising: Improving the Writing

Revising your first draft involves adding, deleting, rearranging, and reworking parts of your writing. Revision begins with a peer review.

Peer Review

Sharing your writing at various stages is important, especially when you review and revise a first draft. The feedback that you receive will help you change and improve your essay.

Respond Complete this response sheet after reading the first draft of a classmate's essay. Then share the sheet with the writer. (Keep your comments helpful and positive.) Answers will vary.

Essay title: ____________________

Writer: ____________________ Reviewer: ____________________

1. Which part of the essay seems to work best—opening, middle, or closing? Why?

____

____

____

2. Which part of the essay needs work—opening, middle, or closing? Why? ____________________

____

____

____

3. Which details in the story caught your attention? Name three.

   a. ____________________

   b. ____________________

   c. ____________________

4. Does the writer include appropriate dialogue? Explain.

____

____

____

5. Identify a phrase or two that show the writer's level of interest.

____

____

Adding Specific Verbs and Modifiers

You can strengthen your essay by adding specific verbs and modifiers. Such improvements in word choice make your writing more interesting.

Verbs

General	Specific
grew	swelled
came	advanced
run	sprint
lives	roams
wear	adorn

Modifiers

General	Specific
baseball hat	flat-billed New York Yankees hat
curly hair	wavy auburn hair
sweet sauce	tangy barbeque sauce

Revising in Action

Read aloud the unrevised and then the revised version of the following excerpt. Note how specific verbs and adjectives make the writing come alive.

> wobbled cushy, leather circulating ceiling
> I ~~walked~~ over to my couch and stared blankly at the blades on the fan.

Revise Improve your writing, using the following checklist and your partner's comments on the response sheet. Continue working until you can check off each item in the list.

Ideas

- ☐ **1.** Do I focus on one specific experience or memory?
- ☐ **2.** Do I include sensory details and dialogue?
- ☐ **3.** Do I use specific verbs and modifiers?

Organization

- ☐ **4.** Does the essay have an opening, a middle, and a closing?
- ☐ **5.** Is the story organized chronologically?
- ☐ **6.** Have I used transitions to connect my sentences?

Voice

- ☐ **7.** Is my interest in the story obvious to the reader?
- ☐ **8.** Does my writing voice fit my personality?

Learning Outcome

Edit the essay.

LO5 Editing: Correcting Your Writing

The main work of editing is correcting your revised first draft.

Quotation Marks and Dialogue

Dialogue enlivens a story and reveals the personalities of its characters. When you recall or create conversations between people using the speaker's exact words, you must use quotation marks before and after the **direct quotation.** However, when you use an **indirect quotation**—one that does not use the speaker's exact words—quotation marks are not needed. See the examples that follow.

Direct Quotation

Before we left class, our teacher said, **"Next week's final will be comprehensive."**

Indirect Quotation

I recall the teacher saying **that the final will be comprehensive.**

Note: The word *that* often indicates dialogue that is being reported rather than quoted.

Punctuation Practice Read the sentences below. Place quotation marks (“”) before and after the speaker's exact words in direct quotations. If the sentence contains no direct quotations, write “C” for correct on the blank following the sentence.

1. "Who is your favorite actress?" asked Veronica. _______
2. The salesman suggested that I should take the truck for a test-drive. __C__
3. Frank said that if we want to make it in time, we should leave by noon. __C__
4. "On my way out today," Jessie said, "I forgot my cell phone." _______
5. "Pull over to the side of the road," said the police officer. _______
6. After glancing at her test score, Jillian said, "Spring break can't come soon enough." _______
7. "And with this new cell phone model," said the saleswoman, "you can play music, get driving directions, and check your e-mail." _______
8. Jana said that she is in love with her new summer dress. __C__

Vocabulary

dialogue
the words spoken by people and set apart with quotation marks

Apply Read your narrative essay. If you included any direct quotations, make sure they are properly marked with quotation marks. If you did not use any direct quotations, you may consider adding one or two to reveal the uniqueness of the people in your story.

Punctuation of Dialogue

As you edit your narrative essay, check for the correct punctuation of dialogue. In general, there are three rules you should follow.

- **When a period or comma follows the quotation, place the period or comma *before* the quotation mark.**

  "You should check your voice messages**,"** advised Mr. Lee.

  "As you will soon discover**,"** advised Reggie, "the wrap station in the cafeteria is the best choice for lunch**."**

- **When a question mark or an exclamation point follows the quotation, place it *before* the quotation mark if it belongs with the quotation. Otherwise, place it after.**

  I asked Sheryl, "Where can I get some good soul food**?"**

  Did you hear Veronica say, "I quit**"?**

- **When a semicolon or colon follows the quotation, place it after the quotation mark.**

  Trey only said, "I have other plans**";** he didn't mention his fear of heights.

Punctuation Practice In each sentence that follows, correct the punctuation and capitalization of the quotations.

1. "Let's focus on solutions, not problems", offered Haley.
2. Jack promised he would, "Try his best to make it;" however, I know he's not coming.
3. "It's not the size of the dog in the fight", suggested Mark Twain ", it's the size of the fight in the dog."
4. "It's about time you showed up"! exclaimed Karen.
5. "Should I apply for the job"? asked my roommate.
6. What did you mean when you said, "There is more to the story than you think?"
7. "We are doing everything in our power to regain your trust", said the company spokesperson.

Apply Read your narrative essay. Closely check the punctuation of your dialogue.

Marking an Essay

Before you finish editing your revised essay, you can practice by editing the following model.

Editing Practice Read the following narrative essay, looking for problems listed in the checklist on the facing page. Also refer to the list of common errors on page 80. Correct the model using the marks listed to the left. One correction has been done for you.

Correction Marks

- 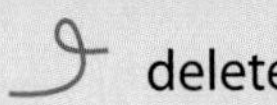 delete
- d (≡) capitalize
- lowercase
- ^ insert
- add comma
- add question mark
- add word
- ⊙ add period
- spelling
- switch

Whale Watchers

On a sunny afternoon off the coast of San Diego my friend Natalie and I set off on our great whale watching adventure. In the winter months some 20,000 gray whales migrate through the Pacific waters along the coast of california, and we wanted to see the majestic creatures in there natural habitat.

As we stepped aboard the 100-foot tour boat nicknamed "Night and Day", Natalie reminded me to take some medication to prevent seasickness. Good thing she did, because the captain announced we would hit 6-foot swells on our journey. Their were about 40 other passengers onboard with us.

About 15 minutes off the shoreline, a passenger shouted, "There she blows"! Indeed, about 20 yards ahead of us, I seen a spray of white water rocket vertically from the ocean surface we had spotted our first whale! As the boat crept closer, we could see the bumpy gray backs of two more whales rising above the undulating waves. I was so excited that high-fived Natalie so hard it made my hand sting.

We ended up seeing five diffrant gray whales two packs of dolphins, and too many pelicans to count. seeing this beautiful sea life in the wild was an experience I'll never forget. Learning that the whales are endangered goes to show that we must boost our efforts to protect them from extinction.

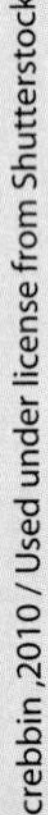

Correcting Your Essay

Now it's time to correct your own essay.

Edit Prepare a clean copy of your essay and use the following checklist to look for errors. Continue working until you can check off each item in the list.

Words

- ☐ **1.** Have I used specific nouns and verbs)? (See page 74.)
- ☐ **2.** Have I used more action verbs than "be" verbs? (See page 348.)

Sentences

- ☐ **3.** Have I used sentences with varying beginnings and lengths? (See pages 264, 266.)
- ☐ **4.** Have I avoided improper shifts in sentences? (See pages 314–315.)
- ☐ **5.** Have I avoided fragments and run-ons? (See pages 297–302, 306–307.)

Conventions

- ☐ **6.** Do I use correct verb forms (*he saw,* not *he seen*)? (See page 356.)
- ☐ **7.** Do my subjects and verbs agree (*she speaks,* not *she speak*)? (See pages 282–291.)
- ☐ **8.** Have I used the right words (*their, there, they're*)?
- ☐ **9.** Have I capitalized first words and proper nouns and adjectives? (See page 414.)
- ☐ **10.** Have I used commas after long introductory word groups and to separate items in a series? (See page 396.)
- ☐ **11.** Have I correctly punctuated any dialogue? (See pages 144–145.)
- ☐ **12.** Have I carefully checked my spelling?

Adding a Title

Make sure to add an attention-getting title. Here are three simple strategies for writing narrative-essay titles.

- **Use a phrase from the paragraph:** Remembering Gramps
- **Use alliteration, the repetition of a consonant sound:** Whale Watchers
- **Use a play on words:** Tripped Up Road Trip

Learning Outcome

Reflect on the experience.

LO6 Reviewing Narrative Writing

Complete these activities as needed to help you better understand how to write narrative essays.

Fill In Description, especially relating to the five senses, makes up a key component of narrative writing. Imagine you are at the carnival in the picture on this page. What sensory details—sights, smells, sounds, and so on—might you experience? Fill in as many as you can in this sensory chart. (See page 137.)

Sights	Sounds	Smells	Tastes	Textures
	Answers will vary.			

Explain What are the three key elements of narrative writing? What purpose does each element serve? Answers will vary.

Sort Circle the transitions that *show time.* (See page 140.)

(after) below (before) near (next) (then)

"The essence of the beautiful is unity in variety."
—William Somerset Maugham

Classification Essay

Say you're starting a flower garden, but you don't know what type of flowers you want to plant. You've got hundreds of options, and you feel overwhelmed. What should you do? Your best plan might be to break down the wide variety of available flowers into categories, or subgroups, that fit your preferences. Think about the color, shape, style, and growing patterns that will work best in your garden. And, eventually, narrow down your choices to a more manageable list.

A classification essay works in the same way: It breaks down a multifaceted topic into manageable subgroups, so that you can look at the individual components and consider the relationships between them.

Learning Outcomes

LO1 Understand classification essays.
LO2 Plan a classification essay.
LO3 Write the first draft.
LO4 Revise the essay.
LO5 Edit the essay.
LO6 Reflect on the experience.

What do you think?

Reread the quotation at the top of the page. How might there be unity in variety? Explain.

Answers will vary.

Learning Outcome

Understand classification essays.

LO1 Reviewing a Classification Essay

A classification essay analyzes a topic by breaking it down into different categories or types.

Read/React Read the following essay. Then complete the analysis on the next page.

Five Branches of the United States Armed Forces

The **opening** gets the reader's attention and establishes criteria for dividing the topic into subgroups.

They serve on land, in the air, and at sea. Their bases reside in at least 135 countries. They are made up of 1.4 million brave men and women, protecting the freedom and ideals of the United States. That's just part of the story behind the United States armed forces, the unified military force of the United States. Look closer and you will find five different branches, each carrying out distinct roles in order to serve one unifying goal.

The **middle paragraphs** describe the subgroups, explain their distinct traits, and show the relationships between them.

The United States Army is the largest and oldest branch of armed forces. Its role is to serve land-based military operations, a responsibility it has had since its formation on June 14, 1775, as the Continental Army during the American Revolution.

Shortly thereafter, another branch of military was founded—the United States Navy (then called the Continental Navy) on October 13,1775. The U.S. Navy is the primary sea branch of the armed forces and is currently the second biggest branch within the armed forces with 332,000 personnel.

The next oldest branch of the armed forces—the United States Marine Corps—is actually a part of the U.S. Navy. Founded on November 10, 1775, the Marine Corps carries out the role of naval infantry, often engaging in amphibious or hybrid warfare. They work closely with but separately from the U.S. Navy.

The United States Coast Guard is a fourth branch of the U.S. armed forces. It was founded in 1790 and is responsible for maritime law enforcement as well as maritime search and rescue. Along with being the smallest branch of the military, the USCG is the only branch under the direction of the Department of Homeland Security. All other branches of the armed forces are under the direction of the Department of Defense.

The newest branch is the United States Air Force. Once a part of the U.S. Army, the USAF was established as a separate branch in 1947 and is responsible for aerial, space, and cyber warfare. It is the third largest military branch.

The **closing** reunites the subgroups for a final look at the topic.

Together the Army, Navy, Marine Corps, Air Force, and Coast Guard make up the United States armed forces. Throughout the last 200 years, each branch has played a role in shaping not only what the United States has become, but also what the world has become.

A Closer Look

List Complete the chart below by writing the names of each branch of military, the role of that branch, and details about it, including the year it was founded. The first one has been done for you.

Branches of U.S. Armed Forces

	Definition/Role	Details
Subgroup 1 Army	Responsible for land-based military operations	- Founding date: June 14, 1775 - Largest branch
Subgroup 2 Navy	Primary sea branch	Founding date: October 13, 1775 Second largest branch
Subgroup 3 Marine Corps	Naval infantry	Founding date: November 10, 1775 Amphibious or hybrid warfare
Subgroup 4 Coast Guard	Maritime law Maritime search/rescue	Founding date: 1790 Smallest branch Only branch reporting to Department of Homeland Security
Subgroup 5 Air Force	Aerial, space, and cyber warfare	Founding date: 1947 Originally part of the Army Third largest branch

Explain The writer chose to distinguish each branch (subgroup) by role, size, and founding date. What other features or points could the writer have used to distinguish the different branches of armed forces? Explain.

Answers will vary.

Learning Outcome

Plan a classification essay.

Olga Lyubkina,2010 / Used under license from Shutterstock.com

LO2 Prewriting: Planning

In your own classification essay, you will explore the categories, or subgroups, of a topic of your choice. These two pages will help you select a topic and gather details about it.

Explore Read through the "Essentials of Life" list below. Select four general subject areas you would like to explore. Then, for each subject, write a possible topic. An example has been done for you.

Essentials of Life

food	intelligence	resources
clothing	personality	energy
shelter	senses	money
education	emotions	government
work	goals	laws
entertainment	health	rights
recreation	environment	science
religion	plants	measurement
family	animals	machines
friends	land	tools
community	literature	agriculture
communication	arts	business

Answers will vary.

1. **Subject Area:** Clothing ______ **Topic:** Types of Athletic shorts ______
2. **Subject Area:** ______ **Topic:** Types of ______
3. **Subject Area:** ______ **Topic:** Types of ______
4. **Subject Area:** ______ **Topic:** Types of ______
5. **Subject Area:** ______ **Topic:** Types of ______

Select Review the topics you've listed above and select one that has three to six types (a number you could comfortably cover in a classification essay).

Researching Your Topic

Once you have selected a topic, you may need to find out more about it. Search Internet sites, encyclopedias, school texts, and other sources as necessary. As you break down your topic into types or categories, consider the following points:

Types or categories should be . . .

- **exclusive**, which means that one example doesn't fit into more than one category.
- **consistent**, which means that examples of this category have the same traits.

Organize In this chart, write your topic within the parentheses. Then list the subgroups, or types, in the first column, define each in the second column, and provide details about each in the third. Answers will vary.

Types of ( )	Definition	Details
Subgroup 1		
Subgroup 2		
Subgroup 3		
Subgroup 4		

WAC

In all classes, research and classification are critical.

Vocabulary

exclusive category
a type that does not overlap with other types

consistent category
a type that contains examples that share the same traits

Learning Outcome

Write the first draft.

LO3 Writing: Creating a First Draft

After you have completed planning and gathering, you are ready to start the drafting stage. Provided below is a sample classification essay.

Read/React Read the essay, noting how the writer classified the topic into four distinct subgroups.

To Work Out or Not to Work Out

Opening paragraph

Thesis statement

The Greek philosopher Plato once said, "Lack of activity destroys the good condition of every human being." The American comedian Phyllis Diller once joked, "My idea of exercise is a good brisk sit." Clearly, different people pursue different levels of physical activity.

Subgroup 1

Diller's attitude best aligns with someone living a "sedentary lifestyle." A person with a sedentary lifestyle exercises fewer than three times per week. This type of lifestyle is linked to weight gain and an increased risk of developing diseases such as type 2 diabetes.

Subgroup 2

A second level of physical activity is known simply as "lifestyle active." This level describes a person who performs everyday lifestyle activities such as walking to and from the grocery store, doing yard work, or playing pick-up basketball. Engaging in regular lifestyle activities can help control cholesterol levels and reduce body fat.

Subgroup 3

Someone who follows a cardio-respiratory exercise program for 20 to 60 minutes, three to five days per week, lives a "moderate physical lifestyle," the third level of physical activity. This type of person might be a regular runner, weight lifter, or power walker. A moderate physical lifestyle helps a person become physically fit while reducing the risk of chronic diseases.

Subgroup 4

Finally, the highest level of physical activity is a "vigorous physical lifestyle." People on this level exercise 20 to 60 minutes most days of the week and follow a routine of aerobic exercises, strength training, and stretching exercises. A vigorous physical lifestyle achieves the same benefits of moderate physical activities, while also promoting a greater level of fitness.

Closing paragraph

Many factors contribute to a person's level of physical activity—work environment, family obligations, and other personal responsibilities. Depending on the time of year, a person may live a moderate physical lifestyle one week and a sedentary lifestyle the next week. What's most important, though, is to live a healthy lifestyle. And a healthy lifestyle requires some level of exercise.

Creating an Opening Paragraph

The objective of the opening paragraph is to gain the reader's attention, introduce the topic, and present your thesis statement. Here are some strategies for beginning your essay:

- **Set the mood.**

  They serve on land, in the air, and at sea. Their bases reside in at least 135 countries. They are made up of 1.4 million brave men and women, protecting the freedom and ideals of the United States.

- **Begin with a question.**

  What makes a baseball so hard to hit?

- **Use a quotation.**

  American comedian Phyllis Diller once joked, "My idea of exercise is a good brisk sit."

Writing a Thesis Statement

To create a thesis statement for your essay, follow this formula.

A Specific Topic	+	Overview of Subgroups	=	Thesis Statement
physical activity		different people pursue different levels		Different people pursue different levels of physical activity.

Write Create your opening paragraph. Start with a sentence that uses one of the strategies above. Then write sentences that build to your thesis statement.

Answers will vary.

Traits

Transition words that classify:

one type / a second / a third / the last / the simplest / a more complex / an advanced / the most complex / the most common / a less common / a rare / a very rare / the earliest / a later / a recent / the newest

Creating Middle Paragraphs

Write Refer to the chart on page 153 to help organize the middle paragraphs of your essay. Use the paragraphs to describe the subgroups of your topic and their respective traits. Include a topic sentence in each paragraph and use transitional words or phrases (like those at the left) to help your writing flow.

Answers will vary.

Creating a Closing Paragraph

The closing paragraph should bring the subgroups together again for a final look at the topic. Consider showing how the subgroups are related to one another, or leave the reader with some other thought.

Write Answer the following questions to help you sum up your essay.

1. What characteristics do the subgroups have in common?

   Answers will vary.

2. What is a key difference between the subgroups?

Write Create the closing paragraph for your classification essay.

Answers will vary.

Learning Outcome

Revise the essay.

Speaking & Listening

Have your partner read your essay aloud. Then complete the response sheet together.

LO4 Revising: Improving the Writing

Revising your first draft involves adding, deleting, rearranging, and reworking parts of your writing. Revision begins with a peer review.

Peer Review

Sharing your writing at various stages is important, especially when you review and revise a first draft. The feedback that you receive will help you change and improve your essay.

Respond Complete this response sheet after reading the first draft of a classmate's essay. Then share the sheet with the writer. (Keep your comments helpful and positive.) Answers will vary.

Essay title: ____________________

Writer: ____________________ Reviewer: ____________________

1. Which part of the essay seems to work best—opening, middle, or closing? Why?

2. Which part of the essay needs work—opening, middle, or closing? Why? ____________

3. Do the middle paragraphs explain the distinct traits of the subgroups? Explain.

4. Name two of your favorite details.

5. Identify a phrase or two that shows the writer's level of interest.

Clarifying Special Terms

Depending on the topic, your essay may contain special terms or words that are unfamiliar to your reader. Keep this potential problem in mind and always clarify such terms in the text of your essay. Consider the following strategies:

- **Provide an actual definition.**

  A person with a sedentary lifestyle exercises fewer than three times per week.

- **Use an appositive before or after the term.**

  The pitcher threw a slider, a pitch that breaks sideways and downward at a slower speed than a straight fastball. (The appositive is set off with a comma and defines the term *slider* in this example.)

- **Give word clues.**

  The African vuvuzelas blared throughout the stadium, a collective buzz from thousands of plastic horns. (Words like *African, blared, buzz, plastic,* and *horns* help the reader understand what *vuvuzelas* are.)

Revising in Action:

Read aloud the unrevised and then the revised version of the following excerpt. Note how the specific words energize the writing.

> , an extremely slow pitch with little to no spin
> Some baseball pitchers will throw a knuckleball^.
> , a pitcher for the Boston Red Sox,
> Tim Wakefield^is known for throwing mostly knuckleballs. Many batters are fooled by this specialty pitch because of its wacky movement.

Respond Improve your writing, using the following checklist and your partner's comments on the response sheet. Continue until you can check off each item.

Ideas

- ☐ **1.** Do I focus on one specific topic?
- ☐ **2.** Do I name and define the types or categories of the topic?
- ☐ **3.** Do I provide details about the traits of each type?
- ☐ **4.** Have I clarified any special terms?

Organization

- ☐ **5.** Does my essay have effective opening, middle, and closing paragraphs?
- ☐ **6.** Do I use transition words and phrases to show the relationship between types?

Voice

- ☐ **7.** Does my voice sound knowledgeable and interested?

Vocabulary

appositive
a word or phrase that identifies or renames a preceding noun or pronoun

Learning Outcome

Edit the essay.

LO5 Editing: Correcting Your Writing

The main work of editing is correcting your revised draft.

Commas Used with Extra Information

When words add information that can be removed from a sentence without changing its basic meaning, those words should be set off with commas. Here are three examples:

> Marc Jacobs, a famous American designer, is the creative director for the Louis Vuitton fashion line.
>
> (The appositive adds information about Marc Jacobs.)

> The road construction barrels, which were orange with white stripes, littered the side of the interstate for miles.
>
> (The clause adds a description of the barrels.)

> A cannoli, found at many Italian-American delis, is a popular Sicilian pastry.
>
> (The phrase adds a tip about where you might find cannolis.)

Insight

For more practice with comma use, see pages 392–402.

Comma Practice Indicate where commas are needed in the following sentences. If no commas are needed, write "correct" on the blank next to the sentence.

1. Internship coordinators, found at most colleges and universities, help students apply for and gain valuable internship experience. ________
2. Shakira, a Colombian recording artist, has enjoyed crossover success in the Latin pop and American pop markets. ________
3. The famous American architect Frank Lloyd Wright was born in a small farming community in Wisconsin. correct
4. In *Slumdog Millionaire*, which won ten Academy Awards, a young man from the slums wins the Indian version of *Who Wants to Be a Millionaire?* ________

Apply Read the sentences in your classification essay and watch for extra information that ought to be set off with commas. If you find any errors, correct them. (For more information, see page 400.)

Commas After Introductory Phrases

Use a comma after a long introductory phrase.

Introductory Phrase

Despite her craving for ice cream, Candace opted for an apple.

Note: The comma is usually omitted if the phrase comes at the end of the sentence.

Candace opted for an apple despite her craving for ice cream.

Note: You may omit the comma after a short (four or fewer words) introductory phrase unless it is needed to ensure clarity.

At 6:30 a.m. Rita would brew her favorite coffee.

Comma Practice Indicate where commas are needed in the following sentences. If no commas are needed, write "correct" on the blank next to the sentence.

1. Even before turning around to check, Vince sensed someone was following him. ________
2. At risk of sounding outlandish, the smell of chocolate-covered bacon is making my mouth water. ________
3. At midnight Willis decided to call it a night. correct
4. After the concert we stopped at a late-night diner for some grub. correct
5. On the left side of the tool shed, I found the circular saw. ________
6. Eventually this rain should subside. correct
7. Before making any harsh judgments, you should know I considered all options prior to deciding. ________
8. Based on her preliminary research, Hanna felt she was ready to begin drafting an essay. ________

Apply Read the sentences in your classification essay, paying special attention to long introductory phrases that ought to be set off with commas. If you find any errors, correct them. (For more information, see page 396.)

Marking an Essay

Before you finish editing your revised essay, you can practice by editing the following model.

Editing Practice Read the following classification essay, looking for problems listed in the checklist on the facing page. Also refer to the list of common errors on page 80. Correct the model using the marks listed to the left. The first correction has been done for you.

Correction Marks

- delete
- capitalize
- lowercase
- insert
- add comma
- add question mark
- add word
- add period
- spelling
- switch

Fast Ballers

What makes a baseball so hard to hit? Well, besides being the size of an orange and traveling at faster velocities than vehicles on an interstate, baseballs do funny things in the air depending on the way their thrown. There are four main types of pitches thrown by baseball players, Each with different speeds and trajectories.

The most frequently thrown pitch is a fastball. As its name suggests, fastball travel at the highest velocity of any pitch. Generally a fastball's trajectry is straight through the air and into the catcher's glove.

A second type of pitch, a changeup, is used to trick hitters into thinking its a fastball. However, the changeup is thrown at a much slower speed and tails slightly downward as it reaches the plate.

A third pitch is called a curveball. It is hard to hit because it travels with topspin that causes it to curve sharply both laterally and downward. A hitter might think a curveball is coming right at ~~them~~ him or her before it curves over the plate and into the strike zone. Because of a curveball's trajectory, its slower than a fastball but faster than a changeup.

A fourth comman pitch is called a slider. The slider is similar to a curveball in that it break laterally and downward as it reaches the batter. However, a slider's break is shorter than a curveball's. It A slider is also thrown at a faster speed than a curveball.

When a pitcher is able to throw all four of these pitches hitting becomes a guessing game for the batter. if the batter is expecting a fastball but receives a changeup, he or she might swing to early. No wonder baseballs is are so hard to hit.

Correcting Your Essay

Now it's time to correct your own essay.

Edit Prepare a clean copy of your essay and use the following checklist to look for errors. Continue working until you can check off each item in the list.

Editing Checklist

Words

- ☐ **1.** Have I used specific nouns and verbs? (See page 74.)
- ☐ **2.** Have I used more action verbs than "be" verbs? (See page 348.)

Sentences

- ☐ **3.** Have I used sentences with varying beginnings and lengths? (See pages 264, 266.)
- ☐ **4.** Have I combined short choppy sentences? (See page 262.)
- ☐ **5.** Have I avoided improper shifts in sentences? (See pages 314–315.)
- ☐ **6.** Have I avoided fragments and run-ons? (See pages 297–302, 306–307.)

Conventions

- ☐ **7.** Do I use correct verb forms (*he saw,* not *he seen*)? (See page 356.)
- ☐ **8.** Do my subjects and verbs agree (*she speaks,* not *she speak*)? (See pages 282–291.)
- ☐ **9.** Have I used the right words *(their, there, they're)*?
- ☐ **10.** Have I capitalized first words and proper nouns and adjectives? (See page 414.)
- ☐ **11.** Have I used commas after long introductory word groups and to set off extra information? (See page 396.)
- ☐ **12.** Have I carefully checked my spelling?

Adding a Title

Make sure to add an attention-getting title. Here are three simple strategies for creating one.

- **Describe the classification:** Five Branches of the United States Armed Forces
- **Think creatively:** To Work Out or Not to Work Out
- **Use a play on words:** Fast Ballers

Create Prepare a clean final copy of your essay and proofread it.

Learning Outcome

Reflect on the experience.

LO6 Reviewing Classification Writing

Complete these activities as needed to help you better understand how to write classification essays.

Classify Study the photo on this page. In the first column of the chart below, break down the peppers into subgroups, or types. Then define each type in the second column and write at least one detail about each in the third.

Victor Medina-San Andrés/Flickr/ Getty Images

Answers will vary.

Types of Peppers	Definition	Details
Subgroup 1		
Subgroup 2		
Subgroup 3		

Match Draw a line from each sentence starter below to the correct description on the right.

1. The opening of a classification essay should . . .
2. The middle of a classification essay should . . .
3. The closing of a classification essay should . . .

- reconnect the subject and its subgroups and present the reader with a final thought.
- introduce the topic and lead up to the thesis statement.
- describe the subgroups and traits relating to those subgroups.

"The vision must be followed by the venture. It is not enough to stare up the steps—we must step up the stairs."

—Vance Havner

Process Essay

From the beginning of this book, you have approached writing as a process. You know that tackling a writing challenge in one giant step won't get the job done. Instead, it takes a series of steps to create a thoughtful and polished piece of writing. As with good writing, many of the great accomplishments we see around us are born out of a process.

By definition a process is a series of actions or operations that produce a particular result. In this chapter, you will describe or explain a process, lay out its steps, and write about it clearly enough for your least knowledgeable reader to understand it.

Learning Outcomes

- LO1 Understand process essays.
- LO2 Plan a process essay.
- LO3 Write the first draft.
- LO4 Revise the essay.
- LO5 Edit the essay.
- LO6 Reflect on the experience.

What do you think?

Reread the definition of a process at the beginning of the second paragraph. Describe the steps you take to get ready for school or work in the morning.

Answers will vary.

Learning Outcome

Understand process essays.

LO1 Reviewing a Process Essay

A process essay explains how something works by laying out the specific steps that will take you to a particular result.

Read/React Read the following essay. Then complete the analysis on the next page.

Making Cheese

The **opening** introduces the topic and gives an overview of the steps.

Can you imagine a pizza without mozzarella? A cheeseburger sans cheddar? A wine and cheese party with no cheese platters? Simply put, cheese packs some powerful eating enjoyment. And while it comes in an assortment of flavors, textures, and forms, every cheese begins as high quality fresh milk. From there, the various types are tweaked from a common cheese-making process.

The first **middle paragraph** describes the first few steps.

Cheese making starts by heating the milk to kill off any unsafe bacteria. The milk comes from a variety of sources—from cows and goats to sheep and buffalo. Once the milk is heated, a starter culture is added to curdle it. The culture contains different enzymes and bacteria that give cheese its unique flavor. For example, Swiss-cheese culture contains the bacterium *Propianibacter shermanii,* while cheddar-cheese culture includes the enzyme *chymosin.* Next, the cheese sits for a day, until the milk has curdled into solids. The solids are called *curds,* while the leftover liquid is called *whey.*

The second **middle paragraph** describes the last few steps.

After the cheese maker separates the curds from the whey, the process continues by reheating the curds, letting them settle, and stirring away as much liquid as possible. This step is repeated until the cheese maker believes the cheese is sufficiently solid. When the cheese solidifies, it is poured into molds of different shapes and sizes. Finally, the cheese is placed in cooler temperatures so that it can ripen. The total ripening time depends on the cheese type and the flavor desired by the cheese maker. Some cheese types take a month to ripen, while others may take just one week. When the cheese is ripened, it's ready to eat.

The **closing** revisits the process as a whole.

Cheese is produced in small batches by hand or mass-produced by machine, but along the way it follows the same process: heating milk, adding culture, separating the curds from the whey, reheating, stirring, pouring, and ripening. The result is a food as diverse as it is delicious. Behold the power of cheese, indeed.

A Closer Look

This essay discusses the process of producing cheese. The writer explains each step in chronological order, using transitions to move logically from one step to the next.

Identity Reread the essay on the facing page paying attention to the steps in the process. Then, in the graphic below, briefly describe each step and the transition word (or words) used to introduce it. The first step has been done for you.

Topic: Making cheese

Transitions	Steps
1. Starts	Heat the milk to kill any bad bacteria.
2. Once	Add a starter culture.
3. Next	Let it sit a day to curdle.
4. After	Reheat and settle repeatedly, to dry the curds.
5. When	Pour it into molds.
6. Finally	Place it in a cooler temperature to ripen.

Explain The writer of this essay clearly shows an interest in the subject in the opening paragraph. What words, phrases, or sentences demonstrate this interest?

Answers will vary.

Traits

Transition words used to show time: after / before / finally / first / second / third / then / later / next / when / once / while

WAC

Process writing is practical writing. In the workplace, the ability to give clear instructions means getting a project done correctly.

Learning Outcome

Plan a process essay.

LO2 Prewriting: Planning

In your own process essay, you will explain how something works or is made. The topic information below will help you select a process to write about.

Selecting a Topic

Use the following ideas to generate possible process-essay topics.

Consider a process that . . .

- relates to your major or academic concentration.
- keeps you healthy or unhealthy.
- relates to your favorite entertainment—sports, music, theater, and so on.
- is in the news.
- impacts the world around you.

Select On the lines below, list four potential topics for your process essay. They may be topics you know a lot about or ones you need to research more thoroughly. Circle the one you would like to write about. Answers will vary.

1. ____________________ 2. ____________________

3. ____________________ 4. ____________________

Researching a Process

Once you have selected a topic, review what you know about it and, if necessary, supplement your information with additional research.

Identify Complete the research questions below. Answers will vary.

1. What is the process? ____________________
2. Why is it important? ____________________
3. What steps are needed to complete it? ____________________
4. What is the outcome? ____________________

Gathering Details

You can use a time line to gather details about the steps in you process. The following example lists the steps needed to purify drinking water.

Topic: *Purifying drinking water*

	Steps
1	*Pretreatment*
2	*Coagulation*
3	*Filtration*
4	*Disinfection*
5	*Outcome: Clean drinking water*

Gather Complete the time line below. Start by writing down the topic of your process essay. Then fill in the steps that will complete the process and bring you to the desired outcome. (Use your own paper if you are writing about a process with more than six steps.) **Answers will vary.**

Topic: ______________________

	Steps
1	______________________
2	______________________
3	______________________
4	______________________
5	______________________
6	______________________
7	**Outcome:** ______________________

Learning Outcome

Write the first draft.

LO3 Writing: Creating a First Draft

Creating a first draft puts all your planning and gathering into concrete form. Provided below is a sample process essay about water treatment.

Read/React Read the essay, noting how the writer uses the opening paragraph to describe the significance of the process, and then uses the middle paragraphs to explain its steps in chronological order.

Making Dirty Water Drinkable

Opening paragraph

One of the most overlooked luxuries of living in the United States is access to clean drinking water. Statistics show roughly one-eighth of the world's population lacks access to safe water supplies, while as many as 2.5 billion people live without sanitized water. Untreated water is full of unhealthy chemicals and contaminants that, if consumed, lead to uncomfortable and sometimes fatal disease, including dysentery and diarrhea. Water purification plants remove these harmful impurities through a process of pretreatment, coagulation, filtration, and disinfection, making our water safe to drink.

First two steps in the process

The first step in water purification is pretreatment. During pretreatment, water is pumped in from its source and screened to remove any large twigs, leaves, or other debris before reaching the holding tanks. Next, coagulation begins. Coagulation removes dirt and other particles from the water by adding a chemical that forms sticky particles called "floc." The floc combines with dirt particles as the water moves to a sedimentary basin. Once inside the basin, the combined weight of the dirt and floc causes it to sink to the floor as sedimentation. The sedimentation is then removed from the water, giving water its clear, colorless quality.

Final two steps in the process

While coagulation removes the sedimentation from the water, the filtration phase pushes the remaining particles and unsettled sedimentation through filters of sand or charcoal. Filtration reduces particles in the water by about 90 to 95 percent. Lastly the water is pumped to a disinfection tank. During disinfection, chlorine is added to kill any lingering viruses or bacteria. Some plants also introduce fluorine into the water to prevent tooth decay. After the process is completed, the water is tested for safety and then released from the treatment plant for safe consumption.

Closing paragraph

Make no mistake: the process of water purification in treatment plants is vitally important to the health of its consumers. By removing dirt and sludge through pretreatment and coagulation, then filtering the lingering particles, and finally disinfecting with chlorine and other chemicals, water purification plants make certain that the water our bodies desperately need to survive will do its job.

Creating an Opening Paragraph

The objective of the opening paragraph is to gain the reader's interest, introduce the topic, state its importance, and provide a thesis statement that gives an overview of the steps. Here are some strategies for beginning your essay:

Building Interest:

- **Find an eye-popping statistic.**
  Roughly one-eighth of the world's population lacks access to safe water supplies, while as many as 2.5 billion people live without sanitized water.
- **Ask a question.**
  Can you imagine a pizza without mozzarella?
- **Make a bold statement.**
  Simply put, cheese packs some powerful eating enjoyment.

Writing a Thesis Statement

To create a thesis statement for your essay, follow this formula.

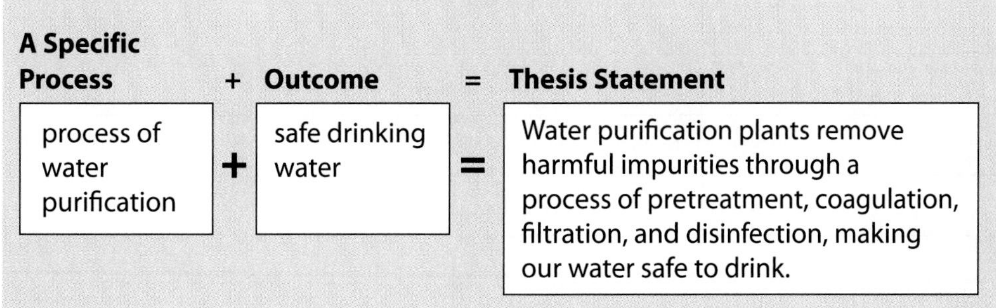

Write Create your opening paragraph. Start with a sentence that uses one of the strategies above. Then write sentences that build to your thesis statement.

Answers will vary.

Creating Middle Paragraphs

Write Clearly describe each step in the process. Cover the first few steps in the first middle paragraph and the last few steps in the second middle paragraph. Present the steps in a way that your least knowledgeable reader will be able to follow and understand. Also remember to include topic sentences in your paragraphs and use transitional words or phrases (see page 167) to make the writing flow.

Answers will vary.

Creating a Closing Paragraph

The closing paragraph should describe the process as a whole, restate the key steps, and provide a closing thought.

Write Create the closing paragraph for your process essay.

Answers will vary.

Learning Outcome

Revise the essay.

Speaking & Listening

Have your partner read your essay aloud. Then complete the response sheet together.

LO4 Revising: Improving the Writing

Revising your first draft involves adding, deleting, rearranging, and reworking parts of your writing. Revision begins with a peer review.

Peer Review

Sharing your writing at various stages is important, especially when you review and revise a first draft. The feedback that you receive will help you change and improve your essay.

Respond Complete this response sheet after reading the first draft of a classmate's essay. Then share the sheet with the writer. (Keep your comments helpful and positive.) Answers will vary.

Essay title: ____________________

Writer: ____________________ Reviewer: ____________________

1. Which part of the essay seems to work best—opening, middle, or closing? Why?

2. Which part of the essay needs work—opening, middle, or closing? Why?

3. Do the middle paragraphs clearly present each step of the process? Explain.

4. Do you understand the process after reading the essay?

5. Identify a phrase or two that shows the writer's level of interest.

Using Transitions That Show Time Order

Transitions or linking words connect ideas by showing the relationships between them. In process writing, time-order transition words provide a link between the steps of the process and add coherence to the writing overall. Refer to the following list of transitional words as you revise your essay.

Transitions That Show Time Order

before, during, after, next, finally, first, second, third, then, later, when, once, while, at, meanwhile

Traits

Transition words signal organization and improve sentence fluency.

Revising in Action

Read aloud the unrevised and then revised version of the following excerpt. Note how transitional words tie the steps of the process together while improving the flow of the writing.

During pretreatment,
The first step in water purification is pretreatment. ^ Water is pumped in from
Next, c
its source. ^ Coagulation begins. Coagulation removes dirt and other particles from the water by adding a chemical that forms sticky particles called "floc."
Once inside the basin,
. . . ^ The combined weight of the dirt and floc causes it to sink to the floor as sedimentation.

Revise Improve your writing, using the following checklist and your partner's comments on the response sheet. Continue revising until you can check off each item in the list.

Revising Checklist

Ideas:

- ☐ **1.** Do I explain an interesting process?
- ☐ **2.** Do I include all the steps in the process?

Organization:

- ☐ **3.** Does the essay have effective opening, middle, and closing paragraphs?
- ☐ **4.** Are the steps in a logical time order?
- ☐ **5.** Have I used transitions to connect my ideas?

Voice:

- ☐ **6.** Do I use an informed, respectful voice?
- ☐ **7.** Does my interest in the topic come through?

Learning Outcome

Edit the essay.

Insight

For more practice with fixing dangling and misplaced modifiers, see page 312.

LO5 Editing: Correcting Your Writing

The main work of editing is correcting your revised draft. The next two activities will help you avoid two common errors that occur with modifiers.

Dangling Modifiers

Dangling modifiers can confuse the reader. Such modifiers describe a word that is not in the sentence.

Dangling modifier:

After handing in his paper, the teacher began the lecture.
(It sounds as if the teacher handed in the paper.)

Corrected:

After Landon handed in his paper, the teacher began the lecture.

Editing Practice Correct any dangling modifiers below by rewriting the sentence. If a sentence contains no modifying error, write a C on the line. (The first one has been done for you.)

1. After radioing for clearance, the plane was landed.

   After radioing for clearance, the pilot landed the plane.

2. While scrambling eggs, the mailcarrier rang the doorbell.

   While I was scrambling eggs, the mail carrier rang the doorbell.

3. After waiting in the lobby for hours, the doctor arrived with an update.

   After we had waited in the lobby for hours, the doctor arrived with an update.

4. After we finished the main course, the server wheeled out the dessert tray.

   C

5. Stretching under the car, my tennis ball was retrieved.

   Stretching under the car, I retrieved my tennis ball.

Apply Read through your essay, looking for dangling modifiers. Correct any that you find by rewriting the sentence so that the modifier clearly describes the correct word.

Misplaced Modifiers

Misplaced modifiers are similar to dangling modifiers in that they create a confusing or illogical idea. They occur when a modifier appears to modify the wrong word in a sentence.

Misplaced modifier:

The tornado siren has **nearly** been **blaring** for an hour.
(Nearly been ringing?)

Corrected:

The tornado siren has been blaring for nearly an hour.

Editing Practice Underline the misplaced modifier in each of the following sentences. Then correct the error by rewriting the sentence. (The first one has been done for you.)

1. That sedan is my favorite car in the showroom with the shiny blue paint.

   That sedan with the shiny blue paint is my favorite car in the showroom.

2. The soda is my first choice with the most caffeine.

   The soda with the most caffeine is my first choice.

3. The car's headlights nearly turned on after three miles.

   The car's headlights turned on after nearly three miles.

4. Please review the report on global warming enclosed.

   Please review the enclosed report on global warming.

Apply Read through your essay, checking for misplaced modifiers. Correct any that you find by rewriting the sentence so that the modifier is placed next to the appropriate word.

Marking an Essay

Before you finish editing your revised essay, you can practice by editing the following model.

Editing Practice Read the following process essay, looking for problems listed in the checklist on the facing page. Also refer to the list of common errors on page 80. Correct the model using the marks to the left. The first correction has been done for you.

Correction Marks

- delete
- capitalize
- lowercase
- insert
- add comma
- add question mark
- add word
- add period
- spelling
- switch

Fighting the Flu

Flu season is a bummer. For some people, its downright dangerous. Every year from November through April, some 60 million Americans will contract the flu bug. Many people opt to receive a yearly flu vaccine, which reduce there chances of getting the flu. The type of influenza vaccine given out each year are created through a multifaceted process.

The first step is surveyllance. Throughout the year, scientists survey the globe to predict which strains of the influenza virus will dominate the next flu season. A vaccine can protect against three different strains, so this step helps decide which strains to put in the vaccine. Next, the World Health Organization confirms the dominant strains and submits their recommendation to the Food and drug Administration (FDA). The FDA then distributes seeds of the three strains to manufacturers for production.

After surveillance and strain selection, the manufacturing of vaccines begins. In this step, each virous strain is produced separately. Later combined to make one vaccine. Manufacturing begins by injecting millions of chicken eggs with the virus strains, which develop. The virus fluid is then given a chemical treatment, so that the virus is disrupted and will stop spreading. What's left of the strain is combined. With the other two strains. Lastly, the FDA tests the vaccine concentrate to make sure it is acceptable for immunization.

The result is an influenza vaccine that is distributed in viles and syringes to clinics throughout the world during flu season. After the vaccine is injected it takes about two weeks for a body to develop immunity to the three strains. When flu season ends, the process of creating next year's vaccine begins again.

Correcting Your Essay

Now it's time to correct your own essay.

Edit Create a clean copy of your essay and use the following checklist to look for errors. Continue working until you can check off each item in the list.

Editing Checklist

Words

- ☐ **1.** Have I used specific nouns and verbs? (See page 74.)
- ☐ **2.** Have I used more action verbs than "be" verbs? (See page 348.)

Sentences

- ☐ **3.** Have I varied the beginnings and lengths of sentences? (See pages 264, 266.)
- ☐ **4.** Have I combined short choppy sentences? (See page 262.)
- ☐ **5.** Have I avoided improper shifts in sentences? (See pages 314–315.)
- ☐ **6.** Have I avoided fragments and run-ons? (See pages 297–302, 306–307.)

Conventions

- ☐ **7.** Do I use correct verb forms *(he saw,* not *he seen*)? (See page 356.)
- ☐ **8.** Do my subjects and verbs agree (*she speaks,* not *she speak*)? (See pages 282–291.)
- ☐ **9.** Have I used consistent verb tense in all steps? (See page 314.)
- ☐ **10.** Have I used the right words (*their, there, they're*)?
- ☐ **11.** Have I capitalized first words and proper nouns and adjectives? (See page 414.)
- ☐ **12.** Have I used commas after long introductory word groups? (See page 396.)
- ☐ **13.** Have I carefully checked my spelling?

Adding a Title

Make sure to add an attention-getting title. Here are two simple strategies for creating one.

- **Use alliteration:** Fighting the Flu
- **Describe the process:** Making Cheese; Making Dirty Water Drinkable

Create Prepare a clean copy of your essay and carefully proofread it.

Learning Outcome

Reflect on the experience.

LO6 Reviewing Process Writing

Complete these activities as needed to help you better understand how to write process essays.

Organize Think about your professional goals. What do you want to do? Where do you want to work? How can you get there? In the graphic below, identify your goal and lay out five steps to achieving it. For each step, write a transition word or phrase that links the first steps to the second and so on. (See page 175.)

Goal: Answers will vary.

Transitions	Steps
1	
2	
3	
4	
5	

Explain In your own words, explain the difference between a dangling modifier and a misplaced modifier. Give an example of each error and show how you would correct it. (See pages 176–177.)

Answers will vary.

"The murals in restaurants are on par with the food in museums."

—Peter De Vries

DreamPictures/Taxi/Getty Images

17

Comparison-Contrast Essay

The photo above is full of contrasts: bare glass versus painted brick, straight lines versus curves and jags, tan walls versus an explosion of color, architecture versus painting. The photo also contains some surprising comparisons. The building and the mural both serve the neighborhood. There are even buildings painted in the mural.

By looking at the similarities and differences between two things, you can come to understand both things better. An essay that examines similarities and differences is called a comparison-contrast essay.

This chapter will guide you through the process of writing an essay that compares and contrasts two places that you know well.

What do you think?

What similarities and differences are there between artwork and food?

Answers will vary.

Learning Outcomes

- **LO1** Understand comparison-contrast essays.
- **LO2** Plan a comparison-contrast essay.
- **LO3** Write the first draft.
- **LO4** Revise the essay.
- **LO5** Edit the essay.
- **LO6** Reflect on the experience.

Learning Outcome

Understand comparison-contrast essays.

LO1 Reviewing a Comparison Essay

A **comparison-contrast** essay shows the similarities and differences between two subjects. In the following essay, a writer compares his bedroom to his sister's.

Read/React Read the following essay. Then complete the analysis on the next page.

Life in a War Zone

The **opening** catches the reader's interest and leads to the thesis statement.

"How do you ever find anything in here?" my sister asks. We're looking for her cell phone, which I borrowed last night, and which I left in my room. "It's like a bomb went off." She's right. Compared to Amaya's room, mine is a disaster. Maybe that's because I'm a guy. Maybe that's because I only sleep there. The differences between my room and Amaya's tell a lot about who we are.

The first **middle paragraph** describes one subject.

I couldn't survive in my sister's room. For one thing, it's pink. She's three years younger than me, and she's still into pink, though the princess posters are down and posters of pop stars cover everything. It's like a hundred people staring at you. Amaya has three chests of drawers, neatly closed, and a closet full of clothes, some of which belong to her friends. She's also got Grandma's old vanity, with three big mirrors and little drawers for makeup. Weirdest of all, she manages to get dirty clothes in the hamper, which means I can see the floor.

The second **middle paragraph** describes the other subject.

Now, Amaya couldn't survive in my room, either. The walls are black. I painted them that way in protest when Amaya painted hers pink. I've got no posters on the walls, only some old high-school art projects I did and never took down. There's just one chest of drawers, and the drawers are never closed, and the clothes are hanging out or stacked on top. I don't have a hamper, so my floor is the hamper. The only important thing in my room is my bed, because that's where I crash. Of course, the bed is never made.

The **closing** sums up the comparison and contrast, providing an additional perspective.

Our two different rooms show our different personalities. Amaya thinks a lot about how she looks and what people think of her. She also spends a lot of time in her room. I don't care about my looks. Engines are my thing, building them and fixing them, which means grease, which means fashion can't be a priority. Amaya might think my room is a health hazard, but I'd die in her room. (By the way, we did find her cell phone, not because I knew where I put it, but because I decided to call it.)

Vocabulary

comparison
a study of the similarities between two things

contrast
a study of the differences between two things

A Closer Look

This essay used a **subject-by-subject pattern of organization**, describing one subject before moving to the other. This organizational pattern works best when focusing on the contrasts between two subjects.

Vocabulary

subject-by-subject pattern of organization
a pattern in which one subject is described before moving on to the other

Analyze Reread the essay on the facing page. As you do, use the following T-chart to analyze the essay. In the first column, write details that describe the author's room. In the second column, write details that describe his sister's room.

Author's Room	Sister's Room
Answers will vary.	

Explain The writer of the essay creates a parallel description of his sister's room and his own room. What do you think a "parallel description" is?

Answers will vary.

Learning Outcome

Plan a comparison-contrast essay.

LO2 Prewriting: Planning

In your own essay, you, too, will compare and contrast two places that you know well. Because you will be using subject-by-subject organization, choose two places with interesting contrasts. The activity below will help you select two places to write about.

Selecting a Topic

Select After each general heading, write the names of two specific places you know enough about to compare and contrast. Then select the two places you would most like to write about in your essay.

Buildings	**1.** Answers will vary.	**2.** ______
Businesses	**1.** ______	**2.** ______
Natural wonders	**1.** ______	**2.** ______
Neighborhoods	**1.** ______	**2.** ______
Restaurants	**1.** ______	**2.** ______
Rooms	**1.** ______	**2.** ______

Describing the Places

Describe Answer each question below, jotting down details about the two places.

1. What three adjectives best describe this place?

Place 1: Answers will vary.

Place 2: ______

2. What is the main feature of this place?

Place 1: ______

Place 2: ______

3. What is the feeling you get in this place?

Place 1: ______

Place 2: ______

4. Why do you want to write about this place?

Place 1: ______

Place 2: ______

Gathering Details

A Venn diagram will help you gather more details as you plan your comparison-contrast essay. The following diagram compares and contrasts two restaurants, listing unique details about each as well as similarities.

Venn Diagram

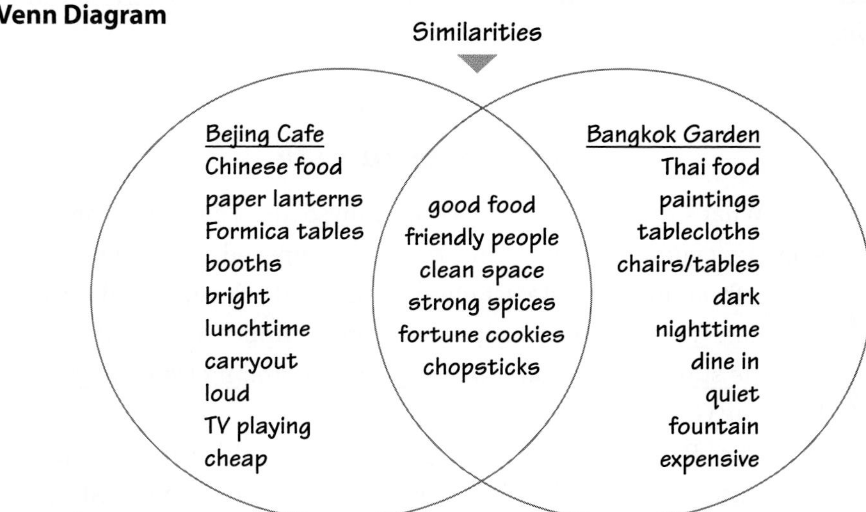

Gather Complete the Venn diagram below. Write the name of one place in one circle and the name of the other place in the other. Next, list the details specific to each place. In the overlapping part, write the things that the two places have in common. Answers will vary.

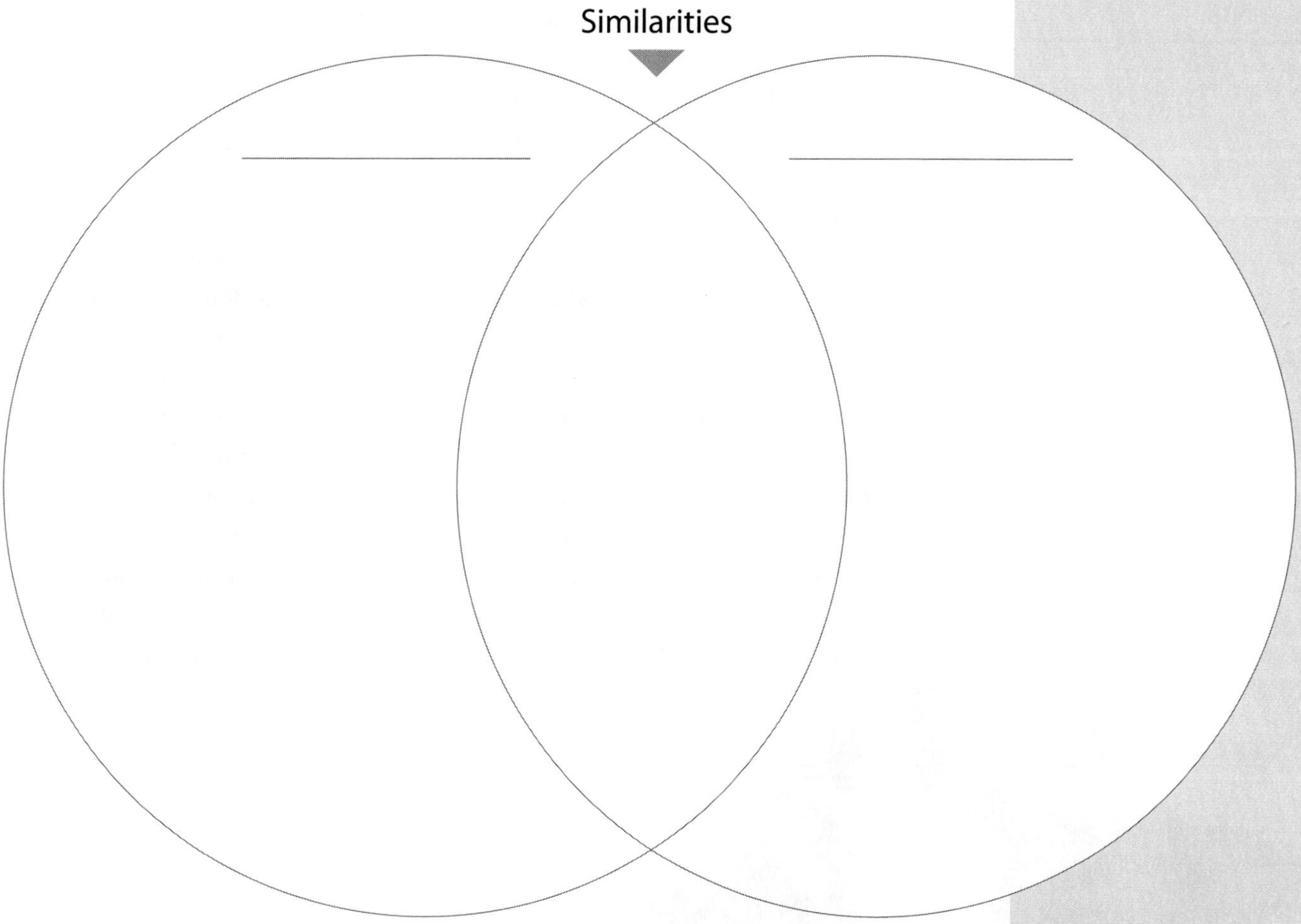

Similarities

Learning Outcome

Write the first draft.

LO3 Writing: Creating a First Draft

Creating a first draft puts all of your planning and gathering into concrete form. Provided below is a sample essay that is organized subject by subject.

Read/React Read the essay, noting how the writer created an effective opening and closing for the subject-by-subject comparison.

Two Tastes of Asia

Opening paragraph

Thesis statement

What's the difference between Chinese and Thai food? That's what I wondered when a Thai restaurant opened just down the street from my favorite Chinese restaurant. Soon, I had two favorites. The difference between Chinese and Thai cuisine is only the start of the differences between the Beijing Café and the Bangkok Garden.

Subject 1

The Beijing Café has been my favorite because of its inexpensive food and bright, busy atmosphere. The food is excellent, from the sizzling Chairman Mao's chicken to the extra spicy Szechuan vegetables, and lunch portions are priced below $5. Such prices mean the restaurant has basic decorations like paper lanterns and a utilitarian interior, with Formica tables and plastic booths. The fluorescent lights overhead make the place bright, and the constant traffic of people on lunch break makes the place a loud, busy hangout.

Subject 2

The Bangkok Garden offers a completely different experience. The food is similar to Chinese food, but with coconut milk and different spices. The prices, though, are higher, partly because Bangkok Garden is more of a dinner place. The walls are covered in elegant paintings and tapestries, and candles give a warm glow to cloth-covered tables. As a result, the Bangkok Garden is a quieter spot, more for dates than for high-schoolers on a lunch break.

Closing paragraph

Both restaurants have great food and friendly staff, and both offer chopsticks and fortune cookies. As I've said, they both are favorites of mine. When I'm hungry at lunchtime and need a quick, inexpensive, and delicious meal, I go with friends over to the Beijing Café. And when I'm hungry at dinnertime and want a romantic dinner, I head to the Bangkok Garden. At first, it seemed a waste to have a Chinese restaurant and a Thai restaurant so close together, but they are more different than they are alike.

Creating an Opening Paragraph

The opening paragraph needs to capture the reader's attention and introduce your thesis statement. Here are some strategies for beginning your essay.

Opening Strategies:

- **Start with a surprising statement.**
  My two favorite restaurants feature food from the other side of the world.
- **Begin with a question.**
  What's the difference between Chinese and Thai food?
- **Use a quotation.**
  "You will soon have two favorites," read the fortune cookie.
- **Share an anecdote.**
  The first time I walked into Bangkok Garden, I was nervous. . . .

Writing a Thesis Statement

To create a thesis statement for your essay, follow this formula.

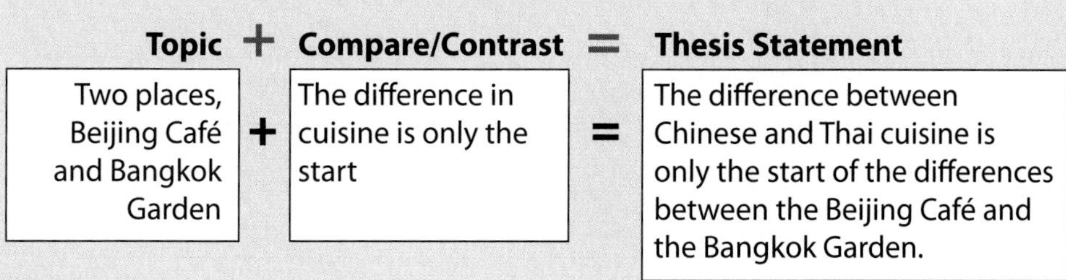

Topic	+	Compare/Contrast	=	Thesis Statement
Two places, Beijing Café and Bangkok Garden	+	The difference in cuisine is only the start	=	The difference between Chinese and Thai cuisine is only the start of the differences between the Beijing Café and the Bangkok Garden.

Write Create your opening paragraph. Start with a sentence that uses one of the strategies above. Then write sentences that build to your thesis statement.

Answers will vary.

Creating Middle Paragraphs

Write Refer to the Venn diagram you completed on page 185 as you develop the middle two paragraphs of your essay. Use one paragraph to describe the first place and another to describe the second place, creating topic sentences for each. Use the transitional words at the left to make your writing flow.

Answers will vary.

Traits

Transitions that compare:
as / as well / also / both / in the same way / much as / much like / one way / like / likewise / similarly

Transitions that contrast:
although / even though / by contrast / but / however / on the other hand / otherwise / though / still / while / yet

Creating a Closing Paragraph

The closing paragraph of your essay should sum up the comparison and contrast and provide a final thought for the reader.

Write Answer the following questions to help you sum up your essay.

1. What key similarity do the two places exhibit?

   Answers will vary.

2. What is the key difference between the two places?

3. What have I learned from writing this essay?

Write Create the closing paragraph for your comparison-contrast essay.

Answers will vary.

Learning Outcome

Revise the essay.

Speaking & Listening

Have your partner read your essay aloud. Then complete the response sheet together.

LO4 Revising: Improving the Writing

Revising your first draft involves adding, deleting, rearranging, and reworking parts of your writing. Revision begins with a peer review.

Peer Review

Sharing your writing at various stages is important, especially when you review and revise a first draft. The feedback that you receive will help you change and improve your essay.

Respond Complete this response sheet after reading the first draft of a classmate's essay. Then share the sheet with the writer. (Keep your comments helpful and positive.) Answers will vary.

Essay title: ______________________________

Writer: ____________________ Reviewer: ____________________

1. Which part of the essay seems to work best—opening, middle, or closing? Why?

____

____

____

____

2. Which part of the essay needs work—opening, middle, or closing? Why? __________

____

____

3. Which contrasting points about the two subjects caught your attention? Name three.

   a. ______________________________

   b. ______________________________

   c. ______________________________

4. Name two favorite details.

   a. ______________________________

   b. ______________________________

5. Identify a phrase or two that shows the writer's level of interest.

____

____

____

Adding Sensory Details

Your essay will be stronger if you show similarities and differences, not just tell about them. Consider the **sensory details** listed below and used to describe one of the restaurants in the essay on page 186. Build your own chart of sensory details to enhance your writing.

Senses	Sensory Detail
Sight	paper lanterns, bright, fluorescents
Hearing	sizzle, loud, traffic
Smell	chicken, szechuan vegetables
Taste	extra spicy
Touch	plastic booths

Revising in Action

Read aloud the unrevised and revised version of the following excerpt. Note how adding sensory details makes the description much richer.

> The food is excellent, from the ^sizzling^ Chairman Mao's chicken to the ^extra spicy^ Szechuan vegetables, and lunch portions are priced below $5. Such prices mean the restaurant has basic decorations ^like paper lanterns^ and a utilitarian interior, with ^Formica^ tables and ^plastic^ booths. . . .

Revise Improve your writing, using the following checklist and your partner's comments on the response sheet. Continue revising until you can check off each item in the list.

Ideas

- ☐ **1.** Do I compare two places?
- ☐ **2.** Do I include sensory details that make the places come to life?

Organization

- ☐ **3.** Does my opening capture the reader's interest and present a thesis statement?
- ☐ **4.** Have I used a subject-by-subject pattern in the middle part?
- ☐ **5.** Have I used transitions to connect my sentences?
- ☐ **6.** Does my closing sum up the comparison and contrast effectively?

Voice

- ☐ **7.** Do I sound knowledgeable about my subjects?
- ☐ **8.** Is my interest obvious to the reader?

Vocabulary

sensory details
what can be seen, heard, smelled, tasted, touched, or otherwise sensed

Learning Outcome

Edit the essay.

Insight

Note that plural nouns often end in *s*, but plural verbs usually do not. Also note that only present tense verbs and *be* verbs have both singular and plural forms.

LO5 Editing: Correcting Your Writing

The main work of editing is correcting your revised first draft.

Correcting Subject-Verb Agreement

A verb must agree in number with the subject of the sentence. If the subject is singular, the verb must be singular. If the subject is plural, the verb must be plural. When a sentence has two or more subjects joined by *and,* the verb should be plural. When a sentence has two or more subjects joined by *or* or *nor,* the verb should agree with the last subject.

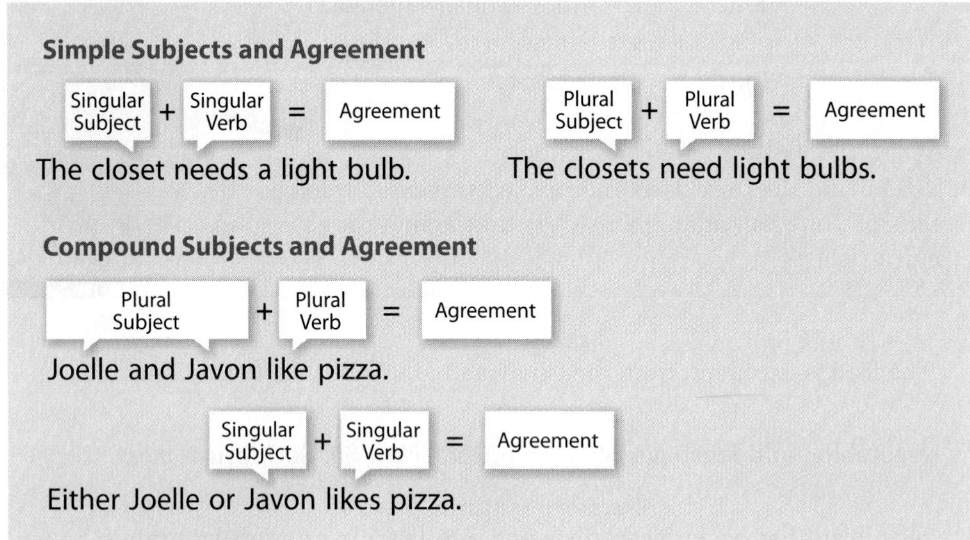

Agreement Practice In the following sentences, correct the subject-verb agreement errors by deleting the wrong verb forms and writing the correct verbs above.

1. My old car ~~have~~ has a stick shift and ~~are~~ is really loud above 55 m.p.h.
2. My new car ~~are~~ is an automatic.
3. Both the new car and the old car ~~is~~ are ice blue.
4. The new one ~~are~~ is a Prius, but the old one ~~are~~ is a Taurus.
5. The Prius ~~have~~ has four speakers, but the Taurus ~~have~~ has just two.
6. Either the Prius or the Taurus ~~were~~ was built in the United States.
7. The Prius and the Taurus ~~has~~ have front-wheel drive.
8. My brother want the Prius, but either he or my sister ~~get~~ gets the Taurus.
9. A car ~~become~~ becomes your best friend when you commute.
10. Both my brother and my sister ~~needs~~ need a car for their jobs.

Apply Read your comparison-contrast essay and watch for agreement errors. If you find any, correct them. (For more information, see page 282.)

Agreement with *I* and *You*

The pronouns *I* and *you* sometimes take plural-form verbs, even though they are singular. Review the examples below.

Agreement Formulas

Correct: Plural verbs agree with *I* and *you*.

I look and see you. You smile at me.

Incorrect: Most singular verbs do not agree with *I* and *you*.

I looks and sees you. You smiles at me.

Note: The pronoun *I* takes the singular verbs *am* and *was*. Do not use *I* with *be* or *is*.

Correct: The singular verbs *am* and *was* agree with *I*.

I am happy. I was wanting to help. I am eager to lend a hand.

Incorrect: The verbs *are*, *is*, or *were* do not agree with *I*.

I are happy. I were wanting to help. I is eager to lend a hand.

Agreement Practice In the following sentences, correct the subject-verb agreement errors by deleting the wrong forms and writing the correct verbs above.

1. I ~~keeps~~ keep a balcony garden at my apartment.
2. You ~~is~~ are tasting some of the fruits I ~~grows~~ grow in my garden.
3. I ~~be~~ am especially good at growing tomatoes.
4. You ~~looks~~ look surprised that I ~~grows~~ grow tomatoes on a balcony.
5. I ~~has~~ have pots for scallions, carrots, and radishes, too.
6. I ~~thinks~~ think you ~~is~~ are the first person, besides me, to eat from my garden.
7. You ~~has~~ have never tasted such tomatoes, ~~has~~ have you?
8. I ~~be~~ am proud of this garden, as you ~~knows~~ know from my expression.
9. You ~~seems~~ seem amazed that I ~~raises~~ raise such good produce on a balcony!
10. I ~~works~~ work hard, but I ~~enjoys~~ enjoy it.

Apply Read your comparison-contrast essay and watch for agreement errors with *I* and *you*. If you find any, correct them. (For more information, see page 286.)

Marking an Essay

Before you finish editing your revised essay, practice editing the following model.

Editing Practice Read this comparison-contrast essay, looking for problems listed in the checklist on the facing page. Also refer to the list of common errors on page 80. Correct the model using the marks listed to the left. One correction has been done for you.

Correction Marks

- delete
- capitalize
- lowercase
- insert
- add comma
- add question mark
- add word
- add period
- spelling
- switch

A Commuter's Best Friend

I spends much of my day in my car, an ice-blue Toyota Prius. Its a hybrid which means it's much better for my commute to school than my old Taurus. Still, I loved that old beater. It carried me safely and faithfully. Through many winters. Aside from being the same color, my new Prius and my old Taurus couldn't be more different.

The Taurus was a fifteen-year-old workhorse it had four doors, room for six, and a trunk to hold all their stuff. The interior is no-frills, with manual windows, a stereo and tape deck, and two speakers. Nothing is digital. In its last years, the Taurus been leaking every fluid I put in it, but still it soldiered on—getting probably twenty miles to the gallon.

The Prius is brand new and a little delicate. It weighs about half as much as the Taurus, and though it has four doors, it really has room only for four people. It has power everything and a GPS navagation system. As I back up the Prius the digital console even shows me a picture of what's behind me. this hybrid is super quiet in the city and gets about twice the mileage of the Taurus.

I think cars have souls, and my taurus was a good friend to me. It read me a lot of books on tape, and it never left me stranded when I needed it. I'm still getting used to this Prius, and I hope we'll be friends, too. Heaven knows, we spend plenty of time together.

TIM MCCAIG/iStockphoto.com

Correcting Your Essay

Now it's time to correct your own essay.

Edit Prepare a clean copy of your essay and use the following checklist to look for errors. Continue working until you can check off each item in the list.

Words

- ☐ **1.** Have I used specific nouns and verbs? (See page 74.)
- ☐ **2.** Have I used more action verbs than "be" verbs? (See page 348.)

Sentences

- ☐ **3.** Have I used sentences with varying beginnings and lengths? (See pages 264, 266.)
- ☐ **4.** Have I combined short choppy sentences? (See page 262.)
- ☐ **5.** Have I avoided improper shifts in sentences? (See pages 314–315.)
- ☐ **6.** Have I avoided fragments and run-ons? (See pages 297–302, 306–307.)

Conventions

- ☐ **7.** Do I use correct verb forms (*he saw,* not *he seen*)? (See page 356.)
- ☐ **8.** Do my subjects and verbs agree (*she speaks,* not *she speak*)? (See pages 282–291.)
- ☐ **9.** Have I used the right words *(their, there, they're)*?
- ☐ **10.** Have I capitalized first words and proper nouns and adjectives? (See page 414.)
- ☐ **11.** Have I used commas after long introductory word groups and to set off extra information? (See page 396.)
- ☐ **12.** Have I carefully checked my spelling?

WAC

You can use this checklist for editing your writing in any class.

Adding a Title

Make sure to add an attention-getting title. Here are three simple strategies for creating one.

- **Use a phrase from the essay:** Cars Have Souls
- **Point to a similarity or difference:** Great Food, Worlds Apart
- **Use the word "versus":** Pink Versus Black

Create Prepare a clean final copy of your essay and proofread it.

Learning Outcome

Reflect on the experience.

LO6 Reviewing Comparison Writing

Complete these activities as needed to help you better understand how to write comparison-contrast essays.

Paul Matthew Photography 2010/used under license from www.shutterstock.com

Compare/Contrast Consider the woman and child in this photograph. How are they alike? How are they different? Fill in the following Venn diagram, describing the two people. Answers will vary.

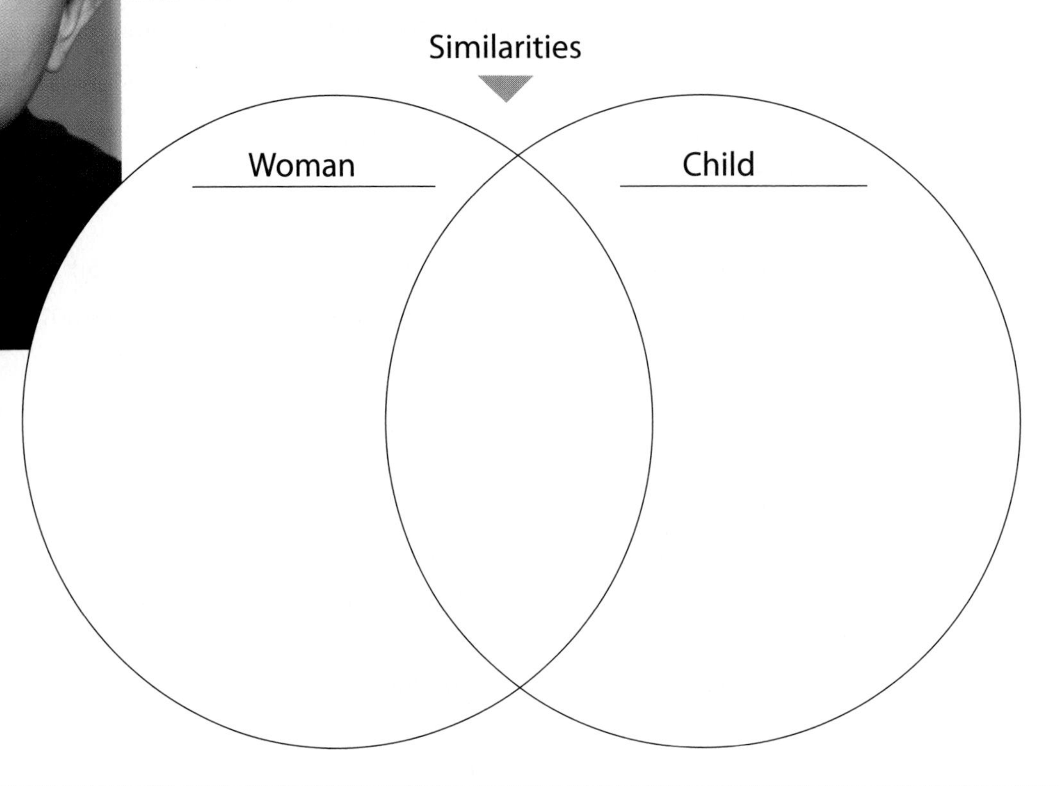

Match For each organizational pattern below, draw a line to connect it to its description.

1. Similarities-differences	an organizational pattern focusing first on one subject and then on the other
2. Point-by-point	a pattern in which one point of comparison is discussed for both subjects before moving on to the next point
3. Subject-by-subject	an organizational pattern dealing with how subjects are alike and how they are different

Sort Circle transitions that *contrast*:

although as well like much as otherwise while similarly

"The cause is hidden. The effect is visible to all."

—Ovid

Julia Christe/fstop/Corbis

Cause-Effect Essay

Why? It's such a simple word, but it digs into the deepest questions. When you ask *why,* you are searching for the cause of something. And there are different causes. A mom who asks why her son has cancer likely needs a different answer than a researcher who asks the same question.

This chapter is all about asking *why* in the form of an essay. You'll read essays that explore the causes and effects of phenomena in the world, and you'll write a similar essay yourself. All the while, keep asking *why?*

Learning Outcomes

LO1 Understand cause-effect essays.

LO2 Plan a cause-effect essay.

LO3 Write the first draft.

LO4 Revise the essay.

LO5 Edit the essay.

LO6 Reflect on the experience.

What do you think?

What are the possible causes of the fire above? What are the likely effects?

Answers will vary.

Learning Outcome

Understand cause-effect essays.

LO1 Reviewing a Cause-Effect Essay

A cause-effect essay shows indicates why something happens (the causes) and what results (the effects). In the following essay, a writer looks at the causes and effects of a spicy diet.

Read/React Read the following essay. Then complete the analysis on the next page.

Why Eat That Stuff?

The **opening** catches the reader's attention and leads to the thesis.

I love spicy food. In fact, I have a theory that food gets better the closer you get to the equator. At the poles, people eat seal blubber and **lutefisk**, but at the equator, people eat tacos and **teriyaki**, **curry** and jalapenos. People who don't like spicy foods wonder what all the fuss is about. There are many reasons people use spices in their foods, and many benefits from doing so.

The first **middle paragraph** discusses causes.

The main reasons for using spice are to make food taste better and to help preserve it. Without salt, pepper, and other basic spices, foods taste bland. In the Middle Ages, explorers like Marco Polo set up trade routes to get desperately needed spices for European foods. Some spices were worth their weight in gold. These spices didn't grow in northern climates, and they weren't needed as much for food preservation as in the equatorial regions, but people still wanted them for taste.

The second **middle paragraph** discusses effects.

New studies show that spicy foods also have surprising health benefits. A recent study published in the *British Journal of Medicine* showed that women who added hot peppers to their food ate fewer calories in later meals than women who didn't. At the University of California, Los Angeles, scientists found that the substance **curcumin**, which makes tumeric yellow, clears **plaque** out of brains, helping stop Alzheimer's disease. And at the State University of New York, researchers found that **capsaicin**—what makes hot peppers hot—causes **endorphins** to be released, making the eater feel happy. Other studies show that capsaicin might even help kill off cancer cells in the digestive tract.

The **closing** sums up the causes and ties them back to the opening.

So, when I order a **Szechuan** chicken lunch special, extra hot, why do I do it? Well, partly it's because of the taste—I've grown to really love hot food. Partly it's for the health benefits that I'm getting eating it. But, to be honest, partly it's because I like to see the look of horror on my friends' faces when I start sweating but keep shoveling it in.

Vocabulary

lutefisk pickled fish; traditional Norwegian dish

teriyaki sweet soy sauce used on many Japanese foods

curry hot spice for Indian and Middle-Eastern foods

curcumin coloring agent in tumeric

plaque unhealthy buildup of material

capsaicin substance that makes hot peppers hot

endorphins natural pain killer released by the body

Szechuan spicy type of food from the Szechuan region of China

A Closer Look

This essay first looks at causes of eating spicy foods, and then looks at effects. This pattern works best for an essay that focuses equally on both—cause and effect.

Analyze Reread the essay on the facing page. As you do, fill in the cause-effect chart below. On the left, write causes of eating spicy food and draw lines to connect them. On the right, write effects of eating spicy foods. Start with the causes and effects in the essay, but feel free to add causes and effects of your own.

Causes	Effects
Answers may include . . . • Improved taste • Food preservation • *And student thoughts*	Answers may include . . . • Reduce calorie intake • Clear plaque from the brain to combat Alzheimer's • Release endorphins for pleasure • Kill cancer cells in the digestive tract • *And student thoughts*

Explain Do you like to eat spicy foods or not? Explain why you do or do not like to eat spicy foods. Describe the effects you experience if you eat something spicy.

Answers will vary.

Learning Outcome

Plan a cause-effect essay.

LO2 Prewriting: Planning

You will also be writing a cause-effect essay about some lifestyle choice. You need a topic that interests you and that you know a good deal about—or are willing to find out about. You also need a topic that has specific causes and effects.

Selecting a Topic

Brainstorm In each column below, brainstorm possible topics for your cause-effect essay. Sample topics have been provided in each category. Try to think of three or four more topics in each. Then select one topic that you would like to explore, tracing causes and effects. Answers will vary.

Lifestyle Choices

Eating	Activities	Style	Pastimes	Habits
vegetarianism	rock climbing	dreadlocks	suduko	smoking

Freewrite After you select a topic that you would like to write a cause-effect essay about, freewrite about the topic. Write about causes of it and effects from it. Then review your freewriting to make sure this is a topic you want to explore. Otherwise, choose a new topic and freewrite about it.

Answers will vary.

Gathering Details

As you gather details about your topic, think of what you already know and what you need to find out. Do whatever research it takes for you to find out about your topic. Then complete a cause-effect chart, like the one below, listing the causes and effects of your topic.

Cause-Effect Chart

Topic: *Vegetarianism*

Causes	Effects
Concern for animals	*Vegans vs. ovo-lacto*
Opposition to "factory farming"	*Greater awareness*
Healthful lifestyle	*Greater health*
Home-grown food	*More sustainable lifestyle*
Personal preference	*Need for proteins*
Peer pressure/social reasons	*Struggles in society*

Gather Complete the following cause-effect chart by writing your topic at the top and listing causes and effects in their columns. Answers will vary.

Cause-Effect Chart

Topic: ________________________________

Causes	Effects

Learning Outcome

Write the first draft.

LO3 Writing: Creating a First Draft

Creating a first draft puts all of your planning and gathering into concrete form. Provided below is a sample essay that is organized subject by subject.

Read/React Read the essay, noting how the writer created an effective opening and closing for the cause-effect essay.

Herbivore, Carnivore, or Omnivore?

Opening paragraph

Thesis statement

"We've spent thousands of years getting to the top of the food chain, so why go back to eating leaves?" That's what people sometimes ask vegans and vegetarians, wondering why anyone would choose that kind of diet. Vegetarians have many reasons for choosing a meat-free diet, but the diet results in the same basic benefits.

Causes

Every vegetarian is unique, with unique reasons for eating what they eat. Many see animals as more than meat—creatures with intelligence and feelings. These vegetarians don't like the idea of killing animals for food, especially not in the overcrowded and inhumane factory farms of today. Other vegetarians reject modern American eating habits, with too much meat and too few vegetables. The US Department of Agriculture recommends that people "go lean on protein" and eat even less fat. However, the average American eats 16 percent of calories in proteins and 44 percent in fat. Vegetarians seek a better diet and a more sustainable lifestyle. And for some, it's just a matter of personal preference. They just would rather have a salad.

Effects

For most vegetarians, their choice has very positive effects. Vegetarians have to think about what they eat and where it comes from, and therefore they tend to eat better quality food and less of it. As a result, vegetarians are often slimmer than omnivores and less prone to arteriosclerosis and colon cancer—caused by fatty red meats. Vegetarians feel they live a more sustainable lifestyle, with less impact on the natural world. Still, vegans and vegetarians have their struggles. Many restaurants have meat in just about every dish, including soups and salads, making it a challenge to eat out. Ads and consumer culture also push vegetarians to eat meat. And vegetarians have to be careful to find proteins that can replace those that others get from eating meat.

Closing paragraph

The vegetarian lifestyle offers numerous benefits physically and spiritually to a person who chooses it. But the lifestyle isn't for everyone. People with poor impulse control will have a hard time resisting the flow of society at large. And growing children and adolescents must be careful to get enough of the proteins and fats they need to keep growing. The lifestyle doesn't work for everyone, but some people wouldn't have it any other way.

Creating an Opening Paragraph

The opening paragraph needs to capture the reader's attention and introduce your thesis statement. Here are some strategies.

Opening Strategies:

- **Start with an interesting quotation:**
"We've spent thousands of years getting to the top of the food chain, so why go back to eating leaves?"
- **Begin with a startling fact:**
For more than four millennia, the "meat of the Orient" hasn't been meat at all, but soybeans.
- **Share an anecdote:**
When I decided to become a vegetarian, my friends looked at me as if I had joined a cult.
- **Begin with a question:**
How many animals does the average American eat in a year?

Writing a Thesis Statement:

To create a thesis statement for your essay, follow this formula.

Topic	+	Compare/Contrast	=	Thesis Statement
vegetarianism		different reasons for choosing it, but the same benefits		Vegetarians have many reasons for choosing a meat-free diet, but the diet results in the same basic benefits.

Traits

Using a variety of details strengthens your ideas and broadens your thinking.

Write Create your opening paragraph. Start with a sentence that uses one of the strategies above. Then write sentences that build to your thesis statement.

Answers will vary.

Creating Middle Paragraphs

Write Refer to the cause-effect chart you created on page 201 as you develop the middle two paragraphs of your essay. Use one paragraph to describe the causes of the lifestyle choice and another to describe the effects of it. Create a topic sentence for each paragraph. Use transitional words at the left to make your writing flow.

Answers will vary.

Traits

Transitions that show causes and effects:
as a result / because / consequently / due to the fact that / every time that / inevitably / resulting in / since / therefore

Creating a Closing Paragraph

The closing paragraph of your essay should revisit the causes and effects of the topic and connect to the ideas in the introduction.

Write Answer the following questions to help you sum up the causes and effects. Answers will vary.

1. What is the most important cause of the lifestyle choice?

2. What is the most important effect?

3. What final point could you leave your reader with?

Write Create the closing paragraph for your cause-effect essay.

Answers will vary.

Learning Outcome

Revise the essay.

Speaking & Listening

Have your partner read your essay aloud. Then complete the response sheet together.

LO4 Revising: Improving the Writing

Revising your first draft involves adding, deleting, rearranging, and reworking parts of your writing. Revision begins with a peer review.

Peer Review

Sharing your writing at various stages is important, especially when you review and revise a first draft. The feedback that you receive will help you change and improve your essay.

Respond Complete this response sheet after reading the first draft of a classmate's essay. Then share the sheet with the writer. (Keep your comments helpful and positive.) Answers will vary.

Essay title: ________________________________

Writer: ____________________ Reviewer: ____________________

1. Which part of the essay seems to work best—opening, middle, or closing? Why?

____

____

____

____

2. Which part of the essay needs work—opening, middle, or closing? Why? __________

____

____

3. Which cause-effect details caught your attention? Name three.

a. ________________________________

b. ________________________________

c. ________________________________

4. Write two other details that might be included.

a. ________________________________

b. ________________________________

5. Identify a phrase or two that shows the writer's level of interest.

____

____

____

Using a Variety of Details

Your essay will be stronger if you use a variety of details to support your point. Different types of details provide different types of support.

Facts ground your essay in reality.

The US Department of Agriculture recommends that people "go lean on protein" and eat even less fat.

Statistics quantify facts.

However, the average American eats 16 percent of calories in proteins and 44 percent in fat.

Quotations from an expert lend support to your point.

Chris Woolston of the Consumer Health interactive says, "Fatty, unbalanced, and oversized: That, in a nutshell, is the American diet."

Anecdotes share an experience from real life.

After a week without meat, some vegetarians report that the smell of cooking hamburger makes them sick.

Revising in Action

Read aloud the unrevised and revised version of the following excerpt. Note how adding in facts and statistics makes the essay much stronger.

Other vegetarians reject modern American eating habits, with too much meat and too few vegetables. Vegetarians seek a better diet and a more sustainable lifestyle.

The US Department of Agriculture recommends that people "go lean on protein" and eat even less fat. However, the average American eats 16 percent of calories in proteins and 44 percent in fat.

Traits

Using a variety of details strengthens your ideas and broadens your thinking.

Revise Improve your writing, using your partner's comments on the response sheet and including sensory details. Continue revising until you can answer *yes* to each question in the following checklist.

Revising Checklist

Ideas:

1. Do I focus on an interesting lifestyle choice?
2. Do I trace the causes and effects of the lifestyle choice?

Organization:

3. Do I have an effective opening, middle, and closing?
4. Have I used one paragraph for causes and the other for effects?
5. Have I used transitions to connect my sentences?

Voice:

6. Do I sound knowledgeable about and interested in my topic?

Learning Outcome

Edit the essay.

LO5 Editing: Correcting Your Writing

The main work of editing is correcting your revised first draft.

Correcting Comma Splices and Run-On Sentences

When you join two sentences together, you need to connect them with a comma and a coordinating conjunction (*and, but, or, nor, for, so, yet*). If you leave out the conjunction, you have an error called a comma splice. If you leave out both the comma and conjunction, you have a run-on sentence. Fix either one by using a comma **and** a coordinating conjunction.

Traits

Coordinating conjunctions:
and, but, or, nor, for, so, yet

Comma Splice: Video games are fun, they shouldn't take over your life.

Run-On: Video games are fun they shouldn't take over your life.

Corrected: Video games are fun, but they shouldn't take over your life.

Correct Correct the following comma splices and run-on sentences by making sure both a comma and a coordinating conjunction are used.

1. I enjoy many types of video games, [and] my friends and I play together.
2. Sometimes we are in the same room, [but (or yet)] often we play together online.
3. We like first-person shooters mostly, [yet (or but)] online role-playing games are also fun.
4. Some games are designed to be addictive, [so] it's important to keep perspective.
5. A balance of life and games is crucial, [for] you can't just live in the game.
6. Game technology is always changing, [so (or and)] it's exciting to see what they invent next.
7. Motion-capture games get you moving, [and] some people exercise to them.
8. Other games have social aspects, [so] we talk to each other over the Internet.
9. Games are like other aspects of life, [for] too much of a good thing is too much.
10. Games should be social, [but (or yet)] they should not replace having friends.

Correction Marks

 delete

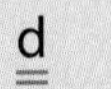 capitalize

 lowercase

 insert

 add comma

 add question mark

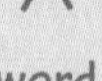 add word

 add period

 spelling

 switch

Apply Read your comparison-contrast essay and watch for comma errors. If you find any, correct them. (For more information, see pages 304–307.)

Correcting Sentence Fragments

A complete sentence has a subject and a verb and expresses a complete thought. If a group of words is missing a subject or a verb (or both) or does not express a complete thought, it is a fragment. Fix fragments by supplying what is missing.

Missing a Subject:	Love to play video games.
Complete Sentence:	**My friends and I** love to play video games.
Missing a Verb:	Bill and I especially.
Complete Sentence:	Bill and I especially **are game fanatics.**
Missing Subject and Verb:	Every weekend for hours at a time.
Complete Sentence:	**We play games** every weekend for hours at a time.
Incomplete Thought:	When we should be studying.
Complete Sentence:	When we should be studying, **the temptation is greatest.**

Correct Fix each fragment below by rewriting it and supplying what is missing. Use your imagination to provide details. Answers will vary.

1. The best game ever

2. After we've played all afternoon

3. Until two in the morning

4. Everyone, including my little brother

5. Whenever somebody wants to quit

Apply Read your essay, watching for sentence fragments. Fix them by providing what is missing—a subject, a verb, a subject and verb, or a complete thought.

Marking an Essay

Before you finish editing your revised essay, you can practice by editing the following model.

Correct Read the following cause-effect essay, looking for problems. Correct the model using the marks listed to the left. One correction has been done for you.

Correction Marks

- delete
- capitalize
- lowercase
- insert
- add comma
- add question mark
- word — add word
- add period
- spelling
- switch

Staying in Step

People have many different ways to stay in shape, from jogging to swimming to bike riding. Different people gravitate toward different types of exercise. Recently, when I was trying to ~~chose~~ choose a type of exercise, I decided on walking. Many factors made me choose walking over other forms of exercise walking has changed my life in a number of ways.

Walking appealed because of its simplicity, safety, cost, and sociability. While other types of exercise require special equipment or special training walking is an activity I do every day anyway. I've been walking since I was ~~1~~ one year old. It requires only normal cloths, comfortable shoes, and a sidewalk. Walking also ~~ain't~~ isn't dangerous like swimming, and walking isn't hard on the knees like joging. To walk, I don't have to belong to a special club or rent any special equipment. And when I walk, I walk with friends, and we talk.

Walking regularly has helped me a lot. First of all, I've dropped ten pounds, I also toned up my legs and the most important muscle of all, my heart. Beyond these benefits, walking has ~~gave~~ given me a chance to talk with best friends about all kinds of things. It has ~~brung~~ brought us closer. Walking also connects me to my community. Many people stop me and say they see me walking and feel they know me. I also like the way that walking connects me to Nature and Weather. Rain or shine, I feel it when I'm walking.

So you can keep your fancy weight machines and thigh busters. I choose walking because it is simple, safe, cheap, and fun. Walking has rewarded me with health and happiness walking is a habit that many people should learn.

Correcting Your Essay

Now it's time to correct your own essay. Use the checklist below.

Apply Create a clean copy of your essay and use the following checklist to search for errors. When you can answer *yes* to a question, check it off. Continue working until all items are checked.

Editing Checklist

Words

- ☐ **1.** Have I used specific nouns and verbs? (See page 74.)
- ☐ **2.** Have I used more action verbs than "be" verbs? (See page 348.)

Sentences

- ☐ **3.** Have I varied the beginnings and lengths of sentences? (See pages 264, 266.)
- ☐ **4.** Have I combined short choppy sentences? (See page 262.)
- ☐ **5.** Have I avoided improper shifts in sentences? (See pages 314–315.)
- ☐ **6.** Have I avoided fragments and run-ons? (See pages 297–302, 306–307.)

Conventions

- ☐ **7.** Do I use correct verb forms (*he saw,* not *he seen*)? (See page 356.)
- ☐ **8.** Do my subjects and verbs agree (*she speaks,* not *she speak*)? (See pages 282–291.)
- ☐ **9.** Have I used the right words (*their, there, they're*)?
- ☐ **10.** Have I capitalized first words and proper nouns and adjectives? (See page 414.)
- ☐ **11.** Have I used commas after long introductory word groups? (See page 396.)
- ☐ **12.** Have I punctuated dialogue correctly? (See pages 144–145.)
- ☐ **13.** Have I carefully checked my spelling?

Adding a Title

Make sure to add an attention-getting title. Here are three simple strategies for writing titles.

- **Ask a question:** Why eat that stuff?
- **Use the word "or":** Herbivore or Carnivore
- **Repeat the sounds of letters:** Staying in Step

Create Prepare a clean final copy of your essay and proofread it.

Learning Outcome

Reflect on the experience.

LO6 Reviewing Cause-Effect Writing

Complete these activities as needed to help you better understand how to write cause-effect essays.

Henglein and Steets/Cultura/Getty Images

Analyze Look at the photograph to the left. Think about the causes and effects shown in it. Fill in the following cause-effect chart with your observations. Answers will vary.

Cause-Effect Chart

Topic: ______________________

Causes	Effects

Freewrite Using your answers in the cause-effect chart above, freewrite about the reason the man is riding the child's car and what is likely to result.

Answers will vary.

"Nothing is as frustrating as arguing with someone who knows what he's talking about."
—Sam Ewing

Argument Essay

Have you ever dismissed a political ad for its over-the-top bias? Or left a lecture shaking your head because you just weren't convinced? Building a persuasive argument is difficult. Convincing others to buy into an argument is even more challenging.

Abraham Lincoln believed the best way to persuade was to present the facts and let logic run its course: "I am a firm believer in the people. If given the truth, they can be depended upon to meet any national crisis. The great point is to bring them the real facts."

In this chapter you will write an essay of argumentation that takes a position on a debatable topic and defends that position with logical and factual supporting details. Along the way you will learn strategies to motivate your audience to side with your argument.

What do you think?

In what ways do you defend your point of view during an argument? Give examples.

Answers will vary.

Learning Outcomes

- LO1 Understand argument essays.
- LO2 Plan an argument essay.
- LO3 Write the first draft.
- LO4 Revise the essay.
- LO5 Edit the essay.
- LO6 Reflect on the experience.

Learning Outcome

Understand argument essays.

LO1 Reviewing an Argument Essay

In an argument essay, a writer takes a stance on a debatable position. In the example below, the writer makes a pitch for preserving America's farmland.

Read/React Read the following essay. Then complete the analysis on the next page.

America the Developed

The **opening** raises concern for the issue with an attention-grabbing story and leads to the thesis (underlined).

Oh beautiful for spacious skies, for amber waves of grain, for purple mountain majesties, above the fruited plain. Sound familiar? These words begin the American classic, "America the Beautiful." Unfortunately, a portion of the American landscape spoken of so eloquently in this song is in danger of vanishing. Strip malls, housing developments, and transportation services are overrunning America's lush farmland, including those amber waves of grain and abundant fruited plains. An American Farmland Trust study estimates two acres of farm and ranch land is lost to development every minute of every day. Beyond the aesthetic loss, the loss of farmland is putting our economy and food supply at risk for future generations. The American public must take greater measures to preserve the country's farmland.

The first **middle paragraph** gives reasons to support the thesis.

From the years 2002 through 2007, America lost more than four million acres of active farmland to development. Much of that development has taken place in the proximity of big cities—areas where land is often most fertile. Studies show that farms closest to cities produce 83 percent of America's fruits and vegetables and 63 percent of its dairy. When development replaces this prime farmland, farmers are forced onto nonfertile land. The result is less production and higher costs for irrigation and transportation. Furthermore, cities lose out on quality of life factors, such as fresh produce, natural flood barriers, and scenic landscapes.

The second **middle paragraph** gives the best reasons to support the thesis.

The most critical case for preserving America's farmland, though, comes down to the nutritional and economic value of food. Food not only feeds bodies but it also supplies jobs. The U.S. food and farming system accounts for nearly $1 trillion of the national economy and employs 17 percent of the national workforce. By some estimates, the world's population will nearly double by 2050, which will greatly increase the demand for food here and abroad. By preserving its farmland, the United States will be able to safely feed itself while gaining a major economic boost from food exports.

The **closing** clarifies the writer's position and outlines what should be done.

It is critical that the United States takes greater steps toward preserving its farmland. By doing so, we will boost our economy and ensure our food supply is safe for future generations. We must build around, not on, farms on the urban edge. Furthermore, we must be more judicious with growth by making already-developed areas more livable. If we don't make it a priority now, the land spoken of in "America the Beautiful" will seem foreign to future generations.

A Closer Look

This argument essay takes a defensible position on farmland and development. The writer's position on farmland is debatable, but it is supported by the details in the middle paragraphs.

Identify The argument essay on the facing page makes a pitch for the preservation of farmland and gives reasons to support it. In the chart below, identify three different reasons that support the thesis statement.

Thesis Statement

Beyond the aesthetic loss, the loss of farmland is putting our economy and food supply at risk for future generations. The American public must take greater measures to preserve the country's farmland.

Reason 1

Development around cities takes the most fertile land, pushing farmers to poorer land.

Reason 2

This drives up food prices and decreases quality of life factors like fresh food, flood barriers, and scenic landscapes.

Reason 3

It also results in fewer jobs and reduced food for expanding populations.

Explain Is the writer's argument convincing? Why or why not? Provide reasons.

Answers will vary.

Learning Outcome

Plan an argument essay.

LO2 Prewriting: Planning

There is no sense in debating a topic about which everyone agrees. In your own essay, you will take a position on a debatable issue. You should pick an issue that you care about and choose the side you want to defend.

Selecting a Topic

If you can't think of a topic, browse newspapers, magazines, and the Internet for current issues that people have strong feelings about.

Select In the space below, list three or four debatable issues you could write about in an essay. Circle your favorite topic.

Answers will vary.

Traits

Consider using one of the following verbs to strengthen the conviction of your position statement: *should, must, ought to, need, needs*

Selecting a Position

Whether in writing or speaking, a convincing argument starts with a strong position on a debatable topic. Once you decide on a topic, consider your initial position on the issue.

Write Write down a defensible **position statement** that introduces the issue and expresses your opinion about it.

Answers will vary.

Refining a Position

With your initial position written, use the following position strategies to develop and refine your opinion of the issue:

- Research all possible positions on your issue of debate. Who supports it and why? Who opposes it and why?
- Gather solid evidence regarding your issue. Does the most compelling evidence support or oppose your position?
- Refine your position. At this point you may have sharpened or changed your mind about your position. Before you are ready to write, clarify your position statement.

Write On the lines below, write your refined position statement.

Answers will vary.

Vocabulary

position statement
a statement that expresses a writer's opinion on a debatable issue

Gathering Details

When you take a stand on an issue, you must gather convincing support to defend your position. You can use four different types of details to support your position: **facts**, **statistics**, **testimonials**, and **predictions**.

Support Chart

Fact	Statistic	Testimony	Prediction
A shield law is a law that gives reporters protection from being forced to reveal confidential information or anonymous sources in a courtroom.	Currently 49 states, including California, offer shield laws of varying degrees.	"We definitely need to have a shield law, but we also need to have a balance." Senator Tom Coburn	Sources may fear being identified and decide against leaking a story of corruption or scandal.

Vocabulary

facts
statements or claims of verifiable information

statistics
concrete numbers about a topic

testimonials
insights from authorities on the topic

predictions
insights into possible outcomes or consequences, forecasting what might happen under certain conditions

Gather Fill in the support chart below with the research you have gathered about your issue. If you have not found supporting details to fit each category, consider doing additional research. **Answers will vary.**

Fact	Statistic	Testimony	Prediction

Learning Outcome

Write the first draft.

LO3 Writing: Creating a First Draft

Creating a first draft puts all your planning and gathering into concrete form. Provided below is a sample argument essay about journalistic shield laws.

Read/React Read the essay, noting the writer's position statement and supporting details.

A Necessary Protection

Opening paragraph

Back in the summer of 2006, investigative journalists Lance Williams and Mark Fainaru-Wada of the *San Francisco Chronicle* faced a dilemma: either reveal the source who leaked confidential information for their story about steroid use in professional baseball or refuse to name names and be found in contempt of court, a punishment carrying 18 months in prison. At the heart of the matter were shield laws. A shield law is a law that gives reporters protection from being forced to reveal confidential information or anonymous sources in a courtroom. Currently 49 states, including California, offer shield laws of varying degrees. However, Williams and Fainaru-Wada's source was involved in a federal investigation, and no shield laws protect journalists in federal court. This fact must change. Passing a federal shield law is a necessary step to ensure the general public's right to know.

Thesis statement

Support paragraph 1

Some of the most consequential stories in American history have surfaced due to anonymous whistleblowers, including the Watergate and Enron scandals. Without a federal shield law, future stories like these may never come to light for two reasons. First, sources may fear being identified and decide against leaking a story of corruption or scandal. Second, news organizations may hold back from supporting their confidential-sources agreements due to the financial responsibility of fighting a case in court. The result is a chilling effect on breaking news.

Support paragraph 2

Furthermore, a federal shield law provides journalists with the basic protections to fulfill their job as watchdogs for the general public. It's the responsibility of a free press to provide a check on government corruption, corporate misconduct, and threats to public health and safety by unearthing stories. But what if a journalist decides against running an important story with an unnamed source out of fear of a subpoena?

Closing paragraph

To be certain, a federal shield law should not provide journalists with unlimited protections. If an unnamed source is an imminent threat to national security or bodily harm, the journalist should be compelled to reveal the source. However, in cases where an unnamed source is absolutely necessary, reporters shouldn't have to fear incarceration for honoring a confidentiality agreement. Trust is the foundation of a source-reporter relationship. Williams and Fainaru-Wada knew this. They decided against revealing their source and would have served jail time if the source had not confessed. But the next journalist might not be so lucky. It's time to pass a federal shield law.

Creating an Opening Paragraph

The opening paragraph of your argument essay needs to capture the reader's interest, raise concern for the issue of debate, and establish your position on the topic.

Consider these attention-grabbing strategies for your opening paragraph.

- **Start with a brief dramatic story.**
  Back in the summer of 2006, investigative journalists Lance Williams and Mark Fainaru-Wada of the *San Francisco Chronicle* faced a dilemma: either reveal the source who leaked confidential information for their story about steroid use in professional baseball or refuse to name names and be found in contempt of court.
- **Ask a thought-provoking question.**
  How would you feel if you were wrongly convicted of a crime?
- **Offer a surprising statistic.**
  An American Farmland Trust study estimates two acres of farm and ranch land is lost to development every minute of every day.
- **Make a personal confession.**
  I can't stand cigarette smoke, but I believe adults should have the freedom to smoke in public.

Speaking & Listening

Imagine that you are giving a speech about your topic. What strategy would you use to get listeners' attention? Try a similar strategy in your writing.

Write Create the opening paragraph for your argument essay.

Answers will vary.

Creating Middle Paragraphs

The middle paragraphs should make a persuasive case for your position. Here is where your supporting details become so important. Each paragraph should use facts, statistics, testimonials, or predictions to deepen, clarify, and build upon your position statement. Address any objections to your position with a clear, well-reasoned defense.

Write Create the two middle paragraphs of your essay.

Answers will vary.

Creating an End Paragraph

The closing paragraph should reaffirm your stance on the issue. If appropriate, make a direct or indirect plea to the reader to adopt your position.

- If the United States wants to maintain its fragile southern ecosystem, it should take a hard look at making the importation of Burmese pythons illegal.
- We must build around, not on, farms on the urban edge. Furthermore, we must be more judicious with growth by making already-developed areas more livable.
- It's time to pass a federal shield law.

Write Create the closing paragraph for your argument essay.

Answers will vary.

Learning Outcome

Revise the essay.

Speaking & Listening

Have your partner read your essay aloud. Then complete the response sheet together.

LO4 Revising: Improving the Writing

Revising your first draft involves adding, deleting, rearranging, and reworking parts of your writing. Revision begins with a peer review.

Peer Review

Sharing your writing at various stages—whether it is with a friend, classmate, or tutor—is an important step to improving your essay.

Respond Complete this response sheet after reading the first draft of a classmate's essay. Then share the sheet with the writer. (Keep your comments helpful and positive.) Answers will vary.

Essay title: ______________________________

Writer: ____________________ Reviewer: ____________________

1. Which part of the essay seems to work best—opening, middle, or closing? Why?

____

____

____

2. Which part of the essay needs work—opening, middle, or closing? Why? __________

____

____

____

3. Do the middle paragraphs support the writer's position statement? How so?

____

____

____

4. Does the writer use a variety of support details? Are more needed? Why or why not?

____

____

____

5. Does the writer build a convincing argument? Why or why not?

____

____

____

Looking Out for Logical Fallacies

A **logical fallacy** is a false assertion that weakens an argument by distorting an issue, drawing faulty conclusions, misusing evidence, or misusing language. Below are four common logical fallacies that should be removed from your writing.

Straw Man This logical fallacy distorts an issue by exaggerating or misinterpreting an opponent's position.

Those who consider themselves pro-choice don't value human life.

Bandwagon Mentality Such a logical fallacy appeals to "popular opinion," by implying that a claim cannot be true because most people oppose it, or must be true because most support it.

It's obvious to everyone that cockroaches live only in the apartments of dirty people.

Broad Generalization This logical fallacy makes an all-or-nothing claim based on little evidence. The claim will often include an intensifier, such as *all, every,* or *never.*

All athletes are driven by money.

Impressing with Numbers In this case, a writer attempts to overwhelm the reader with a deluge of statistics, some of which are unrelated to the issue at hand.

At 35 ppm, CO levels factory-wide are only 10ppm above the OSHA recommendation, which is 25 ppm. Clearly, that 10 ppm is insignificant in the big picture.

Revise Improve your writing using your partner's comments on the response sheet and the following checklist. Continue working until you can answer *yes* to each question.

Revising Checklist

Ideas:

1. Do I take a stance on a debatable issue?
2. Do I support my position with a variety of supporting details?
3. Do I avoid errors in logic?

Organization:

4. Do I have topic, middle, and closing paragraphs?
5. Have I used transitions to connect my sentences?

Voice:

6. Do I sound knowledgeable and passionate about the issue?

Vocabulary

logical fallacy
a false assertion that may distort an issue, sabotage an argument, draw faulty conclusions, misuse evidence, or misuse language

Learning Outcome

Edit the essay.

Insight

For more practice with correcting ambiguous wording, see pages 294–295.

LO5 Editing: Correcting Your Writing

The main work of editing is correcting your revised first draft.

Correcting Ambiguous Wording

Ambiguous wording creates uncertainty among readers. Such wording results in sentences that have multiple meanings. Avoid indefinite pronoun references, incomplete comparisons, and unclear wording.

Indefinite Pronoun Reference
When it is unclear which word or phrase a pronoun refers to, the wording is ambiguous.

Ambiguous: When Mike moved the lamp on to the wobbly chair, **it** fell on the floor.

Clear: When Mike moved the lamp on to the wobbly chair, **the lamp** fell on the floor.

Ambiguous: Monica reminded Misha that **she** needed to buy a new black dress for the party. (*Who needed to buy a black dress—Monica or Misha?*)

Clear: Monica reminded Misha to buy a new black dress for the party.

Practice Rewrite each sentence so that it does not contain any ambiguous pronoun references.

1. When Andy placed the box of macaroni back on the shelf, it tipped over.
   When Andy placed the box of macaroni back on the shelf, the box tipped over.
2. The professor told Tim that he needed to pursue the research opportunity.
   The professor told Tim that Tim needed to pursue the research opportunity.
3. As Brad drove his motorcycle into the garage, it shook.
   As Brad drove his motorcycle into the garage, the garage shook.

Apply Read your argument essay and watch for indefinite pronoun references. If you find any, correct them.

Incomplete Comparisons

Don't confuse readers by leaving out a word or words that are necessary to complete a comparison.

Ambiguous: The head chef said the Kobe steak is tastier. (*The Kobe is tastier than what?*)

Clear: The head chef said the Kobe steak is tastier **than the porterhouse.**

Unclear Wording

Avoid writing a statement that can have two or more meanings.

Ambiguous: Jill decided to take her sister to a movie, which turned out to be a real bummer. (*It is unclear what was a real bummer—taking her sister to the movie or the movie itself.*)

Clear: Jill decided to take her sister to a movie, **but the film turned out to be a real bummer.**

Practice Rewrite each of the following sentences so that it does not contain incomplete comparisons or unclear wording. Answers will vary.

1. Going bowling is more fun.

2. I can handle Mel's personality better.

3. Vera wanted to complete her economics report after reading the latest research, but she didn't.

4. Bryan planned to attend the ice cream social after he registered for class, but he didn't.

Apply Read your argument essay and watch for incomplete comparisons or unclear wording. If you find any problems, correct them.

Marking an Essay

Before you finish editing your revised essay, you can practice by editing the following model.

Editing Practice Read the following argument essay, looking for problems listed in the checklist on the facing page. Correct the model using the marks to the left. The first one has been done for you.

Correction Marks

- delete
- capitalize
- lowercase
- insert
- add comma
- add question mark
- add word
- add period
- spelling
- switch

Ban Burmese Pythons

An invasive species are taking the southern tip of Florida by storm. Thousands of Burmese pythons—giant snakes native to Southern asia—are thriving in the tropical-like environment of Everglades National Park. Their presence in the park is a product of irresponsible pet owners, who intentionally release the snakes into the wild when they become too difficult to care for. as a result, Florida lawmakers have passed a law making it illigal for individuals to own burmese pythons. In order to protect native wildlife and treasured ecosystems of the southern United States, this law should expand nationally.

Reports show some 144,000 pythons have been imported into the United States, many of which end up in homes of irresponsible pet owners. "All of the Burmese pythons that we see in the park are a product of the international pet trade" said Skip Snow, a wildlife biologist at Everglades National Park. The problem is many pet owners doesn't fully understand the responsibility of taking care of a python often the python, which grow up to between 10 and 20 feet becomes too big and to expensive to be kept in a home. In the end, the owner releases the pet into the wild.

It is in the wild where Burmese pythons is causing havoc. The tropical environment of the Everglades provides perfect conditions for the pythons to breed and feed. With no natural competitor the strong and stealthy python is feeding at will on native Everglade's species, Scientists worry the ecological effects could be devastating. Second to habitat loss, invasive species are the leading cause of species endangerment.

To be fair, there are no doubt thousands of responsible pet owners across the United States. But the drawbacks of owning Burmese pythons outweigh the benefits. These species are not meant to be pets. If the United States wants to maintain its fragile southern ecosystem, it should take a hard look at making the importation of Burmese pythons illegal.

Correcting Your Essay

Now it's time to edit your own essay.

Apply Create a clean copy of your essay and use the following checklist to check for errors. When you can answer *yes* to a question, check it off. Continue working until all items are checked off.

Editing Checklist

Words

- ☐ **1.** Have I used specific nouns and verbs? (See page 74.)
- ☐ **2.** Have I used more action verbs than "be" verbs? (See page 348.)

Sentences

- ☐ **3.** Have I varied the beginnings and lengths of sentences? (See pages 264, 266.)
- ☐ **4.** Have I combined short choppy sentences? (See page 262.)
- ☐ **5.** Have I avoided improper shifts in sentences? (See pages 314–315.)
- ☐ **6.** Have I avoided fragments and run-ons? (See pages 297–302, 306–307.)

Conventions

- ☐ **7.** Do I use correct verb forms *(he saw,* not *he seen)*? (See page 356.)
- ☐ **8.** Do my subjects and verbs agree (*she speaks,* not *she speak*)? (See pages 282–291.)
- ☐ **9.** Have I used the right words (*their, there, they're*)?
- ☐ **10.** Have I capitalized first words and proper nouns and adjectives? (See page 414.)
- ☐ **11.** Have I used commas after long introductory word groups? (See page 396.)
- ☐ **12.** Have I punctuated dialogue correctly? (See pages 144–145.)
- ☐ **13.** Have I carefully checked my spelling?

Adding a Title

Make sure to add an attention-getting title. Here are three simple strategies for writing titles

- **Use a play on words:** America the Developed
- **Sum up your argument:** A Necessary Protection
- **Create a slogan:** Ban Burmese Pythons

Learning Outcome

Reflect on the experience.

LO6 Reviewing Argument Writing

Complete these activities as needed to help you further understand how to write argument essays.

Describe A convincing argument essay requires a logical defense, based on supporting details. Describe the four types of supporting details illustrated in this chapter.

Answers will vary.

Match Draw a line to connect each logical fallacy with a claim that best demonstrates that fallacy.

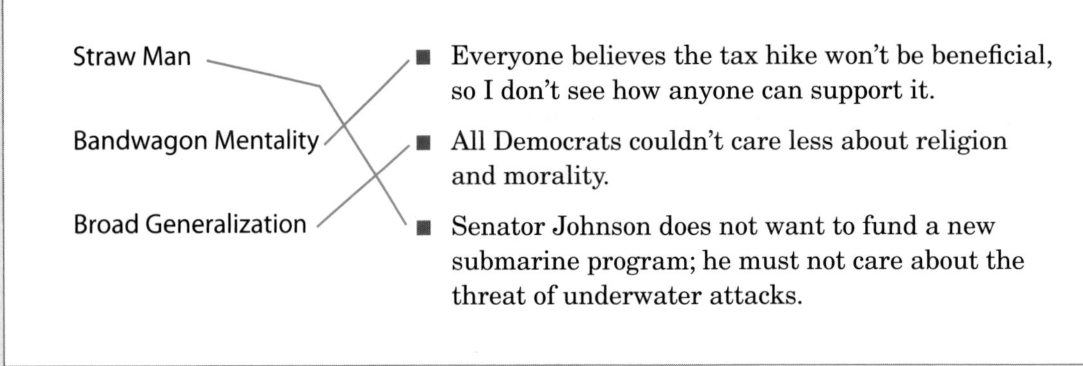

Correct The following sentence contains an indefinite pronoun reference. Rewrite the sentence so it becomes clear what word or phrase the pronoun refers to.

Krunal reminded Reid that he should arrive at the party at half past nine.

Example answers: Krunal reminded Reid to arrive at the party at half past nine.

Krunal reminded Reid that Reid should arrive at the party at half past nine.

89% of students surveyed found the interactive online quizzes valuable.

We know that no two students are alike. **WRITE 2** was developed to help you improve your writing skills in a way that works for you.

Not only is the format fresh and contemporary, it's also concise and focused. **WRITE 2** is loaded with a variety of supplements like portable **In Review** cards, interactive online quizzes, vocabulary flashcards, videos, and more.

At **login.cengagebrain.com**, you'll find plenty of resources to help you become a more successful writer no matter what your learning style!

"We cannot always build the future for our youth, but we can build our youth for the future."
—Franklin Delano Roosevelt

20 Sentence Basics

As you know, sentences are built from some very simple parts—nouns, verbs, and modifiers. Every sentence has, at its base, the pairing of a noun and a verb, or a few of them. The other words in the sentence merely modify the noun and verb.

These are sentence basics—the building blocks of thought. With these blocks, you can build tiny towers or magnificent mansions. It all comes down to understanding how to put the pieces together and deciding what you want to create. This chapter can help.

John Lund/Annabelle Breakey/Blend Images/Getty Images

What do you think?

How do we "build our youth for the future," as Roosevelt suggests in the quotation on the facing page? What part do language and writing have to do with building our youth?

Answers will vary.

Learning Outcomes

LO1 Understand subjects and predicates.

LO2 Work with special subjects.

LO3 Work with special predicates.

LO4 Understand adjectives.

LO5 Understand adverbs.

LO6 Use prepositional phrases.

LO7 Use clauses.

LO8 Apply sentence basics in a real-world context.

Learning Outcome

Understand subjects and predicates.

Eric Isselée,2010 / Used under license from Shutterstock.com

LO1 Subjects and Verbs (Predicates)

The subject of a sentence tells what the sentence is about. The verb (predicate) of a sentence tells what the subject does or is.

Dogs bark.

Subject: what the sentence is about — Predicate: what the subject does

Simple Subject and Simple Predicate

The **simple subject** is the subject without any modifiers, and the **simple predicate** is the predicate without modifiers or objects.

The black and white Schnauzer barked all day long.

simple subject (Schnauzer) — simple predicate (barked)

Complete Subject and Complete Predicate

The **complete subject** is the subject with modifiers, and the **complete predicate** is the predicate with modifiers and objects.

The black and white Schnauzer barked all day long.

complete subject (The black and white Schnauzer) — complete predicate (barked all day long)

Implied Subject

In commands, the subject *you* is implied. Commands are the only type of sentence in English that can have an **implied subject**.

(You) — implied subject

Stop barking! — complete predicate

Inverted Order

Most often in English, the subject comes before the predicate. However, in questions and sentences that begin with *here* or *there*, the subject comes after the predicate.

Why are you so loud? (subject: you; predicate: are)

Here is a biscuit. (subject: biscuit; predicate: is)

Vocabulary

simple subject
the subject without any modifiers

simple predicate
the predicate without modifiers or objects

complete subject
the subject with modifiers

complete predicate
the predicate with modifiers and objects

implied subject
the word *you* implied in command sentences

Creating Subjects and Verbs (Predicates)

Identify/Write For each sentence below, underline and label the simple subject (SS) and simple predicate (SP). Then write a similar sentence of your own and identify the simple subject and simple predicate in the same way.

1. For thousands of years, humans (SS) have bred (SP) dogs.
   Answers will vary.

2. All dog breeds (SS) descended (SP) from wolf ancestors.
   Answers will vary.

3. At the end of the Ice Age, humans (SS) lived (SP) nomadically with their dogs.
   Answers will vary.

4. Ever since that time, dogs (SS) have enjoyed (SP) going for walks.
   Answers will vary.

Identify/Write For each sentence below, underline and label the complete subject (CS) and complete predicate (CP). Then write a similar sentence of your own and identify the complete subject and complete predicate in the same way.

1. An Irish wolfhound (CS) stands as tall as a small pony (CP).
   Answers will vary.

2. Wolfhounds (CS) were bred to hunt their ancestors (CP).
   Answers will vary.

3. Wolfhounds (CS) also were used for hunting boar (CP).
   Answers will vary.

4. Is (CP) that (CS) why boars are extinct in Ireland (CP)?
   Answers will vary.

5. There is (CP) little doubt (CS).
   Answers will vary.

Learning Outcome

Work with special subjects.

LO2 Special Types of Subjects

As you work with subjects, watch for these special types.

Compound Subjects

A **compound subject** is two or more subjects connected by *and* or *or*.

My sister and I like to hike. Terri, Josh, and I love the outdoors.
(sister and I = compound subject; Terri, Josh, and I = compound subject)

"To" Words (Infinitives) as Subjects

An **infinitive** can function as a subject. An infinitive is a verbal form that begins with *to* and may be followed by objects or modifiers.

To become a park ranger is my dream.
(To become a park ranger = infinitive subject)

"Ing" Words (Gerunds) as Subjects

A **gerund** can function as a subject. A gerund is a verb form that ends in *ing* and may be followed by objects or modifiers.

Hiking builds strong calves. Hiking the Appalachian Trail is amazing.
(Hiking = gerund subject; Hiking the Appalachian Trail = gerund subject)

Noun Clause as Subject

A **noun clause** can function as a subject. The clause itself has a subject and a verb but cannot stand alone as a sentence. Noun clauses are introduced by words like *what, that, when, why, how, whatever,* or *whichever*.

Whoever hikes the trail should bring replacement boots.
(Whoever hikes the trail = noun clause subject)

Whatever you need must be carried on your back.
(Whatever you need = noun clause subject)

Traits

Note that each of these special subjects still functions as a noun or a group of nouns. A sentence is still, at root, the connection between a noun and a verb.

Say It

Pair up with a partner and read each sentence aloud. Take turns identifying the type of subject—compound subject, infinitive subject, gerund subject, or noun-clause subject. Discuss your answers.

1. You and I should go hiking sometime.
2. To reach the peak of Mount Rainier would be amazing.
3. Whoever wants to go should train with mountaineering.
4. Hiking the Rockies at altitude is challenging.

Vocabulary

compound subject
two or more subjects connected by *and* or *or*

infinitive
a verb form that begins with *to* and can be used as a noun (or as an adjective or adverb)

gerund
a verb form that ends in *ing* and is used as a noun

noun clause
a group of words beginning with words like *that, what, whoever,* and so on; containing a subject and a verb but unable to function as a sentence

Creating Special Subjects

Identify/Write For each sentence below, underline and label the complete subject: compound subject (CS), infinitive (I), gerund (G), or noun clause (NC). Then write a similar sentence of your own and identify the complete subject in the same way.

1. Planning for success is the key to success. (G: Planning for success)
   Answers will vary.

2. To complete the course in two years is my main goal. (I: To complete the course in two years)
   Answers will vary.

3. The fan and the air conditioner are running. (CS: The fan and the air conditioner)
   Answers will vary.

4. Working through our differences won't be easy. (G: Working through our differences)
   Answers will vary.

5. A donut, a cup of coffee, and good conversation make my morning. (CS: A donut, a cup of coffee, and good conversation)
   Answers will vary.

6. Lifting the ban on street parking will help the neighborhood. (G: Lifting the ban on street parking)
   Answers will vary.

7. To live life to its fullest is not as easy as it sounds. (I: To live life to its fullest)
   Answers will vary.

8. Whoever finds the money will keep it. (NC: Whoever finds the money)
   Answers will vary.

9. Are Hannah, Michelle, and Sharissa going? (CS: Hannah, Michelle, and Sharissa)
   Answers will vary.

10. Whenever he arrives is the starting time. (NC: Whenever he arrives)
    Answers will vary.

Learning Outcome

Work with special predicates.

Tony Campbell,2010 / Used under license from Shutterstock.com

LO3 Special Verbs (Predicates)

As you work with predicates, watch for these special types.

Compound Predicates

A **compound predicate** consists of two or more predicates joined by *and* or *or*.

I watched and laughed. My cat stalked, pounced, and tumbled.
(watched and laughed: compound predicate; stalked, pounced, and tumbled: compound predicate)

Predicates with Direct Objects

A **direct object** follows a transitive verb and tells what or who receives the action of the verb.

I pointed the laser. My cat got the spot. He batted it and nipped the ground.
(laser: direct object; spot: direct object; it, ground: direct objects)

Predicates with Indirect Objects

An **indirect object** comes between a transitive verb and a direct object and tells to whom or for whom an action was done.

I gave him a rest. My cat shot me a puzzled look.
(him: indirect object; me: indirect object)

Passive Predicates

When a predicate is **passive**, the subject of the sentence is being acted upon rather than acting. Often, the actor is the object of the preposition in a phrase that starts with *by*. Using that object as the subject, the sentence can be rewritten to be **active**.

Passive

My cat was exhausted by the game.
(cat: subject; was exhausted: passive verb; game: object of the preposition)

Active

The game exhausted my cat.
(The game: subject; exhausted: active verb; my cat: direct object)

Vocabulary

compound predicate
two or more predicates joined by *and* or *or*

direct object
a word that follows a transitive verb and tells what or who receives the action of the verb

indirect object
a word that comes between a transitive verb and a direct object and tells to whom or for whom an action was done

passive
the voice created when a subject is being acted upon

active
the voice created when a subject is acting

Say It

Pair up with a partner and read each sentence aloud. Take turns identifying the sentence as active or passive. If the sentence is passive, speak the active version out loud.

1. My cat was mesmerized by the laser.
2. The light danced in his paws.
3. The laser glowed red on the wall.
4. The light was chased all down the hallway.

Creating Special Predicates

Identify/Write For each sentence below, underline and label any compound predicate (CP), direct object (DO), and indirect object (IO). Then write a similar sentence of your own and identify the compound predicate and direct or indirect object in the same way.

1. Our pet rabbits hopped and thumped. (CP: hopped and thumped)

   Answers will vary.

2. The lop-ear leaped the gate. (DO: gate)

   Answers will vary.

3. I gave her a carrot. (IO: her; DO: carrot)

   Answers will vary.

4. She crouched and nibbled. (CP: crouched and nibbled)

   Answers will vary.

5. The lionhead sniffed and bounded. (CP: sniffed and bounded)

   Answers will vary.

6. I gave him some dried banana. (IO: him; DO: banana)

   Answers will vary.

7. Those rabbits give me hours of entertainment. (IO: me; DO: hours)

   Answers will vary.

Identify/Write For each passive sentence below, underline and label the simple subject (SS), the simple predicate (SP), and the object of the preposition *by* (O). Then rewrite each sentence, making it active. (See "Passive Predicates" on the previous page.)

1. The rabbits are fed and watered by my sister. (SS: rabbits; SP: are fed; O: sister)

   Answers will vary.

2. Their cages are cleaned by her as well. (SS: cages; SP: are cleaned; O: her)

   Answers will vary.

3. She is seen by them as their food goddess. (SS: She; SP: is seen; O: them)

   Answers will vary.

Learning Outcome

Understand adjectives.

Insight

It's less important to know the name of a phrase or clause than to know how it functions. If a group of words answers one of the adjective questions, the words are probably functioning as an adjective.

Nice One Productions/Flame/Corbis

LO4 Adjectives

To modify a noun, use an adjective or a phrase or clause acting as an adjective.

Adjectives

Adjectives answer these basic questions: *which, what kind of, how many, how much.*

To modify the noun **athletes,** ask . . .

Which athletes? ⟶ college athletes

What kind of athletes? ⟶ female athletes

How many athletes? ⟶ ten athletes

ten female college athletes

Adjective Phrases and Clauses

Phrases and clauses can also act as adjectives to modify nouns.

To modify the noun **athletes,** ask . . .

Which athletes? ⟶ athletes who are taking at least 12 credit hours

What kind of athletes? ⟶ athletes with a 3.0 average

The administration will approve loans for athletes with a 3.0 average who are taking at least 12 credit hours.

Say It

Pair up with a classmate to find adjectives—words, phrases, or clauses—that modify the nouns below. Take turns asking the questions while the other person answers.

1. **Sports**
   Which sports?
   What kind of sports?
   How many sports?
2. **Classes**
   Which classes?
   What kind of classes?
   How many classes?

Using Adjectives

Answer/Write For each noun, answer the questions using adjectives—words, phrases, or clauses. Then write a sentence using two or more of your answers.

Answers will vary.

1. **Tournaments**

   Which tournaments? ____________________

   What kind of tournaments? ____________________

   How many tournaments? ____________________

   Sentence: ____________________

2. **Opponents**

   Which opponents? ____________________

   What kind of opponents? ____________________

   How many opponents? ____________________

   Sentence: ____________________

3. **Victories**

   Which victories? ____________________

   What kind of victories? ____________________

   How many victories? ____________________

   Sentence: ____________________

Learning Outcome

Understand adverbs.

LO5 Adverbs

To modify a verb, use an adverb or a phrase or clause acting as an adverb.

Adverbs

Adverbs answer these basic questions: *how, when, where, why, how long,* and *how often*.

To modify the verb **dance,** ask . . .

How did they dance? → danced vigorously

When did they dance? → danced yesterday

Where did they dance? → danced there

How often did they dance? → danced often

Yesterday, the bride and groom often vigorously danced, there in the middle of the floor.

Adverb Phrases and Clauses

Phrases and clauses can also act as adverbs to modify verbs.

To modify the verb **dance,** ask . . .

How did they dance? → danced grinning and laughing

When did they dance? → danced from the first song

Where did they dance? → danced all around the room

Why did they dance? → danced to celebrate their wedding

How long did they dance? → danced until the last song

Grinning and laughing, the bride and groom danced all around the room from the first song until the last song to celebrate their wedding.

Speaking & Listening

Read the last two sentences aloud. Though they may look imposing on the page, they sound completely natural, probably because adverbs and adjectives are a common part of our speech. Experiment with these modifiers in your writing as well.

Ned Frisk/Blend Images/Getty Images

Using Adverbs

Answer/Write For each verb, answer the questions using adverbs—words, phrases, or clauses. Then write a sentence using three or more of your answers.

Answers will vary.

1. Ran

How did they run? ______________________________

When did they run? ______________________________

Where did they run? ______________________________

Why did they run? ______________________________

How long did they run? ______________________________

How often did they run? ______________________________

Sentence: ______________________________

____

____

____

____

2. Jumped

How did they jump? ______________________________

When did they jump? ______________________________

Where did they jump? ______________________________

Why did they jump? ______________________________

How long did they jump? ______________________________

How often did they jump? ______________________________

Sentence: ______________________________

____

____

____

____

Learning Outcome

Use prepositional phrases.

LO6 Prepositional Phrases

One of the simplest and most versatile types of phrases in English is the **prepositional phrase**. A prepositional phrase can function as an adjective or an adverb.

Building Prepositional Phrases

A prepositional phrase is a preposition followed by an object (a noun or pronoun) and any modifiers.

Preposition	+	Object	=	Prepositional Phrase
at		noon		at noon
in		an hour		in an hour
beside		the green clock		beside the green clock
in front of		my aunt's vinyl purse		in front of my aunt's vinyl purse

As you can see, a prepositional phrase can be just two words long, or many words long. As you can also see, some prepositions are themselves made up of more than one word. Here is a list of common prepositions.

Insight

A preposition is pre-positioned before the other words it introduces to form a phrase. Other languages have post-positional words that follow the words they modify.

Prepositions

aboard	back of	except for	near to	round
about	because of	excepting	notwithstanding	save
above	before	for	of	since
according to	behind	from	off	subsequent to
across	below	from among	on	through
across from	beneath	from between	on account of	throughout
after	beside	from under	on behalf of	'til
against	besides	in	onto	to
along	between	in addition to	on top of	together with
alongside	beyond	in behalf of	opposite	toward
alongside of	but	in front of	out	under
along with	by	in place of	out of	underneath
amid	by means of	in regard to	outside	until
among	concerning	inside	outside of	unto
apart from	considering	inside of	over	up
around	despite	in spite of	over to	upon
as far as	down	instead of	owing to	up to
aside from	down from	into	past	with
at	during	like	prior to	within
away from	except	near	regarding	without

Vocabulary

prepositional phrase
a group of words beginning with a preposition and including an object (noun or pronoun) and any modifiers

Using Phrases

Create For each item below, create a prepositional phrase by writing a preposition in the first box and an object (and any modifiers) in the second box. Then write a sentence using the prepositional phrase. Answers will vary.

1. Preposition + Object (and any modifiers)

Sentence: ______________________________

____

2. Preposition + Object (and any modifiers)

Sentence: ______________________________

____

3. Preposition + Object (and any modifiers)

Sentence: ______________________________

____

4. Preposition + Object (and any modifiers)

Sentence: ______________________________

____

5. Preposition + Object (and any modifiers)

Sentence: ______________________________

____

Learning Outcome

Use clauses.

Speaking & Listening

In each example, read the dependent clause out loud. (The dependent clause is in red.) Can you hear how each dependent clause sounds incomplete? Read it to another person, and the listener will probably say, "What about it?" These clauses depend on a complete thought to make sense.

Vocabulary

independent clause
a group of words with a subject and predicate that expresses a complete thought

dependent clause
a group of words with a subject and predicate that does not express a complete thought

adverb clause
a dependent clause beginning with a subordinating conjunction and functioning as an adverb

adjective clause
a dependent clause beginning with a relative pronoun and functioning as an adjective

noun clause
a dependent clause beginning with a subordinating word and functioning as a noun

LO7 Clauses

A clause is a group of words with a subject and a predicate. If a clause can stand on its own as a sentence, it is an **independent clause**, but if it cannot, it is a **dependent clause**.

Independent Clause

An independent clause has a subject and a predicate and expresses a complete thought. It is the same as a simple sentence.

Clouds piled up in the stormy sky.

Dependent Clause

A dependent clause has a subject and a predicate but does not express a complete thought. Instead, it is used as an **adverb clause**, an **adjective clause**, or a **noun clause**.

An adverb clause begins with a subordinating conjunction (see below) and functions as an adverb, so it must be connected to an independent clause to be complete.

after	before	since	when
although	even though	so that	whenever
as	given that	that	where
as if	if	though	whereas
as long as	in order that	unless	while
because	provided that	until	

Even though the forecast said clear skies, the storms rolled in.

An adjective clause begins with a relative pronoun *(which, that, who)* and functions as an adjective, so it must be connected to an independent clause to be complete.

I don't like a meteorologist who often gets the forecast wrong.

A noun clause begins with words like those below and functions as a noun. It is used as a subject or an object in a sentence.

how	what	whoever	whomever
that	whatever	whom	why

I wish he had known what the weather would be.

Using Clauses

Identify/Write For each sentence below, underline and label any adverb clauses (ADVC), adjective clauses (ADJC), or noun clauses (NC). Then write a similar sentence of your own and identify the clauses.

1. I wonder why weather is so unpredictable. (NC: why weather is so unpredictable)
   Answers will vary.

2. Though we have satellites, storms still surprise us. (ADVC: Though we have satellites)
   Answers will vary.

3. Many different factors determine what will happen in the sky. (NC: what will happen in the sky)
   Answers will vary.

4. Until we can track all factors, we can't predict perfectly. (ADVC: Until we can track all factors)
   Answers will vary.

5. Whoever gives a forecast is making a guess. (NC: Whoever gives a forecast)
   Answers will vary.

6. Since weather is so uncertain, predictions have percentages. (ADVC: Since weather is so uncertain)
   Answers will vary.

7. A 50 percent chance of rain means that there is a 50 percent chance of fair weather. (NC: that there is a 50 percent chance of fair weather)
   Answers will vary.

8. When air crosses a large lake, it picks up moisture. (ADVC: When air crosses a large lake)
   Answers will vary.

9. Because of lake-effect rain, Valparaiso is called "Vapor Rain Snow." (ADVC: Because of lake-effect rain)
   Answers will vary.

10. Buffalo gets as snow whatever moisture Lake Erie dishes up. (NC: whatever moisture Lake Erie dishes up)
    Answers will vary.

Learning Outcome

Apply sentence basics in a real-world context.

LO8 Real-World Application

Identify In the e-mail below, underline simple subjects once and simple predicates twice. Circle dependent clauses.

Send | Attach | Fonts | Colors | Save As Draft

To: Teri Bell

Subject: Revision Suggestions

Hi, Teri:

I enjoyed your article, "What Is New in *BattleTown 2,*" submitted for publication on MMORPNews2.com. We are very interested in publishing your article but would like to request a few revisions before we send contracts.

This is a quick rundown of our revision suggestions:

1. The opening could be more gripping. The title works well to grab the reader's interest, but the opening feels flat. Perhaps you could provide a glimpse of new features of game play, or even give a scenario that wasn't possible in *BattleTown 1.*
2. A direct quotation from Todd Allen would strengthen the center section. Though you allude to your interview on many occasions, Todd never gets to speak for himself, and he is a definite name in the industry.
3. Can you get permission to use the visuals? AssemblyArts would love the free publicity, but you need written permission to include the screenshots.

If you could make these changes, we would be very interested in publishing your article. Once I see the revised piece, I can send a contract for you to sign.

Thanks,
Richard Prince

Expand Answer the adjective and adverb questions below. Then expand the sentence using some of the words, phrases, and clauses you have created.

The agent called. Answers will vary.

Which **agent?** ______

What kind of **agent?** ______

Called ***when?*** ______

Called ***how?*** ______

Sentence: ______

"A complex system that works is invariably found to have evolved from a simple system that works."

—John Gaule

raresirimie,2010 / Used under license from Shutterstock.com

21

Simple, Compound, and Complex Sentences

Most leaves have a central stem with veins extending from it. Sometime this structure forms a simple oval, but at other times, two or more ovals connect to form a compound leaf. And the shape of some leaves is complex, as if a number of leaves were fused together.

Sentences are similar. All have a noun and a verb, but some stop at this simple structure. In other cases, two or more sentences combine to make a compound sentence. And when a sentence has one or more dependent clauses fused to it, it becomes complex.

This chapter shows how to create simple, compound, and complex sentences. As with leaves, variety makes sentences beautiful.

Learning Outcomes

LO1 Create simple sentences.

LO2 Create simple sentences with compound subjects.

LO3 Create simple sentences with compound verbs (predicates).

LO4 Create compound sentences.

LO5 Create complex sentences.

LO6 Create complex sentences with relative clauses.

LO7 Apply simple, compound, and complex sentences in a real-world document.

What do you think?

Which type of leaf is most beautiful—a simple, compound, or complex leaf? Why?

Answers will vary.

Learning Outcome

Create simple sentences.

LO1 Simple Sentences

A **simple sentence** consists of a subject and a verb. The subject is a noun or pronoun that names what the sentence is about. The verb tells what the subject does or is.

Rachel sang.
subject verb

Modifiers

Other words can be added to modify the subject. Words that modify the subject answer the adjective questions: *which, what kind of, how many, how much.*

My new roommate Rachel sang.
(Which Rachel do you mean?)

Other words can also modify the verb. These words and phrases answer the adverb questions: *how, when, where, why, to what degree,* and *how often.*

Rachel sang **in the shower at the top of her lungs.**
(Where and how did Rachel sing?)

Direct and Indirect Objects

The verb might also be followed by a noun or pronoun that receives the action of the verb. Such a word is called the **direct object,** and it answers the question *what* or *whom*?

Rachel sang **"I Need a Hero."**
(What did Rachel sing?)

Another noun or pronoun could come between the verb and the direct object, telling *to whom* or *for whom* an action is done. Such a word is the **indirect object.**

I gave **her** a picture of Chuck Norris.
(I gave a picture of Chuck Norris to whom?)

Vocabulary

simple sentence
a subject and a verb that together form a complete thought

direct object
a noun or pronoun that follows a verb and receives its action

indirect object
a noun or pronoun that comes between a verb and a direct object, telling *to whom* or *for whom* an action is done

Say It

Team up with a partner and follow these steps: One of you speaks the sentence aloud, and the other asks the question in italics. Then the first person says the sentence again, inserting an answer.

1. We sang songs. (*Where did you sing songs?*)
2. The song was our favorite. (*Which song was your favorite?*)
3. Rachel sang. (*What did Rachel sing?*)
4. I sang a song. (*To whom did you sing a song?*)

Insight

In item 1, you are adding modifiers to the verb and in item 2, you are adding modifiers to the subject. In item 3, you are adding a direct object, and in item 4, you are adding an indirect object.

Creating Simple Sentences

Create Provide a noun for a subject and a verb for a predicate. Then write a sentence with the noun and verb, adding details that answer the questions asked.

Answers will vary.

1. **Subject** **Verb**

Which?

2. **Subject** **Verb**

What kind of?

3. **Subject** **Verb**

When?

4. **Subject** **Verb**

Where?

5. **Subject** **Verb**

How?

Learning Outcome

Create simple sentences with compound subjects.

LO2 Simple Sentences with Compound Subjects

A simple sentence can have a **compound subject** (two or more subjects)

A Simple Sentence with Two Subjects

To write a simple sentence with two subjects, join them using *and* or *or*.

One Subject: Lee worked on the Rube Goldberg machine.
Two Subjects: Lee **and** Jerome will add the lever arm that tips the bucket.
Lee **or** Jerome will add the lever arm that tips the bucket.

One Subject: Ms. Claymore will help them attach the flywheel.
Two Subjects: Ms. Claymore **and** her aide will help them attach the flywheel.
Either Ms. Claymore **or** her aide will help them attach the flywheel.

Traits

A compound subject does not make the sentence compound. As long as both (or all) of the subjects connect to the same verb or verbs, the sentence is still considered simple.

A Simple Sentence with Three or More Subjects

To write a simple sentence with three or more subjects, create a series. List each subject, placing a comma after all but the last, and place an *and* or *or* before the last.

Three Subjects: Jerome, Lee, and Sandra are finishing the machine soon.
Five Subjects: Jerome, Lee, Sandra, Ms. Claymore, **and** her aide will enter the machine in a contest.

Note: When a compound subject is joined by *and*, the subject is plural and requires a plural verb. When a compound subject is joined by *or*, the verb should match the last subject.

Ms. Claymore and her aide need to submit the entry form.
Ms. Claymore or her aide needs to submit the entry form.

Say It

Speak each of the following sentences out loud.

1. Jerome *loves* the Rube Goldberg project.
2. Jerome *and* Sandra *love* the Rube Goldberg project.
3. Jerome *or* Sandra *works* on it every day after school.
4. Jerome, Sandra, *and* Lee *have* contributed most.
5. Jerome, Sandra, *or* Lee *has* contributed most.

Vocabulary

compound subject
two or more subjects in a simple sentence

Using Compound Subjects

Create Write subjects in each of the boxes provided. Then write a sentence that includes the subjects as a compound subject using *and* or *or*.

Answers will vary.

1. Subject | Subject

2. Subject | Subject

3. Subject | Subject | Subject

4. Subject | Subject | Subject

5. Subject | Subject | Subject | Subject

6. Subject | Subject | Subject | Subject

Learning Outcome

Create simple sentences with compound verbs (predicates).

LO3 Simple Sentences with Compound Verbs

A simple sentence can also have two or more verbs (predicates). Remember that the predicate tells what the subject is doing or being, so as long as both predicates connect to the same subject, the sentence is still a simple sentence.

Two Verbs

To create a **compound predicate** with two parts, join two verbs using *and* or *or*.

One Verb: The band rocked.
Two Verbs: The band rocked **and** danced.

Remember that the predicate includes not just the verbs, but also words that modify or complete the verbs.

One Predicate: The band played their hit single.
Two Predicates: The band played their hit single **and** covered other songs.

Traits

A compound verb does not make the sentence compound. As long as both (or all) verbs connect to the same subject or subjects, the sentence is still considered simple.

Three or More Verbs

To create a compound predicate with three or more parts, list the verbs in a series, with a comma after each except the last, and the word *and* or *or* before the last.

Three Verbs: The singer crooned, wailed, **and** roared.
Five Verbs: The fans clapped, screamed, danced, cheered, **and** swayed.

If each verb also includes modifiers or completing words (direct and indirect objects), place the commas after each complete predicate.

The crowd members got to their feet, waved their hands back and forth, and sang along with the band.

Ant Strack/Corbis Yellow/Corbis

Vocabulary

compound predicate
two or more predicates in a simple sentence

Using Compound Predicates

Write For each subject below, create predicates in the boxes provided. Then write a simple sentence that joins the compound predicates with *and* or *or*.

Answers will vary.

1. The reporters

Predicate

Predicate

____

____

2. The police

Predicate

Predicate

____

____

3. The manager

Predicate

Predicate

____

____

4. The bouncer

Predicate

Predicate

Predicate

____

____

____

Learning Outcome

Create compound sentences.

Insight

The word *and* indicates that the second clause provides additional information. The words *but, or, nor,* and *yet* create a contrast. The words *for* and *so* indicate that one clause is the cause of the other.

LO4 Compound Sentences

A **compound sentence** is made out of simple sentences joined by a coordinating conjunction: *and, but, or, nor, for, so,* or *yet*.

Compound of Two Sentences

Most compound sentences connect two simple sentences, which are also called independent clauses. Connect the sentences by placing a comma after the first sentence and using a coordinating conjunction after the comma.

Two Sentences: We ordered pizza. I got just one piece.
Compound Sentence: We ordered pizza**, but** I got just one piece.

Compound of Three or More Sentences

Sometimes, you might want to join three or more short sentences in a compound sentence.

Two Sentences: Tim likes cheese. Jan likes veggie. I like pepperoni.
Compound Sentence: Tim likes cheese, Jan likes veggie**, and** I like pepperoni.

You can also join the sentences using semicolons. Authors sometimes use this approach to describe a long, involved process or a flurry of activity.

Tim ate the cheese pizza; Jan ate the veggie pizza; Ray showed up and ate the pepperoni pizza; I got back in time for the last slice.

Note: Remember that a compound sentence is made of two or more complete sentences. Each part needs to have its own subject and verb.

Vocabulary

compound sentence
two or more simple sentences joined with a coordinating conjunction

Radius Images/Radius/Corbis

Creating Compound Sentences

Write Write a simple sentence for each prompt; then combine them as a compound sentence.

Answers will vary.

1. What pizza do you like? ____________________

   What pizza does a friend like? ____________________

   Compound Sentence: ____________________

   ____

2. Where do you go for pizza? ____________________

   What other place do people go? ____________________

   Compound Sentence: ____________________

   ____

3. Who likes thin crust pizza? ____________________

   Who likes pan pizza? ____________________

   Who likes stuffed pizza? ____________________

   Compound Sentence: ____________________

   ____

4. What is the weirdest pizza? ____________________

   What is the grossest pizza? ____________________

   What is the stinkiest pizza? ____________________

   Compound Sentence: ____________________

   ____

   ____

5. When do you eat pizza? ____________________

   When do your friends eat pizza? ____________________

   When does your family eat pizza? ____________________

   Compound Sentence: ____________________

   ____

   ____

Learning Outcome

Create complex sentences.

LO5 Complex Sentences

A **complex sentence** shows a special relationship between two ideas. Instead of connecting two sentences as equal ideas (as in a compound sentence), a complex sentence shows that one idea depends on the other.

Using a Subordinating Conjunction

You can create a complex sentence by placing a subordinating conjunction before the sentence that is less important. Here are common subordinating conjunctions:

after	before	so that	when
although	even though	that	where
as	if	though	whereas
as if	in order that	till	while
as long as	provided that	'til	
because	since	until	

The subordinating conjunction shows that this sentence depends on the other sentence and can't stand without it.

Two Sentences: We played strong offense. We won the football game.

Complex Sentence: **Because** we played strong offense, we won the football game.

We won the football game **because** we played strong offense.

Note: The subordinating conjunction goes at the beginning of the less important clause, but the two clauses could go in either order. When the dependent clause comes second, it usually isn't set off with a comma.

Speaking & Listening

Read the example complex and compound-complex sentences aloud. Despite their daunting names, these sentences aren't that complicated. You use them all the time in speech. Experiment with them in your writing.

Compound-Complex

You can also create a **compound-complex sentence** by placing a subordinating conjunction before a simple sentence and connecting it to a compound sentence.

Simple Sentence: I threw two touchdowns.

Compound Sentence: Jake kicked the extra points and the other team couldn't catch up.

Compound-Complex: **After I threw two touchdowns,** Jake kicked the extra points, and the other team couldn't catch up.

Vocabulary

complex sentence
a sentence with one independent clause and one or more dependent clauses

compound-complex sentence
a sentence with two or more independent clauses and one or more dependent clauses

Creating Complex Sentences

Write Write a simple sentence after each prompt. Then select a subordinating conjunction from the facing page, place it at the beginning of one sentence, and combine the two sentences into a single complex sentence.

Answers will vary.

1. What did you play? ______________________

   Did you win or lose? ______________________

   Complex sentence: ______________________

2. Who did you play? ______________________

   Why did you play the opponent? ______________________

   Complex sentence: ______________________

3. Who won the game? ______________________

   Why did that side win? ______________________

   Complex sentence: ______________________

4. Where did you play? ______________________

   Where else could you have played? ______________________

   Complex sentence: ______________________

5. What surprised you? ______________________

   Why did it surprise you? ______________________

   Complex sentence: ______________________

6. How long did you play? ______________________

   When did you stop? ______________________

   Complex sentence: ______________________

Learning Outcome

Create complex sentences with relative clauses.

LO6 Complex Sentences with Relative Clauses

In a complex sentence, one idea depends on the other. You've seen how a dependent clause can start with a subordinating conjunction. Another type of dependent clause starts with a relative pronoun.

Relative Clauses

A **relative clause** is a group of words that begins with a **relative pronoun** *(that, which, who, whom)* and includes a verb and any words that modify or complete it:

Relative Clauses: that leads into the garden
which usually leans against the shed
who planted the scallions
whom I asked to help me weed

Each relative clause above has a subject and a verb, but none of the clauses is a complete sentence. All need to be connected to a complete sentence.

Complex Sentences: I followed the path that leads into the garden.
I looked for the shovel, which usually leans against the shed.
We have many onions thanks to a friend who planted the scallions.
I worked with Tina, whom I asked to help me weed.

That and *Which*

The pronoun *that* signals that the information after it is necessary to the sentence. The pronoun *which* signals that the information is not necessary, so the clause is set off with a comma.

That: The scallions **that** we planted this spring taste strongest. (*That* defines the scallions.)

Which: I love scallions, **which** I eat raw or fried. (*Which* does not define the scallions but just adds more information about them.)

Who and *Whom*

The pronoun *who* is the subject of the relative clause that it introduces. The pronoun *whom* is a direct object of a clause it introduces.

Who: I helped the woman **who** harvested scallions. (*Who* is the subject.)

Whom: I thanked the woman **whom** I helped. (*Whom* is the direct object.)

Insight

In some languages, if the relative pronoun is the object of the clause it introduces, another pronoun is inserted in the clause: *I liked the gift that my boss gave* it *to me.* In English, no additional pronoun is inserted: *I liked the gift that my boss gave to me.*

Vocabulary

relative clause
a group of words that begins with a relative pronoun and includes a verb but cannot stand alone as a sentence

relative pronoun
a word *(that, which, who, whom)* that relates a relative clause with another word in the sentence

Using Relative Clauses

Create For each item, write a relative clause beginning with the pronoun provided. Then write a complex sentence that includes the relative clause. In case you need a topic idea, think of a party you have attended or one that you would like to attend.

Answers will vary.

1. Relative clause: that ____________________

   Complex sentence: ____________________

2. Relative clause: who ____________________

   Complex sentence: ____________________

3. Relative clause: which ____________________

   Complex sentence: ____________________

4. Relative clause: whom ____________________

   Complex sentence: ____________________

5. Relative clause: that ____________________

   Complex sentence: ____________________

6. Relative clause: which ____________________

   Complex sentence: ____________________

Learning Outcome

Apply simple, compound, and complex sentences in a real-world document.

Workplace

Using a variety of sentences in workplace writing will help ideas flow and will present a polished image.

LO6 Real-World Application

Rewrite Read the following message about a meeting. Note how every sentence is a simple sentence. Rewrite the message, combining sentences into some compound or complex sentences and improving the flow.

Dear Mr. Lindau:

You asked about the Monday production meeting. I will summarize it. The production staff met with the editors. The writers explained their new project. It focuses on twenty-first century skills. The writers presented two chapters. They will become a prototype.

The new project needs to be visual. It should appeal to students and teachers. The design needs to make text accessible. The writing has an open quality. It still feels academic. The book should be available for sale in the fall. A teacher's edition will follow.

The designers are beginning work on a prototype. The writers continue to create chapters.

Dear Mr. Lindau: Answers will vary.

"Never offend people with style when you can offend them with substance."

—Sam Brown

Aurelie and Morgan David de Lossy/cultura/cultura/Corbis

22 Sentence Style

The purpose of makeup is to accentuate a person's natural beauty. Mascara that thickens lashes, blush that lends color to cheeks, lipstick that tastefully outlines the contours of one's lips—these are the appropriate uses of makeup.

Curly mustaches and goatees are not.

In the same way, sentence style is not about putting on a false face or making elaborate curlicues in your writing. It's about saying what you want to say and expressing who you really are. This chapter will help you create effective sentence style.

What do you think?

What will this young man think of his makeup? What do others think? What do readers think of a sentence style that is equally fake and "dressed up"?

Answers will vary.

Learning Outcomes

LO1 Vary sentence lengths.

LO2 Vary sentence beginnings.

LO3 Combine with coordination.

LO4 Combine with subordination.

LO5 Combine by moving parts.

LO6 Combine by deleting.

LO7 Expand sentences.

LO8 Model professional sentences.

LO9 Revise a real-world document for sentence style.

Learning Outcome

Vary sentence lengths.

LO1 Varying Sentence Lengths

To create a smooth flow of thought, use a variety of sentence lengths.

Short Sentences

Short sentences are powerful. They make a point. In dramatic circumstances, a series of short sentences can create a staccato effect:

> I like pigs. Dogs look up to us. Cats look down on us. Pigs treat us as equals.
>
> —Sir Winston Churchill

Sometimes a series of short sentences will start to sound choppy. In such situations, use short sentences in combination with longer sentences.

WAC

Read an article or a speech in your major, noting the lengths of the sentences. Count the words in each. What effect does the variety of sentences (or lack of variety) have on readability?

Medium Sentences

Medium-length sentences do most of the work in everyday writing. They are not overly punchy or overly complicated, and so they communicate well.

> I look to the future because that's where I'm going to spend the rest of my life.
>
> —George Burns

Long Sentences

Long sentences express complex ideas and create an expansive feeling. The long sentence may be the hardest type to pull off because it needs to have a clear sense of direction. Otherwise, it may begin to ramble.

> I write entirely to find out what I'm thinking, what I'm looking at, what I see and what it means, what I want and what I fear.
>
> —Joan Didion

Varying Lengths

The most effective writing includes sentences of different lengths, serving different purposes. Read this call to action, noting the different lengths of sentences and their effect on the whole.

> You're alive. Do something. The directive in life, the moral imperative was so uncomplicated. It could be expressed in single words, not complete sentences. It sounded like this: Look. Listen. Choose. Act.
>
> —Barbara Hall

Varying Sentence Lengths

Create Write the types of sentences requested below.

Answers will vary.

1. Write a short sentence naming your favorite food.

2. Write a medium sentence describing your favorite food.

3. Write a long sentence indicating what you like most about this food.

4. Write a medium sentence providing a final thought about the food.

Create Write the types of sentences requested below.

Answers will vary.

1. Write a short sentence indicating your course of study.

2. Write a medium sentence describing your course of study.

3. Write a long sentence explaining why you chose to follow this course.

4. Write a medium sentence providing a final thought about the course of study.

Learning Outcome

Vary sentence beginnings.

LO2 New Beginnings I

If every sentence begins with the subject, writing can become monotonous. Vary sentence beginnings by starting in these different ways.

Prepositional Phrase

A **prepositional phrase** is formed from a preposition (*in, at, through*) followed by an object (a noun and any modifiers). (For more prepositions, see page 386.)

PR = Preposition
O = Object

After the game . . .	For that matter . . .	With a renewed interest . . .
After = PR, game = O	For = PR, matter = O	With = PR, interest = O

A prepositional phrase functions as an adjective or an adverb. That means that a prepositional phrase can answer any of the adjective or adverb questions:

Adjective Questions	Adverb Questions
Which?	How?
What kind of?	When?
How many?	Where?
How much?	Why?
	How often?
	To what degree?

Test Taking

It is more important to be able to use prepositional phrases and infinitive phrases than to be able to identify them. However, some tests require the ability to identify phrases. For more practice, see pages 242–243 and 386–387.

Infinitive Phrase

An **infinitive phrase** is formed from the word *to* followed by a verb and any objects and modifiers.

V = Verb
O = Object

To prove my point . . .	To complete the comparison . . .	To be specific . . .
prove = V, point = O	complete = V, comparison = O	be = V, specific = O

An infinitive phrase functions as a noun, an adjective, or an adverb. It can answer any of the adjective and adverb questions above, but it can also serve as the subject of the sentence:

To complete my degree is my goal.
(*To complete my degree* functions as the subject of the sentence.)

Vocabulary

prepositional phrase
phrase formed from a preposition followed by an object and any modifiers; functioning as an adjective or adverb

infinitive phrase
verbal phrase that begins with *to* followed by a verb and any objects; functioning as a noun, an adjective, or an adverb

Varying with Prepositional and Infinitive Phrases

Vary For each sentence below, add the requested type of beginning.

Answers will vary.

1. (Prepositional phrase):

   ____

   we decided to go out for ice cream.

2. (Infinitive phrase):

   ____

   we bought homemade frozen custard instead.

3. (Prepositional phrase):

   ____

   the custard was richer and creamier.

4. (Infinitive phrase):

   ____

   an occasional treat like this helps keep life in balance.

Create Write the types of sentences requested below.

Answers will vary.

1. Write a short sentence about a treat you like. (Begin with a prepositional phrase.)

   ____

2. Write a medium sentence about the treat. (Begin with an infinitive phrase.)

   ____

   ____

3. Write a long sentence about the treat. (Begin with a prepositional phrase.)

   ____

   ____

   ____

4. Write a medium sentence about the treat. (Begin with an infinitive phrase.)

   ____

   ____

Learning Outcome

Vary sentence beginnings.

LO2 New Beginnings II

If sentences still sound repetitive, you can start with two other constructions—participial phrases and adverb clauses.

Participial Phrase

A **participial phrase** is formed from a participle (verb ending in *ing* or *ed*) and any objects and modifiers. (For more on participles, see page 362.)

PA = Participle
O = Object

Expecting the best . . .	Considering the source . . .	Concerning the plan . . .
Expecting (PA) the best (O)	Considering (PA) the source (O)	Concerning (PA) the plan (O)

A participial phrase functions as an adjective. That means that the phrase answers one of the adjective questions.

Adjective Questions	
Which?	How many?
What kind of?	How much?

Insight

Participial phrases and gerund phrases both can start with the *ing* form of a verb, but participial phrases function as adjectives, and gerund phrases function as nouns. For a closer look at these phrases, see page 362.

Adverb Clause

An **adverb clause** is formed from a subordinating conjunction followed by a noun (or pronoun) and verb (and any objects and modifiers).

SC = Subordinating Conjunction   N = Noun   V = Verb

When Bill arrived . . .	Because Jan climbed so high . . .	While Ted watched . . .
When (SC) Bill (N) arrived (V)	Because (SC) Jan (N) climbed (V) so high	While (SC) Ted (N) watched (V)

Subordinating Conjunctions			
after	before	since	when
although	even though	so that	whenever
as	given that	that	where
as if	if	though	whereas
as long as	in order that	unless	while
because	provided that	until	

An adverb clause functions as an adverb, answering one of the adverb questions.

Adverb Questions	
How?	Why?
When?	How often?
Where?	To what degree?

Vocabulary

participial phrase
phrase beginning with a participle (*ing* or *ed* form of verb) plus objects and modifiers; used as an adjective

adverb clause
clause beginning with a subordinating conjunction and functioning as an adverb

Varying with Participial Phrases and Adverb Clauses

Vary For each sentence below, add the requested type of beginning.

Answers will vary.

1. (Participial phrase):

   ____

   we worked all through the evening.

2. (Adverb clause):

   ____

   the lights from our office shone out on the people passing by.

3. (Participial phrase):

   ____

   I smiled at my colleagues and shook their hands.

4. (Adverb clause):

   ____

   the project was finished, and we could at last go home.

Create Write the types of sentences requested below.

Answers will vary.

1. Write a short sentence about working. (Begin with a participial phrase.)

   ____

2. Write a medium sentence about working. (Begin with an adverb clause.)

   ____

   ____

3. Write a long sentence about working. (Begin with an adverb clause.)

   ____

   ____

   ____

4. Write a medium sentence about working. (Begin with a participial phrase.)

   ____

   ____

Learning Outcomes

Combine with coordination.

Insight

The word *coordinate* means "to place together." A *coordinating conjunction,* then, is a word that connects ideas in an equal way, placing them together.

Vocabulary

coordinating conjunction
a word that connects sentence parts in an equal way

LO3 Using Coordination

When you have too many short sentences, writing begins to sound choppy. Look for sentences that have related ideas and combine them.

Coordination

If two sentences express ideas of equal importance, you can combine the sentences by connecting them with a **coordinating conjunction**. (See the box below.)

Coordinating Conjunctions						
and	but	or	nor	for	so	yet

Choppy: Human beings are self-aware. Animals may or may not be.

Combined: Human beings are self-aware**, but** animals may or may not be.

Note: Remember to place a comma before the conjunction.

The different coordinating conjunctions make different connections between ideas:

Comparison → and
Contrast → but, yet
Options → or, nor
Cause → so, for

Human beings recognize themselves in mirrors**, and** great apes can as well.
Dolphins recognize themselves in mirrors**, so** they must be self-aware.
Dogs, cats, and babies do not**, so** their self-awareness is in question.

Combining Using Coordination

Coordinate Mark the sentences below to show what coordinating conjunction you would insert to combine them. Use the correction marks as needed to add words and change punctuation and capitalization.

1. Gordon Gallup created the mirror test, for he was testing self-awareness.
2. Gallup put odorless dye on an animal, and spots were in front and in back.
3. The animal looked in a mirror, and some animals noticed the front spot.
4. The animal shifted to see better, and pawing the body part showed awareness.
5. Other animals did not notice the spot, for the mirror image seemed another animal.
6. Great apes, dolphins and orcas, and elephants passed, but (or yet) monkeys did not.
7. Pigeons could be trained to pass, yet (or but) magpies passed without training.
8. A sticker was under the magpie's beak, so the bird tried to pull it off.
9. The other passing creatures had big brains, but magpies have small brains.
10. Magpies are visual creatures, so shiny things attract them.
11. Dogs are more olfactory, so smell is used to identify themselves and others.
12. Dogs might need an olfactory test, for smell is a better indicator for them.
13. Humans would fail an olfactory test, for we don't want to smell ourselves.
14. Pigs passed a modified test, for food was reflected in a mirror.
15. Most pigs turned around to find the food, yet (or but) one in eight looked behind the mirror.
16. Pigs may not be self-aware, but food-aware is a different story.
17. Squid are very intelligent, so perhaps the mirror test would work for them.
18. Squid have big eyes and brains, and both are needed to succeed on the mirror test.

Correction Marks

℘	delete
d (triple underline)	capitalize
Ø	lowercase
∧	insert
∧ with comma	add comma
? with ∧	add question mark
word with ∧	add word
⊙	add period
(oval)	spelling
∽	switch

Learning Outcome

Combine with subordination.

LO4 Using Subordination

If sentences sound choppy, you can combine them using subordination.

Subordination

If one sentence is more important than the other, you can combine the sentences by connecting them with a **subordinating conjunction**. (See the box below). Place the subordinating conjunction before the less important part.

Subordinating Conjunctions			
after	before	since	when
although	even though	so that	whenever
as	given that	that	where
as if	if	though	whereas
as long as	in order that	unless	while
because	provided that	until	

Choppy: Every culture has music. Music is an innate part of being human.
Combined: **Because** every culture has music**,** music is an innate part of being human.

Choppy: Music is a language of emotion. It first touches one's feelings.
Combined: Music is a language of emotion **because** it first touches one's feelings.

Note: If the subordinate clause comes first, put a comma between the clauses.

Different subordinating conjunctions show different kinds of connections:

Time → after, as, as long as, before, since, until, when, whenever, while
Cause → because, given that, if, in order that, provided that, since, so that
Contrast → although, as if, even though, though, unless, whereas, while

Insight

The word *subordinate* means "to place below." A *subordinating conjunction,* then, is a word that makes one idea less important than (or dependent on) another idea.

Vocabulary

subordinating conjunction
a word or phrase that begins a subordinate (adverb) clause, showing that the ideas in the clause are dependent on those in the main clause

Combining Using Subordination

Subordinate Mark the sentences below to show what subordinating conjunction you would use to combine them. Use the correction marks as needed to add words and add and delete punctuation.

Example answers:

1. A note can be high or low because the pitch is the frequency of wavelength.
2. A note can be short or long since the duration is its length in time.
3. Changes in duration make rhythm, whereas changes in pitch make melodies.
4. Sound is waves given that waves move through air, water, and other substances.
5. While we use sound to communicate in speech, music is the cousin of speech.
6. A spoken sentence can become a melody given that the program Autotune can do it.
7. Though language communicates emotion, music communicates emotion even more.
8. Music is also mathematical given that it measures pitch and time.
9. Though mathematical patterns repeat throughout, music makes the math emotional.
10. Although science designs instruments, musicians make science into art.

Correction Marks

ꝸ	delete
d̳	capitalize
Ɖ	lowercase
∧	insert
∧̦	add comma
?∧	add question mark
word ∧	add word
⊙	add period
◯	spelling
∽	switch

Write For each prompt, write a simple sentence, with a subject and predicate. Then combine the sentences, using subordination. Answers will vary.

1. What music do you like most? ______________________

   What music do your friends like? ______________________

   Combine: ______________________

   ____

2. Where do you get your music? ______________________

   Where do your friends get their music? ______________________

   Combine: ______________________

   ____

Learning Outcome

Combine by moving parts.

LO5 Combining by Moving Parts

Sometimes sentences need to be combined because they cover the same material. The way to combine such sentences is to move one part of one sentence into the other sentence.

Moving a Word

Before: Chinese New Year lasts for 15 days. ~~Each day is~~ festive.

After: Chinese New Year lasts for 15 festive days.

Moving a Phrase

Before: Red lanterns (and) scare off the monster Nien. Children dressed in red ~~scare him, too.~~

After: Red lanterns and children dressed in red scare off the monster Nien.

Before: People clean their houses. ~~They try~~ to sweep away bad luck.

After: People clean their houses to sweep away bad luck.

Reworking Sentences

Before: Chinese New Year ~~changes each year. It~~ falls between January 21 and February 20. ~~The date is~~ usually on the second new moon after the winter solstice.

After: Chinese New Year falls between January 21 and February 20, usually on the second new moon after the winter solstice.

Speaking & Listening

On the facing page, read each of the sentence pairs out loud. Then ask yourself how you could say the same thing in one sentence. Say it aloud before writing it down. In this way, your conversational skills can help you improve your writing skills.

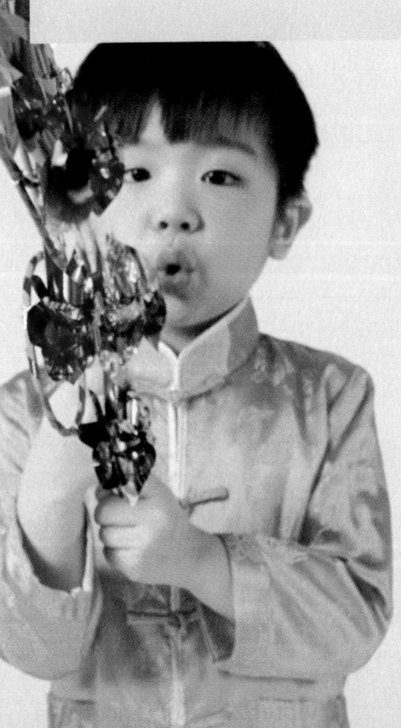

Image Source/Image Source/Corbis

Combining by Moving Parts

Combine Combine each pair of sentences below by moving a word or phrase or by reworking the sentences.

1. Nien used to stalk villages. The monster would devour animals, plants, and people.
The monster Nien used to stalk villages, devouring animals, plants, and people.

2. Villagers left food offerings. The offerings would satisfy Nien's hunger.
Villagers left food offerings to satisfy Nien's hunger.

3. A child wearing red confronted Nien. The child in red scared the monster.
A child wearing red confronted Nien and scared the monster.

4. Red became a lucky color. It was used with lanterns and spring scrolls.
Red, used with lanterns and spring scrolls, became a lucky color.

5. Firecrackers also scared him. They were loud and bright.
Loud and bright firecrackers also scared him.

6. Nien was driven off. The monster was tamed by a Taoist monk.
Tamed by a Taoist monk, Nien was driven off.

7. The monk rode Nien. The monster never bothered anyone again.
The monk rode Nien, and the monster never bothered anyone again.

8. People cleaned house. They wanted to get rid of bad luck.
People cleaned house to get rid of bad luck.

9. The clean houses were ready. Good luck could come into them.
The clean houses were ready for good luck to come into them.

10. Villagers gave each other red envelopes. The envelopes had money inside.
Villagers gave each other red envelopes with money inside.

Learning Outcome

Combine by deleting.

LO6 Combining by Deleting

When writing is wordy or repetitious, the best way to combine sentences is by finding the key pieces of information, deleting the rest, and writing new sentences from what is left.

Finding the Key Pieces

Read the following paragraph, noting how wordy and repetitious it is. Afterward, note the important ideas that the writer underlined.

> What is the difference between science fiction and fantasy? Well, it seems when you look at it at first that the main difference is that science fiction is about technology while fantasy is about magic. That definition might seem pretty good at first, but when you think about it, the difference between science fiction and fantasy goes deeper. Science fiction is all about achieving the new. In a science fiction story, usually the world is changed by what happens in the story and it will never be the same again. Fantasy is just the opposite. In a fantasy story, the whole point is to get things back to the way they used to be, for example restoring a king or rediscovering an ancient and lost treasure or artifact. When you think of it that way, science fiction is revolutionary and fantasy is reactionary. So, though it is true that science fiction features technology and fantasy features magic, the deeper difference is that science fiction looks to the future and change while fantasy looks to the past and continuity.

Workplace

Workplace writing needs to be concise, clear, and compelling. By finding the important points and deleting the unimportant ones, you can create a message that reaches colleagues and clients.

Rewriting and Combining

Now read the much shorter and more effective sentences that the writer wrote from the main ideas.

> What is the difference between science fiction and fantasy? Some say science fiction is about technology while fantasy is about magic, but the difference goes deeper. Science fiction is all about achieving the new, while fantasy is about returning to what is old. In that way, science fiction is revolutionary and fantasy is reactionary.

Combining by Deleting

Underline Read the following wordy, repetitive paragraph. Afterward, go back through and reread the paragraph, looking for important details. Underline them.

Let's look at two classic films, one from science fiction and the other from fantasy. The science fiction film is *2001: A Space Odyssey*. The film shows a lot of technology, which may or may not look really impressive now because the film was made in the '60s. The main point of the film is to show the conflict between the human astronauts and their thinking computer, HAL, who tries to take over the ship. The astronauts manage to shut down the computer, but they and the computer are drawn into connection with a mysterious object in space and the people and computer fuse to become a new life form. The world will never be the same. Now think of *The Lord of the Rings*. In it, the whole point is to stop an ancient evil from rising and save the world from being destroyed. This film is all about trying to save something that is important, and even the last part—*The Return of the King*—tells about restoring the ancient lineage of human beings to return their age of glory. The world is renewed. Note how *2001: A Space Odyssey* focuses on plunging headlong into an unknowable future, while *The Lord of the Rings* focuses on returning to a better past.

Combine Rewrite the paragraph above without unimportant details, combining important details into new sentences. Make the new paragraph concise and smooth.

Answers will vary.

Learning Outcome

Expand sentences.

Speaking & Listening

Imagine each sentence-expanding activity on the facing page as a conversation you are having with a friend. You might even read the sentence aloud and have a friend ask you each of the questions beneath. Then roll some of your answers into a single, more-informative sentence.

LO7 Sentence Expanding

Sometimes a sentence does not say enough, or it is too general. When that happens, the sentence needs to be expanded. Sentence expanding simply means adding details. The best way to expand a sentence is to answer the 5 W's about the topic.

Original Sentence: My friend likes extreme sports.

Who likes extreme sports? my friend Liam

What sports does he like? He likes BMX biking and jumping.

Where does he train? He trains in a field beside his yard.

When did he start? about eight years ago

Why does he do it? He loves the adrenaline rush.

Expanded Sentence: My friend Liam likes the extreme sport of BMX biking and jumping, and he trains in a field beside his house.

Note: The expanded sentence does not use all of the answers to the 5 W's, but a second sentence could cover the other details:

He started BMX jumping about eight years ago and says he loves the adrenaline rush.

Expanding Sentences

Expand Expand the sentences below by answering the questions provided.

Answers will vary.

1. **Short Sentence:** My friend needs help.

   a. Who is your friend?____________________

   b. What help does the person need?____________________

   c. Where does the friend need help?____________________

   d. When does the person need help?____________________

   e. Why does the person need help?____________________

   Expanded Sentence: ____________________

2. **Short Sentence:** My friend got hurt.

   a. Who is your friend?____________________

   b. What happened to the person?____________________

   c. Where did the person get hurt?____________________

   d. When did the person get hurt?____________________

   e. Why did the person get hurt?____________________

   Expanded Sentence: ____________________

Learning Outcome

Model professional sentences.

LO8 Sentence Modeling

Sentence modeling helps you see new ways to put sentences together. Modeling involves reading a well-written sentence and then writing a similar sentence by substituting words. Here is an example original sentence and a sentence modeled after it.

Original Sentence: It seemed the world was divided into good and bad people. The good ones slept better, while the bad ones seemed to enjoy the waking hours much more.

—Woody Allen

Modeled Sentence: I figured the school was divided into talkers and listeners. The talkers dominated in class, while the listeners got better grades on the tests.

Note: The new sentence doesn't *exactly* match the model. The writer made adjustments to make the sentence work.

Original Sentence: Storms are sensual feasts—the cold wet touch of rain, the smell of damp soil, the percussive crack of thunder, the brilliant flashes of lightning.

—Eli King

Modeled Sentence: Morning on the lake was a languid treat—the soft wet slap of oars, the coils of rising mist, the watery murmur of waves, the dark, welling depths.

Note: In the sentence above, the writer chose words that had an opposite feeling from the ones in the original and created a passage with a very different impact. Notice, however, that the sentence still works and makes sense.

WAC

Instead of modeling sentences taken from literature, you can model well-constructed sentences from your academic discipline. When you find a great sentence in one of your books, try to craft a similar sentence. You'll be learning the way professionals write in your field of study.

Modeling Sentences

Model Create sentences that model the ones below.

Answers will vary.

1. Thanks to the Interstate Highway System, it is now possible to travel from coast to coast without seeing anything.

   —Charles Kuralt

2. It was a bright cold day in April, and the clocks were striking thirteen.

   —George Orwell

3. The average, healthy, well-adjusted adult gets up at seven-thirty in the morning feeling just plain terrible.

   —Jean Kerr

4. Arranging a bowl of flowers in the morning can give a sense of quiet in a crowded day—like writing a poem, or saying a prayer.

   —Anne Morrow Lindberg

5. The secret of staying young is to live honestly, eat slowly, and lie about your age.

   —Lucille Ball

6. A boy can learn a lot from a dog: obedience, loyalty, and the importance of turning around three times before lying down.

   —Robert Benchley

7. My mother used to say that there are no strangers, only friends you haven't met yet. She's now in a maximum security twilight home in Australia.

   —Dame Edna Everage

Learning Outcome

Revise a real-world document for sentence style.

LO9 Real-World Application

Expand Read the following cover letter, written to present a résumé for a job. Note how the writer uses a lot of short, say-nothing sentences that could refer to anyone. Then rewrite the letter below, expanding the sentences with details you either make up or take from your own life. Make the letter interesting, informative, and engaging by improving the sentences style and enriching the content.

Workplace

As you can see from this exercise, bland sentences can cost you a job, and great sentences can land you one.

Dear Mr. Dawson:

Do you need a good worker? I need a good employer. My education is good. I have work experience.

Many traits make me a good worker. I do well with many things.

Do you need a good worker? If so, please contact me.

I look forward to hearing from you.

Sincerely,

Dear Mr. Dawson:

Answers will vary.

"My idea of an agreeable person is a person who agrees with me."
—Benjamin Disraeli

Bernd Vogel/Fancy/Corbis

Agreement

When two people agree, they can work together. They have the same goals and outlook, and they can become a team.

Subjects and verbs are much the same. If the subject is plural, the verb needs to be as well, or they can't work together. Pronouns also need to agree with their antecedents in terms of number. Without agreement, these words fight each other, and instead of conveying ideas, they disrupt communication.

This chapter focuses on the agreement between subjects and verbs and between pronouns and antecedents. It also tackles other pronoun problems. After you work through the exercises here, you'll find it easy to write agreeable sentences.

Learning Outcomes

LO1 Make subjects and verbs agree.

LO2 Make two subjects agree with verbs.

LO3 Practice agreement with *I* and *you*.

LO4 Practice agreement with indefinite pronouns.

LO5 Practice pronoun-antecedent agreement.

LO6 Correct other pronoun problems.

LO7 Check agreement in a real-world context.

What do you think?

What makes a person agreeable? What makes subjects and verbs agreeable?

Answers will vary.

Learning Outcome

Make subjects and verbs agree.

LO1 Subject-Verb Agreement

A verb must **agree in number** with the subject of the sentence. If the subject is singular, the verb must be singular. If the subject is plural, the verb must be plural.

singular subject + singular verb = agreement

The truck needs a tune-up.

plural subject + plural verb = agreement

The trucks need tune-ups.

Note how plural subjects often end in *s*, but plural verbs usually do not. Also note that only present tense verbs and certain *be* verbs have separate singular and plural forms.

Present:	singular	plural	Past:	singular	plural
	walks	walk		walked	walked
	sees	see		saw	saw
	eats	eat		ate	ate
	is/am	are		was	were

To make most verbs singular, add just an *s*.

run—runs write—writes stay—stays

The verbs *do* and *go* are made singular by adding an *es*.

do—does go—goes

When a verb ends in *ch, sh, x,* or *z,* make it singular by adding *es*.

latch—latches wish—wishes fix—fixes buzz—buzzes

When a verb ends in a consonant followed by a *y,* change the *y* to *i* and add *es*.

try—tries fly—flies cry—cries quantify—quantifies

Insight

The "Say It" activity below will help you become familiar with the subject-verb agreement patterns in English. Practice it aloud, and for added practice, write the sentences as well.

Say It

Read the following sentences aloud, emphasizing the words in *italics*.

1. The bird *sings*. The birds *sing*. The phone *rings*. The phones *ring*.
2. The person *is*. The people *are*. The child *is*. The children *are*.
3. He *works*. They *work*. She *learns*. They *learn*.
4. The woman *does*. The women *do*. The man *goes*. The men *go*.
5. She *wishes*. They *wish*. He *boxes*. They *box*.

Vocabulary

agree in number
match, as when a subject and verb are both singular, or when they are both plural

Correcting Basic Subject-Verb Agreement

Write In each sentence below, write the correct form of the verb in parentheses.

1. A philosophy major knows about thinking. (know)
2. A philosopher tries to find philosophical work. (try)
3. An employer rarely wishes to hire philosophers. (wish)
4. But such students are able to think (is).
5. My roommate studies philosophy. (study)
6. He also needs to study the want ads for jobs. (need)
7. He says employers need thinkers. (say)
8. That idea makes sense. (make)
9. But that idea doesn't make people hire him. (make)
10. At his job, he fixes lawn mowers very philosophically. (fix)

Speaking & Listening

After completing the sentences in the first activity, say them aloud, emphasizing the underlined verbs.

Correct Read the following paragraph. Correct any agreement errors you find by crossing out the incorrect verb and writing the correct present tense verb above.

The philosopher Plato ~~say~~ says the material world ~~aren't~~ isn't the real world. He ~~say~~ says we ~~sees~~ see shadows on a cave wall. Plato ~~believe~~ believes in eternal forms of perfection. Every real table in the world ~~are~~ is patterned after the perfect form of a table. In that way, people too ~~is~~ are patterned after the perfect form of people. Though Plato ~~live~~ lives more than three hundred years before Jesus, many Christian thinkers ~~likes~~ like his concept of eternal forms. The idea ~~fit~~ fits well with the ideas of a soul and a creator. Many modern thinkers, though, ~~has~~ have the opposite idea. They ~~says~~ say that only physical things ~~is~~ are real. Plato, of course, ~~disagree.~~ disagrees

Write For each plural verb below, write one sentence using the verb in its singular form. Answers will vary.

1. fly ______
2. do ______
3. fish ______
4. wax ______
5. go ______
6. deny ______

Learning Outcome

Make two subjects agree with verbs.

LO2 Agreement with Two Subjects

Sentences with **compound subjects** have special rules to make sure that they agree.

Two or More Subjects

When a sentence has two or more subjects joined by *and,* the verb should be plural.

plural subject + plural verb = agreement

Jumbo and Dumbo march.

When a sentence has two or more subjects joined by *or, nor,* or *but also,* the verb should agree with the last subject.

or

Radius Images/Radius/Corbis

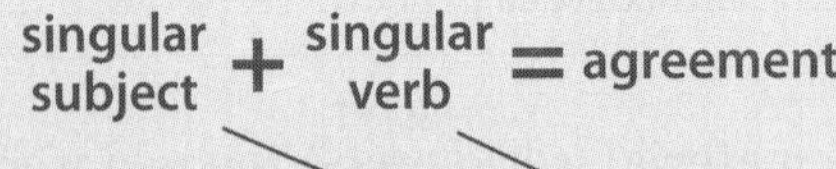

Either Jumbo or Dumbo trumpets.

Not only Jumbo but also Dumbo trumpets.

Test Taking

For more practice with compound subjects, see pages 250–251.

Say It

Read the following sentences aloud, emphasizing the words in *italics.*

1. Jumbo *and* Dumbo *perform.* Jumbo *or* Dumbo *performs.*
2. The man *and* woman *dance.* The man *or* woman *dances.*
3. The Democrat *and* the Republican *agree.* The Democrat *or* the Republican *agrees.*
4. Not only Dave *but also* Tim *writes.*
5. The dog, cat, *and* guinea pig *greet* me. The dog, cat, *or* guinea pig *greets* me.

Vocabulary

compound subject
two or more subjects that share the same verb or verbs

Fixing Agreement with Two Subjects

Write In each sentence below, write the correct form of the verb in parentheses.

1. The acrobat and clown entertain the crowd. (entertain)
2. The acrobat or clown gets a pie in the face. (get)
3. A trapeze artist and a tightrope walker receive an ovation. (receive)
4. Not only the acrobat but also the clown is highly paid. (are)
5. Neither the lion tamer nor the sword swallower has insurance. (have)
6. The human cannonball or the lion tamer has the scariest job. (have)
7. Either Todd or Lewis plans to join the circus. (plan)
8. Thrills and hard work await Todd or Lewis. (await)
9. Not only Todd but also Lewis is a daredevil. (are)
10. The clowns or the ringmaster introduces each act. (introduce)

Correct Read the following paragraph. Correct any agreement errors you find by crossing out the incorrect verb and writing the correct present tense verb above.

Childhood dreams and fantasies rarely ~~comes~~ come true. A firefighter or police officer ~~are~~ is what many children dream of being. Imagine a world filled with firefighters and police! Neither the accountant nor the landscaper ~~figure~~ figures big in childhood plans. A princess or a wizard ~~are~~ is also a popular choice for kids. Job openings and pay for both careers ~~is~~ are pretty slim. Even the job of astronaut or explorer ~~have~~ has become scarce. The trials of joblessness and the responsibilities of adulthood ~~conspires~~ conspire to convince people to seek other careers. Childhood stars sometimes get "real" jobs, too. Johnny Whitaker and Wil Wheaton ~~works~~ work with computers. They traded childhood dreams for adult ones.

Write Write a sentence with a compound subject joined by *and.* Write a sentence with a compound subject joined by *or.* Check subject-verb agreement.

Answers will vary.

Learning Outcome

Practice agreement with *I* and *you*.

Insight

The word *am* exists for one reason only, to go along with the word *I*. There is no other subject for the verb *am*. In academic or formal writing, *I* should never be used with *be* or *is*. Think of René Descartes saying, "I think, therefore I am."

LO3 Agreement with *I* and *You*

The pronouns *I* and *you* usually take plural verbs, even though they are singular.

plural verb

Correct: I go to Great America and ride roller coasters. You do too..

singular verb

Incorrect: I goes to Great America and rides roller coasters. You does too.

Note: The pronoun *I* takes the singular verbs *am* and *was.* **Do not** use *I* with *be* or *is.*

Correct: I am excited. I was nervous. I am eager to ride the roller coaster.

Incorrect: I are happy. I were nervous. I is eager to ride the roller coaster.

Quick Guide

Using *am, is, are, was,* and *were*

	Singular	**Plural**
Present Tense	I *am* you *are* he *is* she *is* it *is*	we *are* you *are* they *are*
Past Tense	I *was* you *were* he *was* she *was* it *was*	we *were* you *were* they *were*

Say It

Read the following word groups aloud, emphasizing the words in *italics.*

1. I *laugh* / You *laugh* / She *laughs* / They *laugh*
2. I *work* / You *work* / He *works* / They *work*
3. I *do* / You *do* / He *does* / They *do*
4. I *am* / You *are* / She *is* / They *are*
5. I *was* / You *were* / He *was* / They *were*

Correcting Agreement with *I* and *You*

Write In each sentence below, write the correct forms of the verb in parentheses. (Do not change the tense.)

1. I __laugh__ louder than he __laughs__ . (laugh)
2. You __climb__ as well as she __climbs__ . (climb)
3. We __work__ together, or you __work__ alone. (work)
4. Stan __washes__ silverware while I __wash__ pans. (wash)
5. I __help__ often, but he __helps__ rarely. (help)
6. The group __watches__ on Sunday, but I __watch__ later. (watch)
7. I __eat__ first and she __eats__ after. (eat)
8. You __are__ tired, and I __am__ too. (is)
9. Last year, I __was__ short, but you __were__ tall. (was)
10. You __are__ helpful; I hope I __am__ also. (is)

Correct Read the following paragraphs. Correct any agreement errors you find by crossing out the incorrect verb and writing the correct verb above.

I ~~is~~ am starting a class in astronomy, and I ~~wonders~~ wonder if I can borrow your telescope. You rarely ~~uses~~ use it anymore, and I ~~needs~~ need it to be able to look at the moons of Jupiter. My professor says that even a moderate-size telescope will show the moons. She ~~have~~ has instructions for finding Jupiter. I ~~knows~~ know how to use the telescope, but if you ~~is~~ are afraid I would break it, you could set it up for me.

Another idea would be for us to stargaze together. I ~~has~~ have a place away from city lights, and I ~~has~~ have lawn chairs and blankets we could use. If you ~~agrees~~ agree to come along and set up the telescope, I ~~agrees~~ agree to bring snacks for us.

What do you think? I ~~hopes~~ hope I'm not asking too much and that you ~~isn't~~ aren't mad about the request. I just ~~is~~ am excited to see Jupiter's moons, and I ~~thinks~~ think you might like to see them, too.

Write Write two sentences using "I" as the subject. Then write two more using "you" as the subject. Check your subject-verb agreement.

Answers will vary.

Speaking & Listening

After completing the sentences in the first exercise, say them aloud, emphasizing the underlined verbs.

Learning Outcome

Practice agreement with indefinite pronouns.

LO4 Agreement with Singular Indefinite Pronouns

An **indefinite pronoun** is intentionally vague. Instead of referring to a specific person, place, or thing, it refers to something general or unknown.

Singular Indefinite Pronouns

Singular **indefinite pronouns** take singular verbs:

Someone cooks every night.
No one gets out of kitchen duty.
Everyone benefits from the chore schedule.

Note that indefinite pronouns that end in *one, body,* or *thing* are singular, just as these words themselves are singular. Just as you would write, "That thing is missing," so you would write "Something is missing." The words *one, each, either,* and *neither* can be tricky because they are often followed by a prepositional phrase that contains a plural noun. The verb should still be singular.

One of my friends is a great cook.

Each of us wants to cook as well as he does.

Remember that a compound subject joined with *and* needs a plural verb, and a compound subject joined with *or* needs a verb that matches the last subject.

Anything and everything taste terrific in his meals.
No one or nothing keeps him from making a wonderful meal.

Singular

someone
somebody
something

anyone
anybody
anything

no one
nobody
nothing

everyone
everybody
everything

one
each
either
neither

"Everybody needs somebody to love."
—Solomon Burke

Say It

Read the following word groups aloud, emphasizing the words in *italics.*

1. No one *is* / Nobody *has* / Nothing *does*
2. Everyone *is* / Everybody *has* / Everything *does*
3. One of my friends *is* / Each of my friends *has* / Either of my friends *does*

Vocabulary

indefinite pronoun
a special type of pronoun that does not refer to a specific person or thing

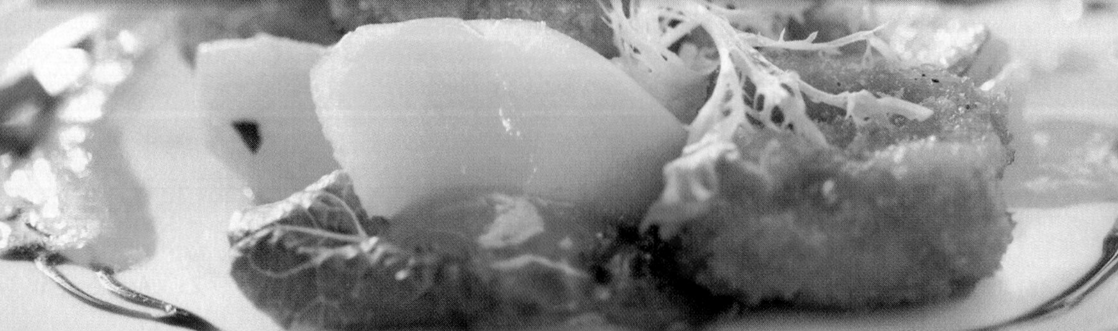
Lew Robertson/Corbis Yellow/Corbis

Correcting Indefinite Pronoun Agreement I

Write In each sentence below, write the correct form of the verb in parentheses. (Do not change the tense.)

1. Everyone completes an application. (complete)
2. Somebody has to get the job. (have)
3. Each of the jobs is available. (are)
4. Neither of the applicants is qualified. (are)
5. Either of the prospects hopes to be trained. (hope)
6. Nobody wants to go home empty-handed. (want)
7. Everybody has bills to pay. (have)
8. Someone or something has to give. (have)
9. Either of the positions pays well. (pay)
10. One of my friends waits for word on the job. (wait)

Write Write sentences using each indefinite pronoun as a subject. Choose present tense verbs and check subject-verb agreement. Answers will vary.

1. Someone ______________________________

____

2. Nothing ______________________________

____

3. Neither ______________________________

____

4. Everyone ______________________________

____

5. Each ______________________________

____

6. Anybody ______________________________

____

Agreement with Other Indefinite Pronouns

Other indefinite pronouns are always plural, or have a singular or plural form, depending on how they are used.

Plural Indefinite Pronouns

Plural indefinite pronouns take plural verbs:

Many of us follow classical music.
Several are big fans.

Plural
- both
- few
- many
- several

Singular or Plural Indefinite Pronouns

Some indefinite pronouns or quantity words are singular or plural. If the object of the preposition in the phrase following the pronoun is singular, the pronoun takes a singular verb; if the object is plural, the pronoun takes a plural verb.

Singular or Plural
- all
- any
- half
- part
- most
- none
- some

Most of the song thrills us.
Most of the songs thrill us.

Notice the shift in meaning, depending on the prepositional phrase. "Most of the song" means that one song is mostly thrilling. "Most of the songs" means that all but a few of many songs are thrilling. Here's another startling difference.

Half of the concert features Tchaikovsky.
Half of the concerts feature Tchaikovsky.

In the first example, half of one concert features the Russian master. In the second, half of a number of concerts features Tchaikovsky's music. What a difference one *s* can make!

Speaking & Listening

The "Say It" activity below will help you become familiar with subject-verb agreement patterns with indefinite pronouns.

Say It

Read the following word groups aloud, emphasizing the words in *italics.*

1. Both *are* / Few *have* / Many *do* / Several *were*
2. All of the piece *is* / Any of the pieces *are* / Half of the piece *does*
3. Part of the song *is* / Most of the songs *are* / None of the instruments *are* / Part of the instrument *is*

Correcting Indefinite Pronoun Agreement II

Write In each sentence below, write the correct forms of the verb in parentheses. (Do not change the tense.) See also page 314.

Speaking & Listening

After completing the sentences in the first exercise, say them aloud, emphasizing the underlined verbs.

1. Several __are__ attending, but all of us __are__ listening. (are)
2. All of the songs __are__ dramatic, but all of the drama __is__ intentional. (is)
3. Some of my friends __have__ the music on MP3, and some of my player __has__ the selections. (have)
4. Everyone __likes__ Tchaikovsky, but few __like__ only him. (likes)
5. One of my friends __listens__ to classical radio; several __listen__ to MP3's. (listen)
6. Half of the album __features__ symphonies, and half of the symphonies __feature__ brass fanfares. (feature)
7. Most of us __read__ about music, and some of us __read__ music, too. (read)
8. Of the music fans, several __are__ hard core, but none of them __is__ a composer. (is)
9. One of my friends __plays__ trombone, and some of my friends __play__ piano. (play)
10. Few __have__ played in an orchestra, but one of us __has__ played in a band. (has)

Write Write sentences using each indefinite pronoun as a subject. Choose present tense verbs and check subject-verb agreement. Answers will vary.

1. Part __________
2. Most __________
3. Few __________
4. Several __________
5. Both __________
6. All __________

Learning Outcome

Practice pronoun-antecedent agreement.

LO5 Pronoun-Antecedent Agreement

A pronoun must agree in **person**, **number**, and **gender** with its **antecedent**. (The antecedent is the word the pronoun replaces.)

The woman brought her briefcase but forgot her computer.

antecedent (third person singular feminine) **+ pronoun** (third person singular feminine) **= agreement**

Quick Guide

	Singular	Plural
First Person:	I, me (my, mine)	we, us (our, ours)
Second Person:	you (your, yours)	you (your, yours)
Third Person:		
masculine	he, him (his)	they, them (their, theirs)
feminine	she, her (her, hers)	they, them (their, theirs)
neuter	it (its)	they, them (their, theirs)

Two or More Antecedents

When two or more antecedents are joined by *and*, the pronoun should be plural.

Kali and Teri filled their baskets with eggs.

When two or more singular antecedents are joined by *or, nor,* or *but also,* the pronoun or pronouns should be singular.

Ada Summer/Fancy/Corbis

Kali or Teri filled her basket with eggs.

Not only Kali but also Teri filled her basket with eggs.

Note: Avoid sexism when choosing pronouns that agree in number.

Sexist: Each child should bring his basket.

Correct: Each child should bring her or his basket.

Correct: Children should bring their baskets.

Workplace

In the workplace, it is important that you avoid sexist language, using masculine pronouns to refer to an anticedent that may be masculine or feminine. Either use alternate pronouns, such as "him or her" or make the antecedent plural and use a plural pronoun.

Vocabulary

person
the person speaking (first person—*I, we*), the person being spoken to (second person—*you*), or the person being spoken about (third person—*he, she, it, they*)

number
singular or plural

gender
masculine, feminine, neuter, or indefinite

antecedent
the noun (or pronoun) that a pronoun refers to or replaces

Correcting Pronoun-Antecedent Agreement

Write In each sentence below, write the pronoun that agrees with the underlined word.

1. Ted has written a patriotic poem and ___he___ will read ___his___ poem at the Fourth of July festival.
2. Shandra and Shelli will bring ___their___ lawn chairs to the fireworks display.
3. Either John or Grace will play ___his___ or ___her___ favorite marches over the sound system.
4. Not only John but also Dave plays trombone and will bring ___his___ instrument to play with the band.
5. Each person should bring ___his___ or ___her___ own flag.
6. Mayor Jenny White or Congressperson Mark Russell will give the invocation, and then ___she___ or ___he___ will introduce the main speaker.
7. Rick and Linda will sing ___their___ rendition of the national anthem.
8. Acrobats will stroll through the park on ___their___ ten-foot-tall stilts.
9. Each acrobat will have to keep ___his___ or ___her___ balance on uneven ground among running children.
10. Ducks and ducklings in the lake will have to make ___their___ way to quieter waters when the fireworks begin.

Revise Rewrite each of the following sentences to avoid sexism. Answers will vary.

1. Every acrobat should check his equipment.

____

____

2. Each acrobat must keep her balance.

____

____

3. One of the acrobats left his stilts at the park.

____

____

Insight

Different languages treat gender differently. For example, Romance languages have masculine and feminine forms for nonliving things. In English, gender is reserved for people and animals.

Learning Outcome

Correct other pronoun problems.

LO6 Other Pronoun Problems

Missing Antecedent

If no clear antecedent is provided, the reader doesn't know what or whom the pronoun refers to.

Confusing: In Illinois, they claim Lincoln as their own.
(Who does "they" refer to?)
Clear: In Illinois, the citizens claim Lincoln as their own.

Vague Pronoun

If the pronoun could refer to two or more words, the passage is **ambiguous**.

Indefinite: Sheila told her daughter to use her new tennis racket.
(To whom does the pronoun "her" refer, Sheila or her daughter?)
Clumsy: Sheila told her daughter to use Sheila's new tennis racket.
Clear: Sheila lent her new tennis racket to her daughter.

Double Subject

If a pronoun is used right after the subject, an error called a double subject occurs.

Incorrect: Your father, he is good at poker.
Correct: Your father is good at poker

Insight

Use *my* before the thing possessed and use *mine* afterward: *my cat,* but *that cat is mine.* Do the same with *our/ours, your/yours,* and *her/hers.*

Incorrect Case

Personal pronouns can function as subjects, objects, or possessives. If the wrong case is used, an error occurs.

Incorrect: Them are funny videos.
Correct: They are funny videos.

The list below tells you which pronouns to use in each case.

Subject	Object	Possessive
I	me	my, mine
we	us	our, ours
you	you	your, yours
he	him	his
she	her	her, hers
it	it	its
they	them	their, theirs

Vocabulary

ambiguous
unclear, confusing

Correcting Other Pronoun Problems

Write In each blank below, write the correct pronoun from the choices in parentheses.

1. ___I___ (I, me, my, mine) need to help ___you___ (you, your, yours) with the taxes.

2. ___You___ (you, your, yours) should help ___her___ (she, her, hers) and see what ___she___ (she, her, hers) needs.

3. ___He___ (he, him, his) can show ___me___ (I, me, my, mine) that account of ___yours___ (you, your, yours).

4. ___You___ (you, your, yours) gave ___your___ (you, your, yours) permission for ___me___ (I, me, my, mine) to see.

5. ___We___ (we, us, our, ours) asked ___our___ (we, us, our, ours) accountant to help ___us___ (we, us, our, ours).

Revise Rewrite each sentence below, correcting the pronoun problems.

1. Bob and Josh took his assignment to class.

   Answers will vary.

2. Lupita needed to visit with Kelly, but she had no time.

3. Before climbing in, it broke.

4. They say that a cure for cancer is coming.

5. Trina and Lois, they bought frozen custard.

6. Carl asked Tim to cook his lunch.

Learning Outcome

Check agreement in a real-world context.

LO7 Real-World Application

Correct In the letter below, correct the agreement errors. Use the correction marks to the left.

Correction Marks

- delete
- capitalize
- lowercase
- insert
- add comma
- add question mark
- add word
- add period
- spelling
- switch

Send | Attach | Fonts | Colors | Save As Draft

From: Rodell Williams

To: Jean Leuinski

Subject: Thank You for You Recommendation

Hi, Ms. Leuinski:

Thank ~~your~~ [you] for recommending me for the position of Research Analyst at Bismark Laboratories. During the interview last Monday, Dr. Jason Lemark said that ~~she~~ [he] had received your letter and had talked with you by phone. On both occasions, ~~him~~ [he] noted, you described ~~mine~~ [my] work as "well-researched, meticulous, and professional." I deeply ~~appreciates~~ [appreciate] your comments and ~~you~~ [your] trust.

The outcome of the application process could not be more positive. Dr. Lemark ~~are~~ [is] offering not just one job, but two! The first position is the one that I applied for in Bismark's San Diego office. The second position ~~have~~ [has] more responsibility and higher pay, but ~~they~~ [it] is in the company's Houston office.

Thanks again for your strong recommendation, Ms. Leuinski! Your positive words clearly affected the decision made by Dr. Lemark and the Research and Development Department. You ~~has~~ [have] my deepest gratitude.

Best wishes,

Rodell

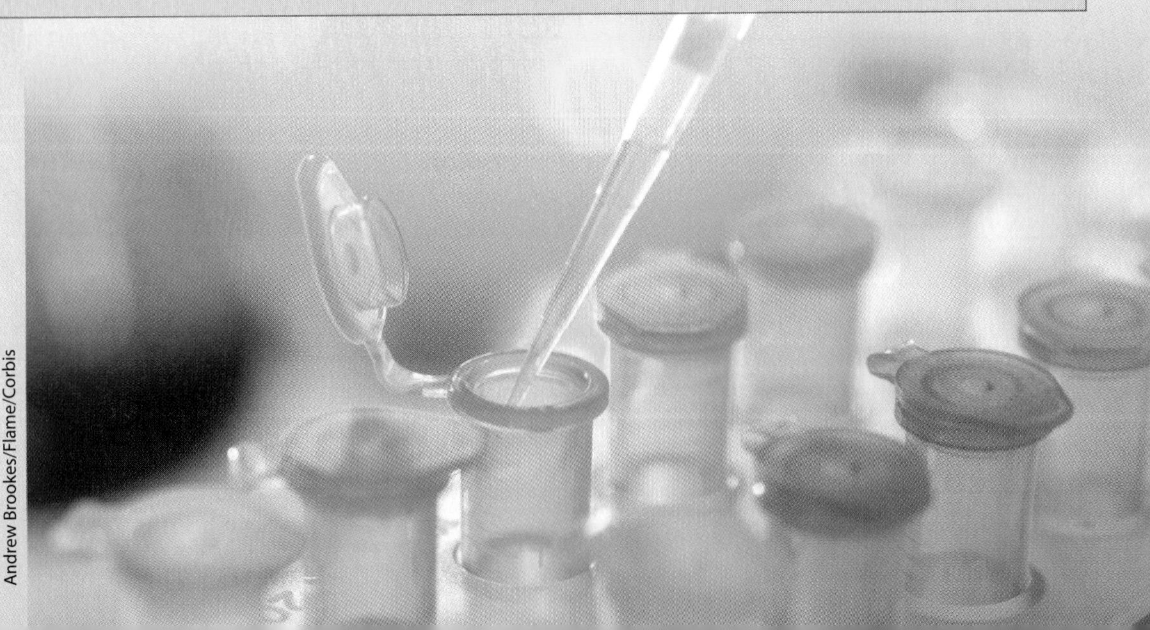

Andrew Brookes/Flame/Corbis

"The fragments of the world seek each other so that the world may come into being."
—Pierre Teilhard de Chardin

Photography by Tyler Bell

Sentence Fragments

Once upon a time, someone spent days carving letters the size of a man's head into a solid block of stone. What message would be important enough to inscribe in that way? A couple thousand years later, we don't know. All that remains is a fragment of the stone, and of the meaning.

Sometimes in writing, sentences get broken into fragments as well. The subject gets knocked away, or the verb drops out, or some other important part goes missing. The reader then has to puzzle out the meaning—or just skips it entirely.

This chapter focuses on sentence fragments, on recognizing them and repairing them. The exercises here will help you to put the pieces back together.

Learning Outcomes

LO1 Correct common fragments.

LO2 Correct tricky fragments.

LO3 Check for fragments in a real-world context.

What do you think?

Read the quotation above. Explain why the fragments of a sentence might "seek each other."

Answers will vary.

Learning Outcome

Correct common fragments.

LO1 Common Fragments

In spoken communication and informal writing, sentence fragments are occasionally used and understood. In formal writing, fragments should be avoided.

Missing Parts

A sentence requires a subject and a predicate. If one or the other or both are missing, the sentence is a **fragment**. Such fragments can be fixed by supplying the missing part.

Fragment:	Went to the concert.
Fragment + Subject:	We went to the concert.
Fragment:	Everyone from Westville Community College.
Fragment + Predicate:	Everyone from Westville Community College may participate.
Fragment:	For the sake of student safety.
Fragment + Subject and Predicate:	The president set up a curfew for the sake of student safety.

Incomplete Thoughts

A sentence also must express a complete thought. Some fragments have a subject and a verb but do not express a complete thought. These fragments can be corrected by providing words that complete the thought.

Fragment:	The concert will include.
Completing Thought:	The concert will include an amazing light show.
Fragment:	If we arrive in time.
Completing Thought:	If we arrive in time, we'll get front-row seats.
Fragment:	That opened the concert.
Completing Thought:	I liked the band that opened the concert.

Say It

Answers will vary.

Read these fragments aloud. Then read each one again, but this time supply the necessary words to form a complete thought.

1. The student union building.
2. Where you can buy used books.
3. Walked to class every morning.
4. When the instructor is sick.
5. The cop was.

Vocabulary

fragment
a group of words that is missing a subject or a predicate (or both) or that does not express a complete thought

Correct Add words to correct each fragment below. Write the complete sentence on the lines provided. Answers will vary.

1. Went to the office. ______________________

2. The photographer, standing at the door. ______________________

3. Will debate the pros and cons of tanning. ______________________

4. Native Americans. ______________________

5. Is one of the benefits of art class. ______________________

Correct The following paragraph contains numerous fragments. Either add what is missing or combine fragments with other sentences to make them complete. Use the correction marks shown to the right. Answers will vary.

Some people are good at memorizing facts. They piece things together. Like the inside of a jigsaw puzzle. Slowly build a big picture. Others are better at grasping overall shapes. Then filling in the middle with facts. Either way, have to finish the puzzle.

Correction Marks

- delete
- capitalize
- lowercase
- insert
- add comma
- add question mark
- add word
- add period
- spelling
- switch

Correct On your own paper or orally, correct the following fragments by supplying the missing parts. Use your imagination. Answers will vary.

1. In the newspaper.
2. We bought.
3. The purpose of sociology class.
4. Somewhere above the clouds tonight.
5. Was the reason.

Learning Outcome

Correct tricky fragments.

LO2 Tricky Fragments

Some fragments are more difficult to find and correct. They creep into our writing because they are often part of the way we communicate in our speaking.

Absolute Phrases

An **absolute phrase** looks like a sentence that is missing its helping verb. An absolute phrase can be made into a sentence by adding the helping verb or by connecting the phrase to a complete sentence.

Absolute Phrase (Fragment): Our legs trembling from the hike.

Absolute Phrase + Helping Verb: Our legs were trembling from the hike.

Absolute Phrase + Complete Sentence: We collapsed on the couch, our legs trembling from the hike.

Informal Fragments

Fragments that are commonly used in speech should be eliminated from formal writing. Avoid the following types of fragments unless you are writing dialogue.

Interjections: Hey! Yeah!

Exclamations: What a nuisance! How fun!

Greetings: Hi, everybody. Good afternoon.

Questions: How come? Why not? What?

Answers: About three or four. As soon as possible.

Note: Sentences that begin with *here* or *there* have a **delayed subject**, which appears after the verb. Other sentences (commands) have an **implied subject** (*you*). Such sentences are not fragments.

Delayed Subject: Here are some crazy fans wearing wild hats.

Implied Subject: Tackle him! Bring him down!

Vocabulary

absolute phrase
a group of words with a noun and a participle (a word ending in *ing* or *ed*) and the words that modify them

delayed subject
a subject that appears after the verb, as in a sentence that begins with *here* or *there* or a sentence that asks a question

implied subject
the word *you*, assumed to begin command sentences

Say It

Answers will vary.

Read these fragments aloud. Then read each one again, but this time supply the necessary words to form a complete thought.

1. Are three types of laptop computers.
2. Our instructor explaining the assignment.
3. About three in the morning.
4. Is my favorite Web site.
5. My friend working at a half-priced disk shop.

Complete Rewrite each tricky fragment below, making it a sentence.

1. Our boisterous behavior announcing our approach.
   Answers will vary.
2. A tidy hedge surrounding the trimmed lawn.
3. The owner's gaze tracking us from the front porch.
4. His dogs barking loudly from the backyard.
5. Our welcome feeling less likely with each step.

Delete The following paragraph contains a number of informal fragments. Identify and delete each one. Reread the paragraph and listen for the difference.

~~Wow!~~ It's amazing what archaeologists can discover from bones. Did you know that Cro-Magnon (our ancestors) and Neanderthal tribes sometimes lived side by side? ~~Sure did!~~ In other places, when climate change drove our ancestors south, Neanderthals took their place. Neanderthals were tough and had stronger arms and hands than Cro-Magnons had. Neanderthal brains were bigger, too. ~~What?~~ So why aren't there any Neanderthals around now? ~~Huh?~~ Well, although Neanderthal tribes used spears and stone tools, our ancestors were much better toolmakers. ~~Yeah!~~ Also, Neanderthals mainly ate big animals, while Cro-Magnon ate anything from fish to pigs to roots and berries. So in the long run, Cro-Magnon hominids prospered while Neanderthal tribes dwindled away.

Learning Outcome

Check for fragments in a real-world context.

Correction Marks

 delete

 capitalize

 lowercase

 insert

 add comma

 add question mark

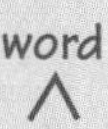 add word

 add period

 spelling

 switch

LO3 Real-World Application

Correct Correct any sentence fragments in the following business memo.

Example answers:

Slovik Manufacturing

Date: August 8, 2011

To: Jerome James, Personnel Director

From: Ike Harris, Graphic Arts Director

Subject: Promotion of Mona Veal from Intern to Full-Time Graphic Artist

For the past five months, Mona Veal has worked as an intern in our Marketing Department. I recommend that she be offered a position as a full-time designer. Here are the two main reasons behind this recommendation.

1. Mona has shown the traits that Slovik Manufacturing values in a graphic designer. She is creative, dependable, and easy to work with.
2. Presently, we have two full-time graphic designers and one intern. While this group has worked well, the full-time designers have averaged 3.5 hours of overtime per week. Given this fact, our new contract with Lee-Stamp Industries will require more help, including at least one additional designer.

If you approve this recommendation, please initial below and return this memo.

Yes, I approve the recommendation to offer Mona Veal a full-time position. _______

Attachment: Evaluation report of Mona Veal

cc: Elizabeth Zoe
Mark Moon

Answer Team up with a classmate to discuss answers to the following questions about sentence fragments.

1. What is a sentence fragment?
2. What is a delayed subject?
3. What is an absolute phrase?
4. What are at least two ways to correct a sentence fragment?

"If we can connect in some tiny way with a human that doesn't agree with us, then maybe we won't blow up the planet."
—Nancy White

Photograph by Erin O'Connor

25 Comma Splices, Run-Ons, and Ramblers

Learning Outcomes

LO1 Correct comma splices.

LO2 Correct run-on sentences.

LO3 Correct rambling sentences.

LO4 Correct comma splices and run-ons in a real-world context.

Sometimes people fail to connect. Two sides try to come together, but they can't communicate.

Sometimes sentences have the same trouble. Comma splices and run-ons occur when sentences are joined in ways that just don't connect. And rambling sentences result when two many ideas get crammed in between the first capital letter and the period. This chapter focuses on fixing such problems.

What do you think?

In what positive way could the protestors and the police in the photo above connect?

Answers will vary.

Learning Outcome

Correct comma splices.

LO1 Comma Splices

Comma splices occur when two sentences are connected with only a comma. A comma splice can be fixed by adding a coordinating conjunction (*and, but, or, nor, for, so,* or *yet*) or a subordinating conjunction (*while, after, when,* and so on). The two sentences could also be joined by a semicolon (;) or separated by a period.

Comma Splice: The Eiffel Tower was a main attraction at the Paris Exposition, the Ferris wheel was its equivalent at the Chicago Exposition.

Corrected by adding a coordinating conjunction:	The Eiffel Tower was a main attraction at the Paris Exposition, and the Ferris wheel was its equivalent at the Chicago Exposition.
Corrected by adding a subordinating conjunction:	While the Eiffel Tower was a main attraction at the Paris Exposition, the Ferris wheel was its equivalent at the Chicago Exposition.
Corrected by replacing the comma with a semicolon:	The Eiffel Tower was a main attraction at the Paris Exposition; the Ferris wheel was its equivalent at the Chicago Exposition.

Comma Splice: An engineer named George Washington Gale Ferris planned the first Ferris wheel, many people thought he was crazy.

Corrected by adding a coordinating conjunction:	An engineer named George Washington Gale Ferris planned the first Ferris wheel, but many people thought he was crazy.
Corrected by adding a subordinating conjunction:	When an engineer named George Washington Gale Ferris planned the first Ferris wheel, many people thought he was crazy.
Corrected by replacing the comma with a period:	An engineer named George Washington Gale Ferris planned the first Ferris wheel. Many people thought he was crazy.

Insight

A comma is not strong enough to join sentences without a conjunction. A semicolon can join two closely related sentences. A period or question mark can separate two sentences.

Vocabulary

comma splice
a sentence error that occurs when two sentences are connected with only a comma

Correcting Comma Splices

Practice A Correct the following comma splices by adding a coordinating conjunction *(and, but, yet, or, nor, for, so)*, adding a subordinating conjunction (*when, while, because,* and so on), or replacing the comma with a semicolon or period. Use the approach that makes the sentence read most smoothly. (The first one has been done for you.)

1. We set out for a morning hike, [but] it was raining.
2. The weather cleared by the afternoon, [so] we hit the trail.
3. Both Jill and I were expecting wonderful scenery, [and] we were not disappointed.
4. The view of the valley was spectacular, [for] it was like a portrait.
5. We snacked on granola bars and apples, [and] we enjoyed the view.
6. Then we strapped on our backpacks, [for] the final leg of the hike awaited us.
7. The trail became rockier, [so (and)] we had to watch our step.
8. We reached the end of our hike, [for] the sun was setting.
9. We're on the lookout for a new trail, [but (yet)] it will be tough to beat this one.
10. We're done with our physical activities, [so (and, for)] it is time to watch a movie.

Practice B Correct any comma splices in the following e-mail message.

Send | Attach | Fonts | Colors | Save As Draft

To: HR Staff

Subject: Agenda for Conference

Example answers:

HR Staff:

At 8:15 a.m. on Friday, we will meet in Conference Room B. Breakfast will be provided.

We will discuss our strategy for the show, and we will then set up our materials at show table 15. The busiest crowd flow is expected from 10 a.m. to 11 a.m. The second busiest should be from 1 p.m. to 3 p.m.

Please bring plenty of energy and enthusiasm to the show, and be ready to discuss the strengths of our products.

Thanks,

Phil Dawson

Learning Outcome

Correct run-on sentences.

LO2 Run-On Sentences

A **run-on sentence** occurs when two sentences are joined without punctuation or a connecting word. A run-on can be corrected by adding a comma and a conjunction or by inserting a semicolon or period between the two sentences.

Run-On: Horace Wilson taught in Tokyo in 1872 he introduced the Japanese to baseball.

Corrected by adding a comma and coordinating conjunction:	Horace Wilson taught in Tokyo in 1872, and he introduced the Japanese to baseball.
Corrected by adding a subordinating conjunction and a comma:	While Horace Wilson taught in Tokyo in 1872, he introduced the Japanese to baseball.
Corrected by inserting a semicolon:	Horace Wilson taught in Tokyo in 1872; he introduced the Japanese to baseball.

Run-On: The first team in Japan was formed in 1878 no one knew how popular the sport would become.

Corrected by adding a comma and a coordinating conjunction:	The first team in Japan was formed in 1878, yet no one knew how popular the sport would become.
Corrected by adding a subordinating conjunction and a comma:	When the first team in Japan was formed in 1878, no one knew how popular the sport would become.
Corrected by inserting a period:	The first team in Japan was formed in 1878. No one knew how popular the sport would become.

Traits

Here's an additional way to correct a run-on sentence: Turn one of the sentences into a phrase or series of phrases; then combine it with the other sentence.

The first team in Japan was formed in 1878 without a thought about how popular the sport would become.

Vocabulary

run-on sentence
a sentence error that occurs when two sentences are joined without punctuation or a connecting word

Correcting Run-On Sentences

Correct Correct the following run-on sentences. Use the approach that makes the sentence read most smoothly. The first one has been done for you.

1. In 1767 English scientist Joseph Priestley discovered a way to infuse water with carbon dioxide. This invention led to carbonated water.
2. Carbonated water is one of the main components of soft drinks. It gives soft drinks the fizz and bubbles we enjoy.
3. The first soft drinks in America were dispensed out of soda fountains. They were most often found at drug stores and ice-cream parlors.
4. Interestingly, soda was sold at drug stores because it promised healing properties.
5. Most of the formulas for American soft drinks were invented by pharmacists. The idea was to create nonalcoholic alternatives to traditional medicines.
6. The first carbonated drink bottles could not keep bubbles from escaping, so it was more popular to buy a soda from a soda fountain.
7. A successful method of keeping bubbles in a bottle was not invented until 1892. It was called a crowned bottle cap.
8. The first diet soda to be sold was known as "No-Cal Beverage." In 1959 the first diet cola hit the stores.

Rewrite Rewrite the following paragraph, correcting any run-on sentences that you find.

Arbor Day is an undervalued holiday in America. On this holiday, people are encouraged to plant trees it is celebrated on the fourth Friday of April. It was created by J. Sterling Morton he was President Grover Cleveland's Secretary of Agriculture. The holiday is now observed in a number of other countries.

Example rewrite:

Arbor Day is an undervalued holiday in America. On this holiday, people are encouraged to plant trees. It is celebrated on the fourth Friday of April. It was created by J. Sterling Morton, President Grover Cleveland's Secretary of Agriculture. The holiday is now observed in a number of other countries.

Learning Outcome

Correct rambling sentences.

LO3 Rambling Sentences

A **rambling sentence** occurs when a long series of separate ideas are connected by one *and, but,* or *so* after another. The result is an unfocused sentence that goes on and on. To correct a rambling sentence, break it into smaller units, adding and cutting words as needed.

Rambling: When we signed up for the two-on-two tournament, I had no thoughts about winning, but then my brother started talking about spending his prize money and he asked me how I would spend my share so we were counting on winning when we really had little chance and as it turned out, we lost in the second round.

Corrected: When we signed up for the two-on-two tournament, I had no thoughts about winning. Then my brother started talking about spending the prize money. He even asked me how I would spend my share. Soon, we were counting on winning when we really had little chance. As it turned out, we lost in the second round.

Say It

Read the following rambling sentences aloud. Afterward, circle all of the connecting words (*and, but, so*), and be prepared to suggest different ways to break each rambling idea into more manageable units.

1. I enjoyed touring the hospital and I would enjoy joining the nursing staff and I believe that my prior work experience will be an asset but I also know that I have a lot more to learn.
2. The electronics store claims to offer "one-stop shopping" and they can take care of all of a customer's computer needs and they have a fully trained staff to answer questions and solve problems so there is really no need to go anywhere else.

Vocabulary

rambling sentence
a sentence error that occurs when a long series of separate ideas are connected by one *and, but,* or *so* after another

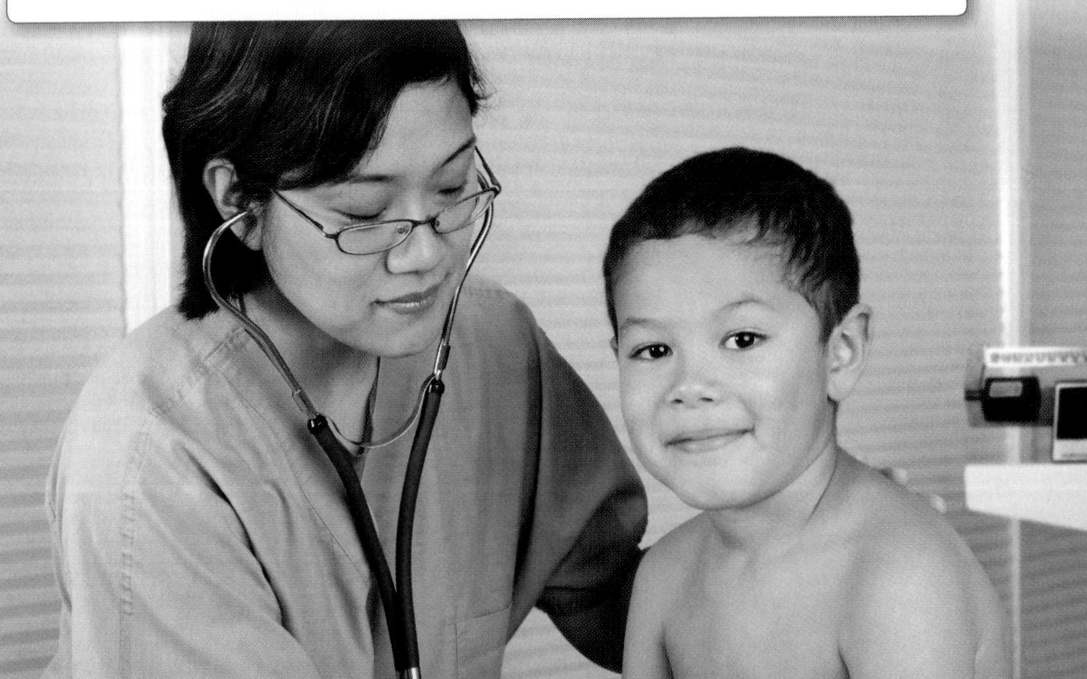

Correcting Rambling Sentences

Correct Correct the following rambling sentences by dividing them into separate sentences. Afterward, share your corrections with a classmate. Did you change each rambling sentence in the same way? Answers will vary.

1. The dancer entered gracefully onto the stage and she twirled around twice and then tiptoed to the front of the stage and the crowd applauded.

___

___

___

2. I went to the movies last night and when I got to the theater, I had to wait in a superslow line and when I finally got to the front, the show I wanted to see was sold out.

___

___

___

3. I like to listen to music everywhere but I especially like to rock out in my car so I scream and dance and I don't care if anyone sees me through the windows.

___

___

___

Answer Answer the following questions about rambling sentences.

1. How can you recognize a rambling sentence?

Answers will vary.

___

___

2. Why is a rambling sentence a problem?

___

___

___

3. How can you correct one?

___

___

___

Extend

Share your corrections with a classmate. Did you change each rambling sentence in the same way?

Learning Outcome

Correct comma splices and run-ons in a real-world context.

LO4 Real-World Application

Correct Correct any comma splices or run-on sentences in the following e-mail message.

Send | Attach | Fonts | Colors | Save As Draft

To: StaplePro Employees

Subject: Agenda for Personnel Meeting

Example corrections:

Good morning:

This Saturday, from 8:00 a.m. to noon, StaplePro will conduct its quarterly inventory check. The warehouse supervisors and I will lead the inventory teams. Please provide any assistance the inventory teams require of you.

After this check, the paper inventory forms will be discontinued, and all shipments in and out must be inventoried using the hand scanners. There should be fewer errors when using StaplePro's electronic system. The supervisors will schedule training for their employees who are unfamiliar with the scanners.

Thanks for your cooperation. StaplePro's new system will help us store and ship staples more effectively and provide better service for our customers.

Best regards,

Kevin Dooley

Warehouse Director

Reflect Reflect on what you have learned about comma splices and run-on sentences by answering the following questions.

1. What is the difference between a comma splice and a run-on sentence?

   Answers will vary.

2. How can you correct comma splices and run-on sentences? (Name at least three ways.)

3. What are three common coordinating conjunctions that you can use to connect two sentences?

"I say that what we really need is a car that can be shot when it breaks down.'"

—Russell Baker

Tim Pannell/Corbis Yellow/Corbis

26 Additional Sentence Problems

Cars are great when they go, but when a car breaks down, it is a huge headache. There's going to be a look under the hood, a bit of scrabbling beneath the thing, maybe a push, maybe a jack, and probably a tow truck and a big bill.

Sentences also are great until they break down. But you don't have to be a skilled mechanic to fix sentences. This chapter outlines a few common sentence problems and shows how to fix them. You'll be on your way in no time!

Learning Outcomes

LO1 Correct misplaced and dangling modifiers.

LO2 Correct shifts in sentence construction.

LO3 Correct sentence problems in a real-world context.

What do you think?

Which can carry you farther, a car or a sentence?

Answers will vary.

Learning Outcome

Correct misplaced and dangling modifiers.

Insight

Avoid placing any adverb modifiers between a verb and its direct object.

Misplaced: *I will throw quickly the ball.*

Corrected: *I will quickly throw the ball.*

Also, do not separate two-word verbs with an adverb modifier.

Misplaced: *Please take immediately out the trash.*

Corrected: *Please immediately take out the trash.*

Vocabulary

dangling modifier
a modifying word, phrase, or clause that appears to modify the wrong word or a word that isn't in the sentence

illogical
without logic; senseless, false, or untrue

misplaced modifier
a modifying word, phrase, or clause that has been placed incorrectly in a sentence, often creating an amusing or illogical idea

LO1 Misplaced / Dangling Modifiers

Dangling Modifiers

A modifier is a word, phrase, or clause that functions as an adjective or adverb. When the modifier does not clearly modify another word in the sentence, it is called a **dangling modifier**. This error can be corrected by inserting the missing word and/or rewriting the sentence.

Dangling Modifier: After strapping the toy cowboy to his back, my cat stalked sullenly around the house. *(The cat could strap the toy cowboy to his own back?)*

Corrected: After I strapped the toy cowboy to his back, my cat stalked sullenly around the house.

Dangling Modifier: Trying to get the cowboy off, the bowl got knocked off the shelf. *(The bowl was trying to get the cowboy off?)*

Corrected: Trying to get the cowboy off, the cat knocked the bowl off the shelf.

Misplaced Modifiers

When a modifier is placed beside a word that it does not modify, the modifier is misplaced and often results in an amusing or **illogical** statement. A **misplaced modifier** can be corrected by moving it next to the word that it modifies.

Misplaced Modifier: My cat was diagnosed by the vet with fleas. *(The vet has fleas?)*

Corrected: The vet diagnosed my cat with fleas.

Misplaced Modifier: The vet gave a pill to my cat tasting like fish. *(The cat tastes like fish?)*

Corrected: The vet gave my cat a pill tasting like fish.

Say It

Read the following sentences aloud, noting the dangling or misplaced modifier in each one. Then tell a classmate how you would correct each error.

1. The climbing tower on the front porch is the place to find my cat called Feline Paradise.
2. You will often see him climbing up the shag-carpeted towers and ramps with sharp claws.
3. Though just three months old, I have taught my cat his name.
4. After tearing up the couch, I decided to get my cat a scratching post.
5. I have worked to teach my cat to beg for three weeks.

Correcting Dangling and Misplaced Modifiers

Rewrite Rewrite each of the sentences below, correcting the misplaced and dangling modifiers. Sample answers:

1. I bought a hound dog for my brother named Rover.
   I bought a hound dog named Rover for my brother.
2. The doctor diagnosed me and referred me to a specialist with scoliosis.
   The doctor diagnosed me with scoliosis and referred me to a specialist.
3. The man was reported murdered by the coroner.
   The coroner reported that the man was murdered.
4. Please present the recommendation that is attached to Mrs. Burble.
   Please present the attached recommendation to Mrs. Burble.
5. Jack drove me to our home in a Chevy.
   Jack drove me in a Chevy to our home.
6. I couldn't believe my brother would hire a disco DJ who hates disco.
   I couldn't believe my brother, who hates disco, would hire a disco DJ.
7. We saw a fox and a vixen on the way to the psychiatrist.
   On the way to the psychiatrist, we saw a fox and a vixen.
8. I gave the secretary my phone number that works in reception.
   I gave the secretary who works in reception my phone number.
9. I found a pair of underwear in the drawer that doesn't belong to me.
   I found a pair of underwear that doesn't belong to me in my drawer.
10. We offer jackets for trendy teens with gold piping.
    We offer jackets with gold piping for trendy teens.

Correct For each sentence, correct the placement of the adverb.

1. Give quickly the report to your boss.
   Quickly give the report to your boss.
2. We will provide immediately an explanation.
   We will immediately provide an explanation.
3. Fill completely out the test sheet.
   Completely fill out the test sheet.

Insight

When a modifier comes at the beginning of the sentence or the end of the sentence, make sure it modifies the word or phrase closest to it. Ask yourself, "Who or what is being described?"

Learning Outcome

Correct shifts in sentence construction.

LO2 Shifts in Sentences

Shift in Person

A **shift in person** is an error that occurs when first, second, and/or third person are improperly mixed in a sentence.

Shift in person: If you exercise and eat right, an individual can lose weight. (The sentence improperly shifts from second person—*you*—to third person—*individual*.)

Corrected: If you exercise and eat right, you can lose weight.

Shift in Tense

A **shift in tense** is an error that occurs when more than one verb tense is improperly used in a sentence. (See pages 354–361 for more about tense.)

Shift in tense: He tried every other option before he agree to do it my way. (The sentence improperly shifts from past tense—*tried*—to present tense—*agree*.)

Corrected: He tried every other option before he agreed to do it my way.

Shift in Voice

A **shift in voice** is an error that occurs when active voice and passive voice are mixed in a sentence.

Shift in voice: When she fixes the radiator, other repairs may be suggested. (The sentence improperly shifts from active voice—*fixes*—to passive voice—*may be suggested*.)

Corrected: When she fixes the radiator, she may suggest other repairs.

Say It

Read the following sentences aloud, paying careful attention to the improper shift each one contains. Then tell a classmate how you would correct each error.

1. David exercises daily and ate well.
2. Marianne goes running each morning and new friends might be met.
3. After you choose an exercise routine, a person should stick to it.
4. Lamar swam every morning and does ten laps.
5. The personal trainer made a schedule for me, and a diet was suggested by her.

Vocabulary

person
first person (*I* or *we*—the person speaking), second person (*you*—the person spoken to), or third person (*he, she, it,* or *they*—the person or thing spoken about)

voice of verb
whether the subject is doing the action of the verb (active voice) or is being acted upon (passive voice) (See page 352.)

shift in person
an error that occurs when first, second, and third person are improperly mixed in a sentence

shift in tense
an error that occurs when more than one verb tense is improperly used in a sentence

shift in voice
an error that occurs when active voice and passive voice are mixed in a sentence

Correcting Improper Shifts in Sentences

Rewrite Rewrite each sentence below, correcting any improper shifts in construction. Sample answers:

1. You should be ready for each class in a person's schedule.
   You should be ready for each class in your schedule.

2. I work for my brother most days and classes are attended by me at night.
   I work for my brother most days and attend classes at night.

3. When you give me a review, can he also give me a raise?
   When you give me a review, can you also give me a raise?

4. As we walked to school, last night's football game was discussed by us.
   As we walked to school, we discussed last night's football game.

5. I hoped to catch the bus until I see it leave.
   I hoped to catch the bus until I saw it leave.

Correct Correct the improper shifts in person, tense, or voice in the following paragraph. Use the correction marks to the right when you make your changes.

Example corrections:

Some people are early adopters, which means they adopt technology ~~is adopted by them~~ when it is new. Other people are technophobes because they ~~you~~ are afraid of technology, period. I am not an early adopter or a technophobe, but I have ~~a person has~~ to see the value in technology before I use it. Technology has to be cheap, intuitive, reliable, and truly helpful before I ~~you~~ start using it. I let others work out the bugs and pay the high prices before I adopt a piece of technology ~~is adopted by me~~. But when I decide it is time to get a new gadget or program, I ~~you~~ buy it and use it until it is worn out. Then I look for something else that is even cheaper and more intuitive, reliable, and helpful, which I ~~is~~ then buy ~~bought by me~~.

Correction Marks

- delete
- capitalize
- lowercase
- insert
- add comma
- add question mark
- add word
- add period
- spelling
- switch

Learning Outcome

Correct sentence problems in a real-world context.

LO3 Real-World Application

Correct Correct any dangling modifiers, misplaced modifiers, or shifts in construction in the following message. Use the correction marks to the left.

Send | Attach | Fonts | Colors | Save As Draft

From: Julia Armstrong

To: Human Resources Staff

Cc: Richard Montgomery

Subject: Monthly Human Resources Staff Meeting with President Smith

Dear HR Team:

Monday, September 12, will be the [first monthly] Human Resources staff meeting with the ~~first monthly~~ president. [You] ~~A person~~ should plan to attend these meetings on the second Monday of each month from 8:30 to 9:30 a.m., and you should go to the Human Resources conference room.

To help make these meetings productive, [you] ~~a staff member~~ can prepare in two ways:

1. You should review and bring any periodic reports that are generated by you—hiring stats, exit interviews, medical or worker's comp claims, and so on. [You] ~~He or she~~ should bring 11 copies and an electronic file of each document.
2. You should bring any questions or concerns. However, if an issue is significant, [you] ~~the person~~ should review it with Richard before you bring it to a monthly meeting.

This monthly meeting is a big commitment of time from everyone [and needs] ~~needing~~ regular attendance. If you can't make the meeting, send an e-mail and attach ~~to~~ [to] Richard a note.

Thanks for your cooperation. If you have questions or suggestions about the meeting, [contact] Richard or [me] ~~I should be contacted by you.~~

Thanks,

Julia

Correction Marks

- delete
- capitalize
- lowercase
- insert
- add comma
- add question mark
- add word
- add period
- spelling
- switch

Rewrite The sentences that follow come from church bulletins and are amusing due to misplaced or dangling modifiers or other sentence problems. Rewrite each sentence to remove these problems. Answers will vary.

1. Remember in prayer the many who are sick of our church and community.

2. For those of you who have children and don't know it, we have a nursery downstairs.

3. The ladies of the church have cast off clothing of every kind. They can be seen in the church basement Saturday.

4. The third verse of "Blessed Assurance" will be sung without musical accomplishment.

Workplace

Journalists and publishers need to be especially careful to avoid mistakes in their writing. But errors in writing reflect badly on all professionals.

Write Write the first draft of a personal narrative (true story) in which you share a time when you misplaced or lost something important to you or to someone else. Here are some tips for adding interest to your story:

- Start right in the middle of the action. Answers will vary.
- Build suspense to keep the reader's interest.
- Use dialogue.
- Use sensory details (what you heard, saw, felt, and so on).

Afterward, exchange your writing with a classmate. Read each other's narrative first for enjoyment and a second time to check it for the sentence errors discussed in this chapter.

Part 6 Word Workshops

"If you want to make an apple pie from scratch, you must first create the universe."

—Carl Sagan

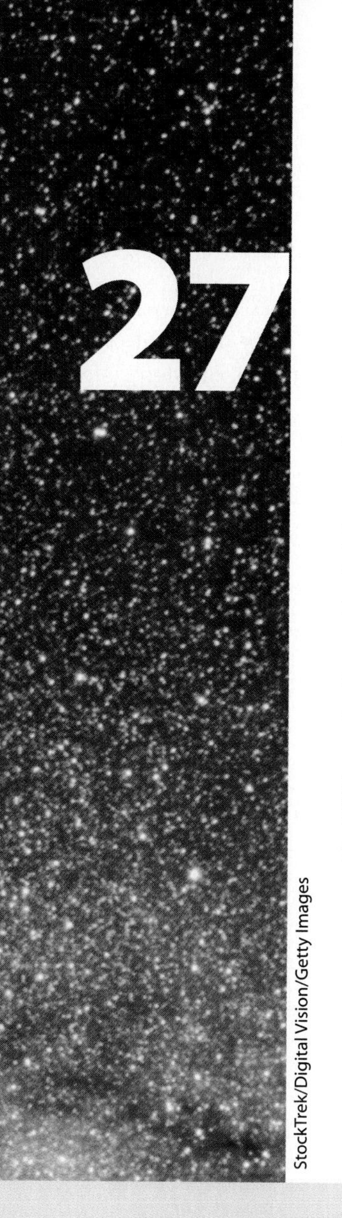

StockTrek/Digital Vision/Getty Images

Noun

Astrophysicists tell us that the universe is made up of two things—matter and energy. Matter is the stuff, and energy is the movement or heat of the stuff.

Grammarians tell us that thoughts are made up of two things—nouns and verbs. Nouns name the stuff, and verbs capture the energy. In that way, the sentence reflects the universe itself. You can't express a complete thought unless you are talking about matter and energy. Each sentence, then, is the basic particle of thought.

This chapter focuses on nouns, which describe not just things you can see—such as people, places, or objects—but also things you can't see—such as love, justice, and democracy. The exercises in this chapter will help you sort out the stuff of thinking.

What do you think?

What is the most beautiful noun? What is the ugliest one? What makes a noun beautiful or ugly?

Answers will vary.

Learning Outcomes

LO1 Understand classes of nouns.

LO2 Use singular and plural nouns.

LO3 Form tricky plurals.

LO4 Use count and noncount nouns.

LO5 Use articles.

LO6 Use other noun markers.

LO7 Use nouns correctly in a real-world context.

Learning Outcome

Understand classes of nouns.

LO1 Classes of Nouns

All nouns are either *common* or *proper*. They can also be *individual* or *collective*, *concrete* or *abstract*.

Common or Proper Nouns

Common nouns name a general person, place, thing, or idea. They are not capitalized as names. **Proper nouns** name a specific person, place, thing, or idea, and they are capitalized as names.

	Common Nouns	Proper Nouns
Person:	politician	Barack Obama
Place:	park	Yellowstone
Thing:	marker	Sharpie
Idea:	religion	Hinduism

Individual or Collective Nouns

Most nouns are **individual**: They refer to one person or thing. Other nouns are **collective**, referring most commonly to a group of people or animals.

	Individual Nouns	Collective Nouns
Person:	secretary	staff
	catcher	team
	student	class
	daughter	family
Animal:	lamb	herd
	locust	swarm
	wolf	pack
	kitten	litter
	goose	gaggle

Concrete or Abstract

If a noun refers to something that can be seen, heard, smelled, tasted, or touched, it is a **concrete noun**. If a noun refers to something that can't be sensed, it is an **abstract noun**. Abstract nouns name ideas, conditions, or feelings.

Concrete Nouns	Abstract Nouns
judge	impartiality
brain	mind
heart	courage
train	transportation

Vocabulary

common noun
noun referring to a general person, place, thing, or idea; not capitalized as a name

proper noun
noun referring to a specific person, place, thing, or idea; capitalized as a name

individual noun
noun referring to one person or thing

collective noun
noun referring to a group of people or animals

concrete noun
noun referring to something that can be sensed

abstract noun
noun referring to an idea, a condition, or a feeling—something that cannot be sensed

Using Different Classes of Nouns

Identify In each sentence below, identify the underlined nouns as common (C) or proper (P).

1. William Faulkner wrote about the death of the Old South.
   P C P
2. His novel *The Unvanquished* tells about the aftermath of the Civil War.
   P C P
3. He chronicles the end of slavery but also of the genteel class in the South.
   C C P
4. His novel *Absalom, Absalom!* describes the creation and end of a plantation.
   P C C

Identify In each sentence below, identify the underlined nouns as individual (I) or collective (CL).

1. Quentin Compson appears often in the collected works of Faulkner.
   I CL
2. The Compson family is the centerpiece of Yoknapatawpha County.
   CL I
3. The novel *The Sound and the Fury* tells of the plight of the Compsons'.
   I CL
4. Benjamin Compson watches a group golf in what was once their farm field.
   I CL

Identify In each sentence below, identify the underlined nouns as concrete (CT) or abstract (A).

1. The Compsons become a symbol of the decline of the South.
   CT A
2. Faulkner depicts the family with compassion and humor.
   CT A A
3. Other novels tell of other denizens of Faulkner's imagination.
   CT A
4. Faulkner won the Pulitzer Prize for his novel *A Fable,* set outside the county.
   CT CT

Learning Outcome

Use singular and plural nouns.

LO2 Singular or Plural

The **number** of a noun indicates whether it is singular or plural. A **singular** noun refers to one person, place, thing, or idea. A **plural** noun refers to more than one person, place, thing or idea. For most words, the plural is formed by adding *s*. For nouns ending in *ch, s, sh, x,* or *z,* add an *es.*

	Most Nouns Add *s*		Nouns Ending in *ch, s, sh, x,* or *z* Add *es*	
	Singular	**Plural**	**Singular**	**Plural**
Person:	sister	sisters	coach	coaches
Place:	park	parks	church	churches
Thing:	spoon	spoons	kiss	kisses
Idea:	solution	solutions	wish	wishes

Same in Both Forms or Usually Plural

Some nouns are the same in both forms, and others are usually plural:

Same in Both Forms		Usually Plural	
Singular	**Plural**	**Plural**	
deer	deer	clothes	series
fish	fish	glasses	shears
moose	moose	pants	shorts
salmon	salmon	proceeds	species
sheep	sheep	savings	tongs
swine	swine	scissors	trousers

Insight

The irregular plurals from Old English are some of the oldest words in our language, so they are used very often. The irregular plurals from Latin are some of the newest, brought in through science. As such, they are used less often.

Irregular Plurals

Irregular plurals are formed by changing the words themselves. That is because the plural form comes from Old English or Latin.

From Old English		From Latin	
Singular	**Plural**	**Singular**	**Plural**
child	children	alumnus	alumni
foot	feet	axis	axes
goose	geese	crisis	crises
man	men	datum	data
mouse	mice	millennium	millennia
person	people	medium	media
tooth	teeth	nucleus	nuclei
woman	women	phenomenon	phenomena

Vocabulary

number
whether a word is singular or plural

singular
referring to one thing

plural
referring to more than one thing

irregular plural
a plural noun formed by changing the word rather than by adding *s.*

Using Singular and Plural Nouns

Identify For each word, fill in the blank with either the singular or plural form, whichever is missing. If the word usually uses the plural form, write an X on the line.

1. crisis — crises
2. x — species
3. child — children
4. automobile — automobiles
5. x — shears
6. tooth — teeth
7. x — clothes
8. deer — deer
9. swine — swine
10. phenomenon — phenomena
11. girl — girls
12. millennium — millennia
13. man — men
14. fish — fish
15. x — pants
16. moose — moose
17. axis — axes
18. boy — boys
19. mouse — mice
20. goose — geese
21. datum — data
22. alumnus — alumni
23. x — savings
24. tree — trees
25. woman — women

Learning Outcome

Form tricky plurals.

LO3 Tricky Plurals

Some plural nouns are more challenging to form. Words ending in *y, f,* or *fe* and certain compound nouns require special consideration.

Nouns Ending in *y*

If a common noun ends in *y* after a consonant, change the *y* to *i* and add *es.* If the noun ends in *y* after a vowel, leave the *y* and add *s*.

y After a Consonant		*y* After a Vowel	
Singular	**Plural**	**Singular**	**Plural**
fly	flies	bay	bays
lady	ladies	key	keys
penny	pennies	toy	toys
story	stories	tray	trays

Nouns Ending in *f* or *fe*

If a common noun ends in *f* or *fe,* change the *f* or *fe* to a *v* and add *es*—unless the *f* sound remains in the plural form. Then just add an *s.*

v Sound in Plural		*f* Sound in Plural	
Singular	**Plural**	**Singular**	**Plural**
calf	calves	belief	beliefs
life	lives	chef	chefs
self	selves	proof	proofs
shelf	shelves	safe	safes

Compound Nouns

A **compound noun** is made up of two or more words that function together as a single noun. Whether the compound is hyphenated or not, make it plural by placing the *s* or *es* on the most important word in the compound.

Important Word First		Important Word Last	
Singular	**Plural**	**Singular**	**Plural**
editor in chief	editors in chief	bird-watcher	bird-watchers
mother-in-law	mothers-in-law	human being	human beings
professor emeritus	professors emeri-tus	test tube	test tubes
secretary of state	secretaries of state	well-wisher	well-wishers

Vocabulary

compound noun
noun made up of two or more words

Forming Tricky Plurals

Form Plurals For each word below, create the correct plural form.

1. day days
2. shelf shelves
3. middle school middle schools
4. pony ponies
5. bay bays
6. life lives
7. chief chiefs
8. loaf loaves
9. tray trays
10. compact car compact cars
11. mother-in-law mothers-in-law
12. ray rays
13. lady ladies
14. carafe carafes
15. stepsister step sisters
16. poof poofs
17. nose tackle nose tackles
18. party parties
19. son-in-law sons-in-law
20. baby babies

Form Plurals In the sentences below, correct the plural errors by circling them and writing the correct forms above.

1. If I give you two pennys (pennies) for your thoughts, will you give me two cents' worths (worth)?
2. Have you read *The Secret Lifes* (Lives) *of Cheves* (Chefs)?
3. The professor emerituses (professors emeritus) are working on two mathematical prooves (proofs).
4. I won't question your believes (beliefs) or insult your wells-wisher (well-wishers).
5. The ladys (ladies) tried to quiet their screaming babys (babies).
6. Time is sure fun when you're having flys (flies).
7. The compacts car (compact cars) are equipped with remote-access keis (keys).
8. I like chicken pattys (patties) but don't like salmons patty (salmon patties).
9. I read about dwarves (dwarfs) and elfs (elves).
10. Stack those books on the shelfs (shelves) above the saves (safes).

Learning Outcome

Use count and noncount nouns.

LO4 Count and Noncount Nouns

Some nouns name things that can be counted, and other nouns name things that cannot. Different rules apply to each type.

Count Nouns

Count nouns name things that can be counted—*pens, people, votes, cats,* and so forth. They can be singular or plural, and they can be preceded by numbers or articles (*a, an,* or *the*).

Singular	Plural
apple	apples
iguana	iguanas
thought	thoughts
room	rooms

Noncount Nouns

Noncount nouns name things that cannot be counted. They are used in singular form, and they can be preceded by *the,* but not by *a* or *an.*

This semester, I'm taking **mathematics** and **biology** as well as **Spanish**.

Substances	Foods	Activities	Science	Languages	Abstractions
wood	water	reading	oxygen	Spanish	experience
cloth	milk	boating	weather	English	harm
ice	wine	smoking	heat	Mandarin	publicity
plastic	sugar	dancing	sunshine	Farsi	advice
wool	rice	swimming	electricity	Greek	happiness
steel	meat	soccer	lightning	Latin	health
aluminum	cheese	hockey	biology	French	joy
metal	flour	photography	history	Japanese	love
leather	pasta	writing	mathematics	Afrikaans	anger
porcelain	gravy	homework	economics	German	fame

Two-Way Nouns

Two-way nouns can function as count or noncount nouns, depending on their context.

Please set a **glass** in front of each place mat. (count noun)

The display case was made of tempered **glass**. (noncount noun)

Insight

Many native English speakers aren't even aware of count and noncount nouns, though they use them correctly out of habit. Listen for their use of count and noncount nouns.

Vocabulary

count noun
noun naming something that can be counted

noncount noun
noun naming something that cannot be counted

two-way noun
noun that can function as either a count or a noncount noun

Using Count and Noncount Nouns

Sort Read the list of nouns below and sort the words into columns of count and noncount nouns.

window	aluminum	holiday	health	rain
English	shoe	tricycle	poetry	ice
bowling	plum	Japanese	lawyer	teaspoon

Count Nouns	Noncount Nouns
window	English
shoe	bowling
plum	aluminum
holiday	Japanese
tricycle	health
lawyer	poetry
teaspoon	rain
	ice

Correct Read the following paragraph and correct the noun errors. The first sentence has been corrected for you.

Our kitchen redesign involved tearing out the plastics that covered the counter and removing the flashings around the edges. We installed new aluminums to replace the old metals. Also, the cupboard doors, which used to be made of woods, were replaced by doors made of glasses. We have a new jar for holding flours and a new refrigerator with a special place for milks and a dispenser for waters. Everything is illuminated by new lightings, and a larger window lets more sunlights in.

Correction Marks

- delete
- capitalize
- lowercase
- insert
- add comma
- add question mark
- add word
- add period
- spelling
- switch

Look Photography/Beateworks/InsideOutPix/Corbis

Learning Outcome

Use articles.

Insight

If your heritage language does not use articles, pay close attention to the way native English speakers use *the* when referring to a specific thing. Note, however, that *the* is not usually used with proper nouns naming people or animals.

Vocabulary

article
the most common type of noun marker (*a, an,* or *the*)

definite article
the word *the*, used to mark a noun that refers to a specific person, place, or thing

indefinite article
the words *a* or *an*, used to mark a noun that refers to a general person, place, or thing

LO5 Articles

Articles help you to know if a noun refers to a specific thing or to a general thing. There are two basic types of articles—definite and indefinite.

Definite Article

The **definite article** is the word *the*. It signals that the noun refers to one specific person, place, thing, or idea.

Look at the rainbow.
(Look at a specific rainbow.)

Note: *The* can be used with most nouns, but usually not with proper nouns.

Incorrect: The Joe looked at the rainbow.

Correct: Joe looked at the rainbow.

Frank Krahmer/Fancy/Corbis

Indefinite Articles

The **indefinite articles** are the words *a* and *an*. They signal that the noun refers to a general person, place, thing, or idea. The word *a* is used before nouns that begin with consonant sounds, and the word *an* is used before nouns that begin with vowel sounds.

I enjoy seeing a rainbow.
(I enjoy seeing any rainbow.)

Note: Don't use *a* or *an* with plural count nouns or noncount nouns.

Incorrect: I love a sunshine.

Correct: I love the sunshine

Note: If a word begins with an *h* that is pronounced, use *a*. If the *h* is silent, use *an*.

Incorrect: I stared for a hour.

Correct: I stared for an hour.

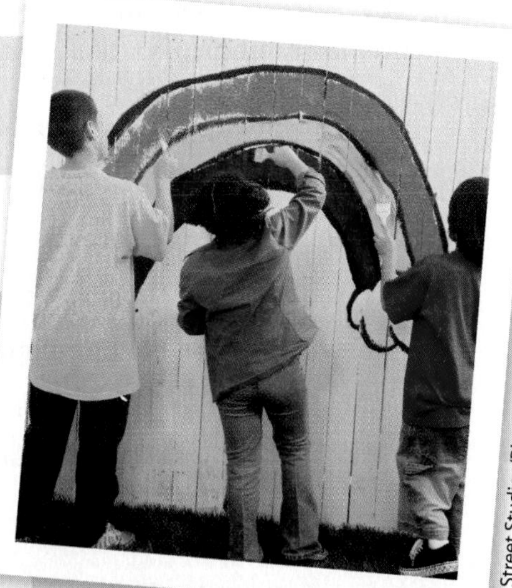

Hill Street Studios/Blend Images/Blend/Corbis

Using Articles

Identify Add the appropriate indefinite article (*a* or *an*) to each of the words below. The first one has been done for you.

1. an orchard	6. an evening	11. an error
2. a petunia	7. a house	12. an opportunity
3. a hose	8. an hour	13. an honest mistake
4. an honor	9. a shark	14. an emblem
5. an avocado	10. an eye	15. a handkerchief

Correct Either delete or replace any articles that are incorrectly used in the following paragraph. The first sentence has been done for you.

Climate scientists see a shift in a weather. With a increase in the levels of carbon dioxide, the atmosphere traps a heat of the sun. More heat in an air means more heat in the oceans. If a ocean gets warmer, the storms it creates are more intense. An hurricane could develop to an higher category, with stronger winds and a increase in a lightning. A Earth is already an storm world, but with a rise in global temperatures, a weather could become more extreme.

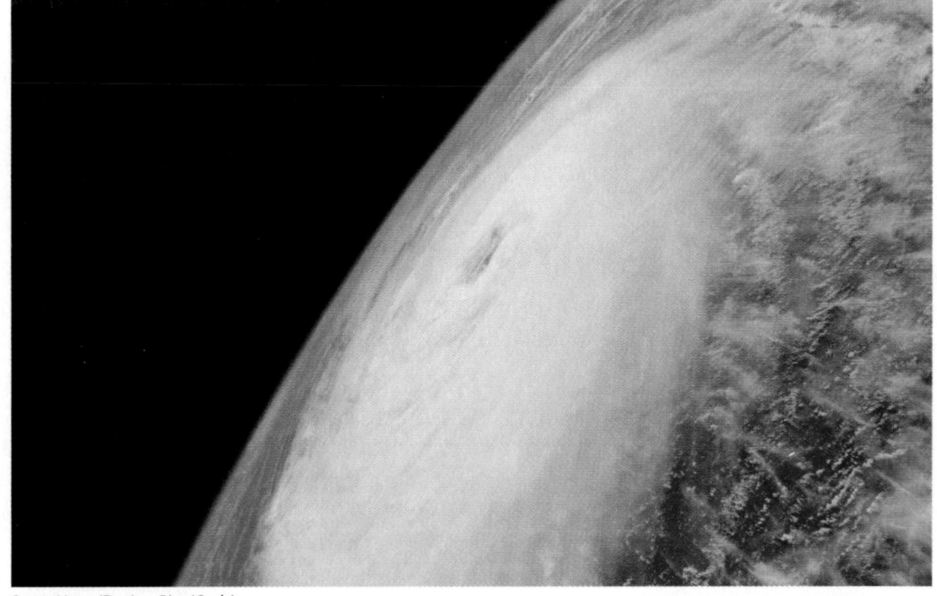

Steve Nagy/Design Pics/Corbis

Correction Marks

- delete
- capitalize
- lowercase
- insert
- add comma
- add question mark
- add word
- add period
- spelling
- switch

Learning Outcome

Use other noun markers.

Traits

These noun markers show if a noun is owned, if it is very general, if it is very specific, or if it is numerous or plentiful.

Vocabulary

possessive adjective
the possessive form of a noun or pronoun, showing ownership of another noun

indefinite adjective
an indefinite pronoun (*many, much, some*) used as an adjective to mark a nonspecific noun

demonstrative adjective
a demonstrative pronoun (*this, that, those*) used as an adjective to mark a specific noun

quantifier
a modifier that tells *how many* or *how much*

LO6 Other Noun Markers

Other words help provide information about nouns.

Possessive Adjective

A **possessive adjective** is the possessive form of a noun or pronoun. Possessive adjectives can be formed by adding *'s* to singular nouns and ' to plural nouns.

Paul's car is in the shop, but **Taylor's** is fixed.

Florida's coast is beautiful.

The **King's** porch has screens.

That is **my** pen. This pen is **mine**.

It's **your** choice. The choice is **yours**.

Possessive Pronouns

	Singular		Plural	
	Before	After	Before	After
First Person	my	mine	our	ours
Second Person	your	yours	your	yours
Third Person	his her its	his hers its	their their their	theirs theirs theirs

Note: One form of a possessive pronoun is used before the noun, and a different form is used after.

Indefinite Adjectives

An **indefinite adjective** signals that the noun it marks refers to a general person, place, thing, or idea. Some indefinite adjectives mark count nouns and others mark noncount nouns.

Each person brought food. **Much** food was set out.

With Count Nouns			With Noncount Nouns	With Count or Noncount		
each	either	every	much	all	any	more
few	many	neither		most	some	
several						

Demonstrative Adjectives

A **demonstrative adjective** marks a specific noun. The words *this* and *that* (singular) or *these* and *those* (plural) demonstrate exactly which one is meant.

These pickles are from **that** jar. **This** taste comes from **those** spices.

Quantifiers

A **quantifier** tells *how many* or *how much* there is of something.

With Count Nouns		With Noncount Nouns		With Count or Noncount		
each	a couple of	a bag of	a little	no	a lot of	most
several	every	a bowl of	much	not any	lots of	all
a number of	many	a piece of	a great deal of	some	plenty of	
both	a few					
nine						

Using Noun Markers

Identify Circle the appropriate noun marker in parentheses for each sentence.

1. I brought one of (**my**, *mine*) favorite recipes, and you brought one of (*your*, **yours**).
2. Is this (**her**, *hers*) recipe, or is it (*their*, **theirs**)?
3. How (*many*, **much**) sugar should I add to the batter?
4. I can't believe the recipe does not use (**any**, *each*) flour.
5. Next, we should make (**this**, *these*) casserole.
6. Your face tells me you don't like (**that**, *those*) idea.
7. After making the dough, we had (*several*, **a little**) butter left over.
8. We liked (**a number of**, *much*) the recipes.
9. The best pie of all was (*her*, **hers**).
10. Let's make sure everyone has a copy in (**their**, *theirs*) recipe files.

Correct Delete and replace any incorrectly used noun markers in the following paragraph. The first one has been done for you.

An omelet can contain as few or as ~~much~~ many ingredients as you wish. Of course, a good omelet starts with three or four eggs. Blend the eggs in ~~yours~~ your biggest bowl and add a ~~couple of~~ little milk. Next, you can include ~~much~~ some vegetables. Try fresh ingredients from ~~yours~~ your garden. Add a cup of chopped scallions, fresh tomatoes, or green peppers. And ~~a number of~~ some spinach can give the omelet a savory flavor. You can also add ~~several~~ meat. Mix in a ~~couple of~~ little bacon or ~~many~~ ham. Or you might include ~~several~~ some sausage. Fry the omelet, fold it, sprinkle it with a ~~couple of~~ little cheese, and enjoy!

Correction Marks

- delete
- capitalize
- lowercase
- insert
- add comma
- add question mark
- add word
- add period
- spelling
- switch

Learning Outcome

Use nouns correctly in a real-world context.

LO7 Real-World Application

Correct In the letter that follows, correct any errors with nouns, articles, or other noun markers. Use the correction marks to the left.

Send | Attach | Fonts | Colors | Save As Draft

From: Melissa St. James

To: Design and Printing Staff

Cc:

Subject: Internship Program for University Students

Hi, Team:

Could you use a assistant—a extra pair of hands at little cost?

The head of the Graphic Arts Department at Northwestern College has asked us if we'd be interested in developing internships for third-year students in a university's four-year graphic-arts program.

Internships could be the real win-win proposition because internes would
- work on tasks that you assign.
- give you 20 hours of work per week for 15 weeks.
- get excellent professional experience by working with you.
- allow us an opportunity to work with potential employees.

Please consider working with an student intern during the fall semester. If you are interested, let me know before January 28.

Thanks for considering these invitation to help future member of a graphic arts profession.

Melissa

Correction Marks

- delete
- capitalize
- lowercase
- insert
- add comma
- add question mark
- add word
- add period
- spelling
- switch

Workplace

Note how the errors in nouns and noun markers make this letter less persuasive. Readers notice errors instead of hearing the persuasive pitch.

"Clothes make the man. Naked people have little or no influence on society."
—Mark Twain

Beathan/Flame/Corbis

28 Pronoun

An old saying goes that clothes make the man. Well, not quite. Just because a suit is sitting there with a laptop on its, well, lap doesn't mean that a living, breathing and thinking person is in the room. The clothes are just temporary stand-ins.

Pronouns, similarly, are stand-ins for nouns. They aren't nouns, but they suggest nouns or refer back to them. That's why it's especially important for the pronouns to clearly connect to whatever it is replacing.

This chapter will help you make sure your pronoun stand-ins work well.

What do you think?

How could clothes make the man (or woman)? How do pronouns help nouns?

Answers will vary.

Learning Outcomes

- LO1 Understand personal pronouns.
- LO2 Create pronoun-antecedent agreement.
- LO3 Correct other pronoun problems.
- LO4 Create agreement with indefinite pronouns.
- LO5 Use relative pronouns.
- LO6 Use other pronouns.
- LO7 Use pronouns correctly in a real-world context.

Learning Outcome

Understand personal pronouns.

LO1 Personal Pronouns

A **pronoun** is a word that takes the place of a noun or another pronoun. The most common type of pronoun is the **personal pronoun**. Personal pronouns indicate whether the person is speaking, is being spoken to, or is being spoken about.

	Singular			Plural		
Person	**Nom.**	**Obj.**	**Poss.**	**Nom.**	**Obj.**	**Poss.**
First (speaking)	I	me	my/mine	we	us	our/ours
Second (spoken to)	you	you	your/yours	you	you	your/yours
Third (spoken about) masculine	he	him	his	they	them	their/theirs
feminine	she	her	her/hers	they	them	their/theirs
neuter	it	it	its	they	them	their/theirs

Nom.=nominative case / **Obj**=objective case / **Poss.**=possessive case

Case of Pronouns

The **case** of a personal pronoun indicates how it can be used.

- **Nominative** pronouns are used as the subjects of sentences or as subject complements (following the linking verbs *am, is, are, was, were, be, being,* or *been*).

  He applied for the job, but the person hired was **she**.

- **Objective** pronouns are used as direct objects, indirect objects, or objects of prepositions.

  The police officer warned **us** about **them**.

- **Possessive** pronouns show ownership and function as adjectives.

  Her lawn looks much greener than **mine**.

Gender

Pronouns can be **masculine**, **feminine**, or **neuter**.

He showed **her** how to fix **it**.

Say It

Read the following aloud.

1. *I* am / *You* are / *He* is / *She* is / *It* is / *We* are / *They* are
2. Show *me* / Show *you* / Show *him* / Show *her* / Show *them* / Show *us*
3. *My* car / *Your* car / *His* car / *Her* car / *Their* car
4. The car is *mine.* / The car is *yours.* / The car is *his.* / The car is *hers.* / The car is *theirs.*

Vocabulary

pronoun
a word that takes the place of a noun or other pronoun

personal pronoun
a pronoun that indicates whether the person is speaking, is spoken to, or is spoken about

case
whether a pronoun is used as a subject, an object, or a possessive

nominative
used as a subject or subject complement

objective
used as a direct object, an indirect object, or an object of a preposition

possessive
used to show ownership

masculine
male

feminine
female

neuter
neither male nor female

Using Personal Pronouns

Select For each sentence below, circle the correct personal pronoun in parentheses.

1. *(I, me, my)* love to hang out at the corner coffee shop.
2. *(I, Me, My)* friends and I gather there on Saturday morning.
3. One friend, Zach, is making a film, and *(he, him, his)* asked me to be in it.
4. We read over the lines, and other patrons listened to *(we, us, our)*.
5. *(We, Us, Our)* friend Rachel is also in the film.
6. At one point, I have to give *(she, her, hers)* a kiss.
7. The other people in the coffee shop applauded *(we, us, our.)*
8. Rachel and *(I, me, my)* blushed and stared into *(we, us, our)* lattes.
9. Zach thought it was great, and *(he, him, his)* set up a shooting schedule.
10. Whoever comes to the coffee shop that day will be *(we, us, our)* extras.

Correct In the following paragraph, correct the pronouns by crossing out the incorrect forms and writing the correct forms above.

Zach, Rachel, and ~~me~~ I went to the coffee shop on Saturday afternoon, when ~~them~~ they are usually closed. The owners agreed to let ~~we~~ us film there. Zach rearranged the tables a little to make room for the camera, and ~~him~~ he and ~~me~~ I set up the equipment. The camera rolled, and Rachel and ~~me~~ I started into our lines. A couple of times, we had to stop because the owners were laughing so much ~~them~~ they couldn't hold a straight face. Rachel and ~~me~~ I had a hard time being straight when it came to ~~ours~~ our kissing scene. It went well, and ~~her~~ she and ~~me~~ I got through it in one take. Zach took the footage away, and he told us he would send a disk of the rough cut to ~~she~~ her and ~~I~~ me.

Learning Outcome

Create pronoun-antecedent agreement.

LO2 Pronoun-Antecedent Agreement

The **antecedent** is the word that a pronoun refers to or replaces. A pronoun must have the same person, number, and gender as the antecedent, which is called **pronoun-antecedent agreement**.

third-person	singular feminine	singular feminine

Colleen thought **she** would need a lift, but **her** car started.

Agreement in Person

A pronoun needs to match its antecedent in **person** (first, second, or third).

	third person	second person

Incorrect: If **people** keep going, **you** can usually reach the goal.
Correct: If **you** keep going, **you** can usually reach the goal.
Correct: If **people** keep going, **they** can usually reach the goal.

Agreement in Number

A pronoun needs to match its antecedent in **number** (singular or plural).

	singular	plural

Incorrect: Each **lifeguard** must buy **their** own uniform.
Correct: **Lifeguards** must buy **their** own uniforms.
Correct: Each **lifeguard** must buy **her** or **his** own uniform.

Agreement in Gender

A pronoun needs to match its antecedent in **gender** (masculine, feminine, or neuter).

	feminine	masculine

Incorrect: **Mrs. Miller** will present **his** speech.
Correct: **Mrs. Miller** will present **her** speech.

Say It

Speak the following words aloud.

1. First person: *I, me, my, mine; we, us, our, ours*
2. Second person: *you, your, yours*
3. Third person feminine: *she, her, hers; they, them, their, theirs*
4. Third person masculine: *he, him, his; they, them, their, theirs*
5. Third person neuter: *it, its; they, them, their, theirs*

Insight

Different languages use gender differently. English reserves gender for people and animals, though some languages use gender for nonliving things. Compare gender use in your heritage language with gender use in English, and note the differences.

Vocabulary

antecedent
the word that a pronoun refers to or replaces

pronoun-antecedent agreement
matching a pronoun to its antecedent in terms of person, number, and gender

person
whether the pronoun is speaking, being spoken to, or being spoken about

number
whether the pronoun is singular or plural

gender
whether the pronoun is masculine, feminine, or neuter

Correcting Agreement Errors

Correct Person Rewrite each sentence to correct the person error.

Sample answers:

1. When you go to the multiplex, a person has a lot of movies to choose from.

   When you go to the multiplex, you have a lot of movies to choose from.

2. Each of us has to buy their own ticket and snacks.

   Each of us has to buy our own ticket and snacks.

3. If the viewer arrives early enough, you can see a triple feature.

   If the viewer arrives early enough, he or she can see a triple feature.

4. One can be overwhelmed by how many movies you can see.

   One can be overwhelmed by how many movies one can see.

Correct Number Rewrite each sentence to correct the number error.

Sample answers:

5. Each moviegoer chooses what movies they want to see.

   Each moviegoer chooses what movies he or she wants to see.

6. A snack-counter attendant serves treats, and they also clean up messes.

   A snack-counter attendant serves treats, and he or she also cleans up messes.

7. Movie critics give his opinion about different films.

   Movie critics give their opinions about different films.

8. A critic shouldn't give away the ending because they would ruin the movie.

   A critic shouldn't give away the ending because he or she would ruin the movie.

Correct Gender Rewrite each sentence to correct the gender error.

Sample answers:

9. A critic shouldn't give away the ending because he would ruin the movie.

   A critic shouldn't give away the ending because he or she would ruin the movie.

10. When Roger Ebert critiques a film, she's right most of the time.

    When Roger Ebert critiques a film, he's right most of the time.

11. Anita accidentally left his purse at the theater.

    Anita accidentally left her purse at the theater.

12. The multiplex sits on a hilltop, and she looks like a palace.

    The multiplex sits on a hilltop, and it looks like a palace.

Learning Outcome

Correct other pronoun problems.

LO3 Other Pronoun Problems

Pronouns are very useful parts of speech, but if they are mishandled, they can cause problems.

Vague Pronoun

Do not use a pronoun that could refer to more than one antecedent.

Unclear: Raul played baseball with his friend and **his** brother.
Clear: Raul played baseball with his friend and **his friend's** brother.

Missing Antecedent

Avoid using *it* or *they* without clear antecedents.

Unclear: **They** say humans share 97 percent of DNA with chimps.
Clear: **Scientists** say humans share 97 percent of DNA with chimps.

Unclear: **It** says in the *Times* that the Democrats back the bill.
Clear: The ***Times*** says that the Democrats back the bill.

Double Subjects

Do not place a pronoun right after the subject. Doing so creates an error called a **double subject**, which is not a standard construction.

Nonstandard: Rudy and Charlie, **they** went fishing.
Standard: Rudy and Charlie went fishing.

Usage Errors *(They're, You're, It's)*

Do not confuse possessive pronouns *(your, their, its)* with contractions *(you're, they're, it's)*. Remember that the contractions use apostrophes in place of missing letters.

Incorrect: Keep **you're** car in **it's** own lane.
Correct: Keep **your** car in **its** own lane.

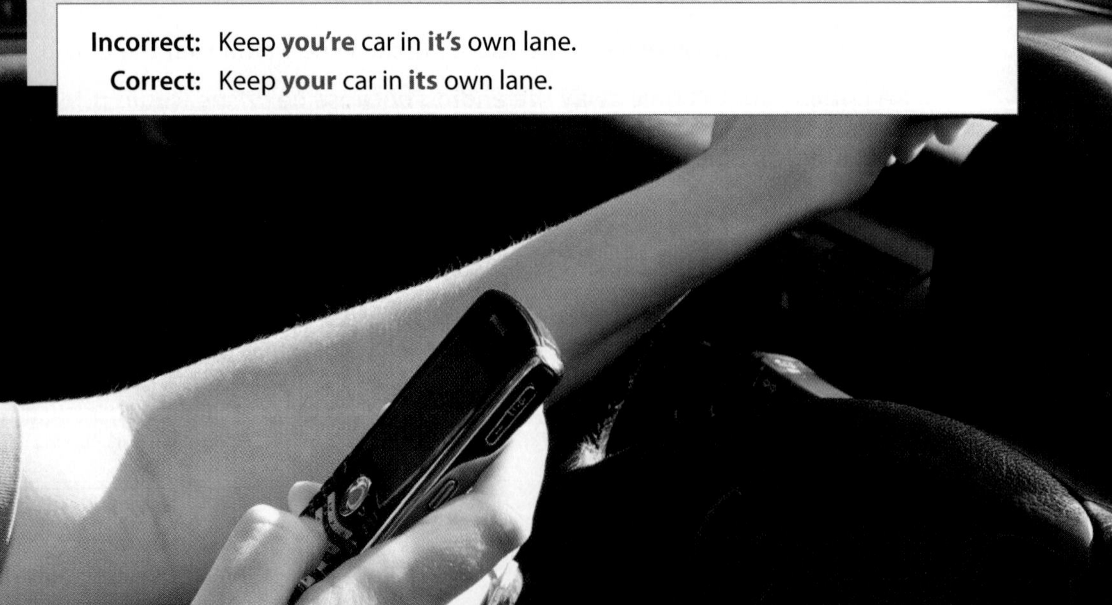

George Fairbairn,2010 / Used under license from Shutterstock.com

Speaking & Listening

The pronoun problems on this page may not cause confusion in spoken English, which is assisted with gestures, body language, and other context cues. In written English, these problems can derail meaning. Watch for them and correct them in your writing.

Vocabulary

vague pronoun
using a pronoun that could refer to more than one antecedent

missing antecedent
using a pronoun that has no clear antecedent

double subject
error created by following a subject with a pronoun

usage error
using the wrong word (e.g., *they're* instead of *their*)

Correcting Other Pronoun Problems

Rewrite Rewrite each sentence to correct the pronoun-reference problems.

Answers will vary.

1. Sarah asked her sister and her friend to help her move.

2. It said on the news that the accident will cost billions to fix.

3. They say that dark energy takes up 75 percent of the universe.

4. Dan wants his father and his friend to help.

5. They have found a way to make deep-water drilling safer.

6. It says on the parking ticket that I have to pay $50.

Correct In the following paragraph, correct the pronoun errors. Use the correction marks to the right.

Answers will vary.

For 28 years, it reported in the *Weekly World News* all kinds of outlandish stories. Often the paper reported about Elvis or the Loch Ness Monster being spotted and his impromptu concerts for die-hard fans. A bat-human hybrid named Bat Boy and an alien named P'lod appeared repeatedly in the tabloid, and he even supposedly had an affair with Hillary Clinton. Since this was during the Monica Lewinski scandal, maybe she was getting back at him. The writers and editors of the *Weekly World News,* they rarely publicly acknowledged that their stories were jokes, but said that he or she had to "suspend disbelief for the sake of enjoyment."

Correction Marks

- delete
- capitalize
- lowercase
- insert
- add comma
- add question mark
- add word
- add period
- spelling
- switch

Learning Outcome

Create agreement with indefinite pronouns.

LO4 Indefinite Pronouns

An **indefinite pronoun** does not have an antecedent, and it does not refer to a specific person, place, thing, or idea. These pronouns pose unique issues with subject-verb and pronoun-antecedent agreement.

Singular Indefinite Pronouns

Some indefinite pronouns are singular. When they are used as subjects, they require a singular verb. As antecedents, they must be matched to singular pronouns.

each	anyone	anybody	anything
either	someone	somebody	something
neither	everyone	everybody	everything
another	no one	nobody	nothing
one			

Nobody is expecting to see Bigfoot on our camping trip.
Someone used **his** or **her** own money to buy a Bigfoot detector at a novelty shop.

Plural Indefinite Pronouns

Some indefinite pronouns are plural. As subjects, they require a plural verb, and as antecedents, they require a plural pronoun.

both	few	several	many

A few of the campers **hear** thumps in the night.
Several of my friends swear **they** can see eyes glowing eight feet off the ground.

Singular or Plural Indefinite Pronouns

Some indefinite pronouns can be singular or plural, depending on the object of the preposition in the phrase that follows them.

all	any	most	none	some

Most of **us are** too frightened to sleep.
Most of the **night is** over already anyway.

Insight

For more practice with indefinite pronouns, see pages 288–290.

Vocabulary

indefinte pronoun
a pronoun that does not refer to a specific person, place, thing, or idea

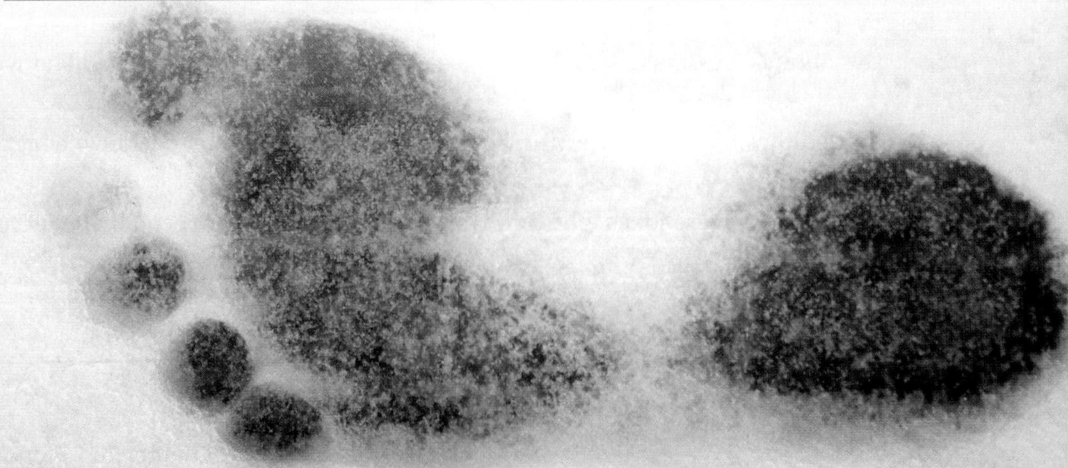

Correcting Agreement

Correct Rewrite each sentence to correct the agreement errors. (Hint: the sentences are about a group of female campers.)

1. Everyone needs to set up their own tent.

   Everyone needs to set up her own tent.

2. No one are getting out of work.

   No one is getting out of work.

3. Anyone who wants to be dry should make sure they have a rain fly.

   Anyone who wants to be dry should make sure she has a rain fly.

4. Nothing are more miserable than a wet sleeping bag.

   Nothing is more miserable than a wet sleeping bag.

5. Few is wanting to end up drenched.

   Few are wanting to end up drenched.

6. Several wants to go hiking to look for Bigfoot.

   Several want to go hiking to look for Bigfoot.

7. Many has doubts that he exists.

   Many have doubts that he exists.

8. A few says they might have dated him in high school.

   A few say they might have dated him in high school.

9. A Bigfoot hunter should make sure they have a camera along.

   A Bigfoot hunter should make sure she has a camera along.

10. Most of the hunters is also going to carry a big stick.

    Most of the hunters are also going to carry a big stick.

11. Most of the afternoon are available for different activities.

    Most of the afternoon is available for different activities.

12. None of the girls is planning to hike after dark.

    None of the girls are planning to hike after dark.

13. None of the food are to be left out to attract animals or Bigfoot.

    None of the food is to be left out to attract animals or Bigfoot.

Learning Outcome

Use relative pronouns.

Insight

For more practice with relative pronouns, see pages 258–259.

Vocabulary

relative pronoun
a pronoun that begins a relative clause, connecting it to a sentence

relative clause
a type of dependent clause that begins with a relative pronoun that is either the subject or the direct object of the clause

LO5 Relative Pronouns

A **relative pronoun** introduces a dependent clause and relates it to the rest of the sentence.

who	whom	which	whose
whoever	whomever	that	

relative clause: I would like to meet the woman **who** discovered dark matter.

Who/Whoever and Whom/Whomever

Who, whoever, whom, and *whomever* refer to people. *Who* or *whoever* functions as the subject of the relative clause, while *whom* or *whomever* functions as the object of the clause.

relative clause: I am amazed by a person **who** could imagine matter that can't be seen.

The woman **whom** I met was named Vera Rubin. (relative clause)

Note: In the second **relative clause**, *whom* introduces the clause even though it is the direct object, not the subject *(I thanked whom).*

That and Which

That and *which* usually refer to things. When *that* introduces the clause, the clause **is not** set off with commas. When *which* introduces the clause, the clause **is** set off with commas.

relative clause: I saw a documentary **that** explained about dark matter and dark energy.

The show is *Into the Wormhole,* **which** is on the Science Channel. (relative clause)

Note: In the first example, the *that* clause is restrictive, or essential to the meaning of the sentence. In the second example, the *which* clause is nonrestrictive, or unnecessary to the meaning of the sentence.

Whose

Whose shows ownership or connection.

relative clause: Morgan Freeman, **whose** voice is soothing, hosts the show.

Note: Do not confuse *whose* with the contraction *who's* (who is).

Using Relative Pronouns

Select For each sentence, circle the correct relative pronoun.

1. Vera Rubin, *(who, whom)* first discovered dark matter, wasn't seeking fame.
2. In the 1960s, she avoided black holes, *(that, which)* were a hot topic.
3. Instead, Rubin focused on the rotation of spiral galaxies, *(that, which)* few other people studied.
4. She expected stars *(that, which)* were on the outside of galaxies would move faster than stars *(that, which)* were near the center.
5. Instead, Rubin discovered the same speed for stars *(that, which)* were in different parts of the galaxy.
6. The only way for the galaxy to move that way would be if it had ten times the mass *(that, which)* was visible.
7. Rubin, *(who, whom, whose)* had never courted fame, became a very controversial figure when she presented her findings about dark matter.
8. Other astrophysicists *(who, whom)* disbelieved her did similar observations and calculations and confirmed her findings.
9. Rubin, *(who, whom, whose)* theory once was radical, became one of the great contributors to modern science.
10. *(Whoever, Whomever)* wrestles with the idea of dark matter should remember that over fifty years ago, one woman was the first to wrestle with the idea.

Stocktrek Images/Alloy/Corbis

Write On your own paper, write a relative clause for each of these relative pronouns: Answers will vary.

1. who
2. whoever
3. whom
4. whomever
5. which
6. that
7. whose

Write a sentence including one of your clauses.

Learning Outcome

Use other pronouns.

LO6 Other Pronoun Types

Other types of pronouns have specific uses in your writing: asking questions, pointing to specific things, reflecting back on a noun (or pronoun), or intensifying a noun (or pronoun).

Interrogative Pronoun

An **interrogative pronoun** asks a question—*who, whose, whom, which, what.*

> **What** should we call our band? **Who** will be in it?

Demonstrative Pronoun

A **demonstrative pronoun** points to a specific thing—*this, that, these, those.*

> **That** is a great name! **This** will look terrific on a cover!

Reflexive Pronoun

A **reflexive pronoun** reflects back to the subject of a sentence or clause—*myself, ourselves, yourself, yourselves, himself, herself, itself, themselves.*

> I credit **myself** for the name. You can credit **yourself** for the logo.

Intensive Pronoun

An **intensive pronoun** emphasizes the noun or pronoun it refers to—*myself, ourselves, yourself, yourselves, himself, herself, itself, themselves.*

> You **yourself** love the name Psycho Drummer. I **myself** couldn't be happier.

Reciprocal Pronoun

A **reciprocal pronoun** refers to two things in an equal way—*each other, one another.*

> We shouldn't fight with **each other**. We should support **one another**.

Traits

To remember these terms, think of the words they came from: *Interrogate* means "ask questions," *demonstrate* means "point out," *reflect* means "show an image of," *intensify* means "make stronger," and *reciprocal* means "working together."

Vocabulary

interrogative pronoun
a pronoun that asks a question

demonstrative pronoun
a pronoun that points to a specific thing

reflexive pronoun
a pronoun that reflects back to the subject of a sentence or clause

intensive pronoun
a pronoun that emphasizes the noun or pronoun it refers to

reciprocal pronoun
a pronoun that refers to two things in an equal way

Say It

Speak the following words aloud.

1. Interrogative: *Who* is? / *Whose* is? / *Which* is? / *What* is? / *Whom* do you see?
2. Demonstrative: *This* is / *That* is / *These* are / *Those* are
3. Reflexive: I helped *myself.* / You helped *yourself.* / They helped *themselves*
4. Intensive: I *myself* / You *yourself* / She *herself* / He *himself* / They *themselves*
5. Reciprocal: We helped *each other.* / We helped *one another.*

Using Other Types of Pronouns

Identify Indicate the type of each underlined pronoun: *interrogative, demonstrative, reflexive, intensive,* or *reciprocal*.

1. That is why this band needs a road crew. demonstrative
2. What are we supposed to do without power cords? interrogative
3. I myself would not mind playing unplugged. intensive
4. You need to remind yourself that we don't have acoustic guitars. reflexive
5. That is the whole problem. demonstrative
6. The guitars themselves prevent us from playing unplugged. intensive
7. Who could hear an unplugged electric guitar? interrogative
8. What person will stand a foot away to listen? interrogative
9. This is ridiculous. demonstrative
10. That won't work as a power cord. demonstrative
11. I myself am about to quit this band. intensive
12. We should be ashamed of ourselves. reflexive
13. We shouldn't blame each other. reciprocal
14. As a band, we should help one another get through this. reciprocal
15. Let's buy ourselves another set of cords. reflexive

Write Create a sentence using *myself* as a reflexive pronoun, and a second using *myself* as an intensive pronoun. Answers will vary.

1. ______________________________

2. ______________________________

Learning Outcome

Use pronouns correctly in a real-world context.

LO7 Real-World Application

Correct In the letter that follows, correct any pronoun errors. Use the correction marks to the left.

Correction Marks

- delete
- capitalize
- lowercase
- insert
- add comma
- add question mark
- add word
- add period
- spelling
- switch

Workplace

In workplace documents, correct grammar is critical to creating a strong impression.

Psycho Drummer

12185 W. 22nd Avenue, Elkhorn, WI 53100 ▪ Ph: 262.555.7188

July 30, 2011

Ms. Marcia Schwamps, Manager
Piedog Studios
350 South Jackson Street
Elkhorn, WI 53100

Dear Ms. Schwamps:

One of your recording technicians says that you are looking for session musicians ~~whom~~ who could play instruments for other artists. My band-mate Jerome and ~~me~~ I would like to offer ~~ours~~ our services.

Jerome and ~~me~~ I are the power duo ~~whom~~ who are called Psycho Drummer, a name that refers to Jerome ~~hisself~~ himself. He is a master percussionist, and ~~him~~ he has trained ~~hisself~~ himself in many styles from heavy metal to rock, pop, jazz, blues, and even classical.

I am the guitarist in Psycho Drummer. I play electric and acoustic (six- and 12-string) guitars as well as electric bass, and I too have trained myself in them.

Attached, you will find ~~ours~~ our résumés, a list of recent gigs ~~us~~ we have played, and a review of ~~we~~ us from the *Walworth County Week*.

Please consider Jerome and ~~I~~ me for work as session musicians at Piedog Studios. We look forward to hearing from ~~yous~~ you and would very much appreciate an interview/audition.

Sincerely,

Terrance "Tear-It-Up" Clark

Terrance "Tear-It-Up" Clark
Guitarist
Enclosures 3

"There are 350 varieties of shark, not counting loan and pool."

—L. M. Boyd

Image Source/Image Source/Corbis

29 Verb

You've probably heard that a shark has to keep swimming or it suffocates. That's not entirely true. Yes, sharks breathe by moving water across their gills, but they can also lie on the bottom and push water through their gills or let currents do the work. Still, most sharks stay on the move, and when a shark is still, it has to work harder to breathe.

Verbs are much the same way. They like to stay on the move. Most verbs are action words, describing what is happening. Some verbs describe states of being—much like sharks sitting on the bottom, breathing. Either way, though, the verb gives life to the sentence, and often it is a word with big teeth. This chapter gives a view into the compelling world of verbs.

What do you think?

Do you prefer doing or being? Why?

Answers will vary.

Learning Outcomes

LO1 Understand and use verb classes.

LO2 Work with number and person.

LO3 Work with voice.

LO4 Form basic verb tenses.

LO5 Form progressive tense.

LO6 Form perfect tense.

LO7 Understand verbals.

LO8 Use verbals as objects.

LO9 Apply learning to real-world examples.

Learning Outcome

Understand and use verb classes.

LO1 Verb Classes

Verbs show action or states of being. Different classes of verbs do these jobs.

Action Verbs

Verbs that show action are called **action verbs**. Some action verbs are **transitive**, which means that they transfer action to a direct object.

Trina **hurled** the softball.
(The verb *hurled* transfers action to the direct object *softball*.)

Others are **intransitive**: They don't transfer action to a direct object.

Trina **pitches**.
(The verb *pitches* does not transfer action to a direct object.)

Linking Verbs

Verbs that link the subject to a noun, a pronoun, or an adjective are **linking verbs**. Predicates with linking verbs express a state of being.

Trina **is** a pitcher.
(The linking verb *is* connects *Trina* to the noun *pitcher*.)

She **seems** unbeatable.
(The linking verb *seems* connects *She* to the adjective *unbeatable*.)

Linking Verbs

is	am	are	was	were	be	being	been	become
grow	feel	seem	look	smell	taste	sound	appear	remain

Note: The bottom-row words are linking verbs if they don't show action.

WAC

If you are mathematically minded, think of a linking verb as an equal sign. It indicates that the subject equals (or is similar to) what is in the predicate.

Helping Verbs

A verb that works with an action or linking verb is a **helping** (or auxiliary) verb. A helping verb helps the main verb form tense, mood, and voice.

Trina **has** pitched two shut-out games, and today she **may be** pitching her third.
(The helping verb *has* works with the main verb *pitched*; the helping verbs *may be* work with *pitching*. Both form special tenses.)

Note: Helping verbs work with verbs ending in *ing* or in past tense form.

Helping Verbs

am	been	could	does	have	might	should	will
are	being	did	had	is	must	was	would
be	can	do	has	may	shall	were	

Vocabulary

action verb
word that expresses action

transitive verb
action verb that transfers action to a direct object

intransitive verb
action verb that does not transfer action to a direct object

linking verb
verb that connects the subject with a noun, a pronoun, or an adjective in the predicate

helping (auxiliary) verb
verb that works with a main verb to form some tenses, mood, and voice

Using Verb Classes

Identify/Write For each sentence below, identify the underlined verbs as transitive action verbs (T), intransitive action verbs (I), linking verbs (L), or helping verbs (H). Then write your own sentence using the same class of verb.

1. I love (T) fast-pitch softball, but I rarely pitch (I).

2. I play (T) first base; it is (L) a pressure-filled position.

3. Runners charge (T) first base, and I tag (T) them out.

4. Double-plays require (T) on-target throws, clean catches, and timing.

5. If a runner steals (I), the pitcher and second baseperson work (I) with me.

6. We catch (T) the runner in a "pickle" and tag (T) her out.

7. Softball is (L) exciting, and I will (H) play all summer.

8. I look (L) worn out after a game, but I feel (L) completely exhilarated.

Learning Outcome

Work with number and person.

LO2 Number and Person of Verb

Verbs reflect number (singular or plural) and person (first person, second person, or third person).

Number

The **number** of the verb indicates whether the subject is singular or plural. Note that most present tense singular verbs end in *s,* while most present tense plural verbs do not.

Singular: A civil war re-enactment **involves** infantry, cavalry, and artillery units.
Plural: Civil war re-enactors **stage** amazing battle scenes from the war.

Person

The **person** of the verb indicates whether the subject is speaking, being spoken to, or being spoken about.

	Singular	Plural
First Person:	(I) am	(we) are
Second Person:	(you) are	(you) are
Third Person:	(she) is	(they) are

Note that the pronoun *I* takes a special form of the *be* verb—*am.*

Correct: I am eager to see the cannons fire.
Incorrect: I is eager to see the cannons fire.

The pronoun *I* also is paired with plural present tense verbs.

Correct: I hope to see a bayonet charge.
Incorrect: I hopes to see a bayonet charge.

In a similar way, the singular pronoun *you* takes the plural form of the *be* verb—*are, were.*

Correct: You are in for a treat when the battle begins.
Incorrect: You is in for a treat when the battle begins.
Correct: You were surprised at how steady the horses were in combat.
Incorrect: You was surprised at how steady the horses were in combat.

Vocabulary

number
singular or plural

person
whether the subject is speaking *(I, we)*, is being spoken to *(you)*, or is being spoken about *(he, she, it, they)*

Using Number and Person

Provide For each sentence below, provide the correct person and number of present tense *be* verb *(is, am, are)*.

1. We ___are___ at the Civil War encampment.
2. It ___is___ a gathering of Union and Confederate regiments.
3. You ___are___ in a uniform of Union blue.
4. I ___am___ in the gray of the Confederacy.
5. A light artillery brigade ___is___ a group of mobile cannon.
6. A cavalry regiment ___is___ a group of mounted soldiers.
7. The camp doctors ___are___ equipped to do amputations.
8. The medicine they use ___is___ sometimes worse than the disease.
9. I ___am___ amazed by all of the tent encampments.
10. You ___are___ interested in becoming a re-enactor.

Rewrite Rewrite each sentence below to fix the errors in the number and person of the verb.

1. I jumps the first time a cannon goes off.

   I jump the first time a cannon goes off.

2. The guns blows huge white smoke rings whirling into the air.

   The guns blow huge white smoke rings whirling into the air.

3. The cavalry regiments charges together and battles with sabers.

   The cavalry regiments charge together and battle with sabers.

4. In the fray, one cavalry officer fall from his horse.

   In the fray, one cavalry officer falls from his horse.

5. The infantry soldiers lines up in two rows and sends out volleys of bullets.

   The infantry soldiers line up in two rows and send out volleys of bullets.

6. After the battle, President Lincoln deliver a solemn address.

   After the battle, President Lincoln delivers a solemn address.

Learning Outcome

Work with voice.

LO3 Voice of the Verb

The **voice** of the verb indicates whether the subject is acting or being acted upon.

Voice

An **active voice** means that the subject is acting. A **passive voice** means that the subject is acted on.

Active: The cast **sang** the song "Our State Fair."
Passive: The song "Our State Fair" **was sung** by the cast.

	Active Voice		Passive Voice	
	Singular	Plural	Singular	Plural
Present Tense	I see you see he/she/it sees	we see you see they see	I am seen you are seen he/she/it is seen	we are seen you are seen they are seen
Past Tense	I saw you saw he saw	we saw you saw they saw	I was seen you were seen it was seen	we were seen you were seen they were seen
Future Tense	I will see you will see he will see	we will see you will see they will see	I will be seen you will be seen it will be seen	we will be seen you will be seen they will be seen
Present Perfect Tense	I have seen you have seen he has seen	we have seen you have seen they have seen	I have been seen you have been seen it has been seen	we have been seen you have been seen they have been seen
Past Perfect Tense	I had seen you had seen he had seen	we had seen you had seen they had seen	I had been seen you had been seen it had been seen	we had been seen you had been seen they had been seen
Future Perfect Tense	I will have seen you will have seen he will have seen	we will have seen you will have seen they will have seen	I will have been seen you will have been seen it will have been seen	we will have been seen you will have been seen they will have been seen

Active voice is preferred for most writing because it is direct and energetic.

Active: The crowd gave the cast a standing ovation.
Passive: The cast was given a standing ovation by the crowd.

Passive voice is preferred when the focus is on the receiver of the action or when the subject is unknown.

Passive: A donation was left at the ticket office.
Active: Someone left a donation at the ticket office.

Workplace

In workplace writing, use active voice for most messages. Use passive voice to deliver bad news.

Vocabulary

voice
active or passive

active voice
voice created when the subject is performing the action of the verb

passive voice
voice created when the subject is receiving the action of the verb

Antenna/fstop/fStop/Corbis

Using Voice of a Verb

Rewrite Read each passive sentence below and rewrite it to be active. Think about what is performing the action and make that the subject. The first one is done for you.

1. *State Fair* was put on by the community theater group.
   The community theater group put on *State Fair.*
2. The Frake family was featured in the musical.
   The musical featured the Frake family.
3. Many songs were sung and danced by the cast.
   The cast sang and danced many songs.
4. Pickles and mincemeat were rated by judges at the fair.
   The judges at the fair rated pickles and mincemeat.
5. Mrs. Frake's mincement was spiked with too much brandy.
   Mrs. Frake spiked her mincemeat with too much brandy.
6. The judges of the contest were overcome by the strength of the mincemeat.
   The strength of the mincemeat overcame the judges of the contest.
7. Two couples were shown falling in love at the fair.
   Two couples fell in love at the fair.
8. The singers were assisted by a stalwart piano player in the orchestra pit.
   A stalwart piano player in the pit assisted the singers.
9. The song "It's a Grand Night for Singing" was the climax of the first half.
   The song "It's a Grand Night for Singing" climaxed the first half.
10. The cast was applauded gratefully by the crowd.
    The crowd gratefully applauded the cast.

Write Using the chart on the facing page, write a sentence for each situation below. Answers will vary.

1. (A present tense singular active sentence) ______________________
2. (A past tense plural passive sentence) ______________________

LO4 Present and Future Tense Verbs

Learning Outcome

Form basic verb tenses.

Basic verb tenses tell whether action happens in the past, in the present, or in the future.

Present Tense

Present tense verbs indicate that action is happening right now.

> Master musicians and new professionals **gather** at the Marlboro Music Festival.

Present tense verbs also can indicate that action happens routinely or continually.

> Every summer, they **spend** seven weeks together learning music.

Present Tense in Academic Writing

Use present tense verbs to describe current conditions.

> Pianist Richard Goode **plays** beside talented young artists.

Use present tense verbs also to discuss the ideas in literature or to use historical quotations in a modern context. This use is called the "historical present," which allows writers to continue speaking.

> The audiences at Marlboro **rave** about the quality of the music, or as the *New York Times* **says**, "No matter what is played . . . the performances at Marlboro are usually extraordinary."

Note: It is important to write a paragraph or an essay in one tense. Avoid shifting needlessly from tense to tense as you write. (See also page 314.)

WAC

Look at writing in your field of study. Is most writing done in present tense or past tense? When writing in your field, use the tense that is most expected.

Future Tense

Future tense verbs indicate that action will happen later on.

> Marlboro music **will launch** the careers of many more young stars.

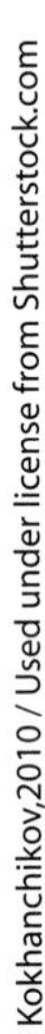

Vocabulary

present tense
verb tense indicating that action is happening now

future tense
verb tense indicating that action will happen later

Using Present and Future Verb Tenses

Write For each sentence below, fill in the blank with the present tense form of the verb indicated in parentheses.

1. Young musicians ___come___ to Marlboro Music by special invitation. (came)
2. Seasoned professionals ___treat___ them like colleagues, not students. (treated)
3. Musicians ___work___ side by side for weeks before performing. (worked)
4. The town of Marlboro, New Hampshire, ___has___ only 987 citizens. (had)
5. Many times that number ___come___ to the concerts each summer. (came)

Change Cross out and replace the verbs in the following paragraph, making them all present tense.

A sixteen-year-old cellist named Yo Yo Ma ~~arrived~~ arrives at Marlboro Music. He ~~couldn't~~ can't believe his fortune to be surrounded by such great musicians. He ~~began~~ begins to play and soon ~~fell~~ falls in love with music. A festival administrator named Jill Hornor also ~~caught~~ catches his eye, and he ~~fell~~ falls in love with her as well. They ~~were~~ are married.

Write Write a sentence of your own, using each word below in the form indicated in parentheses. Answers will vary.

1. thought (present) ______________________________
2. lived (future) ______________________________
3. hoped (present) ______________________________
4. cooperated (future) ______________________________

Past Tense Verbs

Past tense verbs indicate that action happened in the past.

When referring to his campaign in England, Julius Caesar **reported**, "I **came.** I **saw.** I **conquered.**"

Forming Past Tense

Most verbs form their past tense by adding *ed*. If the word ends in a silent *e*, drop the *e* before adding *ed*.

help → helped
look → looked
love → loved
hope → hoped

If the word ends in a consonant before a single vowel and the last syllable is stressed, double the final consonant before adding *ed*.

stop → stopped
plan → planned
occur → occurred
refer → referred

If the word ends in a *y* preceded by a consonant, change the *y* to *i* before adding *ed*.

study → studied
worry → worried
hurry → hurried
carry → carried

Irregular Verbs

Some of the most commonly used verbs form past tense by changing the verb itself. See the chart below:

Present	Past	Present	Past	Present	Past
am	was, were	fly	flew	see	saw
become	became	forget	forgot	shake	shook
begin	began	freeze	froze	shine	shone
blow	blew	get	got	show	showed
break	broke	give	gave	shrink	shrank
bring	brought	go	went	sing	sang
buy	bought	grow	grew	sink	sank
catch	caught	hang	hung	sit	sat
choose	chose	have	had	sleep	slept
come	came	hear	heard	speak	spoke
dig	dug	hide	hid	stand	stood
do	did	keep	kept	steal	stole
draw	drew	know	knew	swim	swam
drink	drank	lead	led	swing	swung
drive	drove	pay	paid	take	took
eat	ate	prove	proved	teach	taught
fall	fell	ride	rode	tear	tore
feel	felt	ring	rang	throw	threw
fight	fought	rise	rose	wear	wore
find	found	run	ran	write	wrote

Traits

Note that the irregular verbs at the bottom of the page are some of the oldest verbs in the English language. That's why they are irregular. Sadly, they are used quite often because they describe the everyday tasks that English speakers have been doing for more than a thousand years.

Vocabulary

past tense
verb tense indicating that action happened previously

Using Past Tense Verbs

Write For each verb, write the correct past tense form.

1. swing swung
2. think thought
3. slip slipped
4. reply replied
5. teach taught
6. cry cried
7. sing sang
8. give gave
9. cap capped
10. fly flew
11. type typed
12. cope coped
13. shop shopped
14. grip gripped
15. gripe griped
16. pour poured
17. soap soaped
18. trick tricked
19. try tried
20. tip tipped

Edit Make changes to the following paragraph, converting it from present tense to past tense. Use the correction marks to the right.

When I ~~am~~ was fresh out of college, I ~~get~~ got my first job as an assistant editor at a sports publisher. At this company, acquisitions editors ~~follow~~ followed trends, ~~talk~~ talked with authors, and ~~work~~ worked with them to create a manuscript. Developmental editors then ~~work~~ worked with the manuscript to develop it into a worthwhile book. Assistant editors ~~help~~ helped with all stages of production. They ~~edit~~ edited manuscripts and ~~typemark~~ typemarked them. Then they ~~check~~ checked the galleys—or long sheets of printout film that paste-up artists cut and ~~wax~~ waxed to create pages. Those ~~are~~ were the days of manual layout. Assistant editors ~~have~~ had to check the paste-up pages for dropped copy. They also proofread and ~~enter~~ entered changes, and ~~check~~ checked bluelines. Publishing is completely different now, but back then, I ~~get~~ got my first experience in real-world work. I ~~am~~ was glad just to have an office of my own.

Correction Marks

- delete
- capitalize
- lowercase
- insert
- add comma
- add question mark
- add word
- add period
- spelling
- switch

Learning Outcome

Form progressive tense.

LO5 Progressive Tense Verbs

The basic tenses of past, present, and future tell when action takes place. The progressive tense or aspect tells that action is ongoing.

Progressive Tense

Progressive tense indicates that action is ongoing. Progressive tense is formed by using a helping verb along with the *ing* form of the main verb.

Work habits **were changing** rapidly.

There are past, present, and future progressive tenses. Each uses a helping verb in the appropriate tense.

For thousands of years, most humans **were working** in agriculture.

Currently in the West, most humans **are working** in nonagricultural jobs.

In the future, people **will be making** their living in unimaginable ways.

Forming Progressive Tense

Past:	was/were	+	main verb	+	ing
Present:	am/is/are	+	main verb	+	ing
Future:	will be	+	main verb	+	ing

BASE/Corbis Yellow/Corbis

Insight

Avoid using progressive tense with the following:

- Verbs that express thoughts, attitudes, and desires: *know, understand, want, prefer*
- Verbs that describe appearances: *seem, resemble*
- Verbs that indicate possession: *belong, have own, possess*
- Verbs that signify inclusion: *contain, hold*

*I **know** your name*, not *I **am knowing** your name.*

Vocabulary

progressive tense
verb tense that expresses ongoing action

Using Progressive Tense

Form Rewrite each sentence three times, changing the tenses as requested in parentheses.

Humans need food, but agribusiness makes food production very efficient.

1. (present progressive) Humans are needing food, but agribusiness is making food production very efficient.

2. (past progressive) Humans were needing food, but agribusiness was making food production very efficient.

3. (future progressive) Humans will be needing food, but agribusiness will be making food production very efficient.

People provide a product or service, and others pay for it.

4. (present progressive) People are providing a product or service, and others are paying for it.

5. (past progressive) People were providing a product or service, and others were paying for it.

6. (future progressive) People will be providing a product or service, and others will be paying for it.

The products and services in greatest demand produce the most wealth.

7. (present progressive) The products and services in greatest demand are producing the greatest wealth.

8. (past progressive) The products and services in greatest demand were producing the greatest wealth.

9. (future progressive) The products and services in greatest demand will be producing the greatest wealth.

Learning Outcome

Form perfect tense.

LO6 Perfect Tense Verbs

The perfect tense tells that action is not ongoing, but is finished, whether in the past, present, or future.

Perfect Tense

Perfect tense indicates that action is completed. Perfect tense is formed by using a helping verb along with the past tense form of the main verb.

Each year of my career, I **have learned** something new.

There are past, present, and future perfect tenses. These tenses are formed by using helping verbs in past, present, and future tenses.

In my first year, I **had learned** to get along in a corporate structure.
This year, I **have learned** new technology skills.
By this time next year, I **will have learned** how to be an effective salesperson.

Forming Perfect Tense

Past:	had	+	past tense main verb
Present:	has/have	+	past tense main verb
Future:	will have	+	past tense main verb

Perfect Tense with Irregular Verbs

To form perfect tense with irregular verbs, use the past participle form instead of the past tense form. Here are the past participles of common irregular verbs.

Present	Past Part.	Present	Past Part.	Present	Past Part.
am, be	been	fly	flown	see	seen
become	become	forget	forgotten	shake	shaken
begin	begun	freeze	frozen	shine	shone
blow	blown	get	gotten	show	shown
break	broken	give	given	shrink	shrunk
bring	brought	go	gone	sing	sung
buy	bought	grow	grown	sink	sunk
catch	caught	hang	hung	sit	sat
choose	chosen	have	had	sleep	slept
come	come	hear	heard	speak	spoken
dig	dug	hide	hidden	stand	stood
do	done	keep	kept	steal	stolen
draw	drawn	know	known	swim	swum
drink	drunk	lead	led	swing	swung
drive	driven	pay	paid	take	taken
eat	eaten	prove	proven	teach	taught
fall	fallen	ride	ridden	tear	torn
feel	felt	ring	rung	throw	thrown
fight	fought	rise	risen	wear	worn
find	found	run	run	write	written

Insight

For the simple past tense form of these irregular verbs, see page 356.

Vocabulary

perfect tense
verb tense that expresses completed action

Using Perfect Tense

Form Rewrite each sentence three times, changing the tenses as requested in parentheses.

I work hard and listen carefully.

1. (past perfect) I had worked hard and had listened carefully.

2. (present perfect) I have worked hard and have listened carefully.

3. (future perfect) I will have worked hard and will have listened carefully.

I gain my position by being helpful, and I keep it the same way.

4. (past perfect) I had gained my position by being helpful, and I had kept it the same way.

5. (present perfect) I have gained my position by being helpful, and I have kept it the same way.

6. (future perfect) I will have gained my position by being helpful, and I will have kept it the same way.

My colleagues depend on me, and I deliver what they need.

7. (past perfect) My colleagues had depended on me, and I had delivered what they need.

8. (present perfect) My colleagues have depended on me, and I have delivered what they need.

9. (future perfect) My colleagues will have depended on me, and I will have delivered what they need.

Learning Outcome

Understand verbals.

LO7 Verbals

A **verbal** is formed from a verb but functions as a noun, an adjective, or an adverb. Each type of verbal—gerund, participle, and infinitive—can appear alone or can begin a **verbal phrase**.

Gerund

A **gerund** is formed from a verb ending in *ing,* and it functions as a noun.

Kayaking is a fun type of exercise. (subject)

I love **kayaking.** (direct object)

A **gerund phrase** begins with the gerund and includes any objects and modifiers.

Running rapids in a kayak is exhilarating. (subject)

I enjoy **paddling a kayak through white water**. (direct object)

Participle

A **participle** is formed from a verb ending in *ing* or *ed,* and it functions as an adjective.

Exhilarated, I ran my first rapids at age 15. (*exhilarated* modifies *I*)

That was an **exhilarating** ride! (*exhilarating* modifies *ride*)

A **participial phrase** begins with the participle and includes any objects and modifiers.

Shocking my parents, I said I wanted to go again.

Infinitive

An **infinitive** is formed from *to* and a present tense verb, and it functions as a noun, an adjective, or an adverb.

To kayak is to live. (noun)

I will schedule more time **to kayak.** (adjective)

You need courage and a little craziness **to kayak.** (adverb)

An **infinitive phrase** begins with an infinitive and includes any objects or modifiers.

I want **to kayak the Colorado River through the Grand Canyon.**

Vocabulary

verbal
gerund, participle, or infinitive; a construction formed from a verb but functioning as a noun, an adjective, or an adverb

verbal phrase
phrase beginning with a gerund, a participle, or an infinitive

gerund
verbal ending in *ing* and functioning as a noun

gerund phrase
phrase beginning with a gerund and including objects and modifiers

participle
verbal ending in *ing* or *ed* and functioning as an adjective

participial phrase
phrase beginning with a participle and including objects and modifiers

infinitive
verbal beginning with *to* and functioning as a noun, an adjective, or an adverb

infinitive phrase
phrase beginning with an infinitive and including objects and modifiers

Using Verbals

Identify Identify each underlined verbal by circling the correct choice in parentheses (gerund, participle, infinitive).

1. Rock climbing is an extreme sport. (gerund, participle, infinitive)
2. I'd like to climb El Capitan one day. (gerund, participle, infinitive).
3. Rappelling down a cliff in Arizona, I almost slipped. (gerund, participle, infinitive).
4. Catching myself, I checked my lines and carabiners. (gerund, participle, infinitive).
5. To fall while climbing could be fatal. (gerund, participle, infinitive).
6. I keep my equipment in top shape to avoid a mishap. (gerund, participle, infinitive).

Form Complete each sentence below by supplying the type of verbal requested in parentheses. Answers will vary.

1. My favorite exercise is ____________________. (gerund)
2. ____________________ would get me into shape. (gerund)
3. ____________________, I could stay in shape (participle)
4. Perhaps I will also try ____________________. (gerund)
5. When exercising, remember ____________________. (infinitive)
6. ____________________, I'll lose weight. (participle)

Write For each verbal phrase below, write a sentence that correctly uses it.

Answers will vary.

1. to work out ____________________
2. choosing a type of exercise ____________________
3. excited by the idea ____________________

Learning Outcome

Use verbals as objects.

LO8 Verbals as Objects

Though both infinitives and gerunds can function as nouns, they can't be used interchangeably as direct objects. Some verbs take infinitives and not gerunds. Other verbs take only gerunds and not infinitives.

Gerunds as Objects

Verbs that express facts are followed by **gerunds**.

admit	deny	enjoy	miss	recommend
avoid	discuss	finish	quit	regret
consider	dislike	imagine	recall	

I miss **walking** along the beach.

not I miss to walk along the beach.

I regret **cutting** our vacation short.

not I regret to cut our vacation short.

fotoadrenalina,2010 / Used under license from Shutterstock.com

Infinitives as Objects

Verbs that express intentions, hopes, and desires are followed by **infinitives**.

agree	demand	hope	prepare	volunteer
appear	deserve	intend	promise	want
attempt	endeavor	need	refuse	wish
consent	fail	offer	seem	
decide	hesitate	plan	tend	

We should plan **to go** back to the ocean.

not We should plan going back to the ocean.

We will endeavor **to save** money for the trip.

not We will endeavor saving money for the trip.

Gerunds or Infinitives as Objects

Some verbs can be followed by either a gerund or an infinitive.

begin	hate	love	remember	stop
continue	like	prefer	start	try

I love **walking** by the ocean.

or I love **to walk** by the ocean.

Vocabulary

gerund
verbal ending in *ing* and functioning as a noun

infinitive
verbal beginning with *to* and functioning as a noun, an adjective, or an adverb

Using Verbals as Objects

Select For each sentence below, circle the appropriate verbal in parentheses.

1. I imagine (walking, to walk) along the Pacific Coast.
2. We want (seeing, to see) whales or dolphins when we are there.
3. I hope (getting, to get) some beautiful shots of the ocean.
4. We should avoid (getting, to get) sunburned when we are on the beach.
5. I enjoy (getting, to get) sand between my toes.
6. Maybe a surfer will offer (showing, to show) me how to surf.
7. We deserve (going, to go) on vacation more often.
8. Later, we will regret not (taking, to take) the time for ourselves.
9. I have never regretted (taking, to take) a vacation.
10. I wish (having, to have) a vacation right now.

Write For each verb below, write your own sentence using the verb and following it with a gerund or an infinitive, as appropriate. Answers will vary.

1. quit ______________________________

____

2. recall ______________________________

____

3. tend ______________________________

____

4. volunteer ______________________________

____

5. discuss ______________________________

____

6. decide ______________________________

____

Learning Outcome

Apply learning to real-world examples.

LO9 Real-World Application

Revise Rewrite the following paragraph, changing passive verbs to active verbs. (See page 352.)

Bedford's school music program should be supported by Grohling Music Suppliers. Our instrument rentals and our sheet-music services have been used extensively by the school system. In these tough economic times, the school should be assisted by us.

Grohling Music Suppliers should support Bedford's school music program. The school system has extensively used our instrument rentals and our sheet-music services. In these tough economic times, we should assist the school.

Revise In the following paragraph, change future perfect verbs into past perfect verbs by crossing out helping verbs and writing new helping verbs. (See page 360.)

We ~~will have~~ had provided reduced-cost sheet music to the school system and ~~will have~~ had added used and refurbished instrument rentals. In addition, we ~~will have~~ had provided best-customer discounts to schools that ~~will have~~ had rented and bought in volume.

Revise In the following paragraph, correct misused verbals by crossing out the gerund or infinitive and replacing it with the correct verbal form. (See page 364.)

I hope ~~exploring~~ to explore these possibilities with you. We could recommend ~~to make~~ making some of these changes the first year. I admit ~~to have~~ having a soft spot for student performers. I recall ~~to get~~ getting my first flute as a student and ~~to begin~~ beginning with music then.

"Where lipstick is concerned, the important thing is not color, but to accept God's final word on where your lips end."

—Jerry Seinfeld

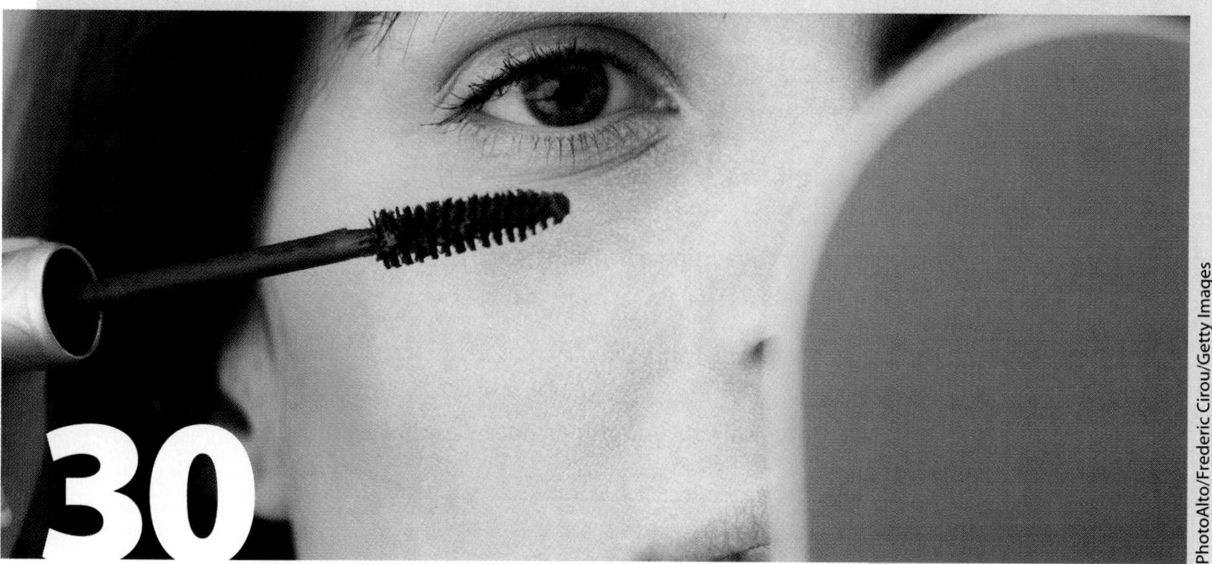

PhotoAlto/Frederic Cirou/Getty Images

30 Adjective and Adverb

The purpose of makeup is to accentuate the beauty that is already in your face. The focus should be on you, not on the mascara, lipstick, foundation, or blush you use.

In the same way, the real beauty of a sentence lies in the nouns and verbs. Adjectives and adverbs can modify those nouns and verbs, bringing out their true beauty, but these modifiers should not overwhelm the sentence. Use them sparingly to make your meaning clear, not to distract with flash. This chapter will show you how to get the most out of those few adjectives and adverbs.

What do you think?

What effect is created when lipstick overwhelms lips? What effect is created when adjectives overload nouns?

Answers will vary.

Learning Outcomes

- LO1 Understand adjective basics.
- LO2 Put adjectives in order.
- LO3 Use adjectivals.
- LO4 Understand adverb basics.
- LO5 Place adverbs well.
- LO6 Use adverbials.
- LO7 Apply adjectives and adverbs in real-world contexts.

Learning Outcome

Understand adjective basics.

Speaking & Listening

Read the first example sentence aloud. Then read it without the adjectives. Note how adjectives add spice to the description. Like spice, though, adjectives should be used sparingly, to "season" nouns, not to overwhelm them.

Vocabulary

adjective
word that modifies a noun or pronoun

articles
the adjectives *a, an,* and *the*

predicate adjective
adjective that appears after a linking verb and describes the subject

positive adjective
word that modifies a noun or pronoun without comparing it

comparative adjective
word that modifies a noun or pronoun by comparing it to something else

superlative adjective
word that modifies a noun or pronoun by comparing it to two or more things

LO1 Adjective Basics

An **adjective** is a word that modifies a noun or pronoun. Even **articles** such as *a, an,* and *the* are adjectives, because they indicate whether you mean a general or specific thing. Adjectives answer these basic questions: *which, what kind of, how many / how much.*

Adjectives often appear before the word they modify.

I saw a **beautiful gray tabby** cat.

A **predicate adjective** appears after the noun it modifies and is linked to the word by a linking verb.

The cat was **beautiful** and **gray**.

Proper adjectives come from proper nouns and are capitalized.

I also saw a **Persian** cat.

Forms of Adjectives

Adjectives come in three forms: positive, comparative, and superlative.

- **Positive adjectives** describe one thing without making any comparisons.

Fred is a **graceful** cat.

- **Comparative adjectives** compare the thing to something else.

Fred is **more graceful** than our dog, Barney.

- **Superlative adjectives** compare the thing to two or more other things

He is the **most graceful** cat you will ever see.

Note: For one- and two-syllable words, create the comparative form by adding *er*, and create the superlative form by added *est*. For words of three syllables or more, use *more* (or *less*) for comparatives and *most* (or *least*) for superlatives. Also note that *good* and *bad* have special superlative forms:

Positive	Comparative	Superlative
good	better	best
bad	worse	worst
big	bigger	biggest
happy	happier	happiest
wonderful	more wonderful	most wonderful

Using the Forms of Adjectives

Identify/Write In each sentence below, identify the underlined adjectives as positive (P), comparative (C), or superlative (S). Then write a new sentence about a different topic, but use the same adjectives.

1. The shelter had a Siamese (P) cat with crossed (P) eyes and black (P) feet.

2. She was more inquisitive (C) than the other cats.

3. Her eyes were the bluest (S) I had ever seen on a cat.

4. Her surprising (P) meow was loud (P) and insistent (P).

5. But her name—Monkey—was the most surprising (S) fact of all.

Correct Read the paragraph below and correct adjective errors, using the correction marks to the right. The first one has been done for you.

Some people say dogs are ~~more~~ tamer than cats, but cats have a ~~more great~~ greater place in some people's hearts. Cats were probably first attracted to human civilizations during the ~~most early~~ earliest days of the agricultural revolution. The sudden surplus of grains attracted many mice, which in turn attracted cats. Cats that were the ~~most~~ best mousers were welcomed by humans. In time, ~~more cute~~ cuter and ~~more cuddly~~ cuddlier cats became pets. But cats have never given up their wildness. Even now, a barn cat that is not used to human touch can be ~~feraler~~ more feral than a dog.

Correction Marks

- delete
- capitalize
- lowercase
- insert
- add comma
- add question mark
- add word
- add period
- spelling
- switch

Learning Outcome

Put adjectives in order.

Insight

As the introduction indicates, native English speakers use this order unconsciously because it sounds right to them. If you put adjectives in a different order, a native English speaker might say, "That's not how anybody says it." One way to avoid this issue is to avoid stacking multiple adjectives before nouns.

Kelly Cheng Travel Photography/Flickr/Getty Images

LO2 Adjective Order

Adjectives aren't all created equally. Native English speakers use a specific order when putting multiple adjectives before a noun, and all speakers of English can benefit from understanding this order.

Begin with . . .

1. articles	a, an, the
demonstrative adjectives	that, this, these, those
possessives	my, our, her, their, Kayla's

Then position adjectives that tell . . .

2. time	first, second, next, last
3. how many	three, few, some, many
4. value	important, prized, fine
5. size	giant, puny, hulking
6. shape	spiky, blocky, square
7. condition	clean, tattered, repaired
8. age	old, new, classic
9. color	blue, scarlet, salmon
10. nationality	French, Chinese, Cuban
11. religion	Baptist, Buddhist, Hindu
12. material	cloth, stone, wood, bronze

Finally place . . .

13. nouns used as adjectives	baby [seat], shoe [lace]

Example:

that ruined ancient stone temple
(**1** + **7** + **8** + **12** + **noun**)

Note: Avoid using too many adjectives before a noun. An article and one or two adjectives are usually enough. More adjectives may overload the noun.

Too many:	their first few expensive delicious French bread appetizers
Effective:	their first French bread appetizers

Placing Adjectives in Order

Order Rearrange each set of adjectives and articles so that they are in the correct order. The first one has been done for you.

1. blue square that
   that square blue button
2. my Scottish rugged
   my rugged Scottish kilt
3. plastic brand-new few
   few brand-new plastic beads
4. worthless a brass
   a worthless brass tack
5. classic many Kenyan
   many classic Kenyan masks
6. aluminum soda Ted's
   Ted's aluminum soda can
7. key Catholic my
   my Catholic key chain
8. dilapidated this old
   this dilapidated old shack
9. wool her woven
   her woven wool cardigan
10. identical seven music
    seven identical music stands
11. young the bright
    the bright young faces
12. last real our
    our last real option

Learning Outcome

Use adjectivals.

LO3 Adjective Questions and Adjectivals

Adjectives answer four basic questions: *which, what kind of, how many / how much.*

Reggie Casagrande/Photodisc/Getty Images

	Guy
Which?	that guy
What kind of?	cool tattooed guy
How many/how much?	one guy

that one cool tattooed guy

Insight

Instead of trying to memorize the names of different types of phrases and clauses, just remember the adjective questions. Turn them into a cheer—*which, what kind of, how many/ how much.*

Adjectivals

A single word that answers one of these questions is called an adjective. If a phrase or clause answers one of these questions, it is an **adjectival** phrase or clause.

	Guy
Which?	guy leaning on the Mustang
What kind of?	guy who exudes attitude

Look at that guy, **who exudes attitude, leaning on the Mustang.**

The following types of phrases and clauses can be adjectivals:

Prepositional phrase:	with his arms crossed
Participial phrase:	staring at something
Adjective clause:	who doesn't even own the Mustang

Vocabulary

adjectival
phrase or clause that answers one of the adjective questions and modifies a noun or pronoun

prepositional phrase
phrase that starts with a preposition and includes an object and modifiers

participial phrase
phrase beginning with a participle (*ing* or *ed* form of verb) plus objects and modifiers; used as an adjective

adjective clause
clause beginning with a relative pronoun and including a verb, but not able to stand alone; functioning as an adjective

Say It

Partner with a classmate. One of you should say the noun, and the other should ask the adjective questions. Then the first person should answer each question with adjectives or adjectivals.

1. **convertibles**
   Which convertibles?
   What kind of convertibles?
   How many convertibles?
2. **detergent**
   Which detergent?
   What kind of detergent?
   How much detergent?

Using Adjectives and Adjectivals

Answer/Write For each word, answer the adjective questions using adjectives and adjectivals. Then write a sentence using two or more of your answers.

Answers will vary.

1. Dogs

Which dogs? ______

What kind of dogs? ______

How many dogs? ______

Sentence: ______

______

______

______

2. Sports

Which sports? ______

What kind of sports? ______

How many sports? ______

Sentence: ______

______

______

______

3. Proposals

Which proposals? ______

What kind of proposals? ______

How many proposals? ______

Sentence: ______

______

______

______

Learning Outcome

Understand adverb basics.

LO4 Adverb Basics

An **adverb** modifies a verb, a **verbal**, an adjective, an adverb, or a whole sentence. An adverb answers five basic questions: *how, when, where, why, to what degree, how often.*

Jacek Chabraszewski,2010 / Used under license from Shutterstock.com

Sheri leaped **fearlessly**.
(*Fearlessly* modifies the verb *leaped.*)

Sheri leaped **quite readily**.
(*Quite* modifies *readily,* which modifies *leaped.*)

Obviously, she wants to fly.
(*Obviously* modifies the whole sentence.)

Note: Most adverbs end in *ly*. Some can be written with or without the *ly*, but when in doubt, use the *ly* form.

loud → loud**ly** tight → tight**ly** deep → deep**ly**

Insight

In the United States, intensifying adverbs such as *very* and *really* are used sparingly. Also, in academic writing, it is considered better to find a precise, vivid verb than to prop up an imprecise verb with an adverb.

Forms of Adverbs

Adverbs have three forms: positive, comparative, and superlative.

- **Positive adverbs** describe without comparing.

Sheri leaped **high** and **fearlessly**.

- **Comparative adverbs** (*-er, more,* or *less*) describe by comparing with one other action.

She leaped **higher** and **more fearlessly** than I did.

- **Superlative adverbs** (*-est, most,* or *least*) describe by comparing with more than one action.

She leaped **highest** and **most fearlessly** of any of us.

Note: Some adjectives change form to create comparative or superlative forms.

well → better → best badly → worse → worst

Vocabulary

adverb
word that modifies a verb, a verbal, an adjective, an adverb, or a whole sentence

verbal
word formed from a verb but functioning as a noun, an adjective, or an adverb

positive adverb
adverb that modifies without comparing

comparative adverb
adverb that modifies by comparing with one other thing

superlative adverb
adverb that modifies by comparing to two or more things

Using the Forms of Adverbs

Provide In each sentence below, provide the correct form of the adverb in parentheses—positive, comparative, or superlative.

1. My friend likes to eat quickly (quickly).
2. She eats more quickly (quickly) than I do.
3. She eats most quickly (quickly) of anyone I know.
4. My brother eats reluctantly. (reluctantly)
5. He eats more reluctantly (reluctantly) than a spoiled child.
6. He eats most reluctantly (reluctantly) of anyone on Earth.
7. I eat slowly. (slowly)
8. I eat more slowly (slowly) than I used to.
9. I eat most slowly (slowly) of anytime in my life.
10. I suppose the three of us eat pretty ________ (badly).

Choose In each sentence, circle the correct word in parentheses. If the word modifies a noun or pronoun, choose the adjective form (good, bad). If the word modifies a verb, a verbal, an adjective, or an adverb, choose the adverb form (well, badly.)

1. My brother went to a (good, well) play.
2. He said the actors did (good, well), and that the plot was (good, well).
3. He even got a (good, well) deal on tickets for (good, well) seats.
4. He wanted (bad, badly) to see this play.
5. The problem was that one patron behaved (bad, badly).
6. He had a (bad, badly) attitude and once even booed.
7. My brother told him to stop, but the guy took it (bad, badly).
8. The ushers did (good, well) when they removed the guy.
9. The audience even gave them a (good, well) ovation.
10. My brother says the overall evening went (good, well).

Learning Outcome

Place adverbs well.

Kapu,2010 / Used under license from Shutterstock.com

LO5 Placement of Adverbs

Adverbs should be placed in different places in sentences, depending on their use.

How Adverbs

Adverbs that tell *how* can appear anywhere except between a verb and a direct object.

Steadily we hiked the trail.
We **steadily** hiked the trail.
We hiked the trail **steadily**.

not We hiked **steadily** the trail.

When Adverbs

Adverbs that tell *when* should go at the beginning or end of the sentence.

We hiked to base camp **yesterday**. **Today** we'll reach the peak.

Where Adverbs

Adverbs that tell *where* should follow the verb they modify, but should not come between the verb and the direct object. (**Note:** Prepositional phrases often function as *where* adverbs.)

The trail wound **uphill** and passed **through rockslide debris**.
We avoided falling rocks **throughout our journey.**

not We avoided **throughout our journey** falling rocks.

To What Degree Adverbs

Adverbs that tell *to what degree* go right before the adverb they modify.

I learned **very** definitely the value of good hiking boots.

How Often Adverbs

Adverbs that tell *how often* should go right before an action verb, even if the verb has a helping verb.

I **often** remember that wonderful hike.
I will **never** forget the sights I saw.

Placing Adverbs Well

Place For each sentence below, insert the adverb (in parentheses) in the most appropriate position. The first one has been done for you.

occasionally
1. In order to scare off bears, we made noise. (occasionally)

usually
2. Bears avoid contact with human beings. (usually)

often
3. A bear surprised or cornered by people will turn to attack. (often)

very
4. A mother bear with cubs is likely to attack. (very)

sometimes
5. If a bear approaches, playing dead may work. (sometimes)

usually
6. Climbing a tree is not the best idea. (usually)

often
7. Black bears climb trees. (often)

usually
8. Grizzly bears just knock the tree down. (usually)

especially
9. Another defense is to open your coat to look large. (especially)

very
10. At the same time, try to make a loud noise. (very)

Revise In the paragraph below, use the transpose mark (⌒‿) to move adverbs into their correct positions.

Spotting wildlife is one often of the highlights of a hiking trip. Deer appear in fields occasionally, and lucky hikers might glimpse a bear sometimes in the distance. Porcupines, raccoons, and other creatures amble out of the woods curiously. Not usually hikers will see mountain lions because the cats are ambush predators. Mountain lions attack groups of people rarely and usually avoid human contact. Do keep children from behind straggling.

Learning Outcome

Use adverbials.

LO6 Adverb Questions and Adverbials

Adverbs answer six basic questions: *how, when, where, why, to what degree,* and *how often*.

Don Smith/Flickr/Getty Images

	Children splashed.
How?	splashed barefoot
When?	splashed today
Where?	splashed outside
Why?	splashed excitedly
To what degree?	splashed very excitedly
How often?	splashed repeatedly

Today, the children **repeatedly** and **very excitedly** splashed **barefoot outside**.

Note: Avoid this sort of adverb overload in your sentences.

Adverbials

Often, the adverb questions are answered by **adverbial** phrases and clauses, which answer the same six questions.

	Children splashed.
How?	splashed jumping up and down
When?	splashed during the downpour
Where?	splashed in the puddles in the driveway
Why?	splashed for the joy of being wet
To what degree?	splashed until they were drenched
How often?	splashed throughout the storm

During the downpour and **throughout the storm**, the children splashed, **jumping up and down in the puddles in the driveway for the joy of being wet** and **until they were drenched.**

Note: Again, avoid this sort of adverbial overload in your sentences.

The following types of phrases and clauses can be adverbials:

Prepositional phrase:	in the puddles in the driveway
Participial phrase:	jumping up and down
Dependent clause:	until they were drenched

Insight

The adverb questions can be memorized by turning them into a cheer: *how, when, where, why, to what degree, how often!*

Vocabulary

adverbial
phrase or clause that answers one of the adverb questions

Using Adverbials

Answer/Write For each sentence, answer the adverb questions using adverbs and adverbials. Then write a sentence using three or more of your answers.

Answers will vary.

1. **They danced.**

How did they dance? ____________________

When did they dance? ____________________

Where did they dance? ____________________

Why did they dance? ____________________

To what degree did they dance? ____________________

How often did they dance? ____________________

Sentence: ____________________

____

____

____

2. **They sang.**

How did they sing? ____________________

When did they sing? ____________________

Where did they sing? ____________________

Why did they sing? ____________________

To what degree did they sing? ____________________

How often did they sing? ____________________

Sentence: ____________________

____

____

____

Learning Outcome

Apply adjectives and adverbs in real-world contexts.

LO7 Real-World Application

Correct In the following document, correct the use of adjectives and adverbs. Use the correction marks to the left.

Correction Marks

- delete
- capitalize
- lowercase
- insert
- add comma
- add question mark
- add word
- add period
- spelling
- switch

Clowning Around

1328 West Mound Road
Waukesha, Wi 53100
262-555-8180

January 6, 2011

Mrs. Judy Bednar
38115 North Bayfield Drive
Waukesha, WI 53100

Dear Ms. Bednar:

It's time for a party birthday! You've thought of everything—balloons, decorations, cake . . . But what about awesome awesomely entertainment? How many kids are coming and how much time do you have to keep them entertained?

Fear not. At Clowning Around, we specialize in making every birthday the most fun funnest and most memorable memorablest it can be. For young kids, we offer balloon colorful animals, magic amazing magic tricks, and backyard goofy games. For older kids, we have water wild games and magic street illusions. And for kids of all ages, we have the funniest most funny clowns, the most bravest superheroes, and most amazing amazingest impressionists.

That's right. You can throw a terrific party for your loved one worrying without about the entertainment—and paying without a lot either. See the enclosed brochure for our services and rates. Then give us a call at Clowning Around, and we'll make your party next an event to remember.

Let's talk soon!

Dave Jenkins

Dave Jenkins
CEO, Clowning Around

Enclosure: Brochure

Workplace

Note the effect of adjectives and adverbs on voice. Errors make the writer sound odd, but careful use can create energy and interest.

"A family is a unit composed not only of children but of men, women, an occasional animal, and the common cold."
—Ogden Nash

Alistair Berg/Digital Vision/Getty Images

31 Conjunction and Preposition

A family is a network of relationships. Some people have an equal relationship, like wives and husbands or brothers and sisters. Some people have unequal relationships, like mothers and daughters or fathers and sons. And the very young or very old are often considered dependent on those in their middle age.

Ideas also have relationships, and conjunctions and prepositions show those relationships. When two ideas are equal, a coordinating conjunction connects them. When two ideas are not equal, a subordinating conjunction makes one idea depend on the other. And prepositions create special relationships between nouns and other words.

Conjunctions and prepositions help you connect ideas and build whole families of thought.

Learning Outcomes

- **LO1** Use coordinating and correlative conjunctions.
- **LO2** Use subordinating conjunctions.
- **LO3** Understand common prepositions.
- **LO4** Use *by, at, on,* and *in.*
- **LO5** Use conjunctions and prepositions in real-world documents.

What do you think?

What equal relationships do you have? What dependent relationships do you have?

Answers will vary.

Learning Outcome

Use coordinating and correlative conjunctions.

LO1 Coordinating and Correlative Conjunctions

A **conjunction** is a word or word group that joins parts of a sentence—words, phrases, or clauses.

Coordinating Conjunctions

A **coordinating conjunction** joins grammatically equal parts—a word to a word, a phrase to a phrase, or a clause to a clause. (A clause is basically a sentence.)

Coordinating Conjunctions

and	but	or	nor	for	so	yet

Equal importance: A coordinating conjunction shows that the two things joined are of equal importance.

Rachel and Lydia enjoy arts and crafts..
(*And* joins words in an equal way.)

They have knitted sweaters and pieced quilts.
(*And* joins the phrases *knitted sweaters* and *pieced quilts.*)

I tried to knit a sweater, but the thing unraveled.
(*But* joins the two clauses, with a comma after the first.)

Items in a series: A coordinating conjunction can also join more than two equal things in a series.

Rachel, Lydia, and I will take a class on making mosaics.
(*And* joins *Rachel, Lydia,* and *I*. A comma follows each word except the last.)

We will take the class, design a mosaic, and complete it together.
(*And* joins three parts of a compound verb.)

Stockbyte/Getty Images

Correlative Conjunctions

Correlative conjunctions consist of a coordinating conjunction paired with another word. They also join equal grammatical parts: word to word, phrase to phrase, or clause to clause.

Correlative Conjunctions

either/or	neither/nor	whether/or	both/and	not only/but also

Stressing equality: Correlative conjunctions stress the equality of parts.

Not only Rachel but also Lydia has made beautiful quilts.
(*Not only / but also* stresses the equality of *Rachel* and *Lydia.*)

Either I will learn quilting, or I will die trying.
(*Either / or* joins the two clauses, with a comma after the first.)

Vocabulary

conjunction
word or word group that joins parts of a sentence

coordinating conjunction
conjunction that joins grammatically equal components

correlative conjunction
pair of conjunctions that stress the equality of the parts that are joined

Using Coordinating and Correlative Conjunctions

Correct In each sentence below, circle the best coordinating conjunction in parentheses.

1. I would like to learn knitting (but, for, or) crocheting.
2. Lydia, Rachel, (and, nor, yet) I enjoy making cloth with our hands.
3. We have different talents, (or, so, yet) we teach each other what we know.
4. Lydia is best at knitting, (nor, but, for) I am best at tatting.
5. Rachel is our weaver, (but, yet, so) she is the loom master.
6. Each week, Lydia, Rachel, (and, but, or) I meet to share our works.
7. We want to broaden our skills, (and, or, yet) it's hard to learn something new.
8. I like needlepoint, Rachel likes quilting, (and, nor, so) Lydia likes construction.
9. Come join us one day, (and, for, so) we love to teach beginners.
10. We'll show you our work, (but, nor, for) you'll decide what you want to learn.

Write Create sentences of your own, using a coordinating conjunction *(and, but, or, nor, for, so, yet)* as requested in each. Answers will vary.

1. joining two words: ____________________
2. joining two phrases: ____________________
3. creating a series: ____________________
4. joining two clauses (place a comma after the first clause, before the conjunction): ____________________

Write Create a sentence using a pair of correlative conjunctions:

Answers will vary.

Traits

When two ideas correlate, they work together. They co-relate. Thinking in this way can help you remember the term *correlative conjunctions.*

Learning Outcome

Use subordinating conjunctions.

LO2 Subordinating Conjunctions

A **subordinating conjunction** is a word or word group that connects two clauses of different importance. (A clause is basically a sentence.)

Subordinating Conjunctions

after	as long as	if	so that	till	whenever
although	because	in order that	than	unless	where
as	before	provided that	that	until	whereas
as if	even though	since	though	when	while

Subordinate clause: The subordinating conjunction comes at the beginning of the less-important clause, making it subordinate (it can't stand on its own). The **subordinate clause** can come before or after the more important clause (the **independent clause**).

Summer is too hot to cook inside. I often barbecue.
(two clauses)

Because summer is too hot to cook inside, I often barbecue.
(*Because* introduces the subordinate clause, which is followed by a comma.)

I often barbecue because summer is too hot to cook inside.
(If the subordinate clause comes second, a comma usually isn't needed.)

Special relationship: A subordinating conjunction shows a special relationship between ideas. Here are the relationships that subordinating conjunctions show:

Time	after, as, before, since, till, until, when, whenever, while
Cause	as, as long as, because, before, if, in order that, provided that, since, so that, that, till, until, when, whenever
Contrast	although, as if, even though, though, unless, whereas

Whenever the temperature climbs, I cook on the grill.
(time)

I grill because I don't want to heat up the house.
(cause)

Even though it is hot outside, I feel cool in the shade as I cook.
(contrast)

Traits

In the military, a *subordinate* is someone who takes orders from a superior. Think of a subordinate clause as one that takes orders from the main clause.

Vocabulary

subordinating conjunction
word or word group that connects clauses of different importance

subordinate clause
word group that begins with a subordinating conjunction and has a subject and verb but can't stand alone as a sentence

independent clause
group of words with a subject and verb and that expresses a complete thought; it can stand alone as a sentence

Using Subordinating Conjunctions

Write Fill in the blank in each sentence with an appropriate subordinating conjunction. Then circle what type of relationship it shows.

Example answers:

1. After I marinated the chicken, I put it on the grill.
   (time, cause, contrast)
2. Grilling bratwurst is tough because the grease causes big flames. (time, cause, contrast)
3. Because of trichinosis, pork should not be pink inside.
   (time, cause, contrast)
4. I like grilling chicken even though my favorite food is steak.
   (time, cause, contrast)
5. I grill my steak rare although the FDA recommends well-done.
   (time, cause, contrast)
6. Some people use barbecue sauce whereas I prefer marinades. (time, cause, contrast)
7. I use a gas grill since it is fast and convenient. (time, cause, contrast)
8. Purists use only charcoal because it creates a nice flavor.
   (time, cause, contrast)
9. When I was in Texas, I had magnificent brisket.
   (time, cause, contrast)
10. Although brisket can be tough, this was totally tender.
    (time, cause, contrast)

Write Create three of your own sentences, one for each type of relationship.

Answers will vary.

1. time: ______________________________

2. cause: ______________________________

3. contrast: ______________________________

Learning Outcome

Understand common prepositions.

LO3 Common Prepositions

A **preposition** is a word or word group that shows a relationship between a noun or pronoun and another word. Here are common prepositions:

Prepositions

aboard	back of	except for	near to	round
about	because of	excepting	notwithstanding	save
above	before	for	of	since
according to	behind	from	off	subsequent to
across	below	from among	on	through
across from	beneath	from between	on account of	throughout
after	beside	from under	on behalf of	'til
against	besides	in	onto	to
along	between	in addition to	on top of	together with
alongside	beyond	in behalf of	opposite	toward
alongside of	but	in front of	out	under
along with	by	in place of	out of	underneath
amid	by means of	in regard to	outside	until
among	concerning	inside	outside of	unto
apart from	considering	inside of	over	up
around	despite	in spite of	over to	upon
as far as	down	instead of	owing to	up to
aside from	down from	into	past	with
at	during	like	prior to	within
away from	except	near	regarding	without

Speaking & Listening

A prepositional phrase can help break up a string of adjectives. Instead of writing "the old, blue-awninged store," you can write "the old store with the blue awning." Read sentences aloud to find stacked-up adjectives and use prepositional phrases to create a better flow.

Prepositional Phrases

A **prepositional phrase** starts with a preposition and includes an object of the preposition (a noun or pronoun) and any modifiers. A prepositional phrase functions as an adjective or adverb.

The Basset hound flopped on his side on the rug.
(*On his side* and *on the rug* modify the verb *flopped*.)

He slept on the rug in the middle of the hallway.
(*On the rug* modifies *slept; in the middle* modifies *rug;* and *of the hallway* modifies *middle*.)

Comstock/Getty Images

Vocabulary

preposition
word or word group that creates a relationship between a noun or pronoun and another word

prepositional phrase
phrase that starts with a preposition, includes an object of the preposition (noun or pronoun) and any modifiers; and functions as an adjective or adverb

Using Common Prepositions

Create In each sentence, fill in the blanks with prepositional phrases. Create them from the prepositions on page 386 and nouns or pronouns of your own choosing. Be creative! Answers will vary.

1. Yesterday, I ran ______________________________.
2. Another runner ______________________________ waved at me.
3. I was so distracted, I ran ______________________________.
4. The other runner then ran ______________________________.
5. We both had looks of surprise ______________________________.
6. I leaped ______________________________.
7. The other runner jogged ______________________________.
8. Then we both were ______________________________.
9. The incident ______________________________ was a lesson.
10. The lesson was not to run ______________________________.

Model Read each sentence below and write another sentence modeled on it. Note how the writer uses prepositional phrases to create specific effects.

Answers will vary.

1. The coupe shot between the semis, around the limousine, down the tunnel, and up into bright sunlight.

   ____

   ____

2. I will look for you, but I also look to you.

   ____

   ____

3. Before the freedom of the road and the fun of the trip, I have finals.

   ____

   ____

4. Walk through the hallway, down the stairs, through the door, and into the pantry.

   ____

   ____

Learning Outcome

Use *by, at, on,* and *in.*

LO4 *By, At, On,* and *In*

Prepositions often show the physical position of things—above, below, beside, around, and so on. Four specific prepositions show position but also get a lot of other use in English.

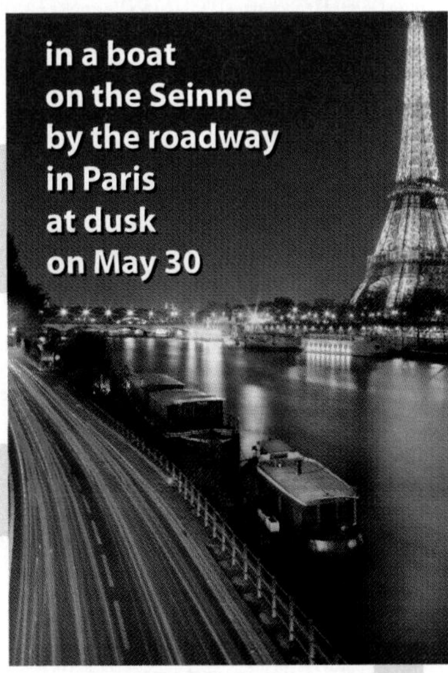

Proframe Photography/Flickr/Getty Images

Uses for *By, At, On,* and *In*

By means "beside" or "up to a certain place or time."

by the creek, by the garage
by noon, by August 16

At refers to a specific place or time.

at the edge, at the coffe shop
at 6:45 p.m., at midnight

On refers to a surface, a day or date, or an electronic medium.

on the table, on the T-shirt
on July 22, on Wednesday
on the computer, on the DVD

In refers to an enclosed space; a geographical location; an hour, a month, or a year; or a print medium.

in the hall, in the bathroom
in Madison, in France
in a minute, in December, in 2014
in the magazine, in the book

Insight

Native English speakers follow these rules without thinking about them. Listen to the way native English speakers use *by, at, on,* and *in*, and practice their use until it seems second-nature.

Say It

Team up with a partner. Have the first person read one of the words below, and have the second person use it in a prepositional phrase beginning with *by, at, on,* or *in*. The first person should check if the form is correct. (Some have more than one correct answer.) Then you should switch roles.

1. the den
2. June 23
3. 9:33 p.m.
4. the MP3 player
5. the corner
6. Pittsburgh
7. the counter
8. the diner
9. sunset
10. the newspaper

Using *By, At, On,* and *In*

Provide In each sentence, circle the correct preposition in parentheses.

1. The guests arrived (by, on, in) 7:30 p.m., so we could eat (at, on, in) 8:00 p.m.
2. Put your suitcase (by, at, on, in) the trunk or (by, at, on) the rooftop luggage rack.
3. I looked for the new album (by, at, on, in) a music store, but could find it only (by, at, on, in) the Internet.
4. We waited (by, at, on, in) the lobby for a half hour, but Jerry didn't show up or even call (by, at, on, in) his cell phone.
5. Three people standing (by, at, in) the corner saw a traffic accident (by, at, on) the intersection of 45th and Monroe.
6. (By, At, On, In) April 1 of 2012, many pranksters may post apocalypse hoaxes (by, at, on, in) the Internet.
7. Let's meet (by, at, on) the convenience store (at, on, in) 7:00 p.m.
8. Place your order form (by, at, on, in) the postage-paid envelope, write your return address (by, at, on, in) the envelope, and post it.
9. A cat lay (by, at, on) the windowsill and looked me (by, at, on, in) the eye.
10. (At, On, In) noon of January 7, the school's pipes (at, on, in) the basement froze and caused flooding.

Write Write a sentence that uses all four of these prepositions in phrases: *by, at, on, in.* Answers will vary.

Learning Outcome

Use conjunctions and prepositions in real-world documents.

LO7 Real-World Application

Revise Read the following e-mail, noting how choppy it sounds because all of the sentences are short. Connect some of the sentences using a coordinating conjunction and a comma, and connect others using a subordinating conjunction. You can also change other words as needed. (Use the correction symbols to the left.) Reread the e-mail to make sure it sounds smooth.

Coordinating Conjunctions

and	but	or	nor
for	so	yet	

Subordinating Conjunctions

after	as long as	if	so that	till	whenever
although	because	in order that	than	unless	where
as	before	provided that	that	until	whereas
as if	even though	since	though	when	while

Correction Marks

- delete
- capitalize
- lowercase
- insert
- add comma
- add question mark
- add word
- add period
- spelling
- switch

Update on Book Revision

From: rhaverson@haversonpublishing.com

To: dkraitsman@delafordandco.com

Subject: Completed Photo Log

Example corrections:

Dear Deirdra:

Attached, please find the photo log. ~~The log~~ that shows all photos on the Website. Some photos are from Getty Images. Others are from Shutterstock, and A few are from Corbis. All photos have been downloaded, and ~~The downloads~~ have the right resolution.

I hope you are pleased with the log. It includes permissions details, ~~It also shows~~ the resolution, ~~I included~~ and a description of each photo.

I am available for more work. I could compile another photo log, or ~~I could also~~ do the permissions work on these photos. I do writing and editing as well.

Thank you for this project. I look forward to hearing from you.

Thanks,

Roger Haverson
Photo Editor

Correct Read the following party invitation, noting the incorrect use of the prepositions *by, at, on,* and *in*. (See pages 388.) Correct the errors by deleting the prepositions and replacing them. Use the correction marks on the facing page.

Workplace

Correct use of *by, at, on,* and *in* will mark you as a writer comfortable with English.

Rankin Technology Annual Picnic

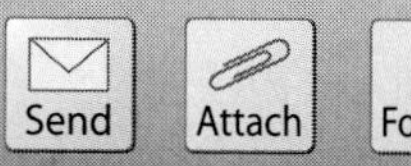

From: Leanna Cartwright

To: Running Man Press Staff

Subject: Annual Running Man Holiday Party

Dear Staff:

It's time for the Running Man Press Holiday Party!

Who? All employees and their significant others

What? Should come for dinner

Where? ~~By~~ At the Hilton ~~in~~ on Grand Avenue ~~on~~ in Ballroom B

When? ~~At~~ On December 12, beginning ~~on~~ at 7:00 p.m. and going until 11:00 p.m.

Why? We're celebrating a great year ~~on~~ at Running Man Press

The event is full of fun, including drinks ~~in~~ at 7:00 p.m., dinner ~~on~~ at 8:00 p.m., awards ~~in~~ at 9:00 p.m., and dancing ~~on~~ at 9:30 p.m. Prime rib, roast chicken, and vegetarian selections are ~~at~~ on the menu, and beverages of all sorts will be available ~~in~~ at the bar.

Please RSVP ~~at~~ by December 2 to let us know how many people will join us ~~on~~ at the Hilton. We look forward to having a great night with everyone ~~at~~ on December 12.

Sincerely,

Leanna Cartwright

Human Resources

Part 7 Punctuation and Mechanics Workshops

"The writer who neglects punctuation, or mispunctuates, is liable to be misunderstood for the want of merely a comma."

—Edgar Allan Poe

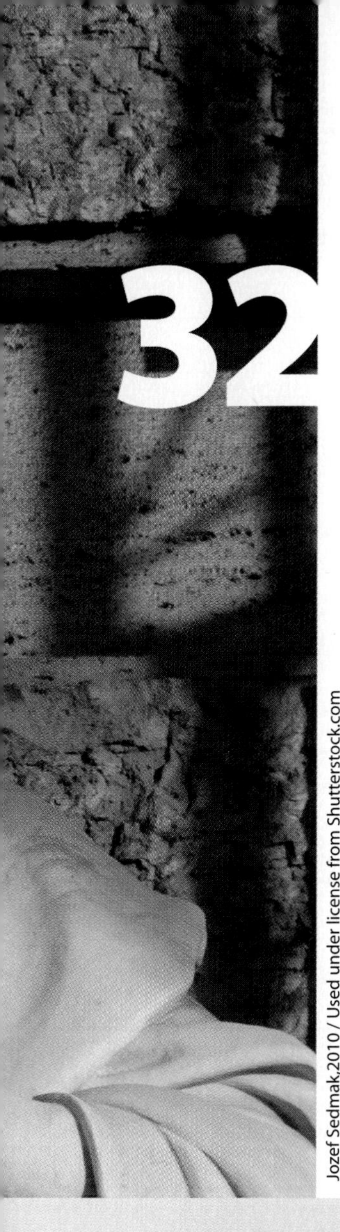

Jozef Sedmak,2010 / Used under license from Shutterstock.com

32 Comma

When you speak, you communicate with much more than words. You pause, raise or lower your pitch, change your tone or volume, and use facial expressions and body language to get your point across.

When you write, you can forget about pitch or volume, facial expressions or body language. You're left with the tone of your words and with the pauses that you put in them. Commas give you one way to create a soft pause. They help to show which words belong together, which should be separated, and which line up in parallel. Commas are key to being understood.

In this chapter you will learn about the conventional use of commas. Understanding the correct comma usage is an important step in becoming a college-level writer.

What do you think?

Imagine reading a book or newspaper without punctuation. What difficulties may you encounter? Explain.

Answers will vary.

Learning Outcomes

- **LO1** Use commas in compound sentences.
- **LO2** Use commas with introductory phrases and equal adjectives.
- **LO3** Use commas between items in a series.
- **LO4** Use commas with appositives and nonrestrictive modifiers.
- **LO5** Use commas in real-world writing.

Learning Outcome

Use commas in compound sentences.

Traits

Make sure to use both a comma and a coordinating conjunction in a compound sentence, or you will create a comma splice or a run-on. For more information, see pages 303–310.

LO1 In Compound Sentences and After Introductory Clauses

The following principles will guide the conventional use of commas in your writing.

In Compound Sentences

Use a comma before the coordinating conjunction *(and, but, or, nor, for, yet, so)* in a compound sentence.

Heath Ledger completed his brilliant portrayal as the Joker in *The Dark Knight*, **but** he died before the film was released.

Note: Do not confuse a compound verb with a compound sentence.

Ledger's Joker became instantly iconic and won him the Oscar for best supporting actor. (compound verb)

His death resulted from the abuse of prescription drugs, but it was ruled an accident. (compound sentence)

After Introductory Clauses

Use a comma after most introductory clauses.

Although Charlemagne was a great patron of learning, he never learned to write properly. (adverb dependent clause)

When the clause follows the independent clause and is not essential to the meaning of the sentence, use a comma. This comma use generally applies to clauses beginning with *even though, although, while,* or some other conjunction expressing a contrast.

Charlemagne never learned to write properly**, even though he continued to practice**.

Note: A comma is *not* used if the dependent clause following the independent clause is needed.

Correcting Comma Errors

Correct For each sentence below, add a comma (^,) before the coordinating conjunction *(and, but, or, nor, for, so, yet)* if the clause on each side could stand alone as a sentence. Write "correct" if the conjunction separates word groups that can't stand alone.

1. Catherine had questions about her class schedule, so she set up an appointment with her academic adviser. ______
2. I was going to play in the sand volleyball league, but it conflicted with my work schedule. ______
3. Trisha picked up some groceries and stopped by the bank. correct
4. I normally don't listen to jazz music, yet I love going to summer jazz concerts in the park. ______
5. Should I finish my essay a day early, or should I go to my friend's house party? ______
6. Kevin has a job interview at the advertisement agency, and he hopes he can make a good impression. ______
7. Creativity is his best quality, but leadership is not far behind. ______

Correct For each sentence below, add a comma after any introductory clauses. If no comma is needed, write "correct" next to the sentence.

1. Even though digital books are the craze, I prefer paperbacks. ______
2. Although the crab dip appetizer was delicious, my entrée left something to be desired. ______
3. Because I'm starved for time, online shopping is a convenient alternative to mall shopping. ______
4. I toggled through radio stations while I waited at the tollbooth. correct
5. Erin worried about giving her speech, even though she had practiced for weeks. ______

Learning Outcome

Use commas with introductory words and equal adjectives.

LO2 With Introductory Words and Equal Adjectives

After Introductory Phrases

Use a comma after introductory phrases.

In spite of his friend's prodding, Jared decided to stay home and study.

A comma is usually omitted if the phrase follows an independent clause.

Jared decided to stay home and study **in spite of his friend's prodding.**

You may omit a comma after a short (four or fewer words) introductory phrase unless it is needed to ensure clarity.

At 10:30 p.m. he would quit and go to sleep.

Speaking & Listening

Try the strategies below by speaking the words aloud. If it sounds strange to switch the order of the adjectives or to insert an *and* between them, do not separate them with a comma.

To Separate Adjectives

Use commas to separate adjectives that equally modify the same noun. Notice in the examples below that no comma separates the last adjective from the noun.

You should exercise regularly and follow a **sensible, healthful** diet.

A good diet is one that includes lots of **high-protein, low-fat** foods.

To Determine Equal Modifiers

To determine whether adjectives modify a noun equally, use these two tests.

1. Reverse the order of the adjectives; if the sentence is clear, the adjectives modify equally. (In the example below, *hot* and *crowded* can be switched, but *short* and *coffee* cannot.)

   Matt was tired of working in the **hot, crowded** lab and decided to take a **short coffee** break.

2. Insert *and* between the adjectives; if the sentence reads well, use a comma when *and* is omitted. (The word *and* can be inserted between *hot* and *crowded,* but *and* does not make sense between *short* and *coffee.*)

Brian K., 2010/used under license from www.shutterstock.com

Correcting Comma Errors

Correct For each sentence below, insert a comma after the introductory phrase if it is needed. If no comma is needed, write "correct" next to the sentence.

1. Before you send the e-mail, make sure you reread it for errors in clarity. ________
2. In accordance with the academic code, plagiarism is deemed a major offense. ________
3. After hitting the 10-mile jogging plateau, Heather felt a great rush of adrenaline. ________
4. Heather felt a great rush of adrenaline after hitting the 10-mile jogging plateau. correct
5. Thankfully DeMarcus stopped the leak before it could do any real damage. correct
6. Based on his past experience, Wilson decided against going to the concert. ________
7. To train for the triathlon, Brent altered his diet. ________
8. At the end of the day, Erin recorded her favorite show. ________

Correct For each sentence below, determine whether or not a comma is needed to separate the adjectives that modify the same noun. Add any needed commas (^). Write "no" next to the sentence if a comma is not needed.

1. I'm expecting this to be a **rocking after** party. no
2. There's nothing like the **warm, emerald** water off the Florida Gulf Coast. ________
3. The exercise program included a **calorie-burning cardio** session. no
4. My **surly economics** professor is one of a kind. no
5. I'm in desperate need of a **relaxing summer** vacation. no
6. Marathon runners favor **light, comfortable** shorts. ________

Learning Outcome

Use commas between items in a series.

LO3 Between Items in a Series and Other Uses

Between Items in Series

Use commas to separate individual words, phrases, or clauses in a series. (A series contains at least three items.)

> Many college students must balance studying with **taking care of a family, working, getting exercise, and finding time to relax**.

Do not use commas when all the items in a series are connected with *or, nor,* or *and.*

> Hmm . . . should I study **or** do laundry **or** go out?

To Set Off Transitional Expressions

Use a comma to set off conjunctive adverbs and transitional phrases.

> Handwriting is not**, as a matter of fact,** easy to improve upon later in life**; however,** it can be done if you are determined enough.

If a transitional expression blends smoothly with the rest of the sentence, it does not need to be set off.

> If you are **in fact** coming**,** I'll see you there.

Traits

Do not use a comma before an indirect quotation.

Incorrect: My roommate said**,** that she doesn't understand the notes I took.

Correct: My roommate said that she doesn't understand the notes I took.

To Set Off Dialogue

Use commas to set off the words of the speaker from the rest of the sentence.

> **"Never be afraid to ask for help,"** advised Ms. Kane
>
> **"With the evidence that we now have,"** Professor Thom said**, "many scientists believe there could be life on Mars."**

To Enclose Explanatory Words

Use commas to enclose an explanatory word or phrase.

> Time management**, according to many professionals,** is an important skill that should be taught in college.

Correcting Comma Errors

Correct Indicate where commas are needed in the following sentences.

1. I considered becoming a lawyer; however, law school wasn't for me.
2. "Don't give up, don't ever give up," advised the late Jim Valvano.
3. MGMT's music is infused with electronic beats, catchy lyrics, and a pop-friendly sound.
4. Western Wisconsin, as opposed to Illinois, is relatively hilly.
5. In Boston I visited Fenway Park, the U.S.S. *Constitution,* and Old North Church.
6. Thomas, as you may have noticed, is eager to share his vast knowledge of random facts.
7. In regard to public transportation, you may decide between the subway, buses, or taxicabs.
8. "While it certainly offers a convenient alternative to paper maps," said Emilie, "my car's navigational system more often gets me lost."
9. Avocados, the key ingredient of guacamole, are a good source of fiber.
10. Secondly, determine if weather, price, or transportation will factor into your decision.

Correct Indicate where commas are needed in the following paragraph.

On an early summer morning in July, I sat slumped in a terminal at JFK airport, reminiscing about my time in Washington, D.C. It had been a fun trip. I visited all the usual landmarks, including the Lincoln Memorial, Arlington National Cemetery, and the Smithsonian Institute. However, my favorite landmark was Mount Vernon, the home and former estate of President George Washington. It's easy to see why Washington adored the location. The estate, located in Alexandria, Virginia, is nestled above the Hudson River. Besides Washington's plantation home, the estate also included a distillery, a blacksmith shop, and acres of farmland. If you're ever in Washington, D.C., I highly recommend a trip to Mount Vernon.

Learning Outcome

Use commas with appositives and nonrestrictive modifiers.

LO4 With Appositives and Other Word Groups

To Set Off Some Appositives

A specific kind of explanatory word or phrase called an **appositive** identifies or renames a preceding noun or pronoun.

Albert Einstein**, the famous mathematician and physicist,** developed the theory of relativity.

Do not use commas if the appositive is important to the basic meaning of the sentence.

The famous physicist **Albert Einstein** developed the theory of relativity.

Traits

Do not use commas to set off necessary clauses and phrases, which add information that the reader needs to understand the sentence.

Example: Only the professors **who run at noon** use the locker rooms in Swain Hall to shower. (necessary clause)

With Some Clauses and Phrases

Use commas to enclose phrases or clauses that add information that is not necessary to the basic meaning of the sentence. For example, if the clause or phrase (in **boldface**) were left out of the two examples below, the meaning of the sentences would remain clear. Therefore, commas are used to set off the information.

The locker rooms in Swain Hall**, which were painted and updated last summer,** give professors a place to shower. (nonrestrictive clause)

Work-study programs**, offered on many campuses,** give students the opportunity to earn tuition money. (nonrestrictive phrase)

Using "That" or "Which"

Use *that* to introduce necessary clauses; use *which* to introduce unnecessary clauses.

Campus jobs **that are funded by the university** are awarded to students only. (necessary)

The cafeteria**, which is run by an independent contractor,** can hire nonstudents. (unnecessary)

Vocabulary

appositive
a noun or noun phrase that renames another noun right beside it

Correcting Comma Errors

Correct Indicate where commas are needed in the following sentences. If no commas are needed, write "correct" next to the sentence.

1. The U.S.S. *Constitution*, a wooden-hulled ship named by George Washington, is the world's oldest, floating, commissioned naval vessel. __________
2. Gordon Ramsay, the fiery chef and television star, specializes in French, Italian, and British cuisines. __________
3. Hall of Fame baseball player and notable philanthropist Roberto Clemente died in a plane crash while en route to Nicaragua to deliver aid to earthquake victims. __________
4. The concert hall, which is on the corner of Meridian Ave and 1st Street, is expected to revitalize the downtown district. __________
5. Press passes that allow for backstage access are given out to special media members. __________
6. John Quincy Adams, who later became the sixth president of the United States, authored the Monroe Doctrine in 1823. __________

Write The following sentences contain clauses using *that*. Rewrite the sentences with clauses using *which*, and insert commas correctly. You may need to reword some parts.

Example answers:

1. The mechanical issue that delayed the flight should be corrected within 25 minutes.

   The mechanical issue, which delayed the flight, should be corrected within 25 minutes.

2. The wind farm that was built along I-95 is scheduled to double in size by 2013.

   The wind farm, which was built along I-95, is scheduled to double in size by 2013.

3. Scholarships that are sponsored by the Kiwanis Club are awarded to local high school students.

   Scholarships, which are sponsored by the Kiwanis Club, are awarded to local high school students.

Learning Outcome

Use commas in real-world writing.

LO5 Real-World Application

Correct Indicate where commas are needed in the following e-mail message.

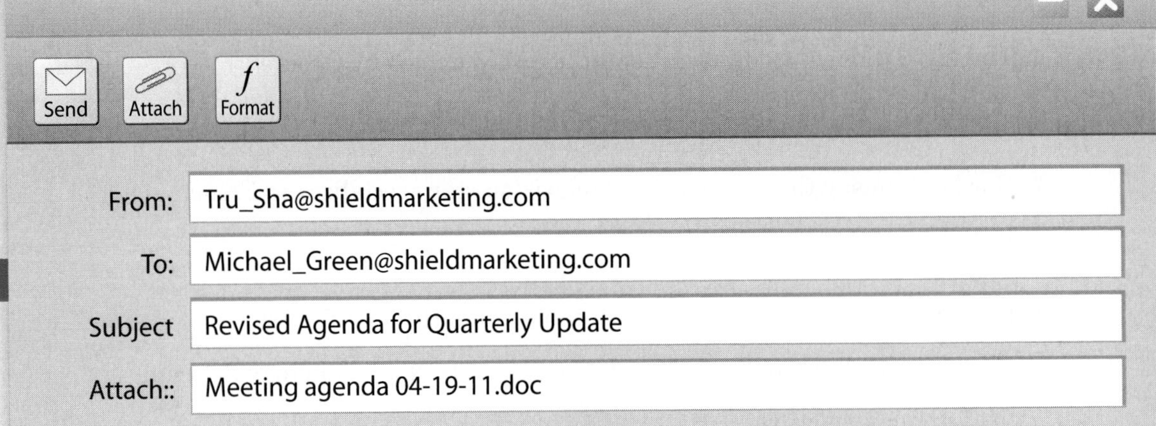

Hi, Michael:

I've attached the agenda for the quarterly update with the marketing team. Daniel Gilchrest, senior marketing coordinator, will moderate the meeting, but I want you to familiarize yourself with the material. Here are some highlights of the new agenda:

1. The advertising allowance for Gillette, Hillsboro Farms, and Justice Inc. has increased by 5 percent.
2. The penetrated market, which accounts for actual users of products, declined in the health-care sector.
3. We will shift the focus of marketing efforts to meet the digital and social media demands of today's market.

Please review the agenda by the end of the day, and let me know if you have any additions or corrections.

Thanks

Tru Sha

Marketing Associate

Pablo Eder, 2010/used under license from www.shutterstock.com

Correction Marks

- delete
- capitalize
- lowercase
- insert
- add comma
- add question mark
- add word
- add period
- spelling
- switch

Workplace

Correct comma use is critical for clear business communication.

"I get the Reese's candy bar. If you read it, there's an apostrophe. The candy bar is his. Next time you're eating a Reese's and some guy named Reese comes up to you and says, 'Let me have that,' you better give it to him."

—Mitch Hedberg

Suzanne Tucker,2010 / Used under license from Shutterstock.com

33 Apostrophe

The position of an apostrophe makes a world of a difference to the meaning of a sentence. Take a close look at the following two examples:

- My brother's girlfriend is having a beach party.
- My brothers' girlfriend is having a beach party.

In the first sentence, an apostrophe and *s* is added to make the singular *brother* possessive. The meaning of the sentence is clear: the girlfriend of the writer's brother is having a beach party. In the second sentence, an apostrophe is positioned after the *s*, forming the plural possessive *brothers'*. In other words, the writer of the second example has more than one brother dating the same girl, who is throwing a beach party.

Apostrophes have two main uses: to form possessives and contractions. The rules and activities in this chapter will help you understand their usage.

Learning Outcomes

LO1 Use apostrophes for contractions and possessives.

LO2 Apply apostrophes in real-world documents.

What do you think?

Have you ever noticed a misplaced apostrophe? Where did you find it? Explain the situation.

Answers will vary.

Learning Outcome

Use apostrophes for contractions and possessives.

LO1 Contractions and Possessives

Apostrophes are used primarily to show that a letter or number has been left out, or that a noun is possessive.

Contractions

When one or more letters are left out of a word, use an apostrophe to form the **contraction**.

don't (*o* is left out)	he'd (*woul* is left out)	would've (*ha* is left out)

Binkski, 2010/used under license from www.shutterstock.com

Missing Characters

Use an apostrophe to signal when one or more characters are left out.

class of '16 (*20* is left out)	rock 'n' roll (*a* and *d* are left out)	good mornin' (*g* is left out)

Possessives

Form possessives of singular nouns by adding an apostrophe and an *s*.

Sharla's pen	the man's coat	*The Pilgrim's Progress*

Singular Noun Ending In *s* (One Syllable)

Form the possessive by adding an apostrophe and an *s*.

the boss's idea	the lass's purse	the bass's teeth

Singular Noun Ending In *s* (Two Or More Syllables)

Form the possessive by adding an apostrophe and an *s*—or by adding just an apostrophe.

Kansas's plains	*or*	Kansas' plains

Plural Noun Ending In *s*

Form the possessive by adding just an apostrophe.

the bosses' preference	the Smiths' home

Note: The word before the apostrophe is the owner.

the girl's ball (*girl* is the owner)	the girls' ball (*girls* are the owners)

Plural Noun Not Ending In *s*

Form the possessive by adding an apostrophe and an *s*.

the children's toys	the women's room

Insight

Pronoun possessives *do not use* apostrophes: *its, whose, hers, his, ours*

Vocabulary

contraction
word formed by joining two words, leaving out one or more letters (indicated by an apostrophe)

Forming Contractions and Possessives

Write For each contraction below, write the words that formed the contraction. For each set of words, write the contraction that would be formed.

1. you're you are
2. John is John's
3. would have would've
4. she'd she would
5. you would you'd
6. shouldn't should not
7. I had I'd
8. they are they're
9. we've we have
10. it is it's

Rewrite Rework the following sentences, replacing the "of" phrases with possessives using apostrophes.

1. I'm going to the house of Jeremy.
   I'm going to Jeremy's house.
2. The ice cream of the corner stand is amazing.
   The corner stand's ice cream is amazing.
3. The pace of the track star is impressive.
   The track star's pace is impressive.
4. I like the early work of the Rolling Stones.
   I like the Rolling Stones' early work.
5. The persona of Texas is well represented in the slogan "Everything is bigger in Texas."
   Texas' persona is well represented in the slogan "Everything is bigger in Texas."
6. The paintings of the artist were outstanding.
   The artist's paintings were outstanding.
7. I discovered the best pizza spot of Portland.
   I discovered Portland's best pizza spot.
8. She reviewed the notes of Kimbra.
   She reviewed Kimbra's notes.
9. The contractor assessed the structure of the house.
   The contractor assessed the house's structure.
10. The position of the politician on health care remained firm.
    The politician's position on health care remained firm.

Learning Outcome

Apply apostrophes in real-world documents.

LO2 Real-World Application

Correct The following letter sounds too informal because it contains too many contractions. Cross out contractions and replace them with full forms of the words. Also, correct any errors with apostrophes. Use the correction marks to the left.

Correction Marks

- delete
- capitalize
- lowercase
- insert
- add comma
- add question mark
- add word
- add period
- spelling
- switch

REDLAND STATE BANK

October 13, 2012

Phillip Jones
2398 10th Ave.
Westchester, NY 10959

Dear Mr. Jones:

This ~~letter's~~ letter is a response to your inquiry about financing your housing project. I enjoyed discussing your project and appreciated your honesty about your current loan.

As of today, ~~we've~~ we have decided to make a commitment to your project. ~~I've~~ I have enclosed Redland State Banks' commitment letter. Please take time to read the terms of agreement.

If ~~there's~~ there is any part you ~~don't~~ do not understand, ~~don't~~ do not hesitate to call or e-mail us. ~~We'd~~ We would be happy to answer any questions. As always's, we look forward to serving you.

Sincerely,

Melinda Erson

Melinda Erson
Loan Officer

Enclosure: Commitment Letter

"Sometimes people give [book] titles to me,
and sometimes I see them on a billboard."
—Robert Penn Warren

Image Source/Getty Images

34 Quotation Marks and Italics

Broadway is plastered with billboards five stories high and is jammed with marquees that flash in the night. They advertise plays and movies, books and magazines, albums and TV shows—all in spotlights or neon trying to make people take notice.

In writing, there are no spotlights, there is no neon. Instead of writing the names of plays, movies, books, and so forth in giant, flashing letters, writers set them off with This chapter will show you how to correctly punctuate titles of works big and small and words used as words.

Learning Outcomes

LO1 Understand the use of quotation marks.

LO2 Understand the use of italics.

LO3 Apply quotation marks and italics in a real-world document.

What do you think?

How are quotation marks and italics like flashing lights in writing? How are they different?

Answers will vary.

Learning Outcome

Understand the use of quotation marks.

LO1 Quotation Marks

To Punctuate Titles (Smaller Works)

Use quotation marks to enclose the titles of smaller works, including speeches, short stories, songs, poems, episodes of audio or video programs, chapters or sections of books, unpublished works, and articles from magazines, journals, newspapers, or encyclopedias. (For other titles, see page 410.)

Speech:	"Ain't I a Woman?"
Song:	"California Gurls"
Short Story:	"The Tell-Tale Heart"
Magazine Article:	"Is Google Making Us Stupid?"
Chapter in a Book:	"The Second Eve"
Television Episode:	"The Empty Child"
Encyclopedia Article:	"Autoban"

Placement of Periods and Commas

When quoted words end in a period or comma, always place that punctuation inside the quotation marks.

"When you leave the kitchen," Tim said, "turn out the light."

Placement of Semicolons and Colons

When a quotation is followed by a semicolon or colon, always place that punctuation outside the quotation marks.

I finally read "The Celebrated Jumping Frog of Calaveras County"; it is a hoot!

Placement of Exclamation Points and Question Marks

If an exclamation point or a question mark is part of the quotation, place it inside the quotation marks. Otherwise, place it outside.

Shawndra asked me, "Would you like to go to the movies?" What could I say except, "That sounds great"**?**

Insight

In British English, a single quotation mark is used instead of double quotation marks. Also, British English has different rules for using other punctuation with quotation marks. When writing in a U.S. setting, use the rules on this page.

For Special Words

Quotation marks can be used (1) to show that a word is being referred to as the word itself; (2) to indicate that it is jargon, slang, or a coined term; or (3) to show that it is used in an ironic or sarcastic sense.

(1) The word "chuffed" is British slang for "very excited."
(2) I'm "chuffed" about my new computer.
(3) I'm "chuffed" about my root canal.

Using Quotation Marks

Correct In the following sentences, insert quotation marks (" ") where needed.

1. Tim loves the short story "Cask of Amontillado" by Edgar Allan Poe.
2. Stephen King's short story "The Body" was made into a movie.
3. Anna Quindlen wrote the article "Uncle Sam and Aunt Samantha."
4. Lisa told Jennie, "Tonight is the pizza and pasta buffet."
5. Jennie asked, "Isn't it buy one, get one free?"
6. Was she thinking, "That's a lot better than cooking"?
7. Here is the main conflict of the story "To Build a Fire": man versus nature.
8. I read an article entitled "The Obese Fruit of Capitalism"; it suggested that our modern obesity epidemic demonstrates the tremendous achievements of fast food and agribusiness.
9. What does the word "hypertrophy" mean?
10. I was "thrilled" to receive the unexpected bill.

Write Write a sentence that indicates the actual meaning of each sentence below.

Sample answers:

1. The fully loaded logging truck "tiptoed" across the one-lane bridge.

   The fully loaded truck drove slowly and carefully across the one-lane bridge.

2. Enjoy our "fast" and "friendly" service.

   Enjoy our slow and unfriendly service.

3. We had a "fun" time at our IRS audit.

   We had an unpleasant time at our IRS audit.

Learning Outcome

Understand the use of italics.

WAC

As you write research reports in different classes, find out which style your discipline uses for reporting titles of larger and smaller works.

LO2 Italics

To Punctuate Titles (Larger Works)

Use italics to indicate the titles of larger works, including newspapers, magazines, journals, pamphlets, books, plays, films, radio and television programs, movies, ballets, operas, long musical compositions, CD's, DVD's, software programs, and legal cases, as well as the names of ships, trains, aircraft, and spacecraft. (For other titles, see page 408.)

Magazine: *The Week*	Newspaper: *Chicago Tribune*
Play: *Cat on a Hot Tin Roof*	Journal: *Nature*
Film: *Casablanca*	Software Program: *Final Draft*
Book: *Death's Disciples*	Television Program: *Doctor Who*

For a Word, Letter, or Number Referred to as Itself

Use italics (or quotation marks—see page 408) to show that a word, letter, or number is being referred to as itself. If a definition follows a word used in this way, place that definition in quotation marks.

The word *courage* comes from the French word *cour,* which means "heart."

In the handwritten note, I couldn't distinguish an *N* from an *M*.

For Foreign Words

Use italics to indicate a word that is being borrowed from a foreign language.

The phrase *et cetera ad nauseum* is a Latin phrase meaning "and so on until vomiting."

For Technical Terms

Use italics to introduce a technical term for the first time in a piece of writing. After that, the term may be used without italics.

Particle physicists are seeking the elusive *Higgs boson*—a subatomic particle thought to provide mass to all other particles. The Higgs boson has become a sort of Holy Grail of quantum mechanics.

Note: If a technical term is being used within an organization or field of study where it is common, it may be used without italics even the first time in a piece of writing.

Using Italics

Correct In the following sentences, underline words that should be in italics.

1. One of my favorite novels is The Curious Incident of the Dog in the Night-Time by Mark Haddon.
2. Have you seen the amazing movie Memento?
3. The name of the paso doble dance comes from the Spanish word for "double step."
4. In 1945, the bomber called the Enola Gay dropped the first atomic bomb, a weapon predicted in 1914 in the H. G. Wells novel The World Set Free.
5. She always has a real joie de vivre.
6. To look at the PDF, you need Adobe Reader or Adobe Acrobat.
7. In this context, the words profane and profanity do not refer to swearing but simply to things that are not divine.
8. The television show Project Runway pits fashion designers against each other.
9. In the musical A Funny Thing Happened on the Way to the Forum, the slave Pseudolus spells out his hope to be F – R – E – E.
10. The enlargement of muscles through weight lifting is known as hypertrophy.

Write Write three sentences, each demonstrating your understanding of one or more rules for using italics. Answers will vary.

1. ______________________________

2. ______________________________

3. ______________________________

Learning Outcome

Apply quotation marks and italics in a real-world document.

LO3 Real-World Application

Practice In the following business letter, underline any words that should be italicized and add quotation marks (“ ”) where needed.

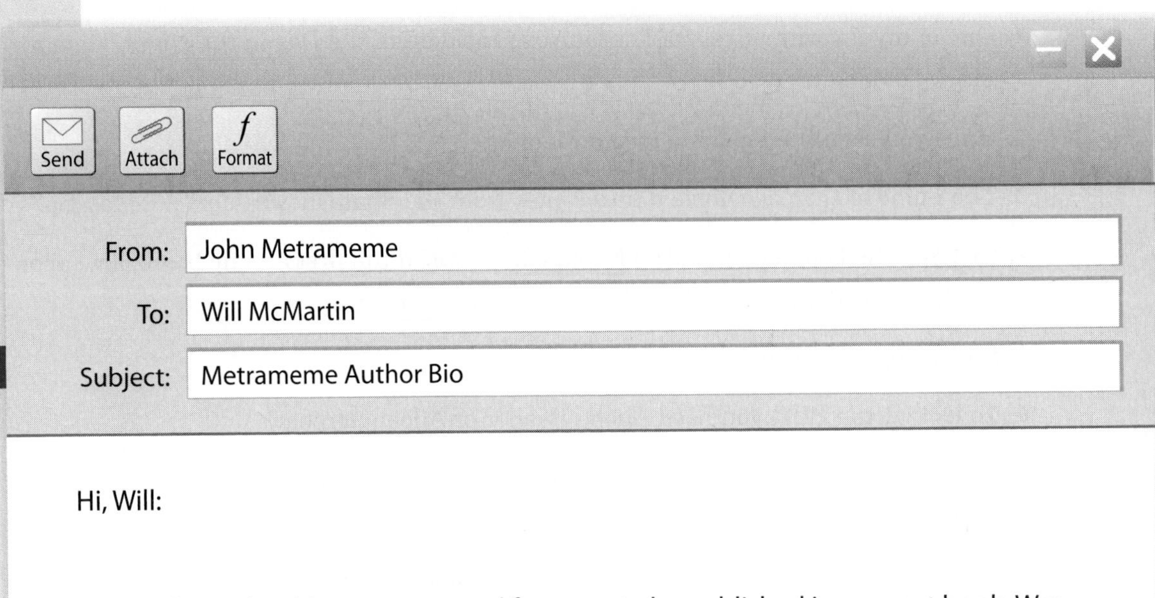

Workplace

Note how improperly punctuated titles can lead to confusion in business writing. Correct punctuation makes for clear communication.

Hi, Will:

Here is the author bio you requested from me to be published in my next book, War Child:

John Metrameme has published over a dozen novels, most recently the historical epic Sons of Thunder and the romp Daddy Zeus. He has written articles also for The Atlantic and The New Yorker, and his short story "Me and the Mudman" won the Rubel Prize. Metrameme is perhaps best known for his novel Darling Buds of May.

In his spare time, Metrameme enjoys acting in productions at his community theater. He played himself in the three-man show The Complete Works of William Shakespeare (Abridged). He also starred as Kit Gill in No Way to Treat a Lady and as Jonathan in Arsenic and Old Lace.

Will, please let me know if you need anything more from me.

Thanks,

John

"Conventions are subject to the vagaries of time and fashion. . . . The writers of the Constitution capitalized words in the middle of sentences."

—Mitchell Ivers

Richard Newstead/Flickr/

35 Capitalization

Why is the word *mom* capitalized in "Did Mom call?" and not in "Did my mom call?" Why is *river* capitalized in "the Ohio River" but not in "the Ohio and Missouri rivers"? These are just two of the vagaries when it comes to proper capitalization in our language. As you page through this section, you will find others.

One of the best ways to learn about the unexpected changes in capitalization is to become a reader and writer yourself. Combine regular reading and writing with the practice in this chapter and you will be well on your way to mastering correct capitalization. You can also use this chapter as a reference whenever you have questions about capitalization. Each left-hand page provides an easy-to-use set of rules and examples.

Learning Outcomes

- LO1 Understand basic capitalization rules.
- LO2 Understand advanced capitalization rules.
- LO3 Understand capitalization of titles, organizations, abbreviations, and letters.
- LO4 Understand capitalization of names, courses, and Web terms.
- LO5 Apply capitalization in real-world documents.

Vocabulary

vagaries
unexpected changes

What do you think?

Why do you suppose that we pay so much attention to the rules of capitalization? Why don't we capitalize words in the middle of sentences?

Answers will vary.

Learning Outcome

Understand basic capitalization rules.

LO1 Basic Capitalization

All first words, proper nouns, and proper adjectives must be capitalized. The following guidelines and examples will help explain these rules.

Proper Nouns and Adjectives

Capitalize all proper nouns and all proper adjectives (adjectives derived from proper nouns). The chart below provides a quick overview of capitalization.

Insight

Different languages use capitalization differently. For example, German capitalizes not just proper nouns but all important nouns. Compare and contrast capitalization styles between your heritage language and English.

Quick Guide: Capitalization at a Glance

Days of the week	**Saturday, Sunday, Tuesday**
Months	**March, August, December**
Holidays, holy days	**Christmas, Hanukah, President's Day**
Periods, events in history	**the Renaissance, Middle Ages**
Special events	**Tate Memorial Dedication Ceremony**
Political parties	**Republican Party, Green Party**
Official documents	**Bill of Rights**
Trade names	**Frisbee disc, Heinz ketchup**
Formal epithets	**Alexander the Great**
Official titles	**Vice-President Al Gore, Senator Davis**
Official state nicknames	**the Garden State, the Beaver State**
Planets, heavenly bodies	**Earth, Mars, the Milky Way**
Continents	**Asia, Australia, Europe**
Countries	**France, Brazil, Japan, Pakistan**
States, provinces	**Montana, Nebraska, Alberta, Ontario**
Cities, towns, villages	**Portland, Brookfield, Broad Ripple**
Streets, roads, highways	**Rodeo Drive, Route 66, Interstate 55**
Sections of the United States and the world	**the West Coast, the Middle East**
Landforms	**Appalachian Mountains, Kalahari Desert**
Bodies of water	**Lake Erie, Tiber River, Atlantic Ocean**
Public areas	**Central Park, Rocky Mountain National Park**

First Words

Capitalize the first word in every sentence and the first word in a full-sentence direct quotation.

Professional sports has become far too important in the United States.

Yvonne asked, "**Why** do baseball players spit all of the time?"

Correcting Capitalization

Practice A In each sentence below, place capitalization marks (≡) under any letters that should be capitalized.

1. Musician louis armstrong helped make jazz popular to american and european audiences.
2. Armstrong grew up in new Orleans in a rough neighborhood called the "battleground."
3. he was sent to reform school because he fired a gun in the air on new year's eve.
4. Upon his release, he visited music halls like funky butt hall to hear king oliver play.
5. Oliver gave armstrong his first real cornet, and he played with oliver's band in storyville, the red-light district in New orleans.
6. He also played with the allen brass band on the strekfus line of riverboats.
7. In 1919, Armstrong left new Orleans for Chicago and played with kid orv.
8. He really began to make a name for himself in the creole jazz band that played at Lincoln gardens in Chicago.

Practice B Read the following paragraph. Place capitalization marks (≡) under any letters that should be capitalized in proper nouns, proper adjectives, or first words.

My great-grandfather Erv grew up in Racine, Wisconsin, during the great depression. He lived in two different houses on villa street just south of the downtown area. Erv attended Holy Name Catholic school and Franklin school when he was a kid. His dad, my great-great-grandfather, came from Poland and started out by selling hot dogs at north beach. Because money was scarce, great-grandfather's family sometimes had only corn on the cob for dinner. After high school, he enlisted in the U.S. navy, but was turned down because of poor eyesight. He then joined the army and fought in Europe during world war II. when Erv returned to Racine, he went to work at massey harris, a company that made tractors.

Learning Outcome

Understand advanced capitalization rules.

LO2 Advanced Capitalization

Sentences in Parentheses

Capitalize the first word in a sentence that is enclosed in parentheses if that sentence is not combined within another complete sentence.

I need to learn more about the health care system in Canada. (**Missy** just married a guy from Toronto.)

Note: Do *not* capitalize a sentence that is enclosed in parentheses and is located in the middle of another sentence.

Missy's husband (his name is Andre) works in a family business.

Sentences Following Colons

Capitalize a complete sentence that follows a colon when that sentence is a formal statement, a quotation, or a sentence that you want to emphasize.

Seldom have I heard such encouraging words: **The** economy is on the rebound.

Salutation and Complimentary Closing

In a letter, capitalize the first and all major words of the salutation. Capitalize only the first word of the complimentary closing.

Dear Governor Doyle: **Sincerely** yours,

Sections of the Country

Words that indicate sections of the country are proper nouns and should be capitalized; words that simply indicate directions are not proper nouns.

The **Southwest** is suffering from a drought. *(section of country)*

I live a few blocks **southwest** of here. *(direction)*

Insight

Some sections of different countries may be unfamiliar to you. For example, the Corn Belt and the Great Plains are sections of this county. The Lake District or The Lakes is a specific district in Great Britain.

Languages, Ethnic Groups, Nationalities, and Religions

Capitalize languages, ethnic groups, nationalities, religions, Supreme Beings, and holy books.

African **Navajo** **Islam** **God** **Allah**
Jehovah **the Koran** **Exodus** **the Bible**

Correcting Capitalization

Practice A In each sentence below, place capitalization marks (≡) under any letters that should be capitalized.

1. The high plains is a subregion in the great plains.
2. Golda Meir once said this about women: "whether women are better than men I cannot say—but I can say they are certainly no worse."
3. The hopi indians come from a group of people called pueblo.
4. My dad is already planning for his retirement. (what will he do with so much free time?)
5. Many people from Mexico prefer Mexican American more than hispanic or latino.
6. Don't visit the deep south in August unless you like stifling heat and humidity.
7. The third largest religion, hinduism, does not have a single founder or a single sacred text.
8. My mechanic made a bad day even worse: he told me that my car needed four new tires.

Practice B Read the following paragraph. Place capitalization marks (≡) under any letters that should be capitalized.

From 1943-1954, the midwest was blessed with the All American Girls Professional Baseball League. There were teams in Racine, Kenosha, Rockford, south Bend, Fort Wayne, grand Rapids, and Minneapolis. The league filled an entertainment need created by World War II: many men, especially minor leaguers, were serving overseas. The women wore dress uniforms with knee-high woolen socks. (they must have been careful about sliding.) The women became heroines for young girls all across the country, from new England to the west coast.

Practice C Place capitalization marks (≡) under any letters that should be capitalized.

kleenex tissue   the koran   holiday   asian   forest

memorial day   sherwood forest   tissue paper   the middle east

Learning Outcome

Understand capitalization of titles, organizations, abbreviations, and letters.

WAC

Note that the American Psychological Association has a different style for capitalizing the titles of smaller works. Be sure you know the style required for a specific class.

LO3 Other Capitalization Rules I

Titles

Capitalize the first word of a title, the last word, and every word in between except articles *(a, an, the),* short prepositions, *to* in an infinitive, and coordinating conjunctions. Follow this rule for titles of books, newspapers, magazines, poems, plays, songs, articles, films, works of art, and stories.

Knight** and **Day (movie)	***Washington Post*** (newspaper)
"What a Wonderful World" (song)	**"Death Penalty's False Promise"** (essay)
Comedy** of **Errors (play)	***Gulliver's Travels*** (novel)

Organizations

Capitalize the name of an organization or a team and its members.

Habitat for **Humanity**	**Libertarian Party**
The Bill & **Melinda Gates Foundation**	**Chicago Cubs**
Special Olympics	**Phoenix Suns**

Abbreviations

Capitalize abbreviations of titles and organizations.

M.D. **Ph.D.** **NAACP** **C.E.** **B.C.E.** **GPA**

Letters

Capitalize letters used to indicate a form or shape.

S-curve **T-shirt** **R-rated** **C-section**

Correcting Capitalization

Practice A In each sentence below, place capitalization marks (≡) under any letters that should be capitalized.

1. To me, *a midsummer night's dream* is one of Shakespeare's best plays.
2. The San Francisco giants used to play in Candlestick park.
3. I enjoyed reading *city of thieves,* a novel by David Benioff.
4. Do you know the song "don't drink the water" by dave matthews?
5. My brother splattered some paint on my favorite Chicago white sox t-shirt.
6. Newman's own foundation donates to charities all net royalties and profits after taxes it receives from Newman's own products.
7. Javier Lopez, an old friend from the neighborhood, earned a ph.d in history.
8. Perhaps the least known of the beatles is George Harrison; I love his song "while my guitar gently weeps."
9. The current hit "the kids are all right" is r-rated according to the *Denver post.*
10. Anna Quindlen's article "uncle sam and aunt samantha" first appeared in *newsweek.*
11. People attend aa (alcoholics anonymous) meetings to support each other as they battle their alcoholism.

Practice B Read the paragraph below, placing capitalization marks (≡) under letters that should be capitalized.

An article in last week's *standard press* promoted the city's farmer's market. The market, held every Thursday afternoon, is sponsored by the Brighton chamber of commerce. The vendors, who must reside within the local area, sell everything from fresh produce to tie-dyed t-shirts. In addition, organizations such as the american red cross and Brighton little league have informational booths at the market. A special feature is the live entertainment supplied by rainbow road, a local folk rock band. They play a lot of Bob Dylan, singing favorites like "blowin' in the wind."

Learning Outcome

Understand capitalization of names, courses, and Web terms.

LO4 Other Capitalization Rules II

Words Used as Names

Capitalize words like father, mother, uncle, senator, and professor only when they are parts of titles that include a personal name or when they are substitutes for proper nouns (especially in direct address).

Hello, **Representative** Baldwin. (*Representative* is part of the name.)

It's good to meet you, **Representative**. (*Representative* is a substitute for the name.

Our **representative** is a member of two important committees.

Who was the volleyball **coach** last year?

We had **Coach Snyder** for two years.

I met **Coach** in the athletic office.

Note: To test whether a word is being substituted for a proper noun, simply read the sentence with a proper noun in place of the word. If the proper noun fits in the sentence, the word being tested should be capitalized. Usually the word is not capitalized if it follows a possessive—*my, his, our, your,* and so on.

Did **Mom** (Yvonne) pick up the dry cleaning?
(*Yvonne* works in the sentence.)

Did your **mom** (Yvonne) pick up the dry cleaning?
(*Yvonne* does not work in the sentence; the word *mom* follows *your*.)

Insight

Do not capitalize common nouns and titles that appear near, but are not part of, a proper noun.

Chancellor John Bohm . . .
(Chancellor *is part of the name.)*

John Bohm, our chancellor, . . .
(Chancellor *appears near, but is not part of, the proper noun.)*

Titles of Courses

Words such as technology, history, and science are proper nouns when they are included in the titles of specific courses; they are common nouns when they name a field of study.

The only course that fits my schedule is **Introduction to Oil Painting**.
(title of a specific course)

Judy Kenner advises anyone interested in **oil painting**.
(a field of study)

Internet and E-Mail

The words *Internet* and *World Wide Web* are capitalized because they are considered proper nouns. When your writing includes a Web address (URL), capitalize any letters that the site's owner does (on printed materials or on the site itself).

When doing research on the **Internet**, be sure to record each site's **Web** address (URL) and each contact's **e-mail** address.

Correcting Capitalization

Practice A In each sentence below, place capitalization marks (≡) under any words that should be capitalized.

1. Every summer, pastor Bachman leads the youth group on a hike around lake geneva.
2. Claude Dickert, our current mayor, writes blog entries on *About brighton,* the city's official web site.
3. At the celebration, dad asked senator ryan about health care.
4. The easiest course I ever took in high school was called leisure reading.
5. When I'm on the internet, I use google to answer all kinds of questions.
6. Whenever mom talks about politics, she eventually criticizes our local congressman.
7. My night course, contemporary history, is always packed because professor scharfenburg presents such interesting lectures.
8. When it comes to shopping for books, I often go to amazon.com for ideas and information.
9. Our instructor had us bookmark *grammar girl,* a web site that provides grammar tips and practice.
10. Make an appointment with the dean if you want to drop cultural geography.

Practice B Read the paragraph below, placing capitalization marks (≡) under any words or letters that should be capitalized.

Internet art does not consist of existing pieces of artwork digitized to be seen using a web browser. Instead, it is art that is created on or with the net, and it comes into being using web sites, e-mail options, virtual worlds such as *second life,* and so on. Steve Dietz, formerly the curator of the Walker art center, defines internet art as art that has "the internet as a necessary condition of viewing/participating/experiencing." Martin Wattenberg has created a Web site called *idea line,* which provides "a timeline of net artwork" to help people experience this type of art.

Learning Outcome

Apply capitalization in real-world documents.

Workplace

Proper capitalization in a business document not only reflects well on the writer, but also shows respect for the names of readers and businesses.

LO5 Real-World Application

Correct In the following basic letter, place capitalization marks (≡) under letters that should be capitalized. If a letter is capitalized and shouldn't be put a lowercase editing mark (/) through the letter.

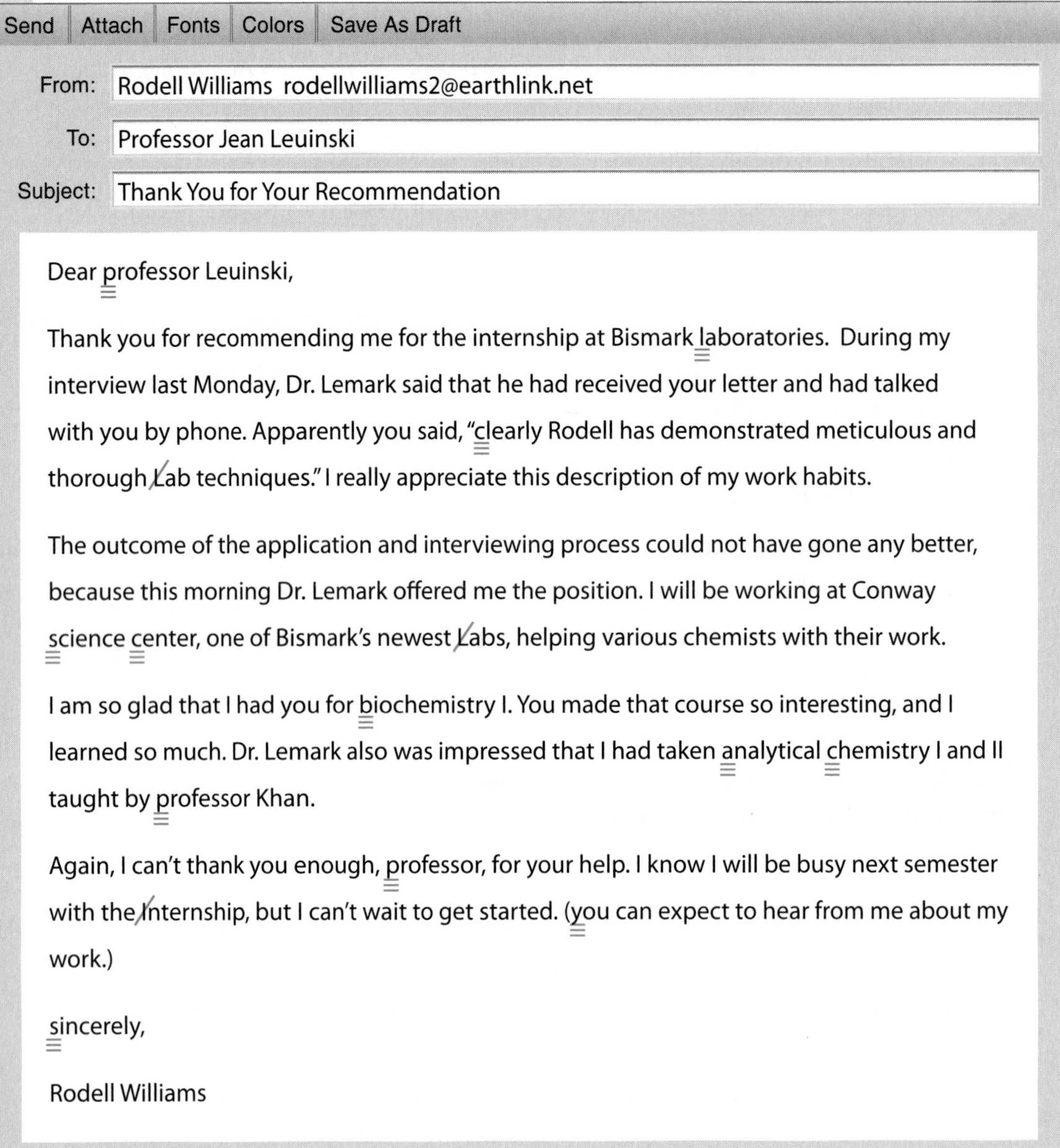

Send | Attach | Fonts | Colors | Save As Draft

From: Rodell Williams rodellwilliams2@earthlink.net

To: Professor Jean Leuinski

Subject: Thank You for Your Recommendation

Dear professor Leuinski,

Thank you for recommending me for the internship at Bismark laboratories. During my interview last Monday, Dr. Lemark said that he had received your letter and had talked with you by phone. Apparently you said, "clearly Rodell has demonstrated meticulous and thorough Lab techniques." I really appreciate this description of my work habits.

The outcome of the application and interviewing process could not have gone any better, because this morning Dr. Lemark offered me the position. I will be working at Conway science center, one of Bismark's newest Labs, helping various chemists with their work.

I am so glad that I had you for biochemistry I. You made that course so interesting, and I learned so much. Dr. Lemark also was impressed that I had taken analytical chemistry I and II taught by professor Khan.

Again, I can't thank you enough, professor, for your help. I know I will be busy next semester with the Internship, but I can't wait to get started. (you can expect to hear from me about my work.)

sincerely,

Rodell Williams

Special Challenge Write one sentence in which you use the same regional or directional word twice—with the word correctly capitalized in one case and correctly lowercase in the other case.

WRITE 2 was built on a simple principle: to create a new teaching and learning solution that reflects the way today's faculty teach and the way you learn.

Through conversations, focus groups, surveys, and interviews, we collected data that drove the creation of the current version of **WRITE 2** that you are using today. But it doesn't stop there. In order to make **WRITE 2** an even better learning experience, we'd like you to **SPEAK UP** and tell us how **WRITE 2** worked for you.

What did you like about it? What would you change? Are there additional ideas you have that would help us build a better product for next semester's students?

At **login.cengagebrain.com,** you'll find a survey form to send us your comments—in addition to all of the resources you need to become a confident and effective writer.

Speak up! Go to **login.cengagebrain.com** today.

Part 8 Reading

"How we remember, what we remember, and why we remember form the most personal map of our individuality."
—Christina Baldwin

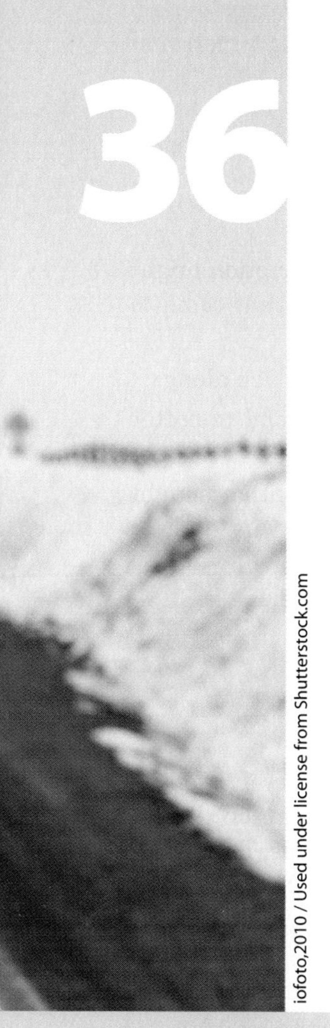

36

Narrative Essays

People have been telling stories since the dawn of time. And listeners have always had a fascination for the "true tale," especially when a speaker could say "I was there."

In relating a personal narrative, the speaker—or author—has an opportunity to revisit the events, choose the most important ones, order them effectively, discard the rest, and perhaps discover some meaning. The listener or reader gains from the tale not only entertainment but a chance to learn something without having to actually experience it.

What do you think?

Study the image and quotation on the previous page; then answer the following question: What do your oldest memories say about you?

Answers will vary.

Learning Outcomes

LO1 Understand, read, and analyze personal narratives.

LO2 Write your own personal narrative.

Learning Outcomes

Understand, read, and analyze personal narratives.

LO1 Understanding Narrative Essays

This chapter contains three example personal essays, along with questions to help analyze each reading. You'll also find writing guidelines for creating a personal essay of your own.

SQ3R When you read, become involved with the text by using the SQ3R approach.

- **Survey:** Prepare by reading "About the Author," skimming the essay, and noting any vocabulary words.
- **Question:** Ask yourself what the title and the author description might lead you to expect from the essay. List any questions that come to mind.
- **Read:** Read the essay for effect, allowing the story to carry you along.
- **Recite:** Recite especially effective or enjoyable sections aloud to better understand and remember them.
- **Review:** Scan the essay again, asking yourself what the author sought to accomplish and how successful you believe he or she was. Answer the questions provided to help you analyze the essay.

Essay List:

"Shark Bait": In this narrative from the book *Dave Barry Is Not Making This Up,* Dave Barry tells of a day spent on a boat, off the shores of Miami, with five other men and four 10-year-olds. Things get interesting when a barracuda shows up where they have been swimming.

"You've Got Hate Mail": Freelance writer Lydie Raschka describes just how unsettling mail can be from an anonymous sender, especially spiteful messages that attack her personally rather than connecting with her work.

"A Doctor's Dilemma": James N. Dillard revisits a life-or-death decision he faced as a young doctor in training, and explains why he would choose differently facing the same situation today.

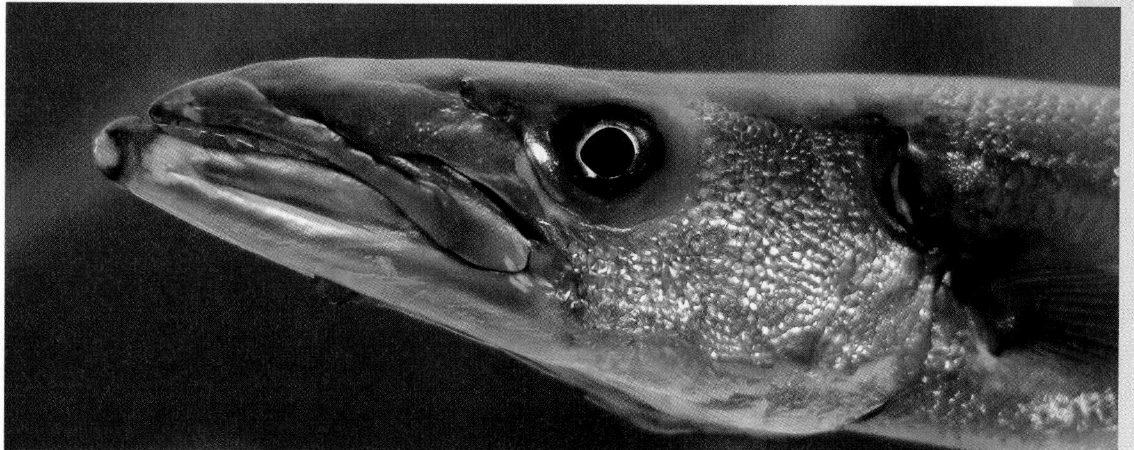

About the Author

Dave Barry is a book author and Pulitzer Prize-winning humor columnist whose work has appeared in over 500 newspapers.

Dave Berry,"Shark Bait," Dave Barry Is Not Making This Up, Random House, 2001.

Shark Bait
by Dave Barry

It began as a fun nautical outing, 10 of us in a motorboat off the coast of Miami. The weather was sunny and we saw no signs of danger, other than the risk of sliding overboard because every exposed surface on the boat was covered with a layer of snack-related grease. We had enough **cholesterol** on board to put the entire U.S. Olympic team into **cardiac arrest**. This is because all 10 of us were guys.

I hate to engage in gender **stereotyping**, but when women plan the menu for a recreational outing, they usually come up with a nutritionally balanced menu featuring all the major food groups, including the Sliced Carrots Group, the Pieces of Fruit Cut into Cubes Group, the Utensils Group, and the Plate Group. Whereas guys tend to focus on the Carbonated Malt Beverages Group and the Fatal Snacks Group. On this particular trip, our food supply consisted of about 14 bags of potato chips and one fast-food fried-chicken Giant Economy Tub o' Fat. Nobody brought, for example, napkins, the theory being that you could just wipe your hands on your stomach. Then you could burp. This is what guys on all-guy boats are doing while women are thinking about their relationships.

The reason the grease got smeared everywhere was that four of the guys on the boat were 10-year-olds, who, because of the way their still-developing digestive systems work, cannot chew without punching. This results in a lot of dropped and thrown food. On this boat, you regularly encountered semi-gnawed pieces of chicken skittering across the deck toward you like small but hostile alien creatures from the Kentucky Fried Planet. Periodically a man would yell "CUT THAT OUT!" at the boys, then burp to indicate the depth of his concern. Discipline is vital on a boat.

We motored through random-looking ocean until we found exactly what we were looking for: a patch of random-looking ocean. There we dropped anchor and dove for Florida lobsters, which protect themselves by using their tails to scoot backward really fast. They've been fooling **predators** with this move for millions of years, but the guys on our boat, being advanced life forms, including a dentist, figured it out in under three hours. I myself did not participate, because I believe that lobsters are the result of a terrible **genetic** accident involving nuclear

Vocabulary

cholesterol
a waxy substance in animal cells, sometimes leading to clogged arteries, heart disease, and/or stroke

cardiac arrest
a heart stoppage, heart attack

stereotyping
applying an oversimplified mental attitude toward some group

predators
animals that survive by hunting and eating other animals

genetic
having to do with DNA, encoded in a creature's genes

radiation and cockroaches. I mostly sat around, watching guys lunge out of the water, heave lobsters into the boat, burp, and plunge back in. Meanwhile, the lobsters were scrabbling around in the chicken grease, frantically trying to shoot backward through the forest of legs belonging to 10-year-old boys squirting each other with gobs of the No. 197,000,000,000 Sun Block that their moms had sent along. It was a total Guy Day, very relaxing, until the arrival of the **barracuda**.

This occurred just after we'd all gotten out of the water. One of the men, Larry, was fishing, and he hooked a barracuda right where we had been swimming. This was **unsettling**. The books all say that barracuda rarely eat people, but very few barracuda can read, and they have far more teeth than would be necessary for a strictly seafood diet. Their mouths look like the entire $39.95 set of **Ginsu knives**, including the handy Arm Slicer.

We gathered around to watch Larry fight the barracuda. His plan was to catch it, weigh it, and release it with a warning. After 10 minutes he almost had it to the boat, and we were all pretty excited for him, when all of a sudden . . .

Ba-DUMP . . . Ba-DUMP . . .

Those of you who read music recognize this as the sound track from the motion picture *Jaws*. Sure enough, cruising right behind Larry's barracuda, thinking **sushi**, was a shark. And not just any shark. It was a hammerhead shark, **perennial** winner of the coveted Oscar for Ugliest Fish. It has a weird, T-shaped head with a big eyeball on each tip, so that it can see around both sides of a telephone pole. This ability is of course useless for a fish, but nobody would dare try to explain this to a hammerhead.

The hammerhead, its fin breaking the surface, zigzagged closer to Larry's barracuda, then surged forward.

"Oh ****!" went Larry, reeling furiously.

CHOMP went the hammerhead, and suddenly Larry's barracuda was in a new weight division.

CHOMP went the hammerhead again, and now Larry was competing in an entirely new category, Fish Consisting of Only a Head.

The boys were staring at the remainder of the barracuda, deeply impressed.

"This is your leg," said the dentist. "This is your leg on *Jaws*. Any questions?"

The boys, for the first time all day, were quiet.

Summarize In one or two sentences, sum up what happened in this narrative.

Answers will vary.

Comment Did you enjoy this story? Why or why not?

Answers will vary.

Vocabulary

barracuda
a long, bony fish native to tropical waters

unsettling
disturbing

Ginsu knives
a brand of cutlery often advertised on television

sushi
cold rice, formed and shaped, often wrapped with raw seafood—not (as assumed in this narrative) equivalent to raw fish

perennial
repeated, consistent

Shannon Fagan/Flirt/Corbis

About the Author

Lydie Raschka is a freelance writer and part-time Montessori educator living in New York City.

Lydie Raschka, "You've Got Hate Mail," Salon.com, February 16, 2001.

You've Got Hate Mail
by Lydie Raschka

First I expected it; now I'm scared.

Hate mail confirms a vague, nagging feeling that you've done something wrong. It's a firm tap on the shoulder that says, "The jig is up." So when the first letter came, it was expected. The second, however, was a shock. By the third I was a wreck. How did he know it would take exactly and only three?

I started writing a few years ago, after I had a baby. I haven't completely figured out what led me to writing, but it was probably tied up with my son's birth and the **attendant** emotions that needed sorting.

I like the solitary work life. I write at a table in the bedroom. I send my ideas out into the **void**. The bedroom seems a safe enough place. I have been told that I am an **introvert**. What on earth makes me want to communicate with strangers in this **perilous** way—standing naked in a field?

"You have to expect these things when you are a writer," my father says about the hate mail. "When you're in the public eye, anyone can read what you write."

The letters are effective and unsettling, to say the least. I have an unusual name, so he thinks I'm foreign. He calls me "**Eurotrash**." It's a relief because it means he doesn't really know me—although he makes some pretty accurate guesses. He doesn't know that my parents simply like unusual names.

He spells my name correctly. I can only hope he's mispronouncing it. He uses it in ways I've never seen it used before—paired with obscenities and crooked thoughts.

It bothers me that he has written my name and my address three different times on three different envelopes. My name is next to the buzzer outside my building so that people will have easier access to me. I am two doors and one buzzer away from danger. But the mail slips through, into the letter box, into my **psyche**.

I call the postal inspector but she never calls me back. One day I leave a message on her machine and I am in tears. Finally she calls. She tells me that letters like these don't usually lead to violence. She says there's nothing we can

Vocabulary

attendant
accompanying

void
empty darkness where nothing exists

introvert
a shy person

perilous
dangerous

Eurotrash
central-European youth who flaunt a supposed world-weariness despite their wealth and arrogance

psyche
soul or personality

do; we have to wait until he makes a mistake.

My fingers shake when I open the mailbox. I pick through the stack. When a letter arrives I open it quickly. You read your mail. You do.

I spend most of a morning sitting in an old school chair at the police station, the kind with a desk attached. The police are standing around. They joke with one another. They drink coffee and ask me what I need in a **skeptical** way, as though there is nothing I can offer that will surprise them.

"I am getting anonymous hate mail," I say.

"Is it threatening?" they ask.

"Not specifically," I answer. "But the first one had feces in it." Sending feces is threatening, in my mind. At the very least it's a health hazard. The policewoman writes down what I say and photocopies the letters. She makes a file.

I am vulnerable to people's opinions of me. I partly believe what he says. When I tell my friends and family, I imagine that they partly believe what he says, too. They ask me what I wrote, what he wrote. "What does it matter what I wrote!?" I say. "Do you think I did something to deserve this?!" I can't yell at him, so I yell at them. I want unconditional support from everyone I know. I want protection. I have revealed too much about who I am.

I cling to his most obvious mistakes—Eurotrash—in the hope that he has gotten other things wrong, too. He is **sarcastic** and angry and a good speller. A person can be a good speller and be crazy, right? But still, it's hard that he's a good speller.

I try to have **rational** conversations with him in my mind, but it's hopeless. We get nowhere.

He owns a dog. It's his dog's feces he has sent. I always thought animal lovers were especially sensitive human beings. In my vulnerable state—in spite of this **blatant** example of insensitivity—dog ownership gives him stature.

He has decided I'm rich because I live in a certain neighborhood. He has decided I've stolen someone's job because I'm foreign. He attacks my writing and everything he can **eke** out about me from what I have written. But he reveals who he is in his writing, too. He has an aunt and a disabled sister. He doesn't know how much we have in common. He doesn't know that I have a sister and a disabled aunt.

I think about changing my **byline**. I will remove my address from the phone book. I will use only a first initial. I will give up writing.

But then he wins, says my editor.

I am unable to write for a month, two months. My editor calls. I say I'm not ready. He hires someone else to write on a topic I wanted to write about. I don't trust my motivations. Perhaps there's truth in what he says. I have been **flippant**. I have been **patronizing**. I have been biased.

At home I put the letters in a brown envelope and write "Anonymous Mail" in the top right-hand corner, avoiding the word "hate." I make a mental note to throw them away before my son can reach the shelf where I have put them. I don't want him to read these letters that have my name written all over them, with their inaccuracies and assumptions and possible wayward truths.

Vocabulary

skeptical
suspiciously unbelieving

sarcastic
ridiculing ironically

rational
logical, sensible

blatant
glaringly obvious

eke
laboriously obtain

byline
name on published essays

flippant
lacking serious respect

patronizing
speaking to someone as to an inferior

The feces were wrapped in a piece of foil; they came in a small padded envelope. I threw the feces away, then fished them out again and put them in a baggie. I washed my hands with soap, and rubbed them red. I am afraid of contamination or disease. I am afraid I will pass on germs to my son.

"Here's a little present from my best friend," he writes. The way he uses language is **absurd**: little present, best friend. He writes in sentences, with periods and commas and capital letters. He ignores the typical friendly greeting—he does not say "Dear."

I imagine him in a room, at a desk or a table. I imagine the light in the room, and the clothes tossed on the bed. He has paper and a pen. He pulls up a chair. Something **compels** him to write. He doesn't know how much we have in common.

Vocabulary

absurd
ridiculous

compels
drives or pushes

Analyze Unlike Dave Barry's "Shark Bait," this narrative does not follow a linear timeline. Make a list of the main events from Raschka's story in the order she presents them. Then write a number next to each in the order you believe they actually happened.

Answers will vary.

Comment Why do you believe Raschka ordered the events as she did?

Answers will vary.

Jose Luis Pelaez, Inc/Surf/Corbis

About the Author

Dr. Dillard served for 12 years as an assistant professor at Columbia University's College of Physicians and Surgeons, and as medical director for its Rosenthal Center for Complementary and Alternative Medicine. Since 2006 he has worked in private practice. He is also an author and television personality.

James Dillard, "A Doctor's Dilemma," Newsweek, June 12, 1995.

A Doctor's Dilemma by James N. Dillard

Helping an accident victim on the road could land you in court.

It was a bright, clear February afternoon in Gettysburg. A strong sun and layers of **down** did little to ease the biting cold. Our climb to the crest of **Little Roundtop** wound past somber monuments, barren trees and polished cannon. From the top, we peered down on the wheat field where men had fallen so close together that one could not see the ground. Rifle balls had whined as thick as bee swarms through the trees, and cannon shots had torn limbs from the young men fighting there. A frozen wind whipped tears from our eyes. My friend Amy huddled close, using me as a wind breaker. Despite the cold, it was hard to leave this place.

Driving east out of Gettysburg on a country blacktop, the gray Bronco ahead of us passed through a rural crossroad just as a small pickup truck tried to take a left turn. The Bronco swerved, but slammed into the pickup on the passenger side. We immediately slowed to a crawl as we passed the scene. The Bronco's driver looked fine, but we couldn't see the driver of the pickup. I pulled over on the shoulder and got out to investigate.

The right side of the truck was smashed in, and the side window was shattered. The driver was partly out of the truck. His head hung forward over the edge of the passenger-side window, the front of his neck crushed on the shattered windowsill. He was unconscious and starting to turn a dusky blue. His chest slowly heaved against a blocked windpipe.

A young man ran out of a house at the crossroad. "Get an ambulance out here," I shouted against the wind. "Tell them a man is dying."

I looked down again at the driver hanging from the windowsill. There were six empty beer bottles on the floor of the truck. I could smell the beer through the window. I knew I had to move him, to open his airway. I had no idea what neck injuries he had sustained. He could easily end up a **quadriplegic**. But I thought: he'll be dead by the time the ambulance gets here if I don't move him and try to do something to help him.

An image flashed before my mind. I could see the courtroom and the driver of the truck sitting in a wheelchair. I could see his attorney pointing at me and

Vocabulary

down
soft flakes of snow (like goose down)

Little Roundtop
a hill south of Gettysburg, site of an important Civil War battle

quadriplegic
a person paralyzed in all four limbs

thundering at the jury: "This young doctor, with still a year left in his **residency training**, took it upon himself to play God. He took it upon himself to move this gravely injured man, condemning him forever to this wheelchair . . ." I imagined the millions of dollars in award money. And all the years of hard work lost. I'd be paying him off for the rest of my life. Amy touched my shoulder. "What are you going to do?"

The automatic response from long hours in the emergency room kicked in. I pulled off my overcoat and rolled up my sleeves. The trick would be to keep enough **traction** straight up on his head while I moved his torso, so that his probable broken neck and spinal-cord injury wouldn't be made worse. Amy came around the driver's side, climbed half in and grabbed his belt and shirt collar. Together we lifted him off the windowsill.

He was still out cold, limp as a rag doll. His throat was crushed and blood from the jugular vein was running down my arms. He still couldn't breathe. He was deep blue-magenta now, his pulse was rapid and **thready**. The stench of alcohol turned my stomach, but I positioned his jaw and tried to blow air down into his lungs. It wouldn't go.

Amy had brought some supplies from my car. I opened an oversize intravenous needle and groped on the man's neck. My hands were numb, covered with freezing blood and bits of broken glass. **Hyoid** bone—God, I can't even feel the thyroid cartilage, it's gone . . . OK, the **thyroid** gland is about there, **cricoid** rings are here . . . we'll go in right here . . .

It was a lucky first shot. Pink air sprayed through the IV needle. I placed a second needle next to the first. The air began whistling through it. Almost immediately, the driver's face turned bright red. After a minute, his pulse slowed down and his eyes moved slightly. I stood up, took a step back and looked down. He was going to make it. He was going to live. A siren wailed in the distance. I turned and saw Amy holding my overcoat. I was shivering and my arms were turning white with cold.

The ambulance captain looked around and bellowed, "What the hell . . . who did this?" as his team scurried over to the man lying in the truck.

"I did," I replied. He took down my name and address for his reports. I had just destroyed my career. I would never be able to finish my residency with a massive lawsuit pending. My life was over.

The truck driver was strapped onto a **backboard**, his neck in a stiff collar. The ambulance crew had controlled the bleeding and started intravenous fluid. He was slowly waking up. As they loaded him into the ambulance, I saw him move his feet. Maybe my future wasn't lost.

A police sergeant called me from Pennsylvania three weeks later. Six days after successful throat-reconstruction surgery, the driver had signed out, against medical advice, from the hospital because he couldn't get a drink on the ward. He was being **arraigned** on drunk-driving charges.

A few days later, I went into the office of one of my senior professors, to tell the story. He peered over his half glasses and his eyes narrowed. "Well, you did the right thing medically of course. But, James, do you know what you put at risk by doing that?" he said sternly. "What was I supposed to do?" I asked.

Vocabulary

residency training
a period of specialty medical training after internship

traction
pull to straighten an injury and avoid pressure

thready
weak

hyoid
a small, U-shaped bone between the tongue and larynx

thyroid
a gland located near the base of the throat

cricoid
cartilage forming part of the larynx

backboard
a board designed for immobilizing and carrying people suspected to have a spinal injury

arraigned
called to a court to face criminal charges

"Drive on," he replied. "There is an army of lawyers out there who would stand in line to get a case like that. If that driver had turned out to be a quadriplegic, you might never have practiced medicine again. You were a very lucky young man."

The day I graduated from medical school, I took an oath to serve the sick and the injured. I remember truly believing I would be able to do just that. But I have found out it isn't so simple. I understand now what a foolish thing I did that day. Despite my oath, I know what I would do on that cold roadside near Gettysburg today. I would drive on.

WAC

This essay focuses on an issue of medical ethics. What ethical considerations do you have in your area of study?

Map Along the time line below, list the most important details of Dr. Dillard's story. Answers will vary.

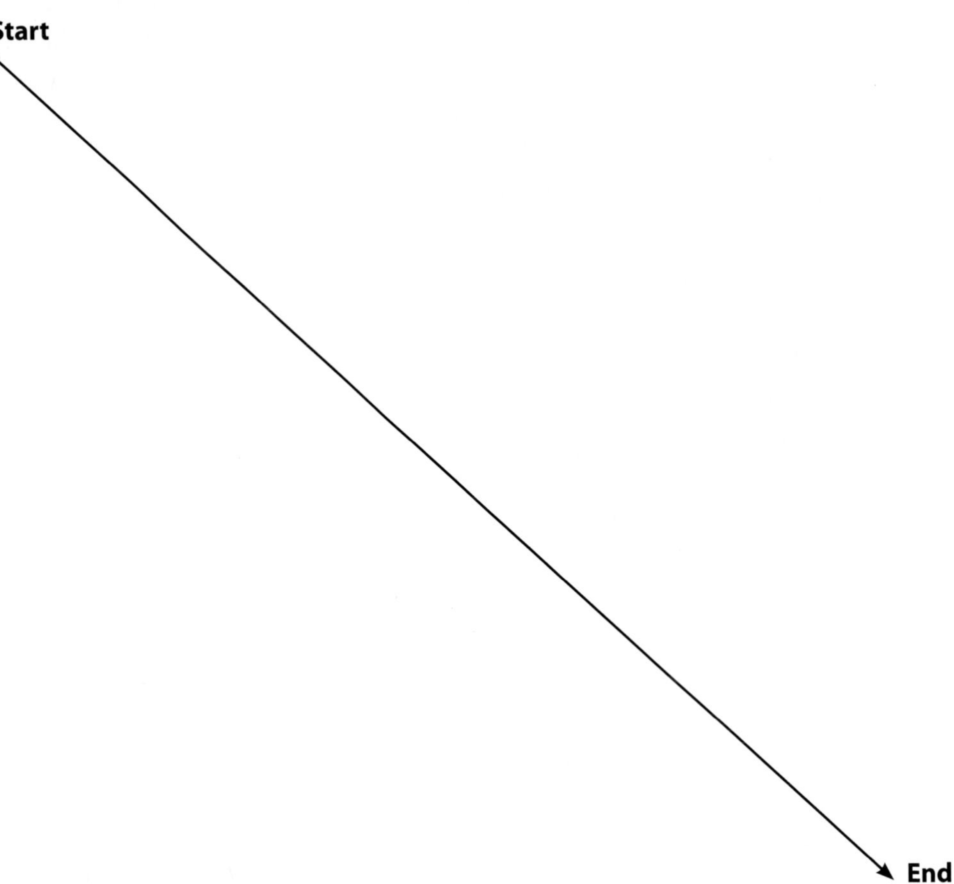

Evaluate What is the doctor's main point in this story? Do his chosen details effectively support that point? Why or why not?

Medical professionals are often forced to choose between providing critical treatment and avoiding legal liability. (Explanations supporting this point will vary.)

LO2 Writing a Narrative Essay

Prewrite To begin writing a personal essay, you need to choose a memorable event from your life. One way to do this is with a life map. At the beginning of the map, write the day you were born. At the end, write today's date. Then begin listing memorable events along the way.

Learning Outcomes

Write your own personal narrative.

Life Map

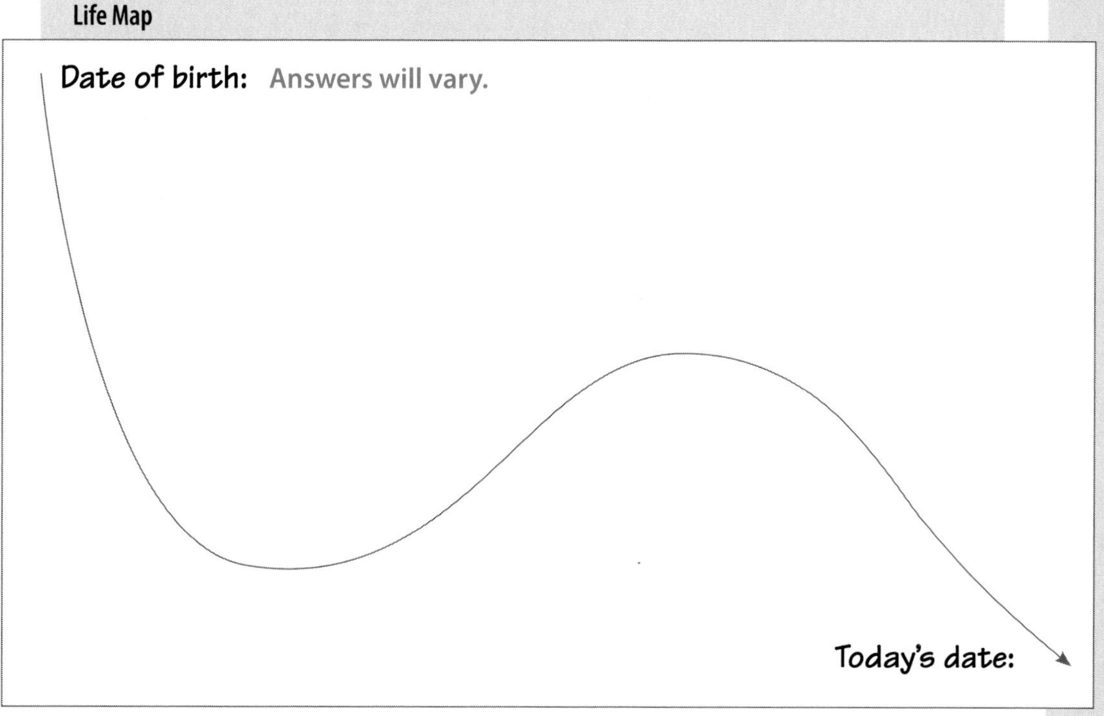

Freewrite Next, choose an event from your life map and ask yourself why it is important to you. How did that event shape you or illustrate who you are today? Spend at least 10 minutes writing whatever comes to mind in explanation.

Prewrite Next, you will need to gather details about the event you have chosen. Most stories occur in a linear fashion, from start to finish. To prepare for your story, begin listing details on a timeline. (Leave space between events to add new details as they occur to you.)

Timeline

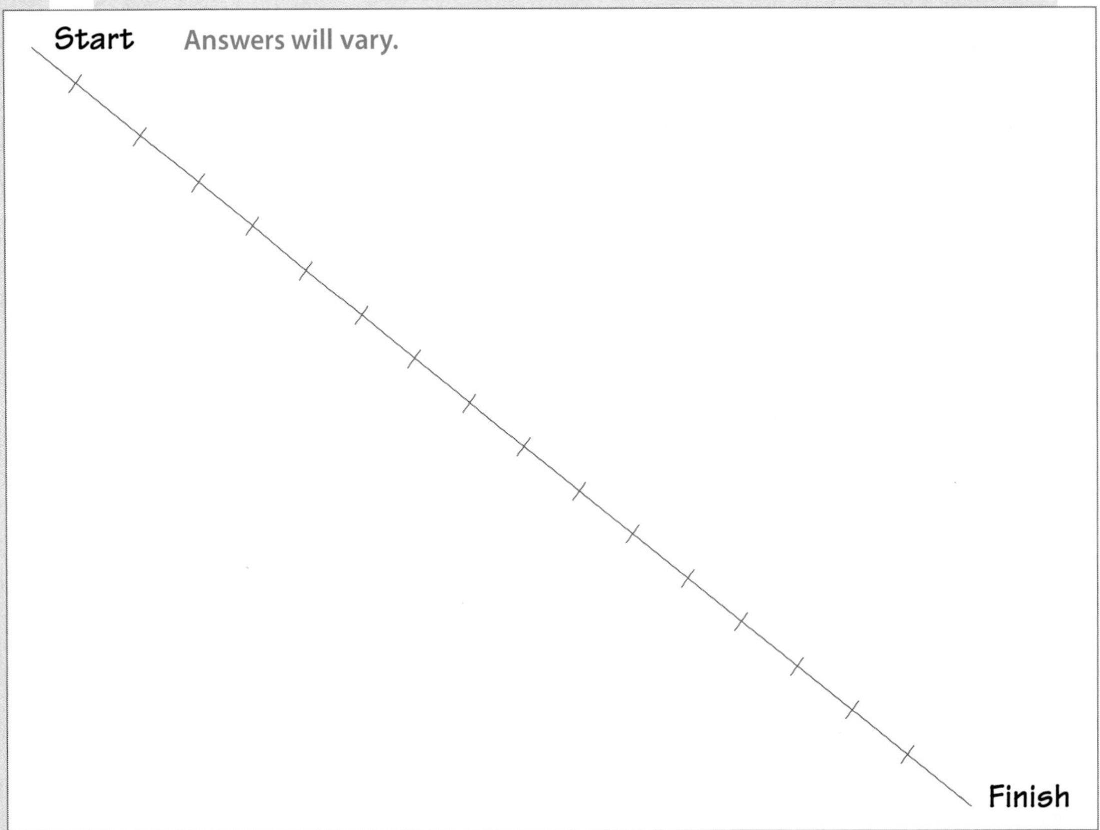

Prewrite A sensory chart is another good way to gather details to use in a personal narrative. As you recall the event, write details of sight, sound, smell, touch, and taste in the appropriate column. Answers will vary.

Sensory Chart

Sight	Sound	Smell	Touch	Taste

Draft Create a strong opening, middle, and closing for your essay. Use the supports below as you create each part. Answers will vary.

Opening Paragraph

Capture your reader's attention in the first line of your personal essay. Use one of the following strategies:

- **Begin with action:** "I was clocking out, sweaty and exhausted after a long shift waiting tables, when he walked in."
- **Ask a question:** "What is it about some people—me for example—that makes travel such an adventure in wrong turns?"
- **Connect to the reader:** "The song starts, and you want to get up and dance, but you feel as big and clumsy as Frankenstein's monster."

Once you have your reader's attention, lead up to your thesis statement. Here is a formula to use as you create your thesis statement.

Memorable Event		Effect on Your Life		Thesis Statement
Caught up in a surge of raw emotion from the crowd	+	I felt just how strong the pull of "mob mentality" can be.	=	Caught up in a surge of raw emotion from the crowd, I felt just how strong the pull of "mob mentality" can be.

Memorable Event + **Effect on Your Life** ______________________

____

____

____

= Thesis Statement

____

____

____

Middle Paragraphs

In your middle paragraphs, provide support for your thesis statement by

- Telling the story (review your timeline for the most important facts).
- Drawing the reader in with details (mine your sensory chart).
- Explaining the significance of what happened.

Closing Paragraph

The final paragraph of a personal essay should reflect back on the whole, if possible making a connection that was not visible at the beginning. At the very least, it should restate and reinforce the thesis of the essay. Review the closing paragraph of the readings in this chapter for examples of effective endings.

Revise Take a break from your writing. Then come back to it with fresh eyes. If possible, read your personal essay aloud to a friend or family member, and ask if any parts are unclear. Then review your writing with the following checklist. Keep polishing until you can answer every question with a "yes."

Ideas

- ☐ **1.** Do I focus on one main event from my life?
- ☐ **2.** Did the event I've chosen have an important effect on me?

Organization

- ☐ **3.** Does my opening grab the reader's attention and present a clear thesis?
- ☐ **4.** Does my middle clearly tell the story (using facts from my timeline)?
- ☐ **5.** Do I include a variety of details?
- ☐ **6.** Does my middle make the significance of the event clear?

Voice

- ☐ **7.** Do I tell the story in a way that keeps the reader interested to the end?

Edit Prepare a clean copy of your personal essay and use the following checklist to check for errors. Continue until you can answer "yes" to each question.

Words

- ☐ **1.** Do I use correct verb forms (*he saw,* not *he seen*)? (See page 356.)
- ☐ **2.** Do my subjects and verbs agree (*she speaks,* not *she speak*)? (See pages 282–291.)
- ☐ **3.** Have I used the right words (*there, their, they're*)?

Sentences

- ☐ **4.** Have I avoided sentence fragments? (See pages 297–302.)
- ☐ **5.** Have I avoided run-on sentences? (See pages 306–310.)
- ☐ **6.** Have I avoided improper shifts in sentences? (See pages 314–315.)

Conventions

- ☐ **7.** Have I used commas after long introductory word groups? (See page 396.)
- ☐ **8.** Have I capitalized first words? (See page 414.)
- ☐ **9.** Have I capitalized proper nouns and proper adjectives? (See page 414.)
- ☐ **10.** Have I carefully checked my spelling?

"Aristotle was famous for knowing everything. He taught that the brain exists merely to cool the blood and is not involved in the process of thinking. This is true only of certain persons."

—Will Cuppy

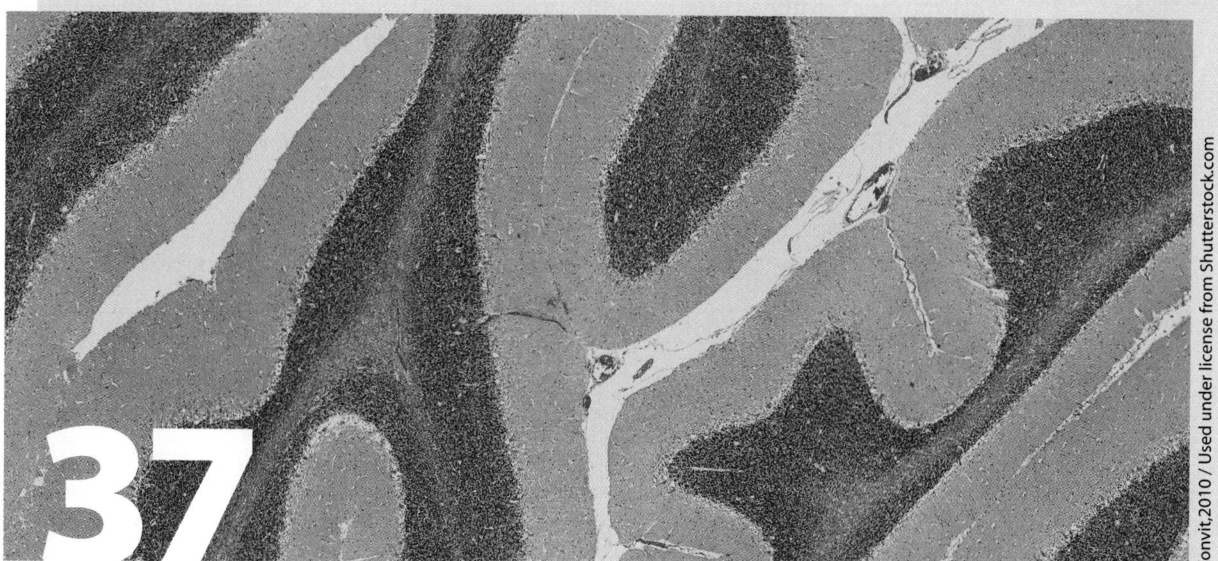

Convit,2010 / Used under license from Shutterstock.com

37 Process Essays

Socrates taught Plato; Plato taught Aristotle; Aristotle taught Alexander the Great; and Alexander conquered the Persian Empire, spreading Greek culture so thoroughly that it affected the Byzantine Empire well into the fifteenth century, nearly two millennia after his death. The fact that we're still familiar with Greek mythology and with cities like Sparta and Athens says something about that effect even today.

Millennia-long though it may be, that spread of thought is a process nevertheless. We can describe it in steps, thereby better understanding the whole.

Learning Outcomes

LO1 Understand, read, and analyze process essays.

LO2 Write your own process essay.

What do you think?

From your own understanding, how is the human brain involved in the process of thinking?

Answers will vary.

Learning Outcomes

Understand, read, and analyze process essays.

LO1 Understanding Process Essays

This chapter contains three example process essays, along with questions you can use as tools to help analyze each reading. At the end of the chapter are writing guidelines for creating a process essay of your own.

SQ3R When you read, become involved with the text by using the SQ3R approach.

- **Survey:** Prepare by reading "About the Author," skimming the essay, and noting any vocabulary words.
- **Question:** Make a list of questions you expect to have answered by the essay.
- **Read:** Read the essay, noting any steps in the process that is being described.
- **Recite:** Recite any steps in order to make sure you understand and remember them.
- **Review:** Scan the essay again, looking for details you might have missed or answers to any remaining questions you may have. Answer the questions provided to help you analyze the essay.

Essay List:

"Conversational Ballgames": Nancy Masterson Sakamoto uses two very different types of ballgames as analogies to contrast Japanese and American conversational styles.

"How Our Skins Got Their Color": Dr. Marvin Harris argues that the natural skin tone of the human race is brown, then explains how Europeans developed white skin from that base, and the parallel development of black skin in sub-Saharan Africa. His essay is based upon explanation of another process: the human body's use of sunlight to create vitamin D, and its use of that substance to absorb calcium.

"Sorry, What's Your Name Again? 6 Steps to Relieve the Most Common Memory Worry": In this how-to process, Roger Seip offers a multi-sensory strategy for remembering the names of new people you meet.

Don Hammond/Design Pics/Corbis

Conversational Ballgames
by Nancy Masterson Sakamoto

After I was married and had lived in Japan for a while, my Japanese gradually improved to the point where I could take part in simple conversations with my husband, his friends, and family. And I began to notice that often, when I joined in, the others would look startled, and the conversation would come to a halt. After this happened several times, it became clear to me that I was doing something wrong. But for a long time, I didn't know what it was.

Finally, after listening carefully to many Japanese conversations, I discovered what my problem was. Even though I was speaking Japanese, I was handling the conversation in a Western way.

Japanese-style conversations develop quite differently from Western-style conversations. And the difference isn't only in the languages. I realized that just as I kept trying to hold Western-style conversations even when I was speaking Japanese, so were my English students trying to hold Japanese-style conversations even when they were speaking English. We were unconsciously playing entirely different conversational ballgames.

A Western-style conversation between two people is like a game of tennis. If I introduce a topic, a conversational ball, I expect you to hit it back. If you agree with me, I don't expect you simply to agree and do nothing more. I expect you to add something—a reason for agreeing, another example, or a remark to carry the idea further. But I don't expect you always to agree. I am just as happy if you question me, or challenge me, or completely disagree with me. Whether you agree or disagree, your response will return the ball to me.

And then it is my turn again. I don't serve a new ball from my original starting line. I hit your ball back again from where it has bounced. I carry your idea further, or answer your questions or objections, or challenge or question you. And so the ball goes back and forth.

If there are more than two people in the conversation, then it is like doubles in tennis, or like volleyball. There's no waiting in line. Whoever is nearest and quickest hits the ball, and if you step back, someone else will hit it. No one stops the game to give you a turn. You're responsible for taking your own turn and no one person has the ball for very long.

About the Author

Nancy Masterson Sakamoto is the author of the book *Polite Fiction: Why Japanese and Americans Seem Rude to Each Other*. Born in Los Angeles in 1931, she went on to marry a Japanese man and taught American studies in Japan from 1972 to 1982. She then returned to the U.S. and became a professor at Shitennoji Gakuen University in Honolulu.

Nancy Masterson Sakamoto, "Conversational Ballgames," Polite Fictions, Tokyo: Kinseido, Ltd., 1982.

A Japanese-style conversation, however, is not at all like tennis or volleyball, it's like bowling. You wait for your turn, and you always know your place in line. It depends on such things as whether you are older or younger, a close friend or a relative stranger to the previous speaker, in a senior or junior position, and so on.

The first thing is to wait for your turn, patiently and politely. When your moment comes, you step up to the starting line with your bowling ball, and carefully bowl it. Everyone else stands back, making sounds of polite encouragement. Everyone waits until your ball has reached the end of the lane, and watches to see if it knocks down all the pins, or only some of them, or none of them. Then there is a pause, while everyone registers your score.

Then, after everyone is sure that you are done, the next person in line steps up to the same startling line, with a different ball. He doesn't return your ball. There is no back and forth at all. And there is always a suitable pause between turns. There is no rush, no impatience.

No wonder everyone looked startled when I took part in Japanese conversations. I paid no attention to whose turn it was, and kept snatching the ball halfway down the **alley** and throwing it back at the bowler. Of course the conversation fell apart, I was playing the wrong game.

This explains why it can be so difficult to get a Western-style discussion going with Japanese students of English. Whenever I serve a volleyball, everyone just stands back and watches it fall. No one hits it back. Everyone waits until I call on someone to take a turn. And when that person speaks, he doesn't hit my ball back. He serves a new ball. Again, everyone just watches it fall. So I call on someone else. This person does not refer to what the previous speaker has said. He also serves a new ball. Everyone begins again from the same starting line, and all the balls run parallel. There is never any back and forth.

Now that you know about the difference in the conversational ballgames, you may think that all your troubles are over. But if you have been trained all your life to play one game, it is no simple matter to switch to another, even if you know the rules. Tennis, after all, is different from bowling.

Vocabulary

alley
in bowling, a single lane with a foul line at one end, pins at the other, and a gutter along each side

Think Critically Review the process diagrams to the left. Which do you think best suits an American conversation and which a Japanese? Explain.

Answers will vary.

Process Diagrams

I. Topic ________________
(Chronological Order)

Step 1
↓
Step 2
↓
Step 3

II.

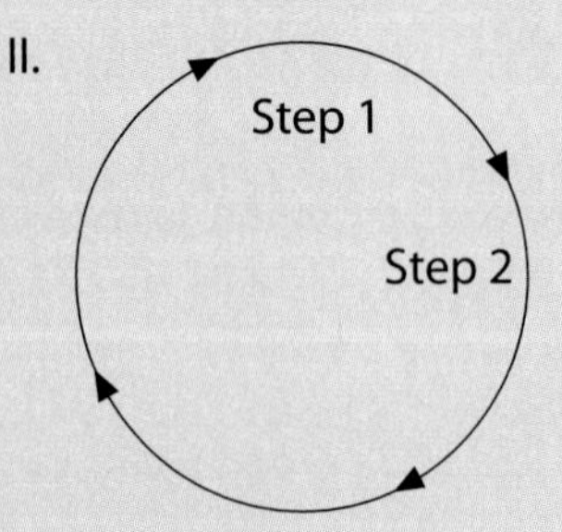

How Our Skins Got Their Color by Marvin Harris

Most human beings are neither very fair nor very dark, but brown. The extremely fair skin of northern Europeans and their descendants, and the very black skins of central Africans and their descendants, are probably special adaptations. Brown-skinned ancestors may have been shared by modern-day blacks and whites as recently as 10,000 years ago.

Human skin owes its color to the presence of particles known as melanin. The primary function of melanin is to protect the upper levels of the skin from being damaged by the sun's ultraviolet rays. This radiation poses a critical problem for our kind because we lack the dense coat of hair that acts as a sunscreen for most mammals. . . . Hairlessness exposes us to two kinds of radiation hazards: ordinary sunburn, with its blisters, rashes, and risk of infection; and skin cancers, including malignant melanoma, one of the deadliest diseases known. Melanin is the body's first line of defense against these afflictions. The more melanin particles, the darker the skin, and the lower the risk of sunburn and all forms of skin cancer. This explains why the highest rates for skin cancer are found in sun-drenched lands such as Australia, where light-skinned people of European descent spend a good part of their lives outdoors wearing scanty attire. Very dark-skinned people such as heavily **pigmented** Africans of Zaire seldom get skin cancer, but when they do, they get it on depigmented parts of their bodies—palms and lips.

If exposure to solar radiation had nothing but harmful effects, natural selection would have favored inky black as the color for all human populations. But the sun's rays do not present an **unmitigated** threat. As it falls on the skin, sunshine converts a fatty substance in the **epidermis** into vitamin D. The blood carries vitamin D from the skin to the intestines (technically making it a hormone rather than a vitamin), where it plays a vital role in the absorption of calcium. In turn, calcium is vital for strong bones. Without it, people fall victim to the crippling diseases **rickets** and **osteomalacia**. In women, calcium deficiencies can result in a deformed birth canal, which makes childbirth lethal for both mother and fetus.

Vitamin D can be obtained from a few foods, primarily the oils and livers of marine fish. But inland populations must rely on the sun's rays and their own

About the Author

Dr. Marvin Harris (1927-2001) was chair of the Anthropology department at Columbia University, then a Graduate Research Professor at the University of Florida. He also served as the Chair of the General Anthropology Division for the American Anthropological Association. During his life he published 16 books and wrote a series of essays he titled *Our Kind.*

Vocabulary

pigmented
colored by pigment

unmitigated
not made less severe

epidermis
uppermost layer of skin

rickets
softening of bones in the young

osteomalacia
softening of bones in adults

skins for the supply of this crucial substance. The particular color of a human population's skin, therefore, represents in large degree a trade-off between the hazards of too much versus too little solar radiation: acute sunburn and skin cancer on the one hand, and rickets and osteomalacia on the other. It is this trade-off that largely accounts for the **preponderance** of brown people in the world and for the general tendency for skin color to be darkest among equatorial populations and lightest among populations dwelling at higher **latitudes**.

At middle latitudes, the skin follows a strategy of changing colors with the seasons. Around the **Mediterranean** basin, for example, exposure to the summer sun brings high risk of cancer but low risk for rickets; the body produces more melanin and people grow darker (i.e., they get suntans). Winter reduces the risk of sunburn and cancer; the body produces less melanin, and the tan wears off.

The **correlation** between skin color and latitude is not perfect because other factors—such as the availability of foods containing vitamin D and calcium, regional cloud cover during the winter, amount of clothing worn, and cultural preferences—may work for or against the predicted relationship. Arctic-dwelling Eskimo, for example, are not as light-skinned as expected, but their **habitat** and economy afford them a diet that is exceptionally rich in both vitamin D and calcium.

Northern Europeans, obliged to wear heavy garments for protection against the long, cold, cloudy winters, were always at risk for rickets and osteomalacia from too little vitamin D and calcium. This risk increased sometime after 6000 B.C., when pioneer cattle herders who did not exploit marine resources began to appear in northern Europe. The risk would have been especially great for the brown-skinned Mediterranean peoples who migrated northward along with the crops and farm animals. Samples of **Caucasian** skin (infant **penile foreskin** obtained at the time of **circumcision**) exposed to sunlight on cloudless days in Boston (42°N) from November through February produced no vitamin D. In Edmonton (52°N) this period extended from October to March. But further south (34°N) sunlight was effective in producing vitamin D in the middle of the winter. Almost all of Europe lies north of 42°N. Fair-skinned, nontanning individuals who could utilize the weakest and briefest doses of sunlight to synthesize vitamin D were strongly favored by natural selection. During the frigid winters, only a small circle of a child's face could be left to peek out at the sun through the heavy clothing, thereby favoring the survival of individuals with **translucent** patches of pink on their cheeks characteristic of many northern Europeans. (People who could get calcium by drinking cow's milk would also be favored by natural selection. . . .)

If light-skinned individuals on the average had only 2 percent more children survive per generation, the changeover in the skin color could have begun 5,000 years ago and reached present levels well before the beginning of the Christian era. But natural selection need not have acted alone. Cultural selection may also have played a role. It seems likely that whenever people consciously or unconsciously had to decide which infants to nourish and which to neglect, the advantage would go to those with lighter skin, experience having show that such individuals tended to grow up to be taller, stronger, and healthier than their darker siblings. White was beautiful because white was healthy.

Vocabulary

preponderance
majority

latitude
imaginary line marking a distance from the earth's equator

Mediterranean
coastal lands of Southern Europe, Southwest Asia, and Northern Africa

correlation
relationship of two things often occurring together

habitat
environment in which a person or an animal lives

Caucasian
light-skinned people originating in the Caucasus Mountains region

penile foreskin
fold of skin surrounding the tip of the penis

circumcision
surgical removal of the foreskin

translucent
nearly transparent

To account for the evolution of black skin in equatorial latitudes, one has merely to reverse the combined effects of natural and cultural selection. With the sun directly overhead most of the year, and clothing a hindrance to work and survival, vitamin D was never in short supply (and calcium was easily obtained from vegetables). Rickets and osteomalacia were rare. Skin cancer was the main problem, and what nature started culture amplified. Darker infants were favored by parents because experience showed that they grew up to be freer of disfiguring and lethal **malignancies**. Black was beautiful because black was healthy.

Vocabulary

malignant
malicious, intending damage

Evaluate What processes are explained in this essay?

Possible answers:

- Development of skin color
- Migration of early people into Europe
- Formation of vitamin D and absorption of calcium

Diagram Label the diagram below with steps from one of the processes in the essay. (Add more arrows as needed.)

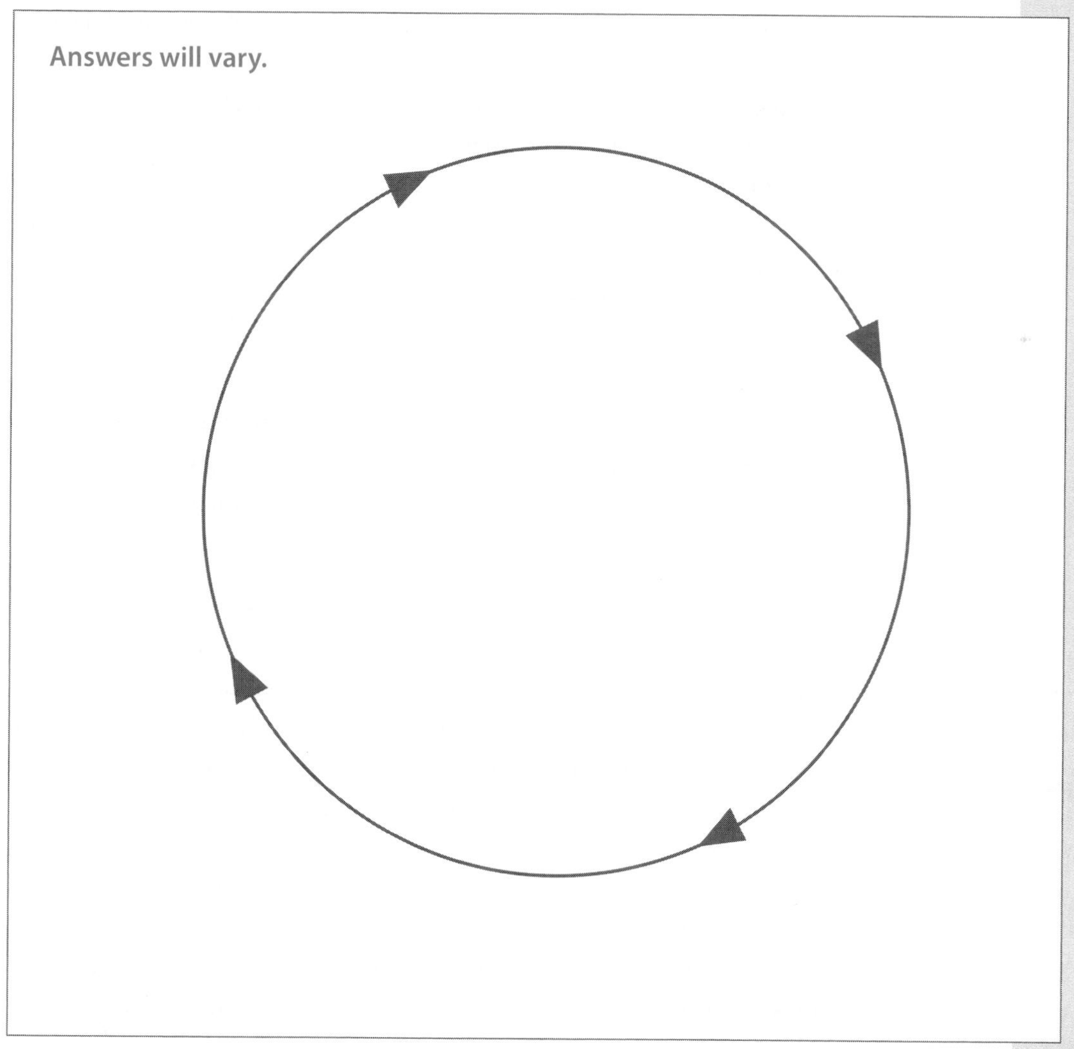

About the Author

A former stand-up comedian, Roger Seip is now a nationally known motivational speaker for organizations such as Harley Davidson, Northwestern Mutual, and the National Association of Realtors.

Roger Seip, "Sorry, What's Your Name Again? 6 Steps to Relieve the Most Common Memory Worry," Freedom Personal Development Blog, July 27, 2009.

Steve Hix/Somos Images/Corbis

Sorry, What's Your Name Again? 6 Steps to Relieve the Most Common Memory Worry by Roger Seip

If you live in fear of forgetting people's names, sometimes within mere seconds of being introduced to them, you're not alone. Surveys show that 83% of the population worries about their inability to recall people's names. Ironically, while most of us hate having our names forgotten or mispronounced, the majority of us claim we just "aren't good at remembering names" or putting faces together with names when we meet people again.

If you have difficulty recalling names, you know that the two most common scenarios are forgetting the name instantaneously upon being introduced to someone new, and failing to recall the name of someone you've met and interacted with in the past and should know but just can't pull up from your memory bank.

Forgetting names becomes more than just an embarrassing social **faux pas** in sales. Straining to recall a name can so preoccupy you that you are unable to fully pay attention to your client or prospect. He or she may perceive you not only as unfocused and easily distracted, but also as not very bright if you're unable to devote your full attention to him or her. Even worse, if you forget the name of a client with whom you've worked in the past, he or she may view your memory **lapse** as a betrayal of trust, which can cost you a great deal of money if that client severs the relationship.

Integrating Learning Styles to Improve Name Recall

While common, this frustrating phenomenon of forgetting names can be relatively easy to overcome when you commit to taking steps to improve your memory. The most important key to really effective learning of any kind is understanding that there are three learning styles: visual, **auditory**, and kinesthetic (physically interactive). The more you can apply all three of these styles to a task, the more quickly and solidly you will learn anything.

Practice each of the following steps to improve your name recollection in every sales and social situation.

1. When you're first introduced to someone, look closely at his or her face and try to find something unique about it. Whether you find a distinctive quality

Vocabulary

faux pas
blunder (French for "false step")

lapse
short break

auditory
involving hearing

or not is **irrelevant**; by really looking for a memorable characteristic in a new face, you're incorporating the visual learning style. And a word of advice: if you do find something that really stands out about someone's face, don't say anything! Within minutes of meeting someone new, it's generally a bad idea to exclaim, "Whoa! That's a huge nose!"

2. The next step **utilizes** both auditory and kinesthetic learning styles. When you meet someone, slow down for five seconds, and concentrate on listening to him or her. Focus on the prospect and repeat his or her name back in a conversational manner, such as "Susan. Nice to meet you, Susan." Also make sure to give a good firm handshake, which establishes a physical connection with the prospect.
3. Creating a mental picture of someone's name incorporates the visual sense again. Many people have names that already are pictures: consider Robin, Jay, Matt, or Dawn to name just a few. Some names will require you to play with them a bit to create a picture. Ken, for example, may not bring an immediate image to your mind, but a "can" is very close. Or you might envision a Ken doll. The point is not to create the best, most creative mental image ever, so don't get caught up in your head during this step of the process, thinking, "Oh, that's not a very good picture. What's a better one?" The worst thing you can do when learning is to stress yourself out and overthink the process. If an image doesn't come to you right away, skip it and do it later. You'll undo all of your good efforts if you're staring dumbly at your prospect, insisting, "Hey. Hold still for a minute while I try to turn your name into a picture!"
4. Once you've identified a mental image that you associate with a person's name, the next step is to "glue" that image to the person's face or upper body. This bridges the gap many people experience between being able to recall faces but not the names that belong to those faces. If you met a new prospect named Rosalind, for example, you might have broken her name down into the memorable image of "rose on land." Now you must create a mental picture that will stick with you as long as you need it and pop into your head every time you meet her; this should be something fun, even a little odd, that will bring "rose on land" to mind when you see her face. You might imagine her buried up to her neck in earth, with roses scattered around her, for example. Because you created the image, it will come up next time you see her and enable you to recall her name.
5. At the end of the conversation, **integrate** auditory learning by repeating the prospect's name one more time, but don't ever overuse someone's name in an effort to place it more firmly in your mind. Use the prospect's name only right at the beginning of the conversation, and then again at the end; if you feel like you can do so naturally, you might insert someone's name once or twice in a natural fashion during the course of the conversation, too. But if you've ever had a **stereotypically** pushy salesperson use your name a dozen times in a five minute conversation, you know how annoying, even weird, this can be, so don't overdo it.

Vocabulary

irrelevant
not applicable

utilize
to put to use

integrate
to merge into a unified whole

stereotypically
in an oversimplified way

6. Writing is a form of kinesthetic learning—you're getting a part of your body involved in the learning process—so if you're really serious about wanting to remember people's names for the long term, keep a name journal or a log of important people you meet, and review it periodically.

Forget Me Not: It's the Effort That Matters Most

The most important thing to know about this memory process is that even when it doesn't work, it still works! For example, if you get stuck trying to make a picture out of someone's name, skip it for now. The next day, when you have a chance, give the matter a few minutes of concentrated thought. If you still can't get a picture, stop and take up the matter a week later. Even if you're still unsuccessful at creating a mental image, you've thought about the prospect's name so much, there's now no way you'll ever forget it! So you've actually accomplished what you set to do in the first place.

People can't remember names for one main reason: they're just not paying attention. This process forces you to think. If, for example, you struggle with the step of creating a mental picture, the other steps—looking at the prospect closely, shaking his or her hand confidently and repeating the name a few times—are easy to do, will solidify the name in your memory, and will ultimately convey a positive image of you to clients and prospects. That positive image will certainly make you memorable to prospects, enabling you to close more deals and increase your bottom line.

Workplace

This essay focuses on a critical skill for success in business and life—remembering people's names.

Respond Do you have trouble remembering names? If so, how do you deal with that trouble? If not, how do you react to people who do?

Answers will vary.

LO2 Writing a Process Essay

Prewrite Brainstorm a cluster to identify processes you are interested in explaining. List possible topics in the bubbles below. (Add more bubbles if necessary.) Answers will vary.

Make an Idea Cluster

Choose one: Put a star next to the process that you think would make the best subject.

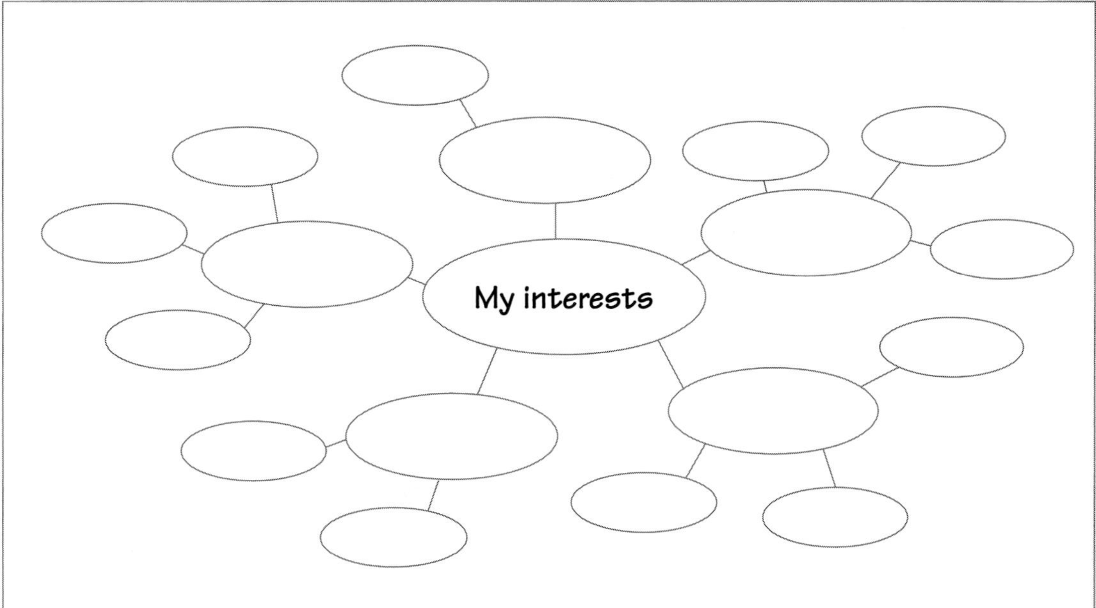

Do Your Research

Make sure you fully understand the subject you have chosen. Read what experts have to say about the process and take careful notes.

Learning Outcomes

Write your own process essay.

Outline the Steps

Prewrite Make a list of the steps from beginning to end of your process. Use one of the diagrams below as a guide.

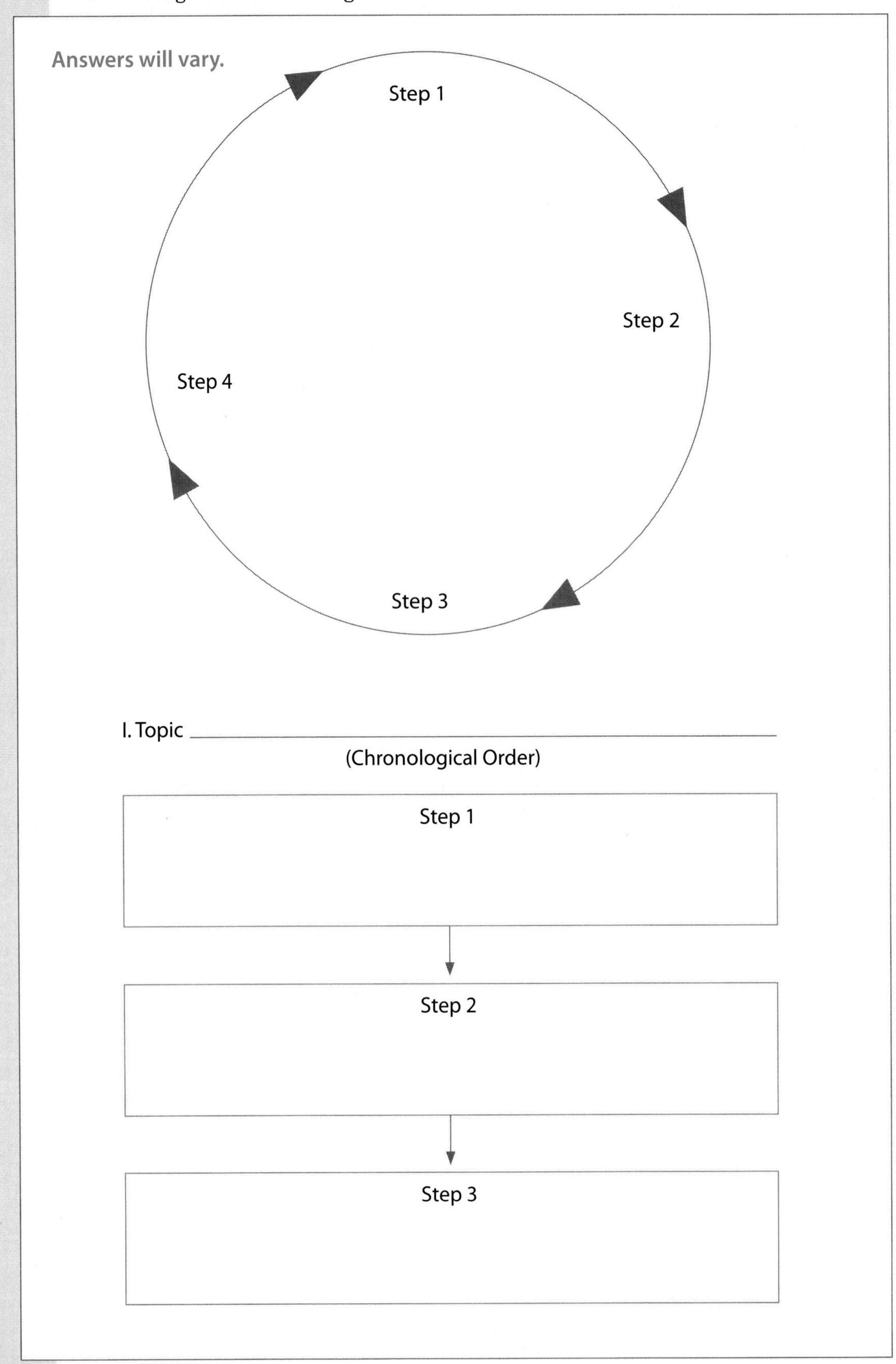

Draft Create a strong opening, middle, and closing for your process essay. Use the supports below as you create each part. Answers will vary.

Opening Paragraph

Capture your reader's attention in the first line of your essay. Think of why your reader should care about this process. Use one of the following strategies:

- **Connect to the reader:** "Saving for the future may seem impossible while you're in school."
- **Ask a question:** "Have you ever wondered how a dolphin, an air-breathing creature, is born at sea?"
- **Begin with action:** "Your chest tightens, throat clenching and unclenching; your tongue undulates, mouth opening and closing; and vibrating puffs of air burst forth—you speak."

Once you have your reader's attention, lead up to your thesis statement. Here is a formula to use as you create your thesis statement.

Main Point		Importance to Reader		Thesis Statement
Setting your blog, newsfeed, and social media to automatically synchronize	+	is actually very easy	=	Setting your blog, newsfeed, and social media to automatically synchronize is actually very easy.

Main Point + **Importance to Reader** ______________________

____

____

____

= **Thesis Statement**

____

____

____

Middle Paragraphs

In your middle paragraphs, expand upon your thesis statement by

- Presenting the steps of the process.
- Defining any special terms.
- Explaining how any needed equipment is to be used.
- Identifying any safety issues.

Closing Paragraph

The final paragraph should help to "set" the process in the reader's mind. You might review the most important details and end by restating your main point, or you might conclude with a reminder of the significance of the process.

WAC

Process writing is very important in science and history.

Revise Take a break from your writing. Then come back to it with fresh eyes. If possible, have a friend or family member read the essay and then perform the process while you watch to see what may not be clear. Then review your writing with the following checklist. Keep polishing until you can answer every question with a "yes."

Ideas

- ☐ **1.** Is the process I have chosen interesting to other people?
- ☐ 2. Do I include all the needed details about steps, equipment, and safety issues?

Organization

- ☐ **3.** Does my opening grab the reader's attention and present a clear thesis?
- ☐ 4. Does my middle fully explain the steps of the process?
- ☐ 5. Are the steps in clear order of sequence or importance?
- ☐ 6. Does my ending remind the reader of the main point and of the significance of the process?

Voice

- ☐ **7.** Is the voice both friendly and professional?

Edit Prepare a clean copy of your personal essay and use the following checklist to check for errors. Continue until you can answer "yes" to each question.

Words

- ☐ **1.** Do I use correct verb forms (*he saw,* not *he seen*)? (See page 356.)
- ☐ **2.** Do my subjects and verbs agree (*she speaks,* not *she speak*)? (See pages 282–291.)
- ☐ **3.** Have I used the right words (*there, their, they're*)?

Sentences

- ☐ **4.** Have I avoided sentence fragments? (See pages 297–302.)
- ☐ **5.** Have I avoided run-on sentences? (See pages 306–310.)
- ☐ **6.** Have I avoided improper shifts in sentences? (See pages 314–315.)

Conventions

- ☐ **7.** Have I used commas after long introductory word groups? (See page 396.)
- ☐ **8.** Have I capitalized first words? (See page 414.)
- ☐ **9.** Have I capitalized proper nouns and proper adjectives? (See page 414.)
- ☐ **10.** Have I carefully checked my spelling?

"In theory, there is no difference between theory and practice. In practice there is."

—Yogi Berra

Sue Hammond/Flickr/Getty Images

38 Comparison-Contrast Essays

In Lewis Carroll's *Alice in Wonderland,* the Mad Hatter wonders aloud, "Why is a raven like a writing desk?" A few pages later, we learn that this riddle has no answer. But the riddle does tickle the mind, so much so that Sam Loyd later quipped that a raven was like a writing desk "because Poe wrote on both."

When you note the similarities between two things—a raven and a writing desk, for example—you are comparing them. When you note the differences, you are contrasting them. An essay that compares and contrasts two things creates a strong understanding of both subjects. It also explores surprising connections between things.

Learning Outcomes

LO1 Understand, read, and analyze comparison-contrast essays.

LO2 Write your own comparison-contrast essay.

What do you think?

In what other ways is a raven like a writing desk? Write as many as you can think of.

Answers will vary.

Learning Outcome

Understand, read, and analyze comparison-contrast essays.

LO1 Understanding Comparison-Contrast Essays

One of the best ways to understand a subject is to compare and contrast it with another. This chapter contains four example comparison-contrast pieces, along with questions and graphics for analyzing each reading. You'll also find writing guidelines for creating a comparison-contrast essay of your own.

SQ3R When you read, become involved with the text by using the SQ3R approach.

- **Survey:** Prepare by reading "About the Author," skimming the writing, and noting any vocabulary words.
- **Question:** Ask yourself what topics are being compared and contrasted and what organizational pattern is used. Here are three common patterns:

Point-by-Point		Subject-to-Subject	Similarities-Differences
Beginning		Beginning	Beginning
Point 1	Subject 1 Subject 2	Subject 1	Similarities
Point 2	Subject 1 Subject 2		
Point 3	Subject 1 Subject 2	Subject 2	Differences
Ending		Ending	Ending

- **Read:** Carefully read the piece, reviewing the vocabulary words as you encounter them, finding answers to your questions, and judging the effectiveness of the author's comparison and contrast.
- **Recite:** Stop to repeat important points silently or aloud.
- **Review:** Analyze the writing by filling in the graphic organizer and answering the questions provided.

Essay List:

"Truth in Advertising: Military Recruitment Ads Versus Reality": Student writer Hector Antinoro responds to military recruitment ads at movie theaters.

"Chinese Space, American Space": Yi-Fu Tuan uses American and Chinese homes to reveal a different attitude toward space, or place, and what it has to say about the two societies.

"Religious Faith Versus Spirituality": Neil Bissoondath uses his mother's death and cremation to distinguish between faith and spirituality.

"Two Views on Social Order: Conflict or Cooperation?": Llewellyn H. Rockwell, Jr., argues that the left and the right in United States politics are alike in many ways.

Tim Tadder/Ivy /Corbis

About the Author

Hector Antinoro is a former National Guard medic who served two terms in Iraq. He is currently finishing a degree as a registered nurse and hopes to specialize in geriatric care. In his spare time, he likes to read poetry by Primo Levi.

Truth in Advertising: Military Recruitment Ads Versus Reality by Hector Antinoro

Attend pretty much any movie nowadays, and you'll sit through two or three military recruitment ads. Although the details vary—an Air Force command station guiding a satellite out of the path of space junk, a Marine strike force clearing a Middle-Eastern building, a National Guard squad rescuing flood victims—they all bear one thing in common: Drama. These ads make military life seem exciting; in reality, it's generally boring, full of what service people call "hurry up and wait." The ads make military service seem full of glory; actually, it's usually thankless and often downright **demeaning**. (Ask anyone who has ever been assigned **KP** duty.) The ads portray an **idealized** individual heroism, but modern soldiers are the most effective in history because of their teamwork. Finally, the ads use the dramatic word "honor"; in reality, most soldiers will tell you what they learn from service is self-respect. Yes, military service is a noble occupation, something every young person should experience. It's just not as glamorous as the movie-theater ads would have you believe.

Think Critically Antinoro uses a point-by-point comparison to contrast recruitment ads and actual military service. His first points are clear opposites, his final ones more subtle. Why do you believe he chose this organization? What effect does it have on your own opinion toward recruitment ads?

Answers will vary.

Write Write your own "Truth in Advertising" paragraph, comparing features of an ad campaign to your experience with reality. Answers will vary.

Vocabulary

demeaning
causing a feeling of low status

KP
manual labor in a military mess hall (literally "kitchen police")

idealized
an imaginary perfection

Clement Cheah Kok Lum,2010 / Used under license from Shutterstock.com

About the Author

Yi-Fu Tuan was born in China and later moved to the United States. He is now a geography professor in Madison, Wisconsin. In this essay, Tuan compares the ways in which American and Chinese cultures create a different perception of place, and what this implies about the two societies.

Yi-Fu Tuan, "Chinese Space, American Space," Connelly, Get Writing: Sentences and Paragraphs 2e, Wadsworth. 1413033504.

Chinese Space, American Space
by Yi-Fu Tuan

Americans have a sense of space, not of place. Go to an American home in exurbia, and almost the first thing you do is drift toward the picture window. How curious that the first compliment you pay your host inside his house is to say how lovely it is outside the house! He is pleased that you should admire his **vistas**. This distant horizon is not merely a line separating earth from the sky; it is a symbol of the future. The American is not rooted in his place, however lovely: his eyes are drawn by the expanding space to a point on the horizon, which is his future.

By contrast, consider the traditional Chinese home. Blank walls enclose it. Step behind the **spirit wall** and you are in a courtyard with perhaps a miniature garden around a corner. Once inside his private compound, you are wrapped in an **ambiance** of calm beauty, an ordered world of buildings, pavement, rock, and decorative vegetation. But you have no distant view: nowhere does the space open out before you. Raw nature in such a home is experienced only as weather, and the only open space is the sky above. The Chinese is rooted in his place. When he has to leave, it is not for the promised land on the terrestrial horizon, but for another world altogether along the vertical, religious axis of his imagination.

The Chinese tie to place is deeply felt. Wanderlust is an alien sentiment. The Taoist classic *Tao Te Ching* captures the ideal of rootedness in place with these words: "Though there may be another country in the neighborhood so close that they are within sight of each other and the crowing of cocks and barking dogs in one place can be heard in the other, yet there is no traffic between them; and throughout their lives the two people have nothing to do with each other." In theory if not in practice, farmers have ranked high in Chinese society. The reason is not only that they are engaged in a "root" industry of producing food but that, unlike **pecuniary** merchants, they are tied to the land and do not abandon their country when it is in danger.

Nostalgia is a recurrent theme in Chinese poetry. An American reader of translated Chinese poems may well be taken aback—even put off—by the

Vocabulary

vista
a distant view

spirit wall
a wall around a courtyard, to keep out evil spirits

ambiance
a feeling or mood associated with a place

pecuniary
involved with money

frequency, as well as the sentimentality, of the lament for home. To understand the strength of this sentiment, we need to know that Chinese desire for stability and rootedness in place is prompted by constant threat of war, exile, and the natural disasters of flood and drought. Forcible removal makes the Chinese keenly aware of their loss. By contrast, Americans move, for the most part, voluntarily. Their nostalgia for hometown is really longing for a childhood to which they can return: in the meantime the future beckons and the future is "out there," in open space.

When we criticize American rootlessness, we tend to forget that it is a result of ideals we admire, namely social mobility and optimism about the future. When we admire Chinese rootedness, we forget that the word "place" means both a location in space and position in society: to be tied to place is also to be bound to one's station in life, with little hope of betterment. Space symbolizes hope; place, achievement and stability.

Insight

Reflect on what sort of space you are most comfortable in. Is it an American space, or one from another society?

Analyze Complete the point-by-point graphic below to analyze Yi-Fu Tuan's comparison of Chinese and American sense of space. In the left column, list details the author provides about Chinese attitudes; in the right column, list corresponding American attitudes.

Sense of Space Example answers:

Chinese Attitudes	American Attitudes
Enclosed	Vistas
Calm	Future
Order	Social mobility
Nostalgia	Optimism
Stability	
Rootedness	

Think Critically Tuan describes both benefits and problems with the Chinese perception of space. What benefits and problems does he describe for the American perception? How would you summarize the primary message of the essay?

Answers will vary.

Write Write an essay about a place that you know well that has changed significantly over time—perhaps your home, your neighborhood, a favorite business, a school you attended, or some other location. Compare the place then (in the past) to the place now (today). Answers will vary.

About the Author

Neil Bissoondath is a journalist and author who was born in Trinidad and later immigrated to Canada. In this essay, he explores his own spiritual experience following his mother's death, comparing and contrasting it with religious faith (and glancingly with scientific certainty).

Neil Bissoondath, "Religious Faith Versus Spirituality," Flachmann/Flachmann/MacLennan, Reader's Choice, Fifth Canadian Edition, Pearson Education Canada, 0131979760.

Remi Benali/Terra /Corbis

Religious Faith Versus Spirituality by Neil Bissoondath

Wait till someone you love dies. You'll see. You'll know God exists. You'll want Him to. The prediction, repeated with minimal variation through the years by believers challenged by my nonbelief, was never offered as a promise but as a vague threat, and always with a sense of satisfied superiority, as if the speakers relished the thought that one day I would get my **comeuppance**.

They were, without exception, enthusiastic practitioners of their respective faiths—Roman Catholics, Presbyterians, Hindus, Muslims, God-fearing people all. Which was, to me, precisely the problem: Why all this fear?

And then one day, without warning, my mother died. Hers was the first death to touch me to the quick. Her cremation was done in the traditional Hindu manner. Under the direction of a **pundit**, my brother and I performed the ceremony, preparing the body with our bare hands, a contact more intimate than we'd ever had when she was alive.

As I walked away from her flaming **pyre**, I felt myself soaring with a lightness I'd never known before. I was suddenly freed from days of physical and emotional **lassitude**, and felt my first inkling of the healing power of ritual, the solace that ceremony can bring.

Still, despite the pain and the unspeakable sense of loss, the oft-predicted discovery of faith eluded me. I remained, as I do today, a nonbeliever, but I have no doubt that I underwent a deeply spiritual experience. This was when I began to understand that religious faith and spirituality do not necessarily have anything to do with each other—not that they are incompatible but that they are often mutually exclusive.

Western civilization has spent two thousand years blurring the distinction between the two, and as we enter the third millennium we are hardly more at peace with ourselves than people were a thousand years ago. Appreciating the distinction could help soothe our anxieties about the days to come.

Spirituality is the individual's ability to wonder at, and delight in, the

Vocabulary

comeuppance
deserved repayment for a wrong attitude

pundit
a Hindu scholar or "wise man"

pyre
a pile of wood for cremating a body

lassitude
weariness, fatigue, or lethargy

indecipherable, like a baby marveling at the wiggling of its own toes. It is to be at ease with speculation, asking the unanswerable question and accepting that any answer would necessarily be incomplete, even false. It is recognizing that if scientific inquiry has inevitable limits, so too do religious explanations, which base themselves on unquestioning acceptance of the unprovable: neither can ever fully satisfy.

A sense of the spiritual comes from staring deep into the formation of a rose or a **hibiscus** and being astonished at the intricate delicacy of its symmetry without needing to see behind its perfection of form the fashioning hand of a deity.

It comes from watching your child being born and gazing for the first time into those newly opened eyes, from holding that child against your chest and feeling his or her heartbeat melding with yours.

It comes from gazing up into the sparkling solitude of a clear midnight sky, secure in the knowledge that, no matter how alone you may feel at moments, the message of the stars appears to be that you most **indisputably** are not.

At such moments, you need no **dogma** to tell you that the world seen or unseen, near or distant, is a wonderful and mysterious place. Spirituality, then, requires neither science nor religion, both of which hunger after answers and reassurance—while the essence of spirituality lies in the opening up of the individual to dazzlement. Spirituality **entails** no worship.

At the very moment of my mother's cremation, her brother, trapped thousands of miles away in England by airline schedules, got out his photographs of her and spread them on his coffee table. He reread her old letters and spent some time meditating on the life that had been lived—his way, at the very moment flames consumed her body, of celebrating the life and saying farewell, his way of engaging with the spiritual.

Analyze Complete the T-graph to analyze Bissoondath's comparison of faith and spirituality. In the left column list details about faith; in the right list details about spirituality. Answers will vary.

Religious Faith	Spirituality

Think Critically How does science fit into Bissoondath's essay? Where would you place it in the T-graph above? How does your placement reflect on your own experiences with science and with religion?

Answers will vary.

Vocabulary

hibiscus
a type of shrub or tree with large flowers

indisputably
without question; unable to be disputed

dogma
an official doctrine concerning faith or religion

entail
to involve or require

About the Author

Llewellyn H. Rockwell, Jr., is chairman of the Ludwig von Mises Institute, a think tank devoted to libertarian political and social theory. He served as Congressman Ron Paul's chief of staff from 1978-1982.

Llewellyn H. Rockwell, Jr., "Two Views on Social Order: Conflict or Cooperation?" http://mises.org/daily/2612.

From "Two Views on Social Order: Conflict or Cooperation?" by Llewellyn H. Rockwell, Jr.

There are two clear and present dangers to liberty in America. One is known as the Left, and the other is known as the Right. They are dangerous because they seek to use government to mold society into a form they seek, rather than the form that liberty achieves if society is left on its own.

I'm going to assume that the Left and the Right come to their views sincerely, that their passion for using government is driven by some fear that the absence of government would yield **catastrophe**. So the burden of my talk today will be to identify and explain the common thread that connects the worldview of the Left and the Right, and suggest that they are both wrong about the capacity of society, whether it is defined locally or internationally, to manage itself. . . .

After the [American] revolution, when government began to regroup and **reconsolidate**, . . . the liberal idea [of pure liberty] began to gain **detractors**. John Adams, whom Jefferson beat in the great presidential election of 1800, never stopped resenting Jefferson's suspicions toward power and opposition to practically everything the federal government wanted to do. It was Jefferson's conviction that liberty yielded social cooperation; it was Adams's view that liberty could only be established and sustained through government authority. These two opposing views persist to this day.

Adams went so far as to level a familiar accusation against Jefferson's faith in pure liberty. Adams wrote him in 1813:

> "You never felt the terrorism of Shays' Rebellion in Massachusetts . . . You certainly never felt the terrorism excited by Genet in 1793, when ten thousand people in the streets of Philadelphia, day by day, threatened to drag Washington out of his house and effect a revolution in the government. . . . I have no doubt you were fast asleep in philosophical tranquility when . . . Market Street was as full of men as could stand by one another, and even before my door when some of my **domestics**, in frenzy, determined to sacrifice their lives in my defence. . . . What think you of terrorism, Mr. Jefferson?"

Vocabulary

catastrophe
a terrible disaster

reconsolidate
to bring scattered elements back together

detractor
someone who insults or argues against

domestic
a household servant

. . . What Adams conveniently overlooked is that the rebellion of which he spoke was actually sparked by taxation and government-backed credit expansion. There would have been no need for a revolt had government not created the conditions that led to it. . . . From Shays' Rebellion to 9-11, we see two worldviews of society at work. One sees the government as a source of liberty and order, and fears society without the state more than any conceivable alternative. The other sees government as a source of disorder that uses that disorder to enhance its power and material resources at the expense of society. . . .

The Left and the Right in this country hold to the first view. The **successors** to Jefferson hold to the second view, which in Jefferson's time was called the liberal view, and which today is called the libertarian view. . . .

Let us begin with the Left. They believe society has fundamental flaws and deep-rooted conflicts that keep it in some sort of structural imbalance. All these conflicts and **disequilibria** cry out for government fixes, for leftists are certain that there is no social problem that a good dose of power can't solve.

If the conflicts they want are not there, they make them up. They look at what appears to be a happy **suburban subdivision** and see pathology. They see an apparently happy marriage and imagine that it is a mask for abuse. They see a thriving church and think the people inside are being manipulated by a **cynical** and corrupt pastor. Their view of the economic system is the same. They see poor peasants in the Third World drinking a Coke or making Nikes, and they cry foul. They figure that prices don't reflect reality but instead are set by large players. There is a power imbalance at the heart of every exchange, domestically and internationally. The labor contract is a **veneer** that covers exploitation.

To the brooding leftist, it is inconceivable that people can work out their own problems, that trade can be to people's mutual advantage, that society can be essentially self-managing, or that attempts to use government power to reshape and manage people might backfire. Their faith in government knows few limits; their faith in people is thin or nonexistent. This is why they are a danger to liberty.

The remarkable fact about the conflict theory of society held by the Left is that it ends up creating more of the very **pathologies** that they believe have been there from the beginning. The surest way to drive a wedge between labor and **capital** is to regulate the labor markets to the point that people cannot make voluntary trades. Both sides begin to fear each other. It is the same with relations between races, sexes, the abled and disabled, and any other groups you can name. It is the same with international relations. A **tariff** or trade sanction is nothing but war by another means. The best path to creating conflict where none need exist is to put a government bureaucracy in charge. . . .

The traditional and correct answer to the conflict theory is that there is essentially nothing government can do to improve the workings of society. During the Great Depression, for example, most everyone on the Left thought that government was the only way out. The hard Left favored communist revolution. The soft Left favored the New Deal. The old liberals pointed out that it was

Vocabulary

successor
person who takes a position after someone else

disequilibria
lack of balance

suburban subdivision
a section of housing outside of a city

cynical
distrustful

veneer
a thin covering to hide a rough inner surface

pathology
study of disease, or diseased condition

capital
money and other such resources

tariff
a tax on imported goods, specifically to raise their price

government itself that brought about the crisis, and that more government intervention could only make matters worse. This was a rational response, but it did not carry the day.

After the Second World War, we saw the emergence of a strange creature in American life, something that called itself conservatism. It was opposed to the Left in American life, particularly that branch that was sympathetic to communism. It counseled vague solutions like **prudence** in public affairs. But in a crucial way, it adopted one **tenet** of the leftist worldview: it rejected old liberalism as a vision for how society can work in the absence of government. It adopted a conflict view of society, a different brand rooted in the **assertions** of Hobbes rather than Marx. The idea that conflict was at the very heart of society, absent government, was a key aspect of this view.

This new thing called conservatism adopted some of the **rhetoric** of the Old Right. It defended property and enterprise in economic affairs. But what was critical was the introduction of a notion that society, if left to its own devices, would collapse into chaos. This was particularly true in international affairs. So while the Cold War was originally an invention of the Democrat Harry Truman, it was tailor-made to appeal to conservatives who were looking for an ideological enemy to slay. It is one thing to say that communism is an evil **ideological** system; it is another to say that we cannot rest until every communist is killed and every communist government wiped off the face of the earth.

What happened to the **noninterventionist** views of the Old Right? They were **predicated** on the idea that there could be a leaderless world order, that nations could get along without one overarching authority and source of law. But after the war, that too began to change. A new conviction arose.

Russell Kirk wrote in 1954 that "civilized society requires distinctions of order, wealth, and responsibility; it cannot exist without true leadership . . . society longs for just leadership. . . ." He contrasted this view with what he considered the **erroneous** opinion of Ludwig von Mises, whom he attacks over the course of many pages. Mises, wrote Kirk, had exaggerated faith in the rationality of individuals. Kirk, in contrast, sees that all of history is governed by two great forces: love and hate. Neither are rational impulses. In order to achieve the triumph of love over hate, wrote Kirk, the conservative "looks upon government as a great power for good."

And so conservatives threw themselves behind the force of government to achieve their aims, and no matter how many wicked things government did over the years under conservative control, they always told themselves that it was surely better than the much-feared alternative of an unmanaged society. . . .

At the end of the Cold War, many conservatives panicked that there would be no more great causes into which the state could enlist itself. There were about 10 years of books that sought to **demonize** someone, somewhere, in the hope of creating a new enemy. Maybe it would be China. Maybe it would be the culture war. Maybe it should be drugs. From their point of view, 9-11 presented the

Vocabulary

prudence
common sense

tenet
a central teaching

assertion
declaration of fact

rhetoric
manner of speaking

ideology
a core social, political, or religious philosophy

noninterventionist
dedication to remaining uninvolved in the conflicts of others

predicate
to base upon

erroneous
in error

demonize
to characterize someone as utterly evil

opportunity they needed, and thus began the newest unwinnable war: the Global War on Terror.

So must government rule every aspect of life until every last terrorist is wiped off the face of the earth? Must we surrender all our liberty and property to this cause, as the regime and its apologists suggest?

This view of society is certainly not sustainable in these times or in the future. Ever more of daily life consists in **seceding** from the state and its **apparatus** of edicts and regulations. In the online world, billions of deals are made every day that require virtually no government law to enforce. The technology that is pushing the world forward is not created by the state but by private enterprise. The places we shop and the communities in which we live are being created by private developers. Most businesses prefer to deal with private courts. We depend on insurance companies, not police, to reduce the risks in life. We secure our homes and workplaces through private firms.

What's more, these days we see all around us how liberty generates order and how this order is self-sustaining. We benefit daily, hourly, minute by minute, from an order that is not imposed from without but rather generated from within, by that remarkable capacity we have for pursuing self-interest while benefiting the whole. Here is the great mystery and majesty of social order, expressed so well in the act of economic exchange.

I've spoken about the problem of those who look at society and see nothing but conflict and no prospect for cooperation. It is a view shared by the Left and the Right. Truly there is an actual conflict at the root of history, but it is not the one most people understand or see. It is the great struggle between freedom and **despotism**, between the individual and the state, between the voluntary means and **coercion**. We know where we stand. We stand with the future of freedom.

Vocabulary

secede
to withdraw from an organization

apparatus
equipment or machinery

despot
a ruler with utter authority

coerce
to compel someone by threat, often implied

Gary Hathaway,2010 / Used under license from Shutterstock.com

Speaking & Listening

Work with a partner to fill in this Venn diagram.

Analyze Complete the following Venn diagram. In the center section, list similarities between the Left and Right. In the outer sections, list details unique to that subject. Answers will vary.

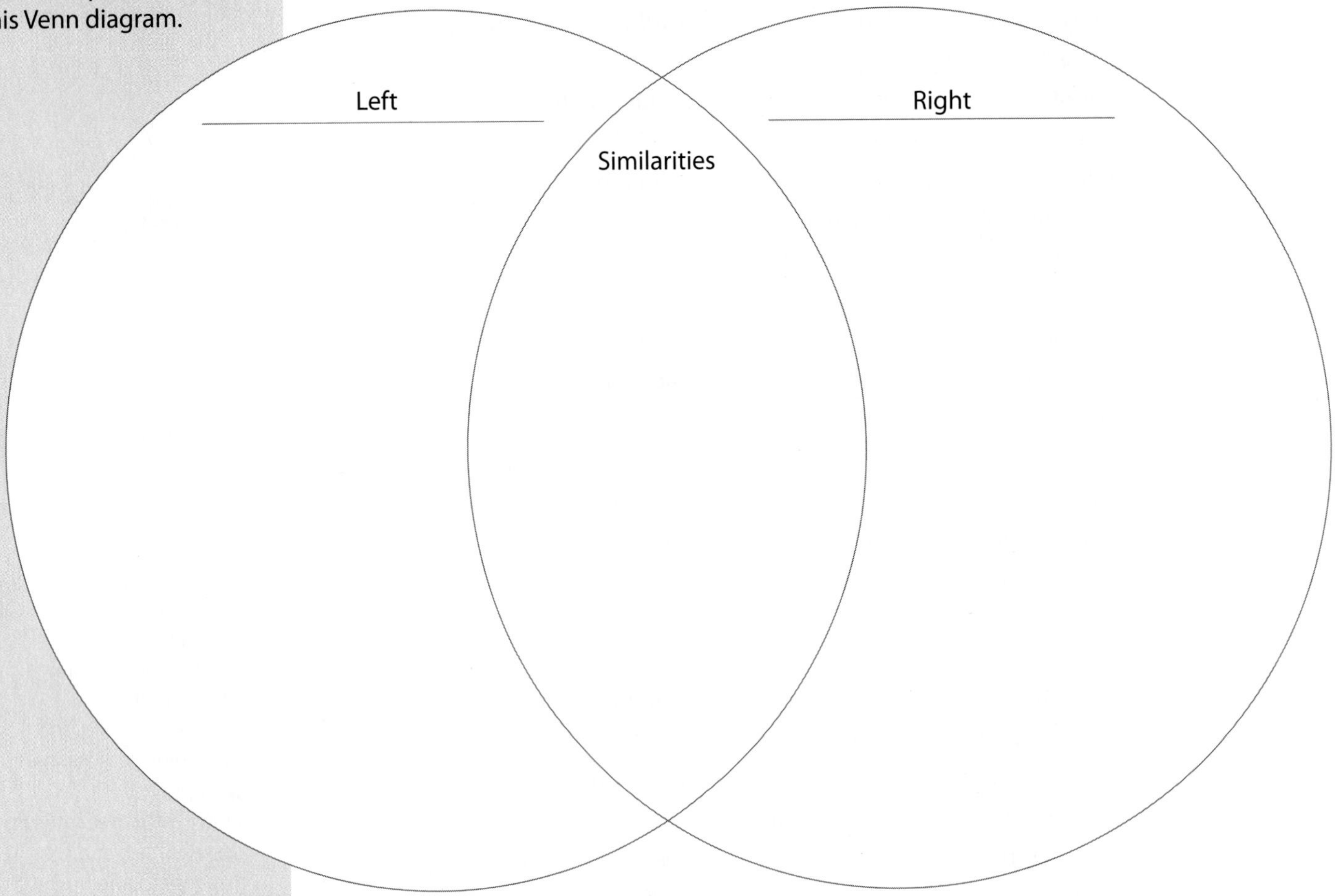

Left

Similarities

Right

Evaluate Write a paragraph explaining in what ways you believe the author is correct. Then write one explaining in what ways you believe he is incorrect. Finally, write a concluding paragraph that summarizes your response to the essay.

Answers will vary.

Read Further Visit the mises.org Web site to read the full essay. Does the additional material there change your understanding of this issue? Explain why or why not. (Use your own paper.) Answers will vary.

LO2 Writing a Comparison-Contrast Essay

Prewrite To begin writing, you need a topic. Using an "essentials of life" checklist like the one below, choose a topic that suggests two subjects to compare. For example, "clothing" might suggest comparing the way two friends dress. Similarly, "technology" might suggest comparing the merits of two different cell phones, or even two different cell-phone plans. Use the list as a springboard for your own ideas. Answers will vary.

Essentials of Life Checklist

Clothing	Goals	Community
Housing	Measurement	Arts
Food	Machines	Faith
Education	Intelligence	Commerce
Family	Agriculture	Heat
Friends	Environment	Laws
Love	Plant life	Science
Senses	Property	Technology
Energy	Health	Work
Entertainment	Medicine	Hobbies
Recreation	Books	Public service
Personality	Tools	Natural resources
Communication	Exercise	Personal rights

In each lettered space, write a topic of your choice from the checklist above. Then, below each topic, list two subjects to compare.

A. Topic

Subject 1:	Subject 2:

B. Topic

Subject 1:	Subject 2:

C. Topic

Subject 1:	Subject 2:

Learning Outcomes

Write your own comparison-contrast essay.

WAC

As this checklist shows, comparing and contrasting are applicable in all subjects and all parts of life.

Prewrite Complete the Venn diagram below. Write your two subjects on the lines provided. In the center section, list similarities between the two subjects. In each outer section, list details that are unique to that subject.

Answers will vary.

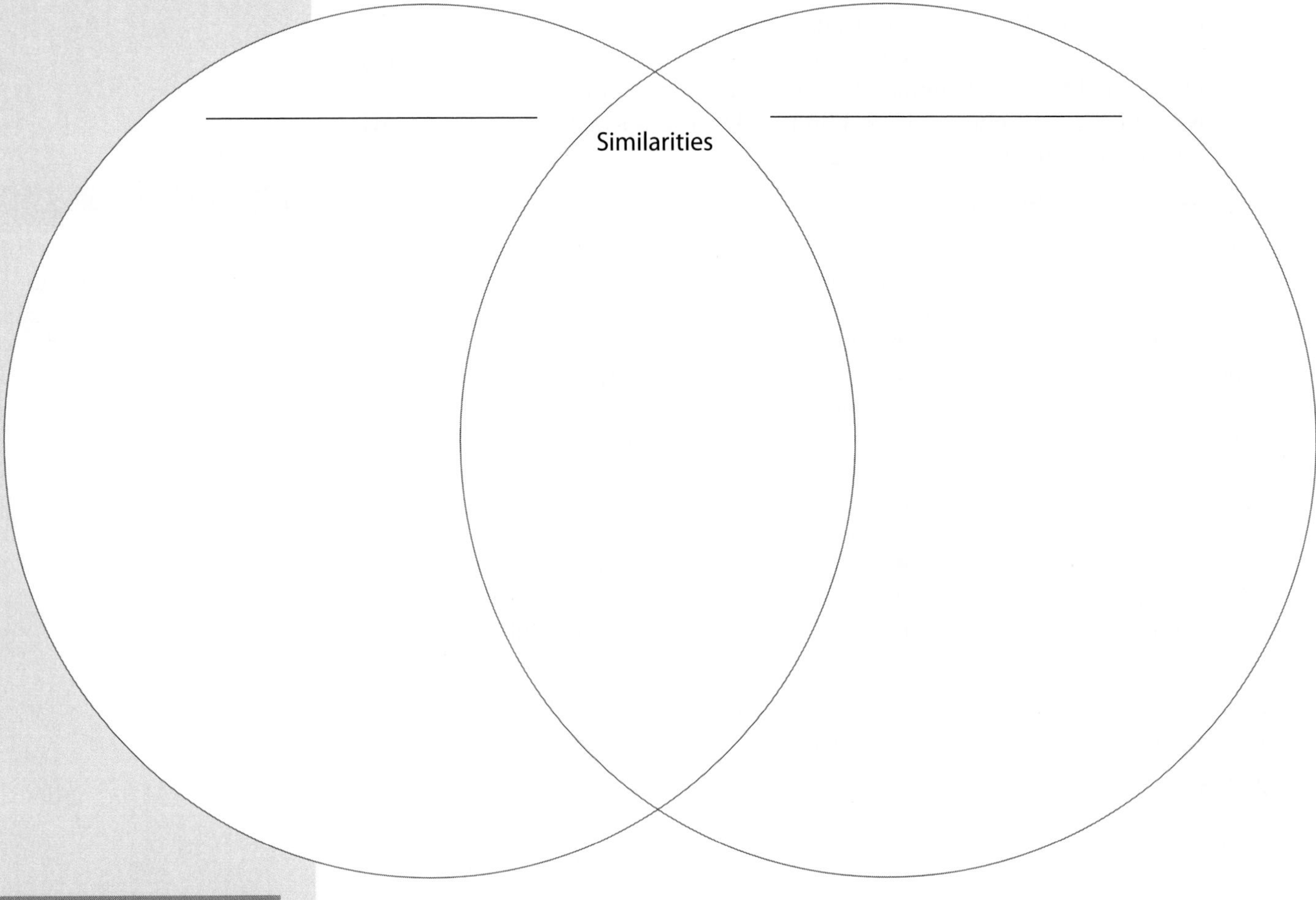

Speaking & Listening

Make sure to share your writing with a classmate. Read your essay aloud to the person, and then discuss the work together. Switch roles and have your partner read her or his writing. Discuss it. Provide positive, helpful feedback.

Choose three or more points to compare and contrast. Then choose a pattern of organization. Use a point-by-point pattern, a subject-to-subject pattern, or a similarities-and-differences pattern.

Point-by-Point		Subject-to-Subject	Similarities-Differences
Beginning		Beginning	Beginning
Point 1	Subject 1	Subject 1	Similarities
	Subject 2		
Point 2	Subject 1		
	Subject 2	Subject 2	Differences
Point 3	Subject 1		
	Subject 2		
Ending		Ending	Ending

Draft Create a strong opening, middle, and closing for your essay. Use the supports below as you create each part. Answers will vary.

Opening Paragraph

Capture your reader's attention in the first line of your essay. Then lead up to your thesis statement. Here is a formula to use as you create your thesis statement.

- **Make a statement:** The barrio of my youth is vanishing.
- **Ask a question:** Why is it that we can never go home again?
- **Use a quotation:** "I've seen this neighborhood change—twice."

Two Subjects		Thought or Feeling		Thesis Statement
Print books and e-books	+	though different, both have their own conveniences	=	Although some people think reading print books or e-books is an either/or decision, both are convenient at different times and places.

Two Subjects + **Thought or Feeling** ______________________

= Thesis Statement

____

Middle Paragraphs

In the middle paragraphs, compare the two subjects, using your organizational pattern. Also use transitions to help the reader follow your ideas:

Transitions That Compare

as	as well	also	both	in the same way	much as
much like	one way	like	likewise	similarly	

Transitions That Contrast

although	even though	by contrast	but
on the one hand	on the other hand	otherwise	though
still	while	yet	however

Closing Paragraph

In your closing, share a final thought, pointing out a key similarity or difference between the subjects you have compared.

Revise Improve your writing. First ask a classmate to read your essay. Then discuss your work, using the following checklist. Continue making improvements until you can answer "yes" to each question.

Ideas

☐ **1.** Do I compare and contrast two subjects?

☐ **2.** Do I include a variety of details (facts, quotations, anecdotes)?

Organization

☐ **3.** Do I introduce my subjects in the opening?

☐ **4.** Have I used a pattern of organization in the middle part?

☐ **5.** Have I used transitions to connect my sentences?

☐ **6.** Do I share a final thought about the comparison in my ending?

Voice

☐ **7.** Do I sound knowledgeable and interested in my subjects?

Edit Prepare a clean copy of your essay and use the following checklist to check for errors. When you can answer "yes" to a question, check it off. Continue working until all items are checked.

Words

☐ **1.** Do I use correct verb forms (*he saw,* not *he seen*)? (See page 356.)

☐ **2.** Do my subjects and verbs agree (*she speaks,* not *she speak*)? (See pages 282–291.)

☐ **3.** Have I used the right words (*there, their, they're*)?

Sentences

☐ **4.** Have I avoided sentence fragments? (See pages 297–302.)

☐ **5.** Have I avoided run-on sentences? (See pages 306–310.)

☐ **6.** Have I avoided improper shifts in sentences? (See pages 314–315.)

Conventions

☐ **7.** Have I used commas after long introductory word groups? (See page 396.)

☐ **8.** Have I capitalized first words? (See page 414.)

☐ **9.** Have I capitalized proper nouns and proper adjectives? (See page 414.)

☐ **10.** Have I carefully checked my spelling?

"The ultimate result of shielding men from the effects of folly is to fill the world with fools."
—Herbert Spencer

Cause-Effect Essays

Set a match to a fuse, and sparks will fly. Let that fuse ignite a stick of dynamite, and the resulting explosion can cause much weightier things to fly—earth, stone, brick, and so on. That simple match becomes the cause of tremendous destruction.

If the explosion was set to bring down a wall of salt in a mine, however, this single destructive act can result in much good—ice melted from winter roads, foods preserved, and meals seasoned, just to name a few benefits.

Match to fuse, fuse to dynamite, explosion to a harvest of salt, salt to roads and foods—each step involves a cause-effect relationship. In this chapter, you will read about several more such relationships and be called upon to evaluate their significance.

Learning Outcomes

LO1 Understand, read, and analyze cause-effect essays.

LO2 Write your own cause-effect essay.

What do you think?

Study the image and quotation. What does each say to you about cause and effect?

Answers will vary.

Learning Outcome

Understand, read, and analyze cause-effect essays.

LO1 Understanding Cause-Effect Essays

Within this chapter you will find three example essays using a cause-effect approach. You will also find questions and graphic organizers you can use as tools to help analyze each reading. At the end of the chapter are writing guidelines for creating a cause-effect essay of your own.

SQ3R When you read, become involved with the text by using the SQ3R approach.

- **Survey:** Prepare by reading "About the Author," skimming the essay, and noting any vocabulary words.
- **Question:** Ask yourself what cause-and-effect relationships you predict from the essay.
- **Read:** Read the essay, noting the causes leading to or effects resulting from the main topic.
- **Recite:** Recite the main details of the cause-and-effect relationship the author provides.
- **Review:** Answer the questions provided and use the graphic organizers to help you analyze the essay.

Essay List:

"Yes, Accidents Happen. But Why?": Robert Strauss discusses the difficulties in determining the causes behind traffic accidents.

"Spanglish Spoken Here": Janice Castro describes the way in which the Spanish language is merging with English in the United States, creating a unique blend of the two.

"Why Schools Don't Educate": New York State Teacher of the Year John Taylor Gatto argues that our modern school system fails our society by turning out students who are disconnected from the real world.

About the Author

Robert Strauss is a journalist whose work has appeared in the *New York Times, Los Angeles Times, Washington Post, Sports Illustrated,* and *Fortune,* among other places. He is also a member of the creative-writing faculty at the University of Pennsylvania.

Robert Strauss, "Yes, Accidents Happen. But Why?" New York Times, October 24, 2007.

Yes, Accidents Happen. But Why?
by Robert Strauss

When Fred Mannering takes his **vintage** MG sports car out for a spin, he always leaves plenty of room between the car in front of him and the MG. He brakes slowly and deliberately. He rarely speeds, and if he were to go fast, it would be only on a superhighway with little traffic.

"My other car is newer, with good antilock brakes and air bags, so I don't take nearly as much care," said Dr. Mannering, a Purdue University professor of **civil engineering** who studies the causes and results of traffic accidents. In that way, he may reflect the behavior of the average driver, governed by hard-to-quantify influences.

Dr. Mannering's study of accidents in Washington State from 1992 to 1997, a period during which air bags and antilock brakes became prevalent, showed that counter to what would seem logical, there was no major reduction in accidents even with the spread of two seemingly effective safety features.

"It just shows how hard it is to determine what causes an accident," he said. "The one thing you might conclude—it's called an offset hypothesis—is that people have an acceptance of a level of safety. If they felt safer because of the air bags and brakes, then maybe they drove faster or switched the radio on and off more to, so to speak, **compensate**.

"What seems like an exact science—determining who or what causes accidents—is actually quite difficult," Dr. Mannering said.

Insurance companies, carmakers, inventors, safety advocates and clearly drivers themselves all have an interest in learning about what might reduce the number of accidents or at least make them less severe. Yet there is surprisingly little data to help them.

"Speeding causes crashes," said Anne McCartt, senior vice president for research at the Insurance Institute for Highway Safety, a nonprofit group financed by auto insurers. "Running through a red light causes crashes. Drinking alcohol certainly causes crashes, but to what extent? That has been difficult to determine."

Rob Foss, a senior research scientist at the University of North Carolina

Vocabulary

vintage
valuable due to its age; classic

civil engineering
the design of public works such as roads and bridges

compensate
balance out or make up for

Highway Safety Research Center, confirmed the **elusive** nature of pinpointing the causes. "I guess all we can safely say we know with certainty is that virtually all crashes are caused by a series of things coming together all at once," he said. "Driving after you have too much to drink is dangerous, but, strangely, we don't know how much, despite laws that have alcohol limits. Many people take trips after having too much to drink and manage to get home."

Part of the problem stems from the limitations of researchers' information. Often they depend on police reports, which can be reliable for some things, like what kind of car is involved or the extent of injuries. But other factors—like distractions—may not exist in police reports. A driver is unlikely, for one, to tell an officer that he was using a cellphone, especially if he thinks it will increase his liability.

"Putting in place a good crash investigation and maintaining good data for these kinds of analyses is complicated and thus expensive," said Peter Kissinger, chief executive of the AAA Foundation for Traffic Safety. "It's not the kind of thing which a political leader in a state has the patience to see through. They would rather put some money for roads as opposed to investing in something as unsexy as maintaining a good crash **database**."

The Strategic Highway Research Program at the National Academy of Sciences may change that. The program will gather raw data from about 1,000 cars equipped with minicameras, motion-detection sensors and other devices to monitor cars and their drivers. The program expands a pilot study done at Virginia Tech University.

The Virginia study came to some **preliminary** conclusions:

- Nearly 80 percent of crashes and 65 percent of near crashes were caused by distractions that made the driver look away for up to three seconds.
- Drivers ages 18 to 20 were up to four times more likely to have an **inattention**-related accident than older drivers.
- Driver drowsiness was involved in 20 percent of all crashes.
- All 14 of the rear-end crashes in the study happened when the lead car was stopped.

"For the last 30 years, the emphasis has been on injury prevention and modification of vehicles because that seemed to be where the payoff was," said Dr. Kenneth Campbell, chief program officer for safety at the Strategic Highway Research Program, who will direct the five-year study. "That has slowed." He said that traffic fatalities in the United States have remained at about 40,000 a year for the last decade or so.

"Now the technology is available to separate out things like alcohol use and different kinds of distractions, and the condition in which people keep a car and all sorts of variables," he said. "It is long in coming, but soon we'll know what really does cause car accidents."

Analyze This essay includes two separate cause-effect relationships. The first suggests reasons (causes) for crashes (the effect); the second describes difficulties (causes) in drawing firm conclusions (an effect).

Make a list of suspected causes for crashes. Next, make a list of reasons those causes are so difficult to pin down. Number the items in each list by supposed order of importance. Write a journal entry describing your thoughts about the subject.

Vocabulary

elusive
difficult to track

database
a computer file that organizes information for easy searching and reference

preliminary
initial, prior to a full set

inattention
lack of attention, distractedness

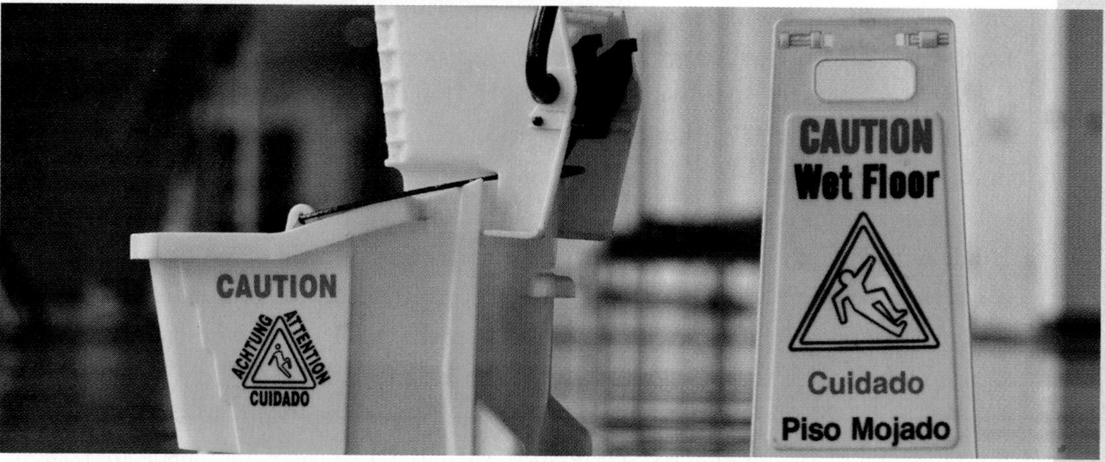

About the Author

Janice Castro is an assistant professor at Northwestern University's journalism school. She served as a reporter, a writer, and an editor at *Time Magazine* for over 20 years and has freelanced for many other publications.

Janice Castro, "Spanglish Spoken Here," Time, July 11, 1988.

Spanglish Spoken Here
by Janice Castro

In Manhattan a first-grader greets her visiting grandparents, happily exclaiming, "Come here, sientate!" Her bemused grandfather, who does not speak Spanish, nevertheless knows she is asking him to sit down. A Miami personnel officer understands what a job applicant means when he says, "Quiero un part time." Nor do drivers miss a beat reading a billboard alongside a Los Angeles street advertising CERVEZA—SIX-PACK!

This free-form blend of Spanish and English, known as Spanglish, is common **linguistic** currency wherever concentrations of Hispanic Americans are found in the U.S. In Los Angeles, where 55 percent of the city's 3 million inhabitants speak Spanish, Spanglish is as much a part of daily life as sunglasses. Unlike the broken-English efforts of earlier immigrants from Europe, Asia and other regions, Spanglish has become a widely accepted conversational mode used casually—even playfully—by Spanish-speaking immigrants and native-born Americans alike.

Consisting of one part **Hispanicized** English, one part Americanized Spanish and more than a little fractured **syntax**, Spanglish is a bit like a Robin Williams comedy routine: a crackling line of cross-cultural **patter** straight from the melting pot. Often it enters Anglo homes and families through the children, who pick it up at school or at play with their young Hispanic contemporaries. In other cases, it comes from watching TV; many an **Anglo** child watching Sesame Street has learned *uno dos tres* almost as quickly as one two three.

Spanglish takes a variety of forms, from the Southern California Anglos who bid farewell with the utterly silly "hasta la bye-bye" to the Cuban-American drivers in Miami who *parquean* their *carros*. Some Spanglish sentences are mostly Spanish, with a quick detour for an English word or two. A **Latino** friend may cut short a conversation by glancing at his watch and excusing himself with the explanation that he must "ir al supermarket."

Many of the English words transplanted in this way are simply handier than their Spanish counterparts. No matter how distasteful the subject, for example, it is still easier to say "income tax" than *impuesto sobre la renta*. At the same time, many Spanish-speaking immigrants have adopted such terms as VCR, microwave

Vocabulary

linguistic
concerning languages

Hispanic
a person of Latin American (see page 474) descent living in the USA

syntax
the ordering of words into phrases and sentences.

patter
rapid speech

Anglo
a Caucasian living in the USA

Latino
See "Hispanic," above.

and dishwasher for what they view as largely American phenomena. Still other English words convey a cultural context that is not **implicit** in the Spanish. A friend who invites you to *lonche* most likely has in mind the brisk American custom of "doing lunch" rather than the **languorous** afternoon break traditionally implied by *almuerzo*.

Mainstream Americans exposed to similar **hybrids** of German, Chinese or Hindi might be mystified. But even Anglos who speak little or no Spanish are somewhat familiar with Spanglish. Living among them, for one thing, are 19 million Hispanics. In addition, more American high school and university students sign up for Spanish than for any other foreign language.

Only in the past ten years, though, has Spanglish begun to turn into a national slang. Its popularity has grown with the explosive increases in U.S. immigration from **Latin American** countries. English has increasingly collided with Spanish in retail stores, offices and classrooms, in pop music and on street corners. Anglos whose ancestors picked up such Spanish words as *rancho, bronco, tornado* and *incommunicado*, for instance, now freely use such Spanish words as *gracias, bueno, amigo* and *por favor.*

Among Latinos, Spanglish conversations often flow easily from Spanish into several sentences of English and back again. "It is done unconsciously," explains Carmen Silva-Corvalan, a Chilean-born associate professor of linguistics at the University of Southern California, who speaks Spanglish with relatives and neighbors. "I couldn't even tell you minutes later if I said something in Spanish or in English."

Spanglish is a sort of code for Latinos: the speakers know Spanish, but their hybrid language reflects the American culture in which they live. Many lean to shorter, clipped phrases in place of the longer, more graceful expressions their parents used. Says Leonel de la Cuesta, an assistant professor of modern languages at Florida International University in Miami: "In the U.S., time is money, and that is showing up in Spanglish as an economy of language." Conversational examples: *taipiar* (type) and *winshi-wiper* (windshield wiper) replace *escribir a maquina* and *limpiaparabrisas.*

Major advertisers, eager to tap the estimated $134 billion in spending power wielded by Spanish-speaking Americans, have ventured into Spanglish to promote their products. In some cases, attempts to sprinkle Spanish through commercials have produced embarrassing **gaffes**. A Braniff airlines ad that sought to tell Spanish-speaking audiences they could settle back *en* (in) luxuriant *cuero* (leather) seats, for example, inadvertently said they could fly without clothes (*encuero*).

A fractured translation of the Miller Lite slogan told readers the beer was "Filling, and less delicious." Similar **blunders** are often made by Anglos trying to impress Spanish-speaking pals. But if Latinos are amused by mangled Spanglish, they also recognize these goofs as a sort of friendly acceptance. As they might put it, *no problema.*

Insight

Do you speak a hybrid language? Which languages are combined? Where do you use this hybrid?

Vocabulary

implicit
clearly conveyed, though not directly expressed

languorous
slow and relaxed

hybrid
a mixture from two or more backgrounds

Latin America
all of the Americas south of the USA

gaffe
an ignorant or careless mistake in language

blunder
a foolish or clumsy error

Analyze Which of these cause/effect diagrams best illustrates the essay? Why?

Cause ↘
Cause → Effect
Cause ↗

Cause → Effect (three effects: Effect, Effect, Effect)

Answers will vary.

Explain What is the main effect or main cause in the essay?

The main effect is the hybridization of Spanish and English.

Analyze How do the details of the essay proceed from that cause or lead to that effect?

Specific examples are given to explain where and why Spanglish occurs. Examples of where include Manhattan, Los Angeles, Miami, and other areas of Hispanic population. Examples of why include children's exposure to both languages, the "economy of language" of "income tax" versus "*impuesto sobre la renta,*" Hispanic adoption of American culture, and advertising adopting Spanish terms.

Reflect How does Spanglish, or the melding of other languages, affect your own life? In what ways is Spanglish unique from other meldings or similar to them?

Answers will vary.

About the Author

New York State Teacher of the Year, and three-time NYC Teacher of the Year, John Taylor Gatto held a variety of jobs—including Army medic, scriptwriter, and audio publisher—before beginning to teach. He is now a public speaker on the topic of education.

John Taylor Gatto, "Why Schools Don't Educate," Acceptance speech for New York City Teacher of the Year Award, January 31, 1990.

Why Schools Don't Educate
by John Taylor Gatto

I accept this award on behalf of all the fine teachers I've known over the years who've struggled to make their transactions with children honorable ones: men and women who are never **complacent**, always questioning, always wrestling to define and redefine endlessly what the word education should mean. A "Teacher of the Year" is not the best teacher around—those people are too quiet to be easily uncovered—but a standard-bearer, symbolic of these private people who spend their lives gladly in the service of children. This is their award as well as mine.

We live in a time of great social crisis. Our children rank at the bottom of nineteen industrial nations in reading, writing, and arithmetic. The world's narcotic economy is based upon our own consumption of this commodity. If we didn't buy so many powdered dreams, the business would collapse—and schools are an important sales outlet. Our teenage-suicide rate is the highest in the world—and suicidal kids are rich kids for the most part, not poor. In Manhattan, 70 percent of all new marriages last less than five years.

Our school crisis is a reflection of this greater social crisis. We seem to have lost our identity. Children and old people are penned up and locked away from the business of the world to an **unprecedented** degree; nobody talks to them anymore. Without children and old people mixing in daily life, a community has no future and no past, only a continuous present. In fact, the term "community" hardly applies to the way we interact with each other. We live in networks, not communities, and everyone I know is lonely because of that. In some strange way, school is a major actor in this tragedy, just as it is a major actor in the widening gulfs among social classes. Using school as a sorting mechanism, we appear to be on the way to creating a **caste system**, complete with untouchables who wander through subway trains begging and sleep on the streets.

I've noticed a fascinating phenomenon in my twenty-nine years of teaching—that schools and schooling are increasingly **irrelevant** to the great **enterprises** of

Vocabulary

complacent
self-satisfied

unprecedented
never before seen

caste system
a society with social divisions, usually based on heredity or wealth

irrelevant
not related or significant

enterprise
a large project

the planet. No one believes anymore that scientists are trained in science classes, or politicians in civics classes, or poets in English classes. The truth is that schools don't really teach anything except how to obey orders. This is a great mystery to me, because thousands of **humane**, caring people work in schools as teachers and aides and administrators, but the abstract logic of the **institution** overwhelms their individual contributions. Although teachers do care and do work very, very hard, the institution is **psychopathic**; it has no conscience. It rings a bell, and the young man in the middle of writing a poem must close his notebook and move to a different cell, where he learns that humans and monkeys derive from a common ancestor.

Our form of **compulsory** schooling is an invention of the state of Massachusetts, from around 1850. It was resisted—sometimes with guns—by an estimated 80 percent of the Massachusetts population, with the last outpost, in Barnstable on Cape Cod, not surrendering its children until the 1880s, when the area was seized by the militia and the children marched to school under guard.

Now, here is a curious idea to ponder: Senator Ted Kennedy's office released a paper not too long ago claiming that prior to compulsory education the state literacy rate was 98 percent, and after it the figure never again climbed above 91 percent, where it stands in 1990. I hope that interests you.

Here is another curiosity to think about: The home-schooling movement has quietly grown to a size where 1.5 million young people are being educated entirely by their own parents. Last month the education press reported the amazing news that children schooled at home seem to be five, or even ten years ahead of their formally trained peers in their ability to think.

I don't think we'll get rid of schools any time soon, certainly not in my lifetime, but if we're going to change what's rapidly becoming a disaster of ignorance, we need to realize that the institution "schools" very well, but it does not "educate"; that's inherent in the design of the thing. It's not the fault of bad teachers or too little money spent. It's just impossible for education and schooling to be the same thing.

Schools were designed by Horace Mann and Barnas Sears and W. R. Harper of the University of Chicago and Edward Thorndike of Columbia Teachers College and others to be instruments for the scientific management of a mass population. Schools are intended to produce, through the application of formulas, formulaic human beings whose behavior can be predicted and controlled.

To a very great extent, schools succeed in doing this. But our society is disintegrating, and in such a society, the only successful people are self-reliant, confident, and individualistic—because the community life that protects the dependent and weak is dead. The products of schooling are, as I've said, irrelevant. Well-schooled people are irrelevant. They can sell film and razor blades, push paper and talk on telephones, or sit mindlessly before a flickering computer terminal, but as human beings they are useless—useless to others and useless to themselves.

Vocabulary

humane
compassionate, sympathetic

institution
an established organization, system, or practice

psychopathic
mentally ill

compulsory
mandatory, enforced

The daily misery around us is, I think, in large measure caused by the fact that—as social critic Paul Goodman put it thirty years ago—we force children to grow up **absurd**. Any reform in schooling has to deal with school's absurdities.

It is absurd and anti-life to be part of a system that compels you to sit in confinement with only people of exactly the same age and social class. The system effectively cuts you off from the immense diversity of life and the **synergy** of variety. It cuts you off from your own past and future, sealing you in a continuous present, much the same way television does.

It is absurd and anti-life to be part of a system that compels you to listen to a stranger reading poetry when you want to learn to construct buildings, or to sit with a stranger discussing the construction of buildings when you want to read poetry.

It is absurd and anti-life to move from cell to cell at the sound of a gong for every day of your youth, in an institution that allows you no privacy and even follows you into the **sanctuary** of your home, demanding that you do its "homework."

"How will they learn to read?" you say, and my answer is: "Remember the lessons of Massachusetts." When children are given whole lives instead of age-graded ones in cell blocks, they learn to read, write, and do arithmetic with ease, if those things make sense in the life that unfolds around them.

But keep in mind that in the United States almost nobody who reads, writes, or does arithmetic gets much respect. We are a land of talkers; we pay talkers the most and admire talkers the most, and so our children talk constantly, following the public models of television and schoolteachers. It is very difficult to teach "the basics" anymore, because they really aren't basic to the society we've made.

Two institutions at present control our children's lives: television and schooling, in that order. Both reduce the real world of wisdom, **fortitude**, **temperance**, and justice to a never-ending, nonstop abstraction. In centuries past, the time of a child or adolescent would be occupied in real work, real charity, real adventure, and the real search for mentors who might teach what he or she really wanted to learn. A great deal of time was spent in community pursuits, practicing affection, meeting and studying every level of the community, learning how to make a home, and dozens of other tasks necessary to becoming a whole man or woman.

But here is the **calculus** of time the children I teach must deal with:

Out of the 168 hours in each week, my children sleep 56. That leaves them 112 hours a week out of which to **fashion** a self.

My children watch 55 hours of television a week according to recent reports. That leaves them 57 hours a week in which to grow up.

My children attend school 30 hours a week, use about 6 hours getting ready, going and coming home, and spend an average of 7 hours a week in homework—a total of 45 hours. During that time, they are under constant **surveillance**, have no private time or private space, and are disciplined if they try to assert individuality in the use of time or space. That leaves 12 hours a week out of which to create

Vocabulary

absurd
ridiculously meaningless

synergy
convergence of mutually beneficial actions

sanctuary
a place of safety and protection

fortitude
strength of will

temperance
self-control

calculus
method of calculation

fashion
as a verb, to craft or create

surveillance
close watch

a unique consciousness. Of course, my kids eat, and that takes some time—not much, because they've lost the tradition of family dining, but if we allot 3 hours a week to evening meals, we arrive at a net amount of private time for each child of 9 hours.

It's not enough. It's not enough, is it? The richer the kid, or course, the less television he watches but the rich kid's time is just as narrowly **proscribed** by a somewhat broader catalog of commercial entertainments and his inevitable assignment to a series of private lessons in areas seldom of his actual choice.

And these things are oddly enough just a more cosmetic way to create dependent human beings, unable to fill their own hours, unable to **initiate** lines of meaning to give substance and pleasure to their existence. It's a national disease, this dependency and aimlessness, and I think schooling and television and lessons—the entire **Chautauqua** idea—has a lot to do with it.

Think of the things that are killing us as a nation—narcotic drugs, brainless competition, recreational sex, the pornography of violence, gambling, alcohol, and the worst pornography of all—lives devoted to buying things, accumulation as a philosophy—all of them are addictions of dependent personalities, and that is what our brand of schooling must inevitably produce.

I want to tell you what the effect is on children of taking all their time from them—time they need to grow up—and forcing them to spend it on abstractions. You need to hear this, because no reform that doesn't attack these specific **pathologies** will be anything more than a **façade**.

1. The children I teach are **indifferent** to the adult world. This defies the experience of thousands of years. A close study of what big people were up to was always the most exciting occupation of youth, but nobody wants to grow up these days and who can blame them? Toys are us.
2. The children I teach have almost no curiosity, and what little they do have is **transitory**; they cannot concentrate for very long, even on things they choose to do. Can you see a connection between the bells ringing again and again to change classes and this phenomenon of **evanescent** attention?
3. The children I teach have a poor sense of the future, of how tomorrow is **inextricably** linked to today. They live in a continuous present; the exact moment they are in is the boundary of their consciousness.
4. The children I teach are ahistorical; they have no sense of how the past has **predestined** their own present, limiting their choices, shaping their values and lives.
5. The children I teach are cruel to each other; they lack compassion for misfortune, they laugh at weakness, and they have contempt for people whose need for help shows too plainly.
6. The children I teach are uneasy with intimacy or **candor**. They cannot deal with genuine intimacy because of a lifelong habit of preserving a secret self inside an outer personality made up of artificial bits and pieces

Vocabulary

proscribed
prohibited

initiate
begin, launch

Chautauqua
a traveling lecture series to entertain and educate

pathology
illness

façade
a false front on a building

indifferent
uncaring

transitory
short-lived

evanescent
vanishing like vapor

inextricable
unable to be separated

predestined
predetermined by destiny

candor
openness in communicating personal feelings

of behavior borrowed from television or acquired to manipulate teachers. Because they are not who they represent themselves to be, the disguise wears thin in the presence of intimacy, so intimate relationships have to be avoided.

7. The children I teach are materialistic, following the lead of schoolteachers who materialistically "grade" everything—and television mentors who offer everything in the world for sale.
8. The children I teach are dependent, passive, and timid in the presence of new challenges. This timidity is frequently masked by surface **bravado**, or by anger or aggressiveness, but underneath is a vacuum without fortitude.

I could name a few other conditions that school reform will have to tackle if our national decline is to be arrested, but by now you will have grasped my thesis, whether you agree with it or not. Either schools, television, or both have caused these pathologies. It's a simple matter of arithmetic: between schooling and television, all the time children have is eaten up. That's what has destroyed the American family; it is no longer a factor in the education of its own children.

What can be done?

First, we need a ferocious national debate that doesn't quit, day after day, year after year, the kind of continuous emphasis that journalism finds boring. We need to scream and argue about this school thing until it is fixed or broken beyond repair—one or the other. If we can fix it, fine; if we cannot, then the success of home schooling shows a different road that has great promise. Pouring the money back into family education might kill two birds with one stone, repairing families as it repairs children.

Genuine reform is possible, but it shouldn't cost anything. We need to rethink the fundamental **premises** of schooling and decide what it is we want all children to learn, and why. For 140 years this nation has tried to impose objectives from a lofty command center made up of "experts," a central **elite** of social engineers. It hasn't worked. It won't work. It is a gross betrayal of the democratic promise that once made this nation a noble experiment. The Russian attempt to control Eastern Europe has exploded before our eyes. Our own attempt to impose the same sort of central **orthodoxy**, using the schools as an instrument, is also coming apart at the seams, albeit more slowly and painfully. It doesn't work because its fundamental premises are mechanical, antihuman, and hostile to family life. Lives can be controlled by machine education, but they will always fight back with weapons of social pathology—drugs, violence, self-destruction, indifference, and the symptoms I see in the children I teach.

It's high time we looked backward to regain an educational philosophy that works. One I like particularly well has been a favorite of the ruling classes of Europe for thousands of years. I think it works just as well for poor children as for rich ones. I use as much of it as I can manage in my own teaching—as much, that is, as I can get away with, given the present institution of compulsory schooling.

Vocabulary

bravado
false bravery

premise
stated ideas

elite
the best or most privileged

orthodox
conventional; conforming to established doctrine

At the core of this elite system of education is the belief that self-knowledge is the only basis of true knowledge. Everywhere in this system, at every age, you will find arrangements that place the child alone in an unguided setting with a problem to solve. Sometimes the problem is fraught with great risks, such as the problem of getting a horse to gallop or making it jump. But that, of course, is a problem successfully solved by thousands of elite children before the age of ten. Can you imagine anyone who has mastered such a challenge ever lacking confidence in his or her ability to do anything? Sometimes the problem is that of mastering solitude, as Thoreau did at Walden Pond, or Einstein did in the Swiss **customshouse**.

One of my former students, Roland Legiardi-Laura, though both his parents were dead and he had no inheritance, rode a bicycle across the U.S. alone when he was hardly out of boyhood. Is it any wonder that in manhood he made a film about Nicaragua, although he had no money and no prior experience with filmmaking, and that it was an international award winner—even though his regular work was as a carpenter?

Right now we are taking from our children the time they need to develop self-knowledge. That has to stop. We have to invent school experiences that give a lot of that time back. We need to trust children from a very early age with independent study, perhaps arranged in school, but which takes place away from the institutional setting. We need to invent a **curriculum** where each kid has a chance to develop uniqueness and self-reliance.

A short time ago, I paid seventy dollars and sent a twelve-year-old girl with her non-English-speaking mother on a bus down the New Jersey coast. She took the police chief of Sea Bright to lunch and apologized for polluting his beach with a discarded Gatorade bottle. In exchange for this public apology, I had arranged for the girl to have a one-day **apprenticeship** in small-town police procedures. A few days later, two more of my twelve-year-old kids traveled alone from Harlem to West Thirty-first Street, where they began apprenticeships with a newspaper editor. Next week, three of my kids will find themselves in the middle of the Jersey swamps at six in the morning studying the mind of a trucking-company president as he dispatches eighteen-wheelers to Dallas, Chicago, and Los Angeles.

Are these "special" children in a "special" program? No, they're just nice kids from central Harlem, bright and alert, but so badly schooled when they came to me that most of them couldn't add or subtract with any **fluency**. And not a single one knew the population of New York City, or how far it is from New York to California.

Does that worry me? Of course. But I am confident that as they gain self-knowledge, they'll also become self-teachers—and only self-teaching has any lasting value.

We've got to give kids independent time right away, because that is the key to self-knowledge, and we must reinvolve them with the real world as fast as possible so that the independent time can be spent on something other than

Vocabulary

customshouse
building where vessels are cleared after paying a tax

curriculum
set of educational courses

apprenticeship
learning by working with an expert

fluency
graceful use of a skill

mere abstractions. This is an emergency. It requires drastic action to correct. Our children are dying like flies in our schools. Good schooling or bad schooling, it's all the same: irrelevant.

What else does a restructured school system need? It needs to stop being a parasite on the working community. I think we need to make community service a required part of schooling. It is the quickest way to give young children real responsibility.

For five years I ran a **guerrilla** school program where I had every kid, rich and poor, smart and **dipsy**, give 320 hours a year of hard community service. Dozens of those kids came back to me years later and told me that this one experience had changed their lives, had taught them to see in new ways, to rethink goals and values. It happened when they were thirteen, in my Lab School program—made possible only because my rich school district was in chaos. When "stability" returned, the lab closed. It was too successful, at too small a cost, to be allowed to continue; we made the expensive, elite programs look bad.

There is no shortage of real problems in this city. Kids can be asked to help solve them in exchange for the respect and attention of the adult world. Good for kids, good for the rest of us.

Independent study, community service, adventures in experience, large doses of privacy and solitude, a thousand different apprenticeships—these are all powerful, cheap, and effective ways to start a real reform of schooling. But no large-scale reform is ever going to repair our damaged children and our damaged society until we force the idea of "school" open—to include family as the main engine of education. The Swedes realized this in 1976, when they effectively abandoned state adoption of unwanted children and instead spent national time and treasure on reinforcing the family so that children born to Swedes were wanted. They reduced the number of unwanted Swedish children from six thousand in 1976 to fifteen in 1986. So it can be done. The Swedes just got tired of paying for the social wreckage caused by children not being raised by their natural parents, so they did something about it. We can, too.

Family is the main engine of education. If we use schooling to break children away from parents—and make no mistake, that has been the central function of schools since John Cotton announced it as the purpose of the Bay Colony schools in 1650 and Horace Mann announced it as the purpose of Massachusetts schools in 1850—we're going to continue to have the horror show we have right now.

The curriculum of family is at the heart of any good life. We've gotten away from that curriculum—it's time to return to it. The way to sanity in education is for our schools to take the lead in releasing the stranglehold of institutions on family life, to promote during school time **confluences** of parent and child that will strengthen family bonds. That was my real purpose in sending the girl and her mother down the Jersey coast to meet the police chief.

I have many ideas on how to make a family curriculum, and my guess is that a lot of you will have many ideas, too, once you begin to think about it. Our

Workplace

Which do you think teaches more effectively, school environments or work environments? Why?

Vocabulary

guerrilla
someone who battles by irregular means, against a superior force

dipsy
variant of "dippy," meaning foolish

confluence
where two or more things flow together

greatest problem in getting the kind of **grass-roots** thinking going that could reform schooling is that we have large, **vested interests** profiting from schooling just exactly as it is, despite **rhetoric** to the contrary.

We have to demand that new voices and new ideas get a hearing, my ideas and yours. We've all had a bellyful of authorized voices on television and in the press. A decade-long, free-for-all debate is called for now, not more "expert" opinions. Experts in education have never been right; their "solutions" are expensive, self-serving, and always involve further **centralization**. Enough.

Time for a return to democracy, individuality, and family.

I've said my piece. Thank you.

Analyze In your opinion, which of these cause/effect diagrams best illustrates the essay? Defend your choice. What is the main effect or main cause in the essay, and what does it result from or lead to?

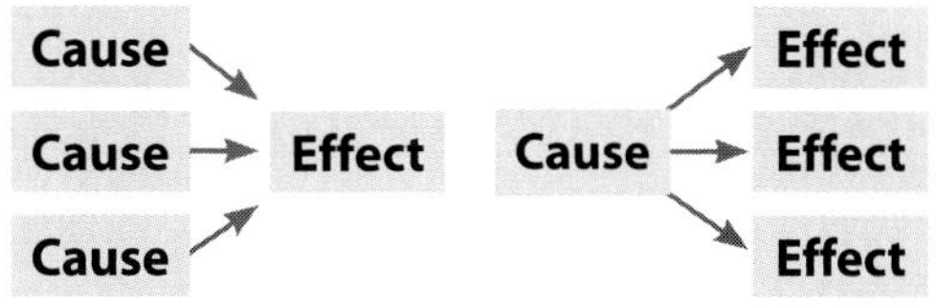

The second diagram: Gatto argues that "our form of compulsory schooling is an invention of the state of Massachusetts," and that statistics show a 98 percent literacy rate for that state before its institution, with a maximum 91 percent literacy rate after. From this cause he explains many educational and societal ills.

Reflect Obviously, not everyone agrees with Mr. Gatto. What do you believe about the future of education in the United States?

Answers will vary.

Vocabulary

grass roots
the basic level of a society rather than its power structures

vested interest
someone with a personal stake or gaining a special benefit

rhetoric
art of speaking effectively, a term often used to describe misleading arguments

centralization
yielding control to a small group

Learning Outcome

Write your own cause-effect essay.

LO2 Writing a Cause-Effect Essay

Prewrite Start by thinking of a cause-and-effect relationship that interests you. Are you concerned about child obesity? Does the effect of an increasingly global economy fascinate you? Make a list of possible topics. Answers will vary.

Make a List

Choose one: Put a star next to a topic that seems doable in the amount of time you have.

Research and Organize

Find out all you can about the topic you have chosen. Then fill in one of the diagrams below with details to include in your essay. Add more boxes if you need them.

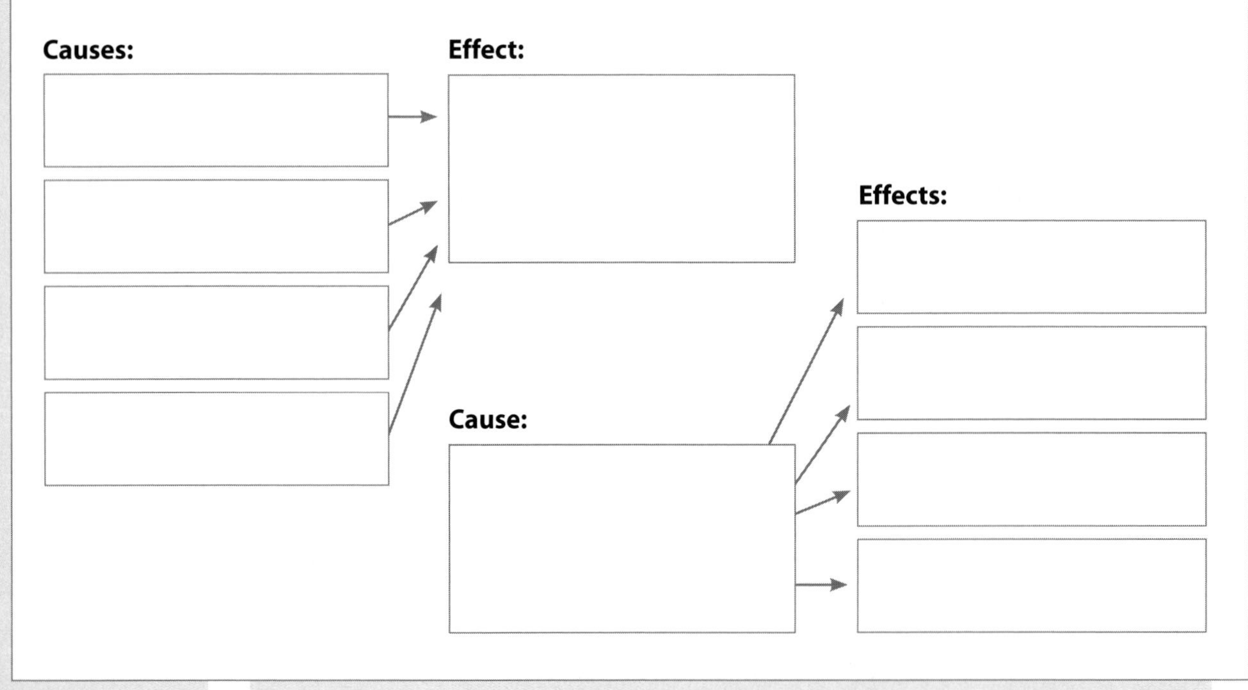

Draft Create a strong opening, middle, and closing for your cause-and-effect essay. Answers will vary.

Opening Paragraph

The opening of your cause-and-effect essay should grab your reader's attention and clearly introduce the topic. It must present your claim that *this* cause results in *these* effects, or *these* causes yield *this* effect. You can use one of the following strategies to start:

- **Ask a question:** "Why is audio and video reporting banned from public courtrooms?"
- **Begin with action:** "Just one year ago, 12-year-old Sana was taken from her home, handed a machete, and sent to fight against soldiers in her government's army."
- **Connect to the reader:** "Picture a street full of people, some real and some imaginary, but because of a psychosis, you are unable to tell which is which."

Once you have your reader's attention, lead up to your thesis statement. Here is a formula to use as you create your thesis statement.

Main Point		Causes or Effects		Thesis Statement
The Niger delta has suffered 50 years of oil contamination.	+	sabotage, theft, corporate mismanagement	=	Africa's Niger delta has suffered 50 years of oil contamination, from a combination of sabotage, theft, and corporate mismanagement.

Main Point + **Importance to Reader** ______________________

____

____

____

= **Thesis Statement**

____

____

____

Middle Paragraphs

In your middle paragraphs, defend your thesis statement by fully explaining each cause or effect of that main point. In general, you should devote at least a paragraph to each cause or effect. Arrange them from most important to least important or vice versa.

Closing Paragraph

The final paragraph should summarize the cause-and-effect relationship to help cement it in the reader's mind. You may also use this paragraph to make recommendations for changes to the situation, or to call the reader to act in some way.

Revise Take a break from your writing. Then come back to it with fresh eyes. If possible, have a friend or family member read the essay and make suggestions. Then review your writing with the following checklist. Keep polishing until you can answer every question with a "yes."

Ideas

- ☐ **1.** Is the cause-and-effect relationship clear?
- ☐ **2.** Do I cover all the important causes or effects of the main topic?

Organization

- ☐ **3.** Does my opening grab the reader's attention and present a clear thesis?
- ☐ **4.** Does my middle fully explain all the causes or effects?
- ☐ **5.** Are the causes or effects covered in the most effective order?
- ☐ **6.** Does my ending summarize the cause-and-effect relationship and leave the reader with something more to think about?

Voice

- ☐ **7.** Is the voice both friendly and professional?

Edit Prepare a clean copy of your personal essay and use the following checklist to check for errors. Continue until you can answer "yes" to each question.

Words

- ☐ **1.** Do I use correct verb forms (*he saw,* not *he seen*)? (See page 356.)
- ☐ **2.** Do my subjects and verbs agree (*she speaks,* not *she speak*)? (See pages 282–291.)
- ☐ **3.** Have I used the right words (*there, their, they're*)?

Sentences

- ☐ **4.** Have I avoided sentence fragments? (See pages 297–302.)
- ☐ **5.** Have I avoided run-on sentences? (See pages 306–310.)
- ☐ **6.** Have I avoided improper shifts in sentences? (See pages 314–315.)

Conventions

- ☐ **7.** Have I used commas after long introductory word groups? (See page 396.)
- ☐ **8.** Have I capitalized first words? (See page 414.)
- ☐ **9.** Have I capitalized proper nouns and proper adjectives? (See page 414.)
- ☐ **10.** Have I carefully checked my spelling?

"Truth springs from argument amongst friends."
—David Hume

Argument Essays

You may think of the word "argue" as meaning heated conversation, with shouts flying. Actually, the word is more related to discussion, reasoning, and debate, as when lawyers argue a case in court. Obviously, a judge wouldn't allow them to bellow at each other, and a jury wouldn't be convinced if they did. Instead, lawyers lay out their evidence and reasoning, seeking to convince. In the same way, the essay writers in this chapter each present an argument, hoping to convince you. Notice the different ways in which they make their case.

Learning Outcomes

LO1 Understand, read, and analyze argument essays.

LO2 Write your own argument essay.

What do you think?

What experience have you had with presenting an argument? How effective have your efforts been?

Answers will vary.

Learning Outcomes

Understand, read, and analyze argument essays.

WAC

Argumentation is very important for all classes. Knowing how to state a position, support it, and defend it will serve you well throughout college and life beyond.

LO1 Understanding Argument Essays

Within this chapter you will find three example argument essays. Each is followed by questions to help analyze the reading. At the end of the chapter are writing guidelines for creating an argument essay of your own.

SQ3R When you read, become involved with the text by using the SQ3R approach.

- **Survey:** Prepare by reading "About the Author," skimming the essay, and noting any vocabulary words.
- **Question:** Ask yourself to predict what the writer hopes to convince you of.
- **Read:** Read the essay, noting the value of supporting arguments and concessions the author makes.
- **Recite:** Recite the main points of the argument.
- **Review:** Answer the questions provided to help you analyze the essay.

Essay List:

"Why I Changed My Mind on the Death Penalty": Lance Morrow argues that while state executions are part of a social contract to maintain civilization, our own culture has become so chaotic that executions no longer serve that purpose.

"A Modest Proposal: Guys Shouldn't Drive Till 25": In the tradition of Jonathan Swift, Joyce Gallagher points out that great tragedy could be avoided, and many public benefits gained, by refusing a driver's license to the most accident-prone sector of our society: young males aged 15-25.

"Choosing Virginity": Lorraine Ali and Julie Scelfo interview a handful of young people who have committed themselves to abstaining from sex until after marriage.

Christian Schmidt/Cusp/Corbis

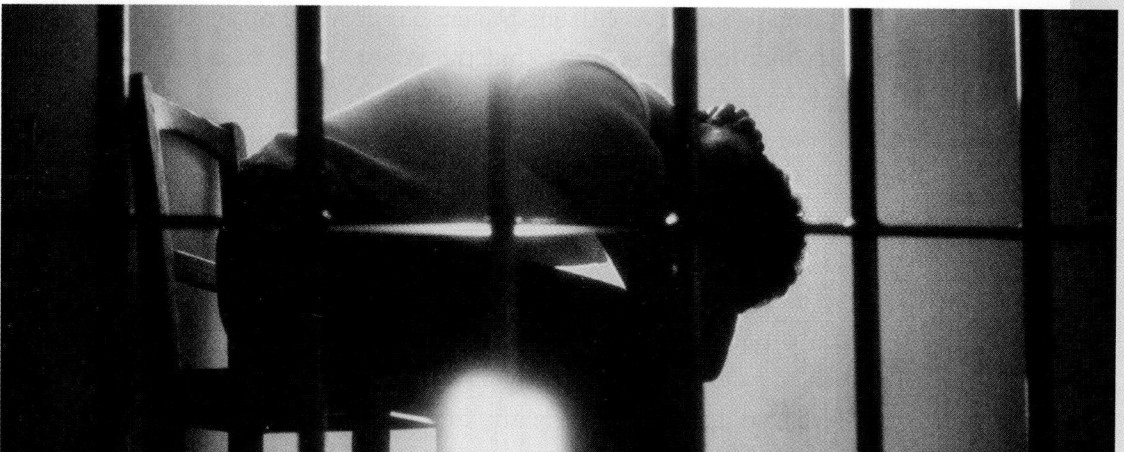

About the Author

Lance Morrow has been a professor of journalism at Boston University and a journalist and essayist for *Time* magazine. He is also the author of several nonfiction books.

Lance Morrow, "Why I Changed My Mind on the Death Penalty," Time, May 3, 2000.

Why I Changed My Mind on the Death Penalty
by Lance Morrow

Christina Marie Riggs, a nurse in Arkansas and a single mother, killed her two children—Justin, 5, and Shelby Alexis, 2—by giving them injections of **potassium chloride** and then smothering them with a pillow. She wrote a suicide note, and apparently tried to kill herself with an overdose of 28 antidepressant tablets. She survived.

Or she did until last night, when the state of Arkansas put Riggs to death by lethal injection at the state prison in Varner. She was the first woman to be executed in Arkansas since 1845.

The state of Arkansas played the part of Jack Kevorkian in a case of assisted suicide. Christina Riggs said she wanted to die. She had dropped all legal appeals. She wanted to be with her children in heaven. Just before Riggs died, she said, "I love you, my babies." Some people said she had killed them because she was severely depressed. The prosecutor, on the other hand, called her "a self-centered, selfish, **premeditated** killer who did the unspeakable act of taking her own children's lives."

So where do we stand on capital punishment now? (And, incidentally, isn't it grand that we seem to be overcoming, at the speed of light, our reluctance to execute women? Bless you, Gloria Steinem.)

Review the state of play:

Deterrence is an unreliable argument for the death penalty, I think, because deterrence is unprovable.

The fear of executing the wrong man (a more popular line of **demurral** these days) is an unreliable argument against all capital punishment. What if there are many witnesses to a murder? What if it's Hitler? Is capital punishment OK in cases of unmistakable guilt? George W. Bush says that he reviews each case to make sure he is absolutely certain a person did it before he allows a Texas execution to go ahead.

I have argued in the past that the death penalty was justified, in certain brutal cases, on the basis of the social contract. That is: Some hideous crimes demand the ultimate punishment in order to satisfy the essentially civilizing deal

Vocabulary

potassium chloride
an odorless salt used in some state executions

premeditated
planned ahead of time

deterrence
a preventative

demurral
hesitation or objection

that we make with one another as citizens. We forgo individual revenge, **deferring** to the law, but depend upon a certainty that the law will give us a justice that must include appropriate harshness. I favored the Texas folk wisdom: "He needs killing." If the law fails in that task, I said, and people see that evil is **fecklessly** tolerated, then the social contract disintegrates. Society needs a measure of **homeopathic** revenge.

But I have changed my mind about capital punishment.

I think the American atmosphere, the American imagination (news, movies, books, music, fact, fiction, entertainment, culture, life in the streets, **zeitgeist**) is now so filled with murder and violence (gang wars, random shootings not just in housing projects but in offices and malls and schools) that violence of any kind—including solemn execution—has become merely a part of our cultural routine and joins, in our minds, the passing parade of stupidity/**psychosis**/chaos/entertainment that Americans seem to like, or have come to deserve. In Freudian terms, the once forceful (and patriarchal) American **Superego** (arguably including the authority of law, of the presidency, of the military, etc.) has collapsed into a great dismal swamp of **Id**.

And in the Swamp, I have come to think, capital punishment has lost whatever cautionary social force it had—its exemplary meaning, its power to proclaim, as it once arguably did, that some deeds are, in our fine and virtuous company, intolerable.

I think those arguing in favor of capital punishment now are indulging in a form of **nostalgia**. Capital punishment no longer works as a morality play. Each execution (divorced from its moral meaning, including its capacity to shock and to warn the young) simply becomes part of the great messy **pageant**, the vast and **voracious** stupidity, the Jerry Springer show of American life.

Maybe most of our moral opinions are formed by emotions and **aesthetic** reactions. My opinion is this: Capital punishment has lost its moral meaning. Having lost its moral meaning, it has become as immoral as any other expression of violence. And therefore we should stop doing it.

Analyze What is Morrow's main argument?

Capital punishment has become just another spectacle, has lost its meaning, and should be done away with.

What are his supporting points?

Answers will vary.

Do you agree or disagree? Why?

Answers will vary.

Vocabulary

defer
delegate to someone else

fecklessly
weakly, irresponsibly

homeopathic
a medical treatment to create immunity by small, repeated exposure

zeitgeist
the spirit of a cultural time period

psychosis
insanity involving a break with reality

Superego
sense of moral responsibility, conscience

Id
instinctual drives

nostalgia
longing for the past

pageant
a spectacle or an exhibition

voracious
endlessly hungry

aesthetic
artistic sense of beauty

Joe Bator/Surf/Corbis

About the Author

Joyce Gallagher is a freelance writer. In this essay, she suggests a radical solution for a problem commonly ignored.

Joyce Gallagher, "A Modest Proposal: Guys Shouldn't Drive Till 25," Brandon/Brandon, Sentences, Paragraphs, and Beyond: With Integrated Readings 6e, Wadsworth, 2011. 0495802131.

A Modest Proposal: Guys Shouldn't Drive Till 25
By Joyce Gallagher

In the year 2001, 57,480 people were killed in motor vehicle accidents.* That figure is within a few hundred of being the same number as those killed in the Vietnam War. We took drastic measures back in the early 1970s and ended that war in a way shocking to some: we left. The time has come for another drastic scheme. We need to recognize the main causes of this highway **carnage** and take action. According to the U.S. Department of Transportation, 25.1 percent of the roadway fatalities involve an age group **constituting** only 14.5 percent of the driving public. That group is in the age range from 15 to 25. Within that group, one half are males. They are three times more likely to be involved in roadway fatalities, meaning that about 7 percent of males are responsible for more than 16 percent of roadway fatalities. This proposal may be a hard sell for politicians, but it is time for us to step forward boldly and raise the legal driving age for males nationally to 25.

Some may protest that it is unfair to punish the good young male drivers for the sins of their irresponsible peers. But we're already discriminating by group. Surely we all agree that drivers of a certain age should not be allowed to drive. That age varies from state to state, but it is around 15. We have concluded that those younger than 15 are too immature. We don't say that those under 15 should be treated individually, not even on the basis of gender. Instead, we exclude the offending group. With my proposal, we would simply move the legal age of male drivers to 25, lumping those of similar age and sex together for the good of society.

For you who would like to point out that some oldsters are also menaces on the roadways, I would say that those over 88 are equal only to those between 15 and 25 for being involved in fatal crashes. Moreover, the crashes by super-seniors are likely to be caused by physical and mental **impairments**, which can be detected by periodic tests and remedied by pulled licenses, whereas the young, often irresponsible and impatient, are more likely to be guided by thrill-seeking impulses, tantrums, and other byproducts of **testosterone**, all of which are hopelessly **glandular**.

*All statistics in this article are from the U.S. Bureau of Transportation Statistics: www.bts.gov.

Vocabulary

carnage
bloody slaughter

constitute
form or compose

impairment
something that damages or reduces an ability

testosterone
a hormone responsible for male characteristics

glandular
produced by glands

Although one **salient** reason—that this group of young males is responsible for the deaths of so many fellow citizens—is enough support for the proposed law, there are many side benefits for society.

- While the male 15-25 age group is waiting to drive motor vehicles, they would have time to improve their cultural lives and lay groundwork for better driving skills and improved mental and physical health.
- Many youngsters would customarily ride with statistically superior female or elder drivers and could learn from the relatively good examples they witness.
- Being no more dependent on driving almost everywhere, the male youngsters would walk more or ride bikes or skateboards, providing them wholesome exercise so often neglected in our **paunchy**, weight-challenged society.
- As a group they would also use more public transportation, relieving traffic congestion on our roadways and reducing congestion in the air we breathe.
- Support for public transportation projects would soar, and cars might cease to be near the center of our lives.
- Car payment money now **impoverishing** so many young males might go toward savings, education, home improvement, self-improvement, and family activities.
- Gratitude from young male drivers for the rides provided by female spouses and other loved ones could promote affectionate and appreciative relationships and diminish road rage.

The only exceptions to this new national law would be for the military and for public security and emergency agencies. Within the armed services, male **personnel** under 25 would be allowed to drive on foreign soil or on military property at any time. Male drivers working for police, fire, rescue, and ambulance services would drive only when on duty and their permits would be terminated for any serious traffic **infraction**. No doubt, some male youngsters, obsessed with driving motor vehicles, would join our public service **sectors**, making our national security and **infrastructural** services stronger so we could all sleep more peacefully.

Probably some males would protest this law and would try to **circumvent** it with devious strategies. Such resistance could be easily combated. For example, those who attempt to cross-dress or dye their hair gray for the purpose of obtaining a driver's license could be charged with a felony.

Several people who have read my modest proposal have suggested that young men are victims of their own bodies and could plead a "testosterone **dementia** defense." Therefore, they should be allowed to take injections of **estrogen** to neutralize the male hormones raging like tiny bulls within their systems. However, even these critics would surely concede that there could be a feminizing reaction to estrogen, one both psychological and physiological. Because of those possible side effects, wives of young men might find estrogen therapy unacceptable. A youthful bride might willingly bear the burden of transporting her husband to work and back, whereas she would almost certainly **recoil** at the thought of his wearing her bra.

Some might argue that improved drivers' education programs in our school

Vocabulary

salient
notably significant, rising above

paunchy
fat

impoverishing
making poor

personnel
the people employed in an organization

infraction
violation

sector
a subdivision of a society

infrastructural
dealing with the framework of an organization, the resources of a society

circumvent
find a way around

dementia
a type of insanity

estrogen
a hormone responsible for female characteristics

recoil
shrink back, flinch away in disgust

systems, better public transportation, the production of vehicles that are no more powerful and threatening than they need be, a reduced speed limit, counseling and restrictions for repeat offenders, and a stricter enforcement of existing laws represent a wiser approach to our national problem. However, because those ideas have failed to **resonate**, and young males have continued to put the pedal to the metal in a flood of blood, it is time for a simple statement that will fit on your bumper sticker:

Guys Shouldn't Drive Till 25

Vocabulary

resonate
to echo within or spread throughout

Joe Bator/Surf/Corbis

React How does this essay make you feel? If you are male, how do you think a female would react to the essay? If you are female, how do you think a male would react?

Answers will vary.

Analyze What is Gallagher truly suggesting?

We should better implement current programs like driver education, public transportation, reasonable vehicles, reduced speed limits, treatment of repeat offenders, and enforcement of existing laws.

Think Critically Is Gallagher's approach effective? Why or why not? What suggestions might you have for a different approach?

Answers will vary.

About the Author

Lorraine Ali is a contributing editor for *Newsweek* and a reporter for various other publications. Julie Scelfo is a *New York Times* reporter.

Lorraine Ali and Julie Scelfo, "Choosing Virginity," Newsweek, December 9, 2002.

Jacques M. Chenet/Documentary/Corbis

Choosing Virginity
by Lorraine Ali and Julie Scelfo

A New Attitude: Fewer teenagers are having sex. As parents and politicians debate the merits of abstinence programs, here's what the kids have to say.

There's a sexual revolution going on in America, and believe it or not, it has nothing to do with Christina Aguilera's bare-it-all video "Dirty." The uprising is taking place in the real world, not on "The Real World." Visit any American high school and you'll likely find a growing number of students who watch **scabrous** TV shows like "Shipmates," listen to Eminem—and have decided to remain **chaste** until marriage. Rejecting the get-down-make-love **ethos** of their parents' generation, this wave of young adults represents a new counterculture, one clearly at odds with the mainstream media and their routine use of sex to boost ratings and peddle product.

According to a recent study from the Centers for Disease Control, the number of high-school students who say they've never had sexual intercourse rose by almost 10 percent between 1991 and 2001. Parents, public-health officials and sexually **beleaguered** teens themselves may be relieved by this "let's not" trend. But the new **abstinence** movement, largely fostered by cultural conservatives and **evangelical** Christians, has also become hotly controversial. . . .

The debate concerns public policy, but the real issue is personal choice. At the center of it all are the young people themselves, whose voices are often drowned out by the political **cacophony**. Some of them opened up and talked candidly to *Newsweek* about their reasons for abstaining from sex until marriage. It's clear that religion plays a critical role in this extraordinarily private decision. But there are other factors as well: caring parents, a sense of their own unreadiness, the desire to gain some **semblance** of control over their own destinies. Here are their stories.

The Wellesley Girl

Alice Kunce says she's a **feminist**, but not the "army-boot-wearing, shaved-head, I-hate-all-men kind." The curly-haired 18-year-old Wellesley College sophomore—she skipped a grade in elementary school—looks and talks like what she is: one of the many bright, outspoken students at the liberal Massachusetts women's college. She's also a virgin. "One of the empowering things about the feminist movement," she says, "is that we're able to assert ourselves, to say no to sex and not feel pressured about it. And I think guys are kind of getting it. Like, 'Oh, not everyone's doing it.'"

Vocabulary

scabrous
suggestive, scandalous

chaste
celibate, pure

ethos
moral beliefs

beleaguered
harassed

abstinence
voluntary avoidance

evangelical
devoted to preaching rather than ritual

cacophony
harsh noise

semblance
appearance

feminist
someone who promotes women's rights

But judging by just about every TV program or movie targeted at teens, everyone is doing it. Alice grew up with these images, but as a small-town girl in Jefferson City, Mo., most teen shows felt alien and alienating. "You're either a prudish person who can't handle talking about sex or you're out every Saturday night getting some," she says. "But if you're not sexually active and you're willing to discuss the subject, you can't be called a prude. How do they market to that?" The friend from back home she's been dating since August asked not to be identified in this story, but Alice doesn't mind talking candidly about what they do—or don't do. "Which is acceptable? Oral, vaginal or anal sex?" she asks. "For me, they're all sex. In high school, you could have oral sex and still call yourself a virgin. Now I'm like, 'Well, what makes one less **intimate** than the other?'"

Alice, a regular churchgoer who also teaches Sunday school, says religion is not the reason she's chosen abstinence. She fears **STDs** and pregnancy, of course, but above all, she says, she's not mature enough emotionally to handle the deep intimacy sex can bring. Though most people in her college, or even back in her Bible-belt high school, haven't made the same choice, Alice says she has never felt **ostracized**. If anything, she feels a need to speak up for those being **coerced** by aggressive abstinence groups. "Religious pressure was and is a lot greater than peer pressure," says Alice, who has never taken part in an abstinence program. "I don't think there are as many teens saying 'Oh come on, everybody's having sex' as there are church leaders saying 'No, it's bad, don't do it. It'll ruin your life.' The choices many religious groups leave you with are either no sex at all or uneducated sex. What happened to educating young people about how they can protect themselves?"

The Dream Team

Karl Nicoletti wasted no time when it came to having "the talk" with his son, Chris. It happened five years ago, when Chris was in sixth grade. Nicoletti was driving him home from school and the subject of girls came up. "I know many parents who are wishy-washy when talking to their kids about sex. I just said, 'No, you're not going to have sex. Keep your pecker in your pants until you graduate from high school.'"

Today, the 16-year-old from Longmont, Colo., vows he'll remain abstinent until marriage. So does his girlfriend, 17-year-old Amanda Wing, whose parents set similarly strict rules for her and her two older brothers. "It's amazing, but they did listen," says her mother, Lynn Wing. Amanda has been dating Chris for only two months, but they've known each other for eight years. On a Tuesday-night dinner date at Portabello's (just across from the Twin Peaks Mall), Amanda asks, "You gonna get the chicken parmesan again?" Chris nods. "Yep. You know me well." They seem like a long-married couple—except that they listen to the Dave Matthews Band, have a 10:30 weeknight **curfew** and never go beyond kissing and hugging. (The guidelines set by Chris's dad: no touching anywhere that a soccer uniform covers.)

"Society is so run by sex," says Chris, who looks like Madison Avenue's **conception** of an All-American boy in his **Abercrombie** sweat shirt and faded baggy jeans. "Just look at everything—TV, movies. The culture today makes it seem OK to have sex whenever, however or with whoever you want. I just disagree with that." Amanda, who looks **tomboy** comfy in baggy brown **cords**, a white T shirt, and chunky-soled shoes, feels the same way. "Sex should be a special thing that doesn't need to be public," she says. "But if you're abstinent, it's like you're the one set aside from society because you're not 'doing it.'"

The peer pressure in this town of 71,000 people in the shadow of the Rocky Mountains is **substantially** less than in cosmopolitan Denver, 45 minutes away. ("It

Vocabulary

intimate
very closely associated, as in something privately shared

STDs
Sexually Transmitted Diseases

ostracized
excluded from a group, shunned

coerced
compelled by forcefulness or threat

curfew
requirement to return home

conception
in this case, an idea

Abercrombie
short for "Abercrombie & Fitch," a clothing store specializing in outdoor fashions

tomboy
a girl who behaves in traditionally boyish ways

cords
short for "corduroy" pants, made of a ribbed cotton fabric

substantial
real, true, not imaginary

figures you had to come all the way out here to find a virgin," one local said.) Chris joined a Christian abstinence group called Teen Advisors this year. "We watched their slide show in eighth grade and it just has pictures of all these STDs," he says. "It's one of the grossest things you've ever seen. I didn't want to touch a girl, like, forever." He now goes out once a month and talks to middle schoolers about abstinence. Amanda saw the same presentation. "It's horrible," she says. "If that doesn't scare kids out of sex, nothing will." Could these gruesome images put them off sex for life? Chris and Amanda say no. They're sure that whoever they marry will be disease-free.

To most abstaining teens, marriage is the golden light at the end of the **perilous** tunnel of dating—despite what their parents' experience may have been. Though Amanda's mother and father have had a long and stable union, Karl Nicoletti separated from Chris's mother when Chris was in fifth grade. His **fiancée** moved in with Chris and Karl two years ago; Chris's mother now has a year-and-a-half-old son out of **wedlock**. Chris and Amanda talk about marriage in the abstract, but they want to go to college first, and they're looking at schools on opposite sides of the country. "I think we could stay together," Chris says. Amanda agrees. "Like we have complete trust in each other," she says. "It's just not hard for us." Whether the bond between them is strong enough to withstand a long-distance relationship is yet to be seen. For now, Chris and Amanda mostly look ahead to their next weekly ritual: the Tuesday pancake lunch.

The Survivor

Remaining a virgin until marriage is neither an easy nor a common choice in Latoya Huggins's part of Paterson, N.J. At least three of her friends became single mothers while they were still in high school, one by an older man who now wants nothing to do with the child. "It's hard for her to finish school," Latoya says, "because she has to take the baby to get shots and stuff."

Latoya lives in a chaotic world: so far this year, more than a dozen people have been murdered in her neighborhood. It's a life that makes her sexuality seem like one of the few things she can actually control. "I don't even want a boyfriend until after college," says Latoya, who's studying to be a beautician at a technical high school. "Basically I want a lot out of life. My career choices are going to need a lot of time and effort."

Latoya, 18, could pass for a street-smart 28. She started thinking seriously about abstinence five years ago, when a national outreach program called Free Teens began teaching classes at her church. The classes reinforced what she already knew from growing up in Paterson—that discipline is the key to getting through your teen years alive. Earlier this year she dated a 21-year-old **appliance** salesman from her neighborhood, until Latoya heard that he was hoping she'd have sex with him. "We decided that we should just be friends," she explains, "before he cheated on me or we split up in a worse way."

So most days Latoya comes home from school alone. While she waits for her parents to return from work, she watches the Disney Channel or chills in her basement bedroom, which she's decorated with construction-paper cutouts of the names of her favorite pop stars, such as Nelly and Aaliyah. She feels safe there, she says, because "too many bad things are happening" outside. But bad things happen inside, too: last year she opened the door to a neighbor who forced his way inside and attempted to rape her. "He started trying to take my clothes off. I was screaming and yelling to the top of my lungs and nobody heard." Luckily, the phone rang. Latoya told the intruder it was her father, and that if she didn't answer he would come home right away. The man fled. Latoya tries not to think about what happened, although she feels "like dying" when she sees her attacker

Vocabulary

perilous
dangerous

fiancée
French term for a woman engaged to be married; *fiancé,* a man engaged to be married.

wedlock
marriage

appliance
any of a variety of household machines

on the street. (Her parents decided not to press charges so she wouldn't have to **testify** in court.) Her goal is to graduate and get a job; she wants to stay focused and independent. "Boys make you feel like you're special and you're the only one they care about," she says. "A lot of girls feel like they need that. But my mother loves me and my father loves me, so there's no gap to fill."

The Beauty Queen

Even though she lives 700 miles from the nearest ocean, Daniela Aranda was recently voted Miss Hawaiian Tropic El Paso, Texas, and her parents couldn't be prouder. They've displayed a picture of their bikini-clad daughter **smack-dab** in the middle of the living room. "People always say to me 'You don't look like a virgin'," says Daniela, 20, who wears super sparkly eye shadow, heavy lip liner and a low-cut black shirt. "But what does a virgin look like? Someone who wears white and likes to look at flowers?"

Daniela models at Harley-Davidson fashion shows, is a cheerleader for a local soccer team called the Patriots and hangs out with friends who work at Hooters. She's also an evangelical Christian who made a vow at 13 to remain a virgin, and she's kept that promise. "It can be done," she says. "I'm living proof." Daniela has never joined an abstinence program; her decision came from strong family values and deep spiritual convictions.

Daniela's arid East El Paso neighborhood, just a mile or so from the Mexican border, was built atop desert dunes, and the sand seems to be reclaiming its own by swallowing up back patios and sidewalks. The city, predominantly Hispanic, is home to the Fort Bliss Army base, breathtaking **mesa** views—and some of the highest teen-pregnancy rates in the nation. "There's a lot of girls that just want to get pregnant so they can get married and get out of here," Daniela says.

But she seems content to stay in El Paso. She studies business at El Paso Community College, dates a UTEP football player named Mike and works as a sales associate at the A'gaci Too clothing store in the Cielo Vista Mall. She also tones at the gym and reads—especially books by the Christian author Joshua Harris. In *Boy Meets Girl,* she's marked such passages as "Lust is never satisfied" with a pink highlighter. She's also saved an article on A. C. Green, the former NBA player who's become a spokesman for abstinence. "My boyfriend's coach gave it to him because the other guys sometimes say, 'Are you gay? What's wrong with you?' It's proof that if a famous man like Green can do it, so can he."

Daniela has been dating Mike for more than a year. He's had sex before, but has agreed to remain abstinent with her. "He's what you call a born-again virgin," she says. "Or a secondary abstinent, or something like that. We just don't put ourselves in compromising situations. If we're together late at night, it's with my whole family."

Daniela knows about temptation: every time she walks out onstage in a bathing suit, men take notice. But she doesn't see a contradiction in her double life as virgin and beauty queen; rather, it's a personal challenge. "I did Hawaiian Tropic because I wanted to see if I could get into a bikini in front of all these people," she says. "I wasn't thinking, 'Oh, I'm going to win.' But I did, and I got a free trip to Houston's state finals. I met the owner of Hawaiian Tropic. It's like, wow, this is as good as it gets."

The Ring Bearer

Lenee Young is trying to write a paper for her Spanish class at Atlanta's Spelman College, but as usual she and her roommates can't help getting onto the subject of guys. "I love Ludacris," Lenee gushes. "I love everything about him. Morris Chestnut, too. He has a really pretty smile. Just gorgeous." But Lenee, 19,

Insight

What views of sexuality are typical in your culture? How do these views match up with those of U. S. society at large?

Vocabulary

testify
make sworn statements

smack-dab
exactly

mesa
Spanish word for "table"; a rock formation with steep sides and a flat top

has never had a boyfriend, and has never even been kissed. "A lot of the guys in high school had already had sex," she says. "I knew that would come up, so I'd end all my relationships at the very beginning." Lenee decided back then to remain a virgin until marriage, and even now she feels little temptation to do what many of her peers are doing behind closed **dormitory** doors. "I feel that part of me hasn't been triggered yet," she says. "Sex is one of those things you can't miss until you have it."

Last summer she went with a friend from her hometown of Pittsburgh to a Silver Ring Thing. These popular free events **meld** music videos, **pyrotechnics**, and live teen comedy sketches with **dire** warnings about STDs. Attendees can buy a silver ring—and a Bible—for $12. Then, at the conclusion of the program, as techno music blares, they recite a pledge of abstinence and don their rings. "My friend, who's also a virgin, said I needed to go so I could get a ring," Lenee says. "It was fun, like the music and everything. And afterwards they had a dance and a bonfire."

The idea of abstinence was not new to Lenee. In high school she participated in a program sponsored by the University of Pittsburgh Medical Center called Postponing Sexual Involvement. Her mother had discussed it with her—once—the week before she left for college. Two of her closest friends are also virgins; the trio jokingly call themselves The Good Girls Club. But student life can sometimes be a shock to her **sensibilities**. "Another friend of mine and this guy were talking about how they didn't use a **condom**. He said, 'I like it raw.' I was like, 'Oh, my goodness.'"

And then there was the recent party that began with truth-or-dare questions. The first one: have you ever kissed a boy? Young was the only woman who said no, and everybody in the room was stunned. "Are you serious? We gotta find you a boyfriend!" But Lenee wasn't embarrassed. "I don't feel like I've missed out," she says. "I just feel like my time will come." Until then, she sports that shiny silver ring.

The Renewed Virgin

Lucian Schulte had always planned to wait until he was married to have sex, but that was before a warm night a couple of years ago when the green-eyed, lanky six-footer found himself with an unexpected opportunity. "She was all for it," says Lucian, now 18. "It was like, 'Hey, let's give this a try.'" The big event was over in a hurry and lacked any sense of intimacy. "In movies, if people have sex, it's always romantic," he says. "Physically, it did feel good, but emotionally, it felt really awkward. It was not what I expected it to be."

While the fictional teens of *American Pie* would have been clumsily overjoyed, Lucian, raised Roman Catholic, was plagued by guilt. "I was worried that I'd given myself to someone and our relationship was now a lot more serious than it was before," he says. "It was like, 'Now, what is she going to expect from me?'" Lucian worried, too, about disease and pregnancy. He promised himself never again.

Lucian, now an engineering major at the University of Alberta in Canada, is a "renewed virgin." His parents are strong proponents of chastity, and he attended school-sponsored abstinence classes. But the messages didn't hit home until he'd actually had sex. "It's a pretty special thing, and it's also pretty serious," he says. "Abstinence has to do with 'Hey, are you going to respect this person?'" He has dated since his high-school affair, and is now hoping a particular cute coed from Edmonton will go out with him. "But I'll try to restrict myself to kissing," he says. "Not because I think everything else is bad. But the more you participate with someone, the harder it's going to be to stop."

Vocabulary

dormitory
in college, a residence hall

meld
mix into a whole

pyrotechnics
fireworks

dire
involving disaster

sensibilities
emotional sensitivity

condom
a sheath covering the penis during sexual intercourse, to prevent pregnancy and transmission of disease

It's not easy to practice such restraint, especially when those around him do not. Lucian lives in a single room, decorated with ski-lift tickets and a "Scooby-Doo" poster, in an all-male dorm, but he says most students "get hitched up, sleep around, and never see each other again." Meanwhile he does his best to push his own sexual urges from his mind. "I try to forget about it, but I have to say it sucks. Homework is a good thing to do, and going out for a run usually works." He also goes to Sunday mass. Lucian figures he can hold out until he's married, which he hopes will be by the time he's 30. "I'm looking forward to an intimate experience with my wife, who I'll truly love and want to spend the rest of my life with," says Lucian. "It's kind of corny, but it's for real."

Teens & Sexuality

Raised in the age of AIDS and better educated about sex and abstinence, more teens are saying "no." Condom use is up and teen pregnancy is down. A look at the trends:

Safer Sex: Today, 25% more students say they used a condom during their last sexual encounter than those surveyed a decade ago.

Sex Ed: 89% have been educated about **AIDS**.

Race: Black students are 40% more likely to have had sex than whites.

Vocabulary

AIDS
acquired immunodeficiency syndrome, a sexually transmitted disease

Reflect How would you summarize the authors' own opinions about teen abstinence? Answers will vary.

____

____

____

Do the authors ever actually state those opinions? What words seem to express them? List specific examples.

____

____

____

____

Summarize the argument of one young person who was interviewed for this essay. Are any counterarguments offered? How does this affect the overall message?

____

____

____

____

____

____

____

Learning Outcomes

Write your own argument essay.

LO2 Writing an Argument Essay

Prewrite To select a topic for an argument essay, start by making a cluster of subjects you have opinions about. Answers will vary.

Make a Cluster

Add more bubbles and lines as needed. Continue clustering until an idea excites you. Put a star next to that idea.

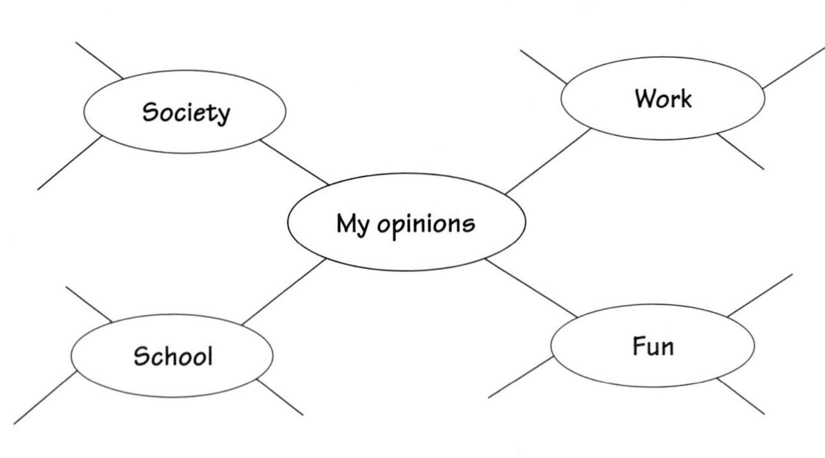

Freewrite

Prepare to write your argument essay by freewriting. Write until you run out of ideas for supporting your position. Then freewrite every argument you can imagine against your position.

Draft Create a strong opening, middle, and closing for your argument essay.
Answers will vary.

Opening Paragraph

The opening paragraphs of an argument essay should catch your reader's attention, provide any needed background to introduce the topic, and then make that introduction. You can use one of the following rhetorical strategies to start:

- **Make a logical claim:** "Judging films by their special effects is like judging people by their looks."
- **Present yourself as an authority:** "Having grown up with country-western music, I can attest to its essentially moral nature."
- **Appeal to the reader's emotion:** "Lowering a student's grades for poor class attendance is double punishment, intended to cause failure, not encourage success."

Once you have your reader's attention, lead up to your thesis statement. Here is a formula to use as you create your thesis statement.

Your Topic		Your Feeling About It		Thesis Statement
nuclear weapons	+	are a necessary deterrent to other nuclear weapons	=	In a world where nuclear weapons are possible, owning nuclear weapons is a necessity.

Your Topic + **Your Feeling About It** ______________________

____

____

____

= Thesis Statement

____

____

____

Middle Paragraphs

In your middle paragraphs, defend your thesis statement by providing supporting reasons. Follow the rhetorical approach of your opening paragraphs, making a logical argument, speaking as an authority, or appealing to your audience's feelings about the subject. To strengthen your position, also address opposing views and make any needed concessions.

Closing Paragraph

Your final paragraph should make a firm conclusion based on the support presented in your middle paragraphs. You may also use this paragraph to call for action from the reader or to point out related subjects for further discussion.

Speaking & Listening

Imagine that you were delivering a speech about your topic. How would you get your audience's attention? Try a similar strategy in writing.

Revise Take a break from your writing for a while. Then come back to it with fresh eyes or have a friend or family member read the essay and make suggestions. When you are confident of the contents, review your writing with the following checklist. Keep polishing until you can answer every question with a "yes."

Ideas

- ☐ **1.** Is my position clear clear?
- ☐ **2.** Do I include the most persuasive reasons for taking this position?

Organization

- ☐ **3.** Does my opening grab the reader's attention?
- ☐ **4.** Does my middle convincingly present support, address counterarguments, and make necessary concessions?
- ☐ **5.** Does my ending make an effective conclusion?
- ☐ **6.** Does my ending make a call to action?

Voice

- ☐ **7.** Does the voice convey an effective rhetorical position: arguing logic, establishing my authority, or appealing to the reader's concerns?

Edit Prepare a clean copy of your personal essay and use the following checklist to check for errors. Continue until you can answer "yes" to each question.

Words

- ☐ **1.** Do I use correct verb forms (*he saw,* not *he seen*)? (See page 356.)
- ☐ **2.** Do my subjects and verbs agree (*she speaks,* not *she speak*)? (See pages 282–291.)
- ☐ **3.** Have I used the right words (*there, their, they're*)?

Sentences

- ☐ **4.** Have I avoided sentence fragments? (See pages 297–302.)
- ☐ **5.** Have I avoided run-on sentences? (See pages 306–310.)
- ☐ **6.** Have I avoided improper shifts in sentences? (See pages 314–315.)

Conventions

- ☐ **7.** Have I used commas after long introductory word groups? (See page 396.)
- ☐ **8.** Have I capitalized first words? (See page 414.)
- ☐ **9.** Have I capitalized proper nouns and proper adjectives? (See page 414.)
- ☐ **10.** Have I carefully checked my spelling?

Index

A

B

C

P

S

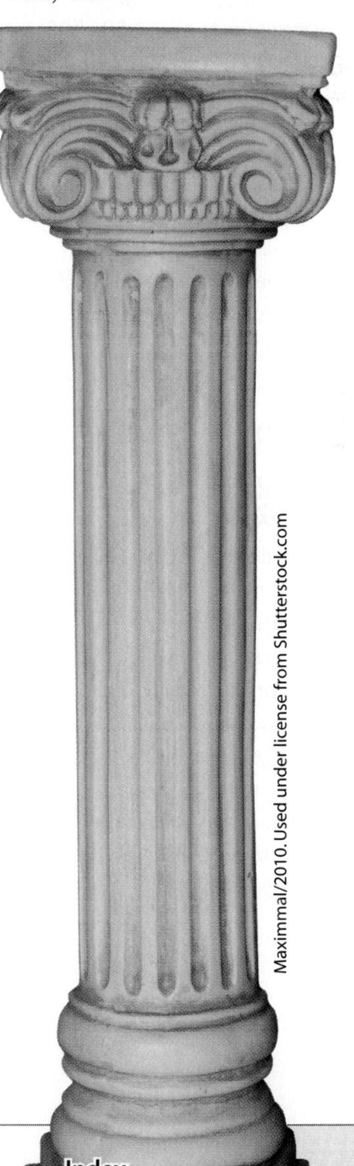

Reading-Writing Connection

To succeed in college, students must approach writing and reading not as assignments to complete, but rather as opportunities to learn and to think. In this way, writing and reading are means to an end, rather than ends unto themselves. Students also must appreciate the unique relationship between the two tasks. Writing aids reading; reading provides ideas for writing.

Writing to Learn (page 2-3)

Writing to learn is ungraded writing, carried out to help students understand concepts introduced in lectures, discussions, lab work, and readings. Essentially, writing to learn consists of having students write freely about the subjects and concepts they are studying. In these writings, students can explore topics under discussion, argue for or against particular points of view, reflect on their work on specific projects, and so on. Writing as a learning strategy is part of the larger writing-across-the-curriculum movement.

Writing to Share Learning (page 4)

The focus of *WRITE 1* and *WRITE 2* is writing to share learning—the paragraphs, essays, and reports students turn in for evaluation. Both texts cover the writing process, writing paragraphs, writing essays, the conventions of the language, and so on. While writing to learn helps students explore and form their thoughts, writing to share learning helps them clarify and fine-tune them. In this way, both types of writing stimulate thinking and learning.

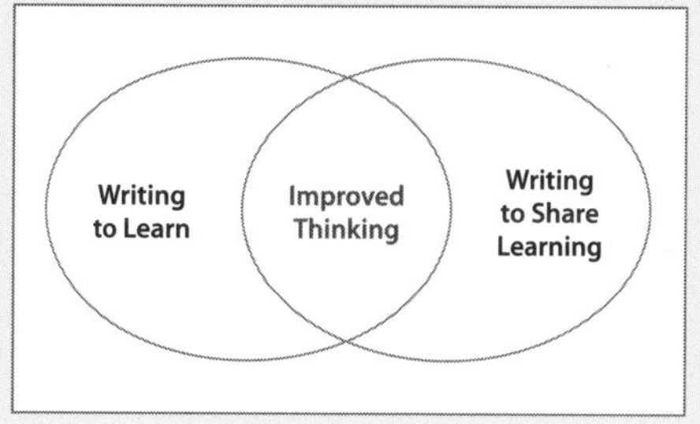

Reading to Learn (pages 8-13)

Reading to learn is an approach that leads to more productive academic reading. It includes, among other things, previewing the text, reading the text, making annotations, engaging in exploratory writing during the reading, and summarizing the text after the reading. Employing such strategies helps students take control of their college-level reading.

Reading Graphics (pages 14-15)

In college-level texts, significant portions of information is communicated via charts, tables, and diagrams. As a result, students need to understand how to read a graphic: scanning it, studying the specific parts, considering and questioning the image, and reflecting on its effectiveness. This skill is often overlooked in developmental and introductory courses.

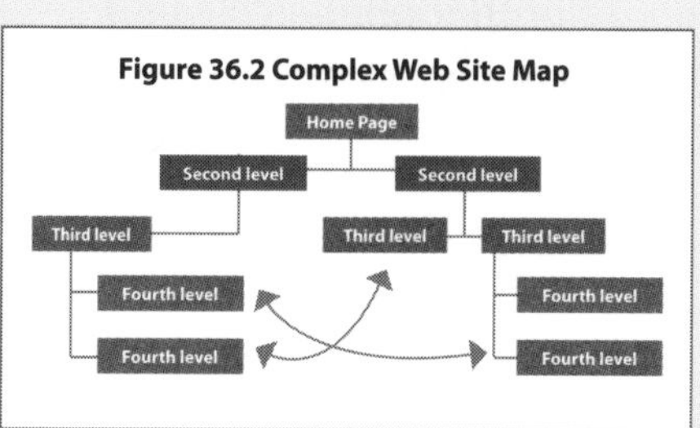

Understanding Assignments (pages 18-19)

Students, too often, approach their writing and reading assignments without the proper forethought, and as a result, they don't carry out their work in the appropriate way. So students must be made aware that understanding the dynamics of each assignment is critical: Are they expected to inform or to persuade in a writing assignment? Who is the intended audience in the material they are reading? *WRITE 1* and *WRITE 2* introduce students to the STRAP strategy, which helps them identify the dynamics of both writing and reading assignments. (*See the back of this card.*)

Students use the STRAP strategy to analyze their writing and reading assignments. The strategy consists of answering questions about these five features: *subject, type, role, audience,* and *purpose*. Once they answer the questions, they'll be ready to get to work. This chart shows how the strategy works:

For Writing Assignments		For Reading Assignments
What specific topic should I write about?	**Subject**	What specific topic does the reading address?
What form of writing *(essay, article)* will I use?	**Type**	What form *(essay, text chapter, article)* does the reading take?
What position *(student, citizen, employee)* should I assume?	**Role**	What position *(student, responder, concerned individual)* does the writer assume?
Who is the intended reader?	**Audience**	Who is the intended reader?
What is the goal *(to inform, to persuade)* of the writing?	**Purpose**	What is the goal of the material?

Using the Traits (pages 20-21)

Students sometimes struggle to understand why a text works or does not work. Without this understanding, they have a hard time developing their own writing, discussing the writing of their peers, and/or analyzing reading material. *WRITE 1* and *WRITE 2* use the traits of writing as a guide to effective prose. A working knowledge of the traits helps students become more thoughtfully involved in their writing and reading. (Traits side notes appear throughout the text.)

- **Ideas** The main points and supporting details in writing and reading material
- **Organization** The overall structure of the material
- **Voice** The personality of the writing—how the writer speaks to the reader
- **Word Choice** The writer's use of words and phrases
- **Sentence Fluency** The flow of the sentences
- **Conventions** The correctness or accuracy of the language
- **Design** The appearance of the writing

Using Graphic Organizers (pages 22-23)

Struggling students find visuals such as graphic organizers helpful when they are writing and learning. Graphic organizers work well for collecting details during the prewriting stage; they also work well when students are gleaning key concepts and ideas from essays and articles they are assigned to read.

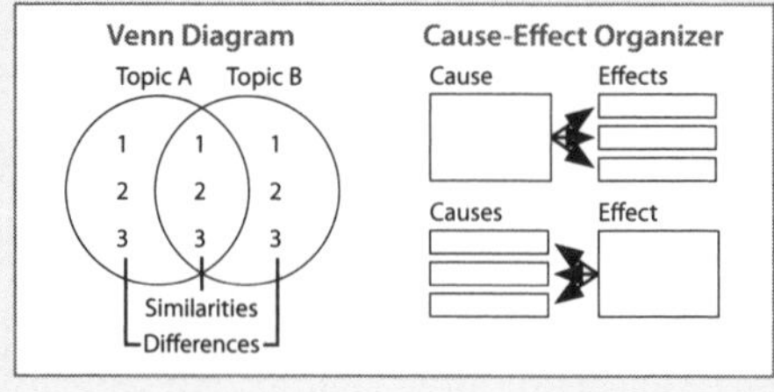

Further Readings

To learn more about writing to learn and the traits of writing, refer to the following publications.

Collins, James L. *Strategies for Struggling Writers.* Guilford Press, 1998.

Mayher John S., Nancy Lester, and Gordon M. Pradl. *Learning to Write / Writing to Learn.* Heinemann, 1983.

Spandel, Vickie. *Creating Writers Through 6-Trait Writing.* Allyn & Bacon, 2008.

Writing Process

Educators Donald M. Murray and Donald H. Graves led a group of others in shifting the focus of writing from product to process. They explored the "moves" that different writers made at different stages as they developed a piece of writing. Though the steps in the process have had various names throughout time, the terms used in *WRITE 1* and *WRITE 2* are prewriting, writing, revising, editing, and publishing.

Prewriting

This phase begins when the writer first starts to think about an idea. Prewriting may begin with a formal writing assignment (as is often the case in academic writing), or it may begin with inspiration, or even a niggling idea that won't let go. During prewriting, the writer focuses on ideas and organization and does the following:

- **Analyzes the rhetorical situation**—the writer's role, the subject of the writing, the purpose, the medium or form, the audience, and the context. In terms of academic writing, this task involves understanding the assignment.
- **Selects a topic** by brainstorming possible ideas and narrowing them down to a specific topic that fits all parts of the rhetorical situation.
- **Gathers information about the topic** through personal reflection, questioning, and research. At this stage, graphic organizers, lists, and notes help writers generate or discover ideas and keep track of them.

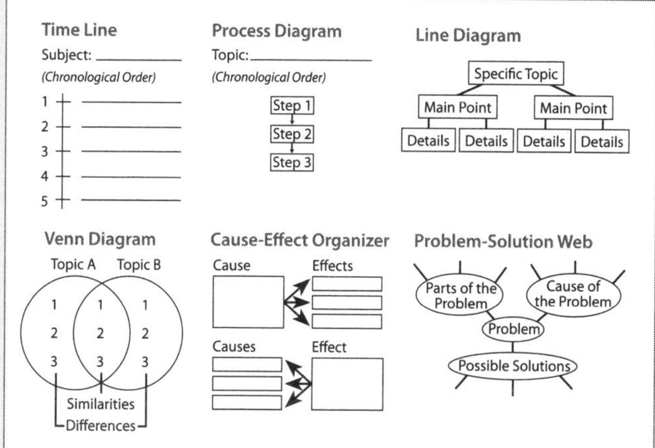

- **Finds a focus,** deciding which specific thought or feeling about the topic that the writer wants to explore. Finding a focus involves sizing the project, making sure it is not too large or too small to be covered in the form required.
- **Organizes details** by creating a quick list or a more formal topic or sentence outline. The organizational structure is often dictated by the writer's purpose (to inform, persuade, entertain, reflect) and by the form of the writing.

Writing

This phase involves creating a first draft—pouring words onto a page or into a computer. The writing phase is informed and guided by the prewriting work, but the writer should feel free to innovate and experiment. At this phase, the writer should focus on ideas, organization, and voice while creating a three-part structure:

- **Opening:** The opening should catch the reader's attention and identify the writer's subject and focus. In a paragraph, the opening is the topic sentence. In an essay, the opening is the first paragraph or so, providing background and introducing the topic.
- **Middle:** The middle should support the opening. In a paragraph, the middle consists of sentences of different levels, presenting main points and supporting details. In an essay, the middle consists of paragraphs, each of which focuses on a main point and develops it.
- **Closing:** The closing should bring the writing to an effective end, perhaps by revisiting the opening, by summing up the main points, or by providing an important final thought. In a paragraph, the closing is a final sentence, and in an essay, it is a paragraph.

Revising

Revising involves making large-scale changes to writing, improving it in the most important ways. A peer review at this stage can help the writer discover what is working and what could work better in a specific piece of writing. During revising, the writer (and peer reviewers) should focus on the "Big Three" traits: ideas, organization, and voice. There are four basic revising moves:

- **Adding**—providing answers to some of the 5 W's and H, or adding engaging, surprising, or varied details to bolster a claim
- **Cutting**—removing ideas that are off topic, redundant, obvious, or otherwise unhelpful in conveying the writer's message
- **Rearranging**—putting it in a more effective order or creating a smoother flow of thought, often using transition words and phrases
- **Rewriting**—experimenting to find the best way to express each idea, and reworking parts that did not convey the message in the first draft

Correction Marks

- delete
- capitalize
- lowercase
- insert
- add comma
- add question mark
- add word
- add period
- spelling
- switch

Editing

Editing involves making small-scale changes to improve style and correctness. During editing, the writer should focus on the "Little Three" traits:

- **Words**—using specific nouns, active verbs, and modifiers that clarify, and avoiding wordiness, deadwood, and clichés
- **Sentences**—varying sentence beginnings, lengths, and style
- **Conventions**—correcting punctuation, capitalization, usage, spelling, and grammar

Publishing

Publishing is simply the act of sharing writing, whether in an official publication or simply by reading it aloud to classmates or family members. Publishing is the step in which writing becomes true communication, the ideas in the writer's mind entering the minds of a real audience.

A Recursive Process

Writing rarely moves straight forward through this process. Instead, writers in one stage may go back to a previous stage, or jump ahead to a later one. The needs of the rhetorical situation dictate the order of steps.

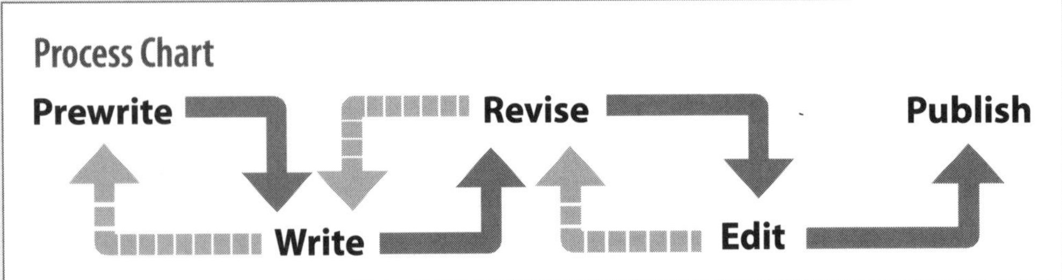

Further Readings

For further readings into the writing process, see the following publications.

Graves, Donald H. *Writing: Teachers & Children at Work.* Heinemann, 2003.
Murray, Donald M. *Learning by Teaching.* Boyton/Cook Heinemann, 1982.
VanderMey, Randall et al. *COMP: Write.* Wadsworth Cengage Learning, 2010.

History of the Traits of Writing

The writing traits date back to the 1960s, when researcher Paul Diederich gathered a group of 50 professionals to determine what elements make up strong writing. In reviewing numerous student papers, the group uncovered a common pattern of characteristics, or traits, that made some papers more effective than others. Years later a group of teachers in Beaverton, Oregon, and Missoula, Montana, replicated Diederich's work and settled on a similar set of traits. Since then, the traits—ideas, organization, voice, word choice, sentence fluency, correctness—have become a cornerstone of writing instruction in schools throughout the world. *WRITE 1* and *WRITE 2* describe the six traits in detail, as well as adding a seventh trait—appropriate design.

The Traits of Writing

Strong Ideas

Good writing starts with an interesting idea. A writer should include plenty of effective ideas and details in his or her writing. And all of the information needs to hold the reader's interest.

Logical Organization

Effective writing has a clear overall structure—with a beginning, a middle, and an ending. Each paragraph should have a topic sentence, and transitions should link the ideas.

Fitting Voice

In the best writing, the writer's voice comes through. Voice is a writer's unique way of saying things. It shows that he or she cares about the writing. Furthermore, voice should fit the form. A personal essay should convey a different voice than a formal expository essay.

Well-Chosen Words

In strong writing, nouns and verbs are specific and clear, and modifiers add important information. The word choice should also fit the purpose and audience.

Smooth Sentences

The sentences in good writing should read smoothly from one to the next. Sentence variety gives the writing flow and energy, while each sentence carries the meaning of the essay or article.

Correct Copy

Strong writing is easy to read because it follows the conventions or rules of the language.

Appropriate Design

The design should follow the guidelines established by the instructor.

Connecting the Process and the Traits

The writing process makes writing easy by breaking the job into five recursive steps. The traits identify the key elements to consider at each step. Together the process and the traits help writers assess and improve their writing. The first three traits—ideas, organization, and voice—deal with big issues and thus dominate the early stages of the writing process (prewriting and writing). Meanwhile, words, sentences, conventions, and design become important later in the process (revising, editing, and publishing). See how the process and traits connect in the chart below.

Process	Traits
Prewriting	**Ideas:** selecting a topic, collecting details about it, forming a thesis **Organization:** arranging the details **Voice:** establishing your stance (objective, personal)
Writing	**Ideas:** connecting your thoughts and information **Organization:** following your planning **Voice:** sounding serious, sincere, interested, . . .
Revising	**Ideas:** reviewing for clarity and completeness **Organization:** reviewing for structure/arrangement of ideas **Voice:** reviewing for appropriate tone
Editing	**Word choice:** checking for specific nouns, verbs, and modifiers **Sentences:** checking for smoothness and variety **Conventions:** checking for correctness
Publishing	**Design:** evaluating the format

Traits Across the Spectrum

The writing traits work well with all writing forms and disciplines. Each discipline has its own specific ideas and organizational structures that writers should follow. And any form of writing benefits from strong words, smooth sentences, correctness, and effective design.

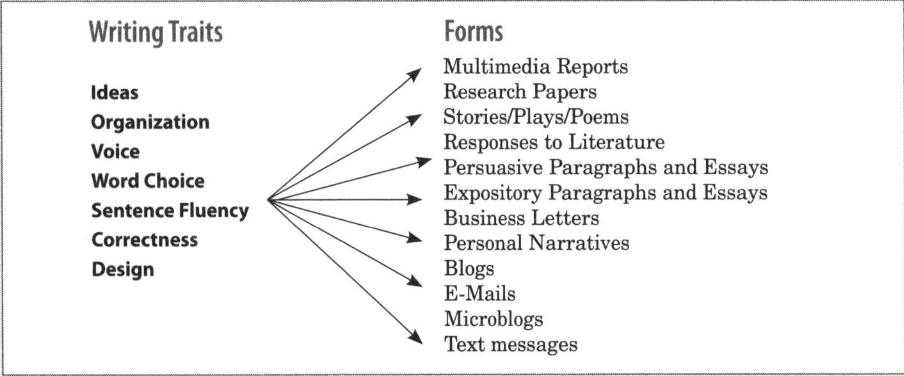

Further Readings

For further readings into the traits of writing, see the following publications.

Diederich, Paul B. *Measuring Growth in English.* National Council of Teachers of English, 1974.
VanderMey, Randall et al. *COMP: Write.* Wadsworth Cengage Learning, 2010.

Paragraph Patterns

Before writers can throw themselves into the drafting stage, they must first find a focus and consider the various patterns of organization. In college-level writing, students will need to introduce their focus in the form of a thesis statement (or in a topic sentence if they are writing a paragraph). A strong thesis statement states a particular feeling, feature, or part of a specific topic.

Forming a Thesis Statement

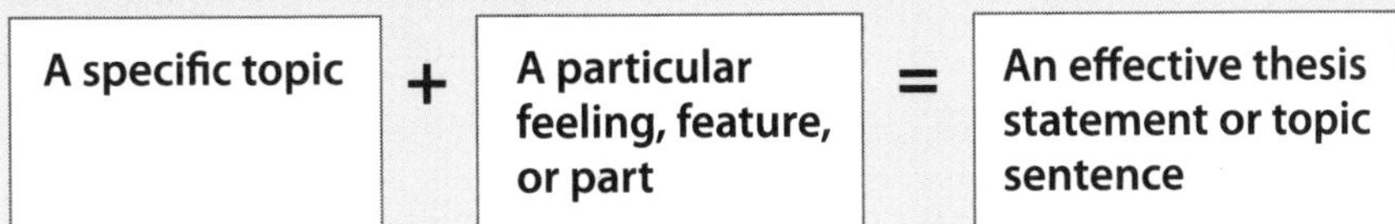

Once students establish a thesis, they should identify an appropriate pattern of organization to organize the information that supports it. As a result, students will begin drafting with a sense of purpose, focus, and organization.

Patterns of Organization

- Use **chronological order** (time) when you are sharing a personal experience, telling how something happened, or explaining how to do something.
- Use **spatial order** (location) for descriptions, arranging information from left to right, top to bottom, from the edge to the center, and so on.
- Use **order of importance** when you are taking a stand or arguing for or against something. Either arrange your reasons from most important to least important or the other way around.
- Use **deductive organization** if you want to follow your thesis statement with basic information—supporting reasons, examples, and facts.
- Use **inductive organization** when you want to present specific details first and conclude with your thesis statement.
- Use **compare-contrast organization** when you want to show how one topic is different from and similar to another one.

Choosing a Pattern of Organization

How do students decide on an appropriate pattern of organization? Here are two strategies they can use:

1. **Study the thesis statement or topic sentence.** It will indicate how to organize the ideas.
2. **Review the information or research gathered during prewriting.** Decide which ideas support the thesis and arrange them according to the appropriate method of organization.

Forming a Meaningful Whole

A meaningful whole in writing means the writer connects all of his or her thoughts and feelings about a specific topic into a complete draft—one with clear beginning, middle, and ending parts. Forming a meaningful whole for a paragraph means including a topic sentence, body sentences, and a closing sentence. For an essay, it means including an opening part (including a thesis statement), a number of supporting paragraphs, and a closing paragraph.

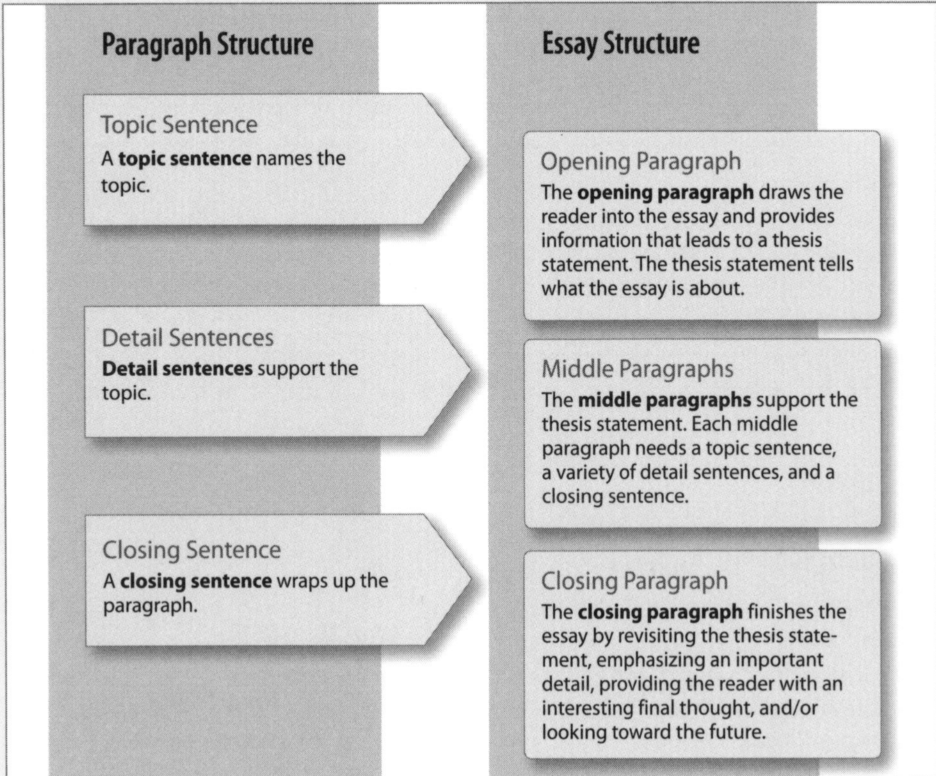

Levels of Detail

College writing requires students use a certain level of depth in their writing. When they make a point, they should fully explain it with specific examples and details before they move to the next point. The process of making important points and supporting them with details is at the core of most writing. To write with depth, students should include different levels of detail. Here are three basic levels:

- **Level 1:** A **controlling sentence** (usually a topic sentence) names a topic or makes a main point.
- **Level 2:** A **clarifying sentence** explains a level 1 sentence.
- **Level 3:** A **completing sentence** adds details to complete the point.

Exceptional writers may add a fourth level of detail, elaborating on the point with anecdotes, examples, quotations, and so on.

Teaching Complete Sentences

Students learn less from worksheets about identifying and correcting sentences than from writing and correcting their own sentences. As a result, many of the activities in this book prompt students to write their own simple, compound, and complex sentences, to create their own prepositional and participial phrases, and so on. Real writing is key.

Subjects and Verbs

At base, every sentence is the connection between a subject and verb. The instruction in the "Sentence Basics" chapter thus focuses on subjects and verbs, and then on special types of subjects and special types of verbs. The other words in the sentence either complete these words (as is the case with direct and indirect objects and object complements) or modify them.

Adjectives and Adverbs

Adjectives, of course, modify nouns and words that function as nouns. Adverbs modify verbs, adjectives, and other adverbs or words that function as such. These definitions might seem a bit esoteric to students, so instead of focusing on definitions, focus on function. Adjectives and adverbs answer basic questions.

Adjective Questions	Adverb Questions
Which?	*How?*
What kind of?	*When?*
How many?/How much?	*Where?*
	Why?
	To what degree?
	How often?/How long?

Impress on students that words that answer these questions are functioning as adjectives or adverbs. These questions become important not so much for identifying words and phrases in writing, but for helping students expand their sentences and create deeper, more thought writing.

Simple, Compound, and Complex Sentences

A simple sentence is a subject and a verb that express a complete thought. A compound sentence is a pair of simple sentences joined with a comma and a coordinating conjunction *(and, but, or, nor, for, so, yet.)* The conjunction coordinates the sentences by showing they are of equal importance. A complex sentence is a pair of simple sentences joined with a subordinating conjunction. The conjunction subordinates one sentence to another by making one sentence into a dependent clause.

The chapter "Simple, Compound, and Complex Sentences" goes into detail about these sentence structures, giving students practice forming each type. Students should then apply their learning in the writing they are doing elsewhere.

Subordinating Conjunctions

after	so that
although	that
as	though
as if	till
as long as	unless
because	until
before	when
even though	whenever
if	where
in order that	whereas
provided that	while
since	

Avoiding Sentence Fragments

A sentence must have a subject and verb and must express a complete thought. To check sentences, have students find the subject (single underline) and the verb (double underline) and then determine if the words express a complete thought. A fragment is missing one or more of these features, but it can be fixed by supplying what is missing.

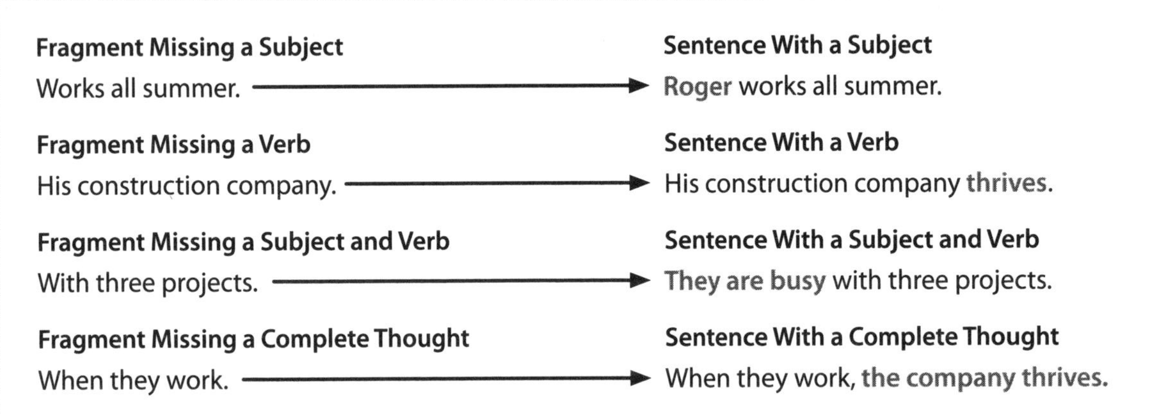

Fragment Missing a Subject Works all summer.	→	**Sentence With a Subject** **Roger** works all summer.
Fragment Missing a Verb His construction company.	→	**Sentence With a Verb** His construction company **thrives.**
Fragment Missing a Subject and Verb With three projects.	→	**Sentence With a Subject and Verb** **They are busy** with three projects.
Fragment Missing a Complete Thought When they work.	→	**Sentence With a Complete Thought** When they work, **the company thrives.**

Note: When a subject and verb are present but a complete thought is not, usually the words are a dependent clause. A dependent clause begins either with a subordinating conjunction *(after, because, though, etc.)* or with a relative pronoun *(who, which, that).*

Avoiding Run-On Sentences and Comma Splices

Just as fragments can result from splitting up a complex sentence, run-ons and comma splices can result from incorrectly creating a compound sentence. A run-on is a pair of sentences joined without a comma and coordinating conjunction. A comma splice occurs when only a comma is used to join sentences. Either error can be corrected by supplying **both** a comma and a coordinating conjunction (or by joining the sentences with a semicolon).

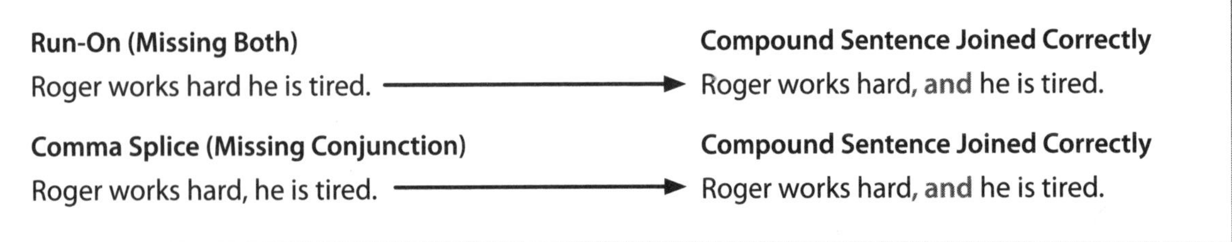

Run-On (Missing Both) Roger works hard he is tired.	→	**Compound Sentence Joined Correctly** Roger works hard**, and** he is tired.
Comma Splice (Missing Conjunction) Roger works hard, he is tired.	→	**Compound Sentence Joined Correctly** Roger works hard, **and** he is tired.

Note: Fragments, run-ons, and comma splices in student writing may be signs that students are experimenting with sentences, trying to combine them in compound and complex forms. Treat these errors, then, as signs of growth. Help students recognize and correct them, but do so in the context of authentic writing.

Teaching Sentence Variety

Variety is more than just the spice of life. The reason the Food and Drug Administration recommends a varied diet is not for sake of spice, but because our bodies need different types of nutrients from different sources. Sentence variety is similar. Yes, varied sentences spice up writing and read more smoothly, but the deeper reason for variety is that different types, kinds, and structures of sentences convey different kinds of thoughts. Sentence variety makes for deeper and more "nutrient-rich" thinking.

Simple, Compound, and Complex

Simple, compound, and complex sentences are covered in their own chapter, which focuses on creating these structures rather than identifying them. Students need to understand that these three structures work well for different kinds of thinking:

- **Simple sentences** provide ideas in a straightforward way.
- **Compound sentences** connect simple sentences equally. Different coordinating conjunctions create different connections.

  additions: *and*   contrasts: *but, yet*

  options: *or, nor*   causes: *for, so*
- **Complex sentences** connect simple sentences in a more nuanced way, making one depend on the other. Note the relationships created by the subordinating conjunctions in complex sentences.

  time: *after, as, as long as, before, since, until, when, whenever, while*

  contrasts: *although, as if, even though, though, unless, until, whereas, while*

  causes: *as, as long as, because, if, in order that, since, so that, when, whenever*

Medium, Long, and Short

Just as different sentence structures create special relationships between ideas, different sentence lengths are suited to different sizes of ideas. Students should not vary the length of sentences randomly. Instead, they should use different lengths for different purposes in their writing.

- **Medium sentences** (10-20 words) work well to express most ideas.

  When I read the advertisement online, I wrote my résumé and cover letter and sent them in.
- **Long sentences** (over 20 words) work well to express complex ideas.

  After waiting anxiously to hear from the employer, I received a call requesting an interview, went in to meet the department manager, toured the facility, and completed a test.
- **Short sentences** (under 10 words) work well to make a point.

  I got the job!

Varied Beginnings

On the surface, the reason to vary the beginnings of sentences is to keep them from sounding repetitive and predictable. At a deeper level, varying beginnings provides the chance to insert a transition word, phrase, or clause that helps make clear the connection between a sentence and what has come before.

- Transition word: However, I won't start work until July.
- Transition phrase: With all the arrangements, I won't start work until July.
- Transition clause: Though I am eager to begin, I won't start work until July.

...ng the Kinds of Sentences

Throughout *WRITE 1* and *WRITE 2,* students are prompted to create statements, questions, commands, and conditional sentences. These kinds of sentences are taught in context—for example, using command verbs when teaching the reader how to perform a process. Additional instruction in the kinds of sentences appear in the online bonus chapters "End Punctuation" and "Sentence Analysis." The key point is for students to understand the uses of the different kinds of sentences in their writing:

- **Statements** provide information about the subject. Use them most often.
  I was one of 25 applicants for the job.
- **Questions** ask for information about the subject. Use them to engage the reader.
  What made me stand out from the other applicants?
- **Exclamations** express strong emotion. Use them sparingly in academic writing.
  I had the best attitude!
- **Commands** tell the reader what to do. (They have an implied subject—*you.*) Use them to call the reader to act.
  Show a positive attitude when you interview.
- **Conditional** sentences show that one situation depends on another.
  If you have a good attitude and résumé, then the interviewer will notice.

Note: Each of these kinds of sentences represents a different kind of thinking. Using a variety of sentence kinds in writing stimulates deeper and broader thought.

Modifying Phrases and Clauses

The "Sentence Basics" chapter deals with creating sentence style by adding modifying phrases and clauses. Instead of focusing on the daunting names of such word groups—participial phrases, infinitive phrases, subordinate clauses—the exercises focus on the function of these groups. Do they answer an adjective question or an adverb question?

Adjective Questions	Adverb Questions
Which?	*How?*
What kind of?	*When?*
How many?/How much?	*Where?*
	Why?
	To what degree?
	How often?/How long?

If you ask one of these questions, students will likely respond verbally with a modifying phrase or clause that you could identify but they could not. Identification is not as important as use. Help students see that if the words answer an adjective or adverb question, those words can be used like an adjective or adverb.